INSTRUCTIONAL DESIGN FOR TEACHING PHYSICAL ACTIVITIES

A Knowledge Structures Approach

Joan N. Vickers, EdD
University of Calgary
Calgary, Alberta, Canada

Human Kinetics Books
Champaign, Illinois

Library of Congress Cataloging-in-Publication Data

Vickers, Joan N., 1945-
    Instructional design for teaching physical activities : a
knowledge structures approach / Joan N. Vickers.
        p.   cm.
    Includes bibliographical references.
    ISBN 0-87322-226-1
    1. Physical education and training--Study and teaching.
I. Title.
    GV363.V515   1990
    613.7'107--dc20   89-48116
                                     CIP

ISBN: 0-87322-226-1

Note: Materials from the following Steps to Success Activity Series books (© 1989 by Leisure Press) have been used throughout this publication: *Teaching Tennis: Steps to Success* and *Tennis: Steps to Success* by J. Brown; *Archery: Steps to Success* and *Teaching Archery: Steps by Success* by K.M. Haywood & C.F. Lewis; *Golf: Steps to Success* and *Teaching Golf: Steps to Success* by D. Owens & L.K. Bunker; *Soccer: Steps to Success* (in press) and *Teaching Soccer: Steps to Success* (in press) by J. Luxbacher; *Softball: Steps to Success* and *Teaching Softball: Steps to Success* by D.L. Potter & G.A. Brockmeyer; *Bowling: Steps to Success* and *Teaching Bowling: Steps to Success* by R.H. Strickland; *Swimming: Steps to Success* and *Teaching Swimming: Steps to Success* by D.G. Thomas; and *Volleyball: Steps to Success* and *Teaching Volleyball: Steps to Success* by B.L. Viera & B.J. Ferguson. This material is used by permission of the publisher.

Developmental Editor: Judy Patterson Wright, PhD
Assistant Editors: Timothy Ryan and Robert King
Photo Editor: Valerie Hall
Copyeditor: Peter Nelson
Proofreader: Laurie McGee
Production Director: Ernie Noa
Typesetters: Angela K. Snyder and Yvonne Winsor
Text Design: Keith Blomberg
Text Layout: Kimberlie Henris and Denise Lowry
Cover Design: Jack Davis
Cover Photo: Wilmer Zehr
Illustrations: Joan Vickers and Kathy Fuoss
Printer: Braun-Brumfield

Printed in the United States of America

10 9 8 7 6 5 4 3 2 1

Human Kinetics Books
A Division of Human Kinetics Publishers, Inc.
Box 5076, Champaign, IL 61825-5076
1-800-747-4HKP

This book is dedicated to my sons, Robert and James.

Contents

Preface

When I first began teaching curriculum and instruction in physical education, I believed that I could not possibly teach how to teach every sport and activity in our diverse physical education programs. Consequently, I was reluctant to include any specific content of sports and activities because it seemed too expansive and complicated to deal with.

My defense mechanisms against teaching subject matter were both elaborate and extensive. First, I was teaching the equivalent of master's students, who had spent years earning their specialist degrees in physical education. Given their solid grounding in the essential knowledges of the field and their broad experience in different activity areas, I assumed they didn't need content information. Second, the literature in curriculum and instruction stressed the "how" of teaching, not the "what" of the subject matter, which implied that a course like mine should concentrate on teaching methodologies and styles, management skills, observation methods, discipline, teacher-student interaction, and so on. Third, I thought there just wasn't enough time to teach the content of each sport. Fourth, because each sport or activity appeared unique, each seemed to need its own treatment by a specialist. Fifth, any content or curricular issues that were emphasized in the field concentrated on the philosophical, societal, or cultural foundations for teaching certain concepts or activities in school physical education. Curriculum per se articulated little actual program content.

So for several years these were the assumptions underlying my teaching. As time went on, however, I found that my students did not seem to apply to their teaching what they knew. And they continually asked to know more about the actual subject matter of the activities they were teaching. Even though all my students had an extensive physical education knowledge base, their problems seemed nevertheless to be rooted in deficiencies in that knowledge base, rather than in their awareness of teaching methodologies or processes.

It seemed that student teachers and coaches needed a way to see how the subject matter of an activity was structured and how, once identified, a structure could be used as a basis and guide for teaching and coaching. This model would link the knowledge of sport with the extensive literature on methodologies and strategies for teaching. More importantly, they needed a way to identify their own knowledge structures for teaching and coaching and the types of instructional processes they could use.

The model that I developed to meet these needs is the KS (Knowledge Structures) Model. The KS Model identifies the subject matter of an activity from the outset and structures it as a hierarchy that constantly informs the process of teaching. Knowledge-based design is an empowering process for new teachers for it helps them feel they have something very important to teach. The KS Model has also been developed specifically for teaching and coaching physical activity. Although it borrows generously from cognitive psychology, the sport sciences, instructional design, and computing science, it is a model created specifically for those of us who teach and coach complex physical skills.

The KS Model has been shaped by a variety of people and experiences. I was fortunate to have been coached very well, and when I went out myself to teach in the junior and senior high school I found that students, even the "too cool to care" bunch, really became interested when they were challenged to learn complicated physical skills and to experience an activity in its fullest form. I also had the privilege of teaching curriculum and instruction for 11 years to students who had all survived a very tough selection process to enter their certification year. Their willingness to experiment with me on new approaches fostered many of the ideas in this book.

During my doctoral studies at the University of British Columbia, Robert Morford and Hal Lawson challenged me to define the knowledge base of physical education. It was the first that I had heard we didn't have one. As an athlete

I knew what the knowledge base was; as a physical education major I took courses that I thought defined it; and it seemed my student teachers told me what it was every day. But Bob and Hal opened another door. They helped me realize that although both teachers and students sensed what was important in physical education, it had not been formally articulated as subject matter, especially for teaching and coaching. A professional field does not have a true knowledge base if the knowledge is solely at the experiential level. The assumptions I described having when I first began teaching curriculum and instruction are symptomatic of a field without a defined knowledge base.

Bob and Hal introduced me to the cross-disciplinary approach to physical education, which is a critical foundation of the KS Model. At the same time, I met Anne Treisman, Daniel Kahneman, and Stan Coren, three gifted perception and cognitive psychologists, and a whole psychology department devoted to explaining how humans represent and use knowledge. They never questioned the possibility that knowledge existed as an aspect of physical skills.

The final piece of the KS Model puzzle came from Brian Gaines and Mildred Shaw. They had spent years developing techniques for eliciting knowledge from experts and developing computer programs (known as expert systems or knowledge acquisition tools) to facilitate this approach. By using these techniques, it is possible to unearth knowledge that eludes discovery through the standard methods of science.

The culmination of developing the KS model is this textbook on instructional design and the Steps to Success Activity Series, which is a breakthrough in skill instruction through the development of complete learning progressions—the *steps to success*. The unique features of the Steps to Success Activity Series are the result of comprehensive development and real-world applications of the KS Model. For each activity within the Steps to Success Activity Series there is both a self-paced participant's book and a comprehensive teacher's guide that emphasizes how to individualize instruction. If you want to design a program for an activity, use the Steps to Success Activity Series and this textbook, *Instructional Design for Teaching Physical Activities*, and create effective physical education programs for the school, recreation, or community teaching and coaching setting.

Strategy for the Future

The KS Model and the Steps to Success Activity Series hold the promise for a dramatic turn-around for our public schools. As the basis for a complete physical education curriculum, the KS Model serves as a theoretical framework, the Steps to Success participant's books serve as textbooks for your students, and the Steps to Success instructor's guides are your curriculum guide. We have never before had textbooks for students of physical education in our schools, and it is time we did.

Following are six important reasons that the KS Model and the Steps to Success Activity Series can be the basis for developing a complete curriculum for your school:

1. The Steps to Success Activity Series is activity specific, which means that activities are the primary building blocks of your curriculum.
2. Each activity book has been designed from a knowledge-based perspective that reflects a cross-disciplinary framework; that is, it identifies the skills and strategies in the sport and shows how sport science concepts from exercise physiology, motor learning, biomechanics, sport psychology, sport history, sport sociology, and other areas have affected performance, teaching, and coaching.
3. The knowledge structures were created by eliciting knowledge from master teachers and coaches, using knowledge elicitation techniques such as structured interview, text analysis, analogical derivation, and stimulated recall. During their development, the knowledge structures were constantly validated against the appropriate sport science authorities.
4. Each activity book shows how the knowledge structure should be taught or coached. This methodology is reflected as a series of steps; by sequencing the steps across grades, or by using a competency approach, you offer students new material and help them grow every year.
5. A top-down sequencing approach has been primarily adopted for the Steps to Success Activity Series for two reasons: First, it places the learning of skills and strategies into the context of game play as

soon as possible, and second, it is the approach used by most of the master teachers and coaches.

6. Because each Steps to Success Activity Series book highlights one or more of the sport science concepts, a curriculum that encompasses a number of activities should provide good coverage of these concepts across a total program. For example, mental skills and goal setting are presented in golf (Owens & Bunker, 1989a, 1989b); concentration is discussed in tennis (Brown, 1989a, 1989b); fear reduction in swimming (Thomas, 1989a, 1989b); teamwork in volleyball (Viera & Ferguson, 1989a, 1989b); developing confidence in archery (Haywood & Lewis, 1989a, 1989b); anticipation in softball (Potter & Brockmeyer, 1989a, 1989b); and mental discipline in bowling (Strickland, 1989a, 1989b).

The KS Model and the Steps to Success Activity Series represent a far-reaching innovation in teaching and coaching sport and physical activity. I hope that both you and your students will find yourselves enjoying a new dimension in developing physical skills as you put the KS Model into practice.

Acknowledgments

New ideas take a long time to foster. The growth process has good days and bad days, and all real leaps seem to occur when one has interaction, support, and encouragement from others. I have received a lot of help in developing the KS Model. For over a decade I taught curriculum and instruction to graduate students in physical education, and their support, acceptance, and use of the ideas in the KS Model have been fundamental to its development. In particular, I want to thank David Brecht, Kevin Johnston, Don Kelm, Robin Laycock, Lori Livingston, and Wendy and Doug Rodney, all of whom did extensive instructional design projects using the KS Model.

Bob Morford, who saw the potential of a knowledge structures approach before I did, has the unique ability to encourage individuals to pursue ideas even in the face of disappointment. Bob introduced me to Kuhn's *The Structure of Scientific Revolutions* (1962), and the challenge of academic work as described there has been immensely helpful to me. He and Hal Lawson also developed the cross-disciplinary model for sport studies, which is fundamental to how knowledge of sport and physical activity is defined within the KS Model. Also, while at the University of British Columbia, I was introduced to the field of cognitive psychology by Anne Treisman, Stan Coren, and Daniel Kahneman. They have no idea how meaningful their seminars, classes, projects, and discussions were.

Brian Gaines introduced me to the powerful tool of knowledge acquisition, which can unlock knowledge that would otherwise lie dormant. He and Mildred Shaw are at the forefront of this area, and together they have provided me with scaffolding critical to defining a knowledge structure for teaching and coaching sport and physical activity.

Rainer Martens and Judy Patterson Wright provided the resources and foresight that have moved the KS Model from theory to application in teaching and coaching. My 3 years of work with Judy have been distinguished by her patience, hard work, and depth of understanding of physical education, which is evident in every page of this book and the Steps to Success Activity Series.

I have also enjoyed working with the authors of the Steps to Success Activity Series and especially want to thank those with whom I have had meetings and interviews: Tom Baechle, Jim Brown, Linda Bunker, Kathie Haywood, Joe Luxbacher, Joan Nelson, Diane Potter, Bob Strickland, Barbara Viera, Hal Wissel, and my colleague from the University of Calgary, George Kingston.

Linda Bain, Shirl Hoffman, and Ann Jewett took special care in reviewing my original manuscript, and their comments helped me to zero in on aspects that needed rewriting, clarification, and elaboration.

The Social Sciences Research Council of Canada, through a Major Strategic Grant, has allowed me to move many of the ideas in the KS Model forward and to develop a HyperMedia System for Sports Coaching and Teaching. The process of working with instructional designers, videodisc specialists, script writers, programmers, and others on the project has facilitated the writing of this book. I especially want to thank Nancy Buzzell, who coordinated my laboratory, and Sandee Greatrex, videodisc and tape specialist, as well as the team of programmers who have worked on the ActionMark program discussed in Module 8: Brian Gaines, David Johnson, Maurice Sharpe, Shawn Abbott, and Mark Morrill.

Finally, I want to thank my sons, Robert and James. In the 12 or so years that I have been developing this idea, they have never once complained about my work and have been a source of constant help and support. Over the years, they have provided a kind of stability that can be understood only when you work early in the morning in the quiet of the house as they sleep.

Part I

Introduction to Instructional Design and the KS Model

Chapters in Part I

Topics

for Chapter 1

- Why the KS Model?
- Instructional design as defined by the KS Model
- Curriculum and instruction defined
- Cognitive science and its contribution to educational thought and instructional design
- The growth of process-based approaches in education
- A critical analysis of process models and approaches
- Expert children and novice adults
- Glaser's Competency Model of Instructional Design
- The emergence of expert systems and their impact upon instructional design
- Shulman's "missing paradigm" in teacher education
- The impact of process- and knowledge-based approaches upon curriculum and instruction in physical education
- Summary of assumptions and goals of the KS Model

1

Photo by Nancy Buzzell.

Foundations and Goals of the KS Model of Instruction

Why the KS Model?

The KS Model brings a knowledge-based perspective to the teaching and coaching of sport and physical activity. What do I mean by a knowledge-based perspective? For all of us who have been involved in sport, physical activity, and physical education, we have lived with the dilemma of being teachers in an area that has no defined knowledge base, or subject matter. In the eyes of the public, especially the North American public, sport and physical activity is just something you do, it defies description, it is in the public domain, and it exists as portrayed by athletes on a field of play or in experiences you had as a youngster in your physical education classes or as an athlete.

So exactly what is it you teach? And what do you say to a parent or a superintendent who asks you to describe your program? If you teach

mathematics, English, or one of the other classroom subjects, your answer is relatively easy. You begin by displaying the curriculum, the textbooks, and the resources assigned by the school board or the state or province. You then show how you have created units or other plans from this base and explain how you expect your students to progress constantly to the end of the year.

But what do you say if you teach physical education? It's hard to answer your questioners beyond giving a statement of the different activities that each student will be involved in. However, it is no longer adequate that we as a profession present ourselves in this way. Parents, teachers, and superintendents want physical education programs to be educational experiences where constant learning occurs, where the values important to society are fostered, and where children are able to develop positive attitudes about

3

physical activity as it relates to health and wellness through the lifespan. The students should have rewarding experiences and activities in which they can experience the joy of learning and personal improvement. There should also be the feeling that students are being educated in a discipline, an area of knowledge that is valuable and needs to be taught in the formal school environment. So with all of these powerful forces at work today, how does this book on instructional design and the larger Steps to Success Activity Series provide a solution?

To the Teacher Educator

Let's begin by looking at the assumptions at work in this book. An assumption is a position taken that serves as a foundation for an idea or set of ideas. Assumptions are most often the parts of your belief system that you do not question, but others do, and it is important to thoroughly understand and be able to explain your assumptions.

The KS Model (Knowledge Structures Model) of instructional design is an activity-specific approach to teaching and coaching. That is, the curriculum is built around the teaching of specific activities. This is because activities are natural mediums for students and teachers to work in, lifetime constructs that can be easily designed to accommodate sport science and other concepts important in our society. Second, The KS Model presents a number of instructional design principles that are the same for all sports and activities. Once you have learned the KS Model process, you can apply it to any areas you see fit. Third, the KS Model places at the forefront a knowledge-based approach; all sports and activities are analyzed using knowledge acquisition and representation techniques, with skills, strategies, and concepts displayed as a hierarchical knowledge structure. Fourth, the categories of knowledge are derived from an analysis of expert sources and adherence to recognized cross-disciplinary foundations.

The final assumption is the need to use this book with a sensitivity to the teaching or coaching demands placed upon your student teachers. This book is best used for a half or full semester, with your students given field experiences of a controlled nature throughout. In order to use the book as intended, your students need time to study and analyze a sport or activity. However, if your students are going immediately into real teaching environments, they need to concentrate upon the immediate skills that will help them deal effectively with a class or team setting. If this is the case, you need to begin not with an in-depth analysis of an activity but instead with lesson planning, observation, time management, and other "must know now" types of knowledge (Module 8, "Real-World Applications"). However, if your students do not have to face the day-to-day challenges of a teaching environment, it is appropriate to work straight through Modules 1 to 8.

Another strategy is to combine theory and practice; for example, consider running an on-campus teaching laboratory at the same time you present Modules 1 to 8. In my situation, I meet with my students in September for 3 hours of lecture and 2 hours of laboratory per week. I begin the semester by introducing the on-campus teaching laboratory described in Module 8. My first lectures concentrate on an introduction to and development of this lab, with an emphasis upon observation skills, management skills, and sequential lesson planning. Following this, the students are actively involved in teaching and observing a class given to junior high students once each week. In groups of three, teachers plan and deliver a unit of nine lessons.

Once the teaching is underway, I introduce the KS Model and the instructional design process, which culminates in their development of a unit plan for one activity. I make it clear to them that they are experiencing two very different things. In the teaching laboratories, they must prepare so as to be effective in a 45-minute class with real students. In the instructional design situation, they shift their focus to a bigger view, one that encompasses the eight modules in the KS Model and the questions salient to planning in the long term. About midway through the semester, the two approaches appear to merge. The practical experiences of the laboratories start to have impact on how the students design instruction; the instructional design process starts to affect the content of the classes, the organization of the laboratories, the role of objectives and evaluation, and the delivery of instruction.

To the Student Teacher and Coach

This book is designed to address your needs in two ways: It presents the tools for planning and delivering instruction in both the teaching setting and the coaching setting. At the outset, it is important to be aware of the very different demands of a single class session as opposed to those of instruction carefully planned to be put into effect over years. When you are preparing yourself for a single session, you should see the event as a director of a play sees the stage. You are totally in charge of the environment, and your students will follow the lead you provide. Often student teachers enter the classroom without this realization. This book teaches you how to observe a class and be aware of the best use of time, how your students move about, and why you must be able to anticipate their transitions and needs and to provide leadership that may take different forms, from very direct to indirect.

In Part I the underlying foundations of the KS Model are first introduced, followed by an overview of the eight modules. Part II describes how knowledge is elicited from expert sources (master teacher and coaches and sport science authorities) and provides a rationale for defining expert knowledge in physical activity within a cross-disciplinary framework (Lawson & Morford, 1979; Morford & Lawson, 1978; Morford, Lawson, & Hutton, 1981). In Part III, Module 1 describes the specific steps to follow in analyzing an activity, thus creating a personalized knowledge structure that you will use to guide your teaching and coaching. Module 2 describes how you can analyze the teaching or coaching environment. Module 3 discusses ways of understanding your students before you design a formal plan of instruction. Modules 4 through 7 show you how to select and sequence content from the knowledge structures, to set objectives, and to design an evaluation scheme that is appropriate for the specific group you are teaching. Finally, Module 8, the applications phase, shows you how the information you analyzed and structured in Modules 1 through 7 can be used to design the different vehicles used in teaching and coaching: lesson and unit plans, practices and season plan, and curriculum design for single and multiple activity programs. Examples are drawn from the Steps to Success Activity Series to show how each module has been implemented in the series. There are also strategies for individualizing instruction and for designing computer-based hypermedia applications. Instructional design exercises given with each module will assist you in understanding the concepts presented; just look for the following KS symbol:

Instructional Design as Defined by the KS Model

The KS Model, or Knowledge Structures Model, of instructional design is presented as a vehicle for linking the subject matter of a sport or activity with teaching and coaching methodology. This model is made up of the eight modules shown in Figure 1.1.

Instructional design is defined within the KS Model as an eight-part process:

1. You must become knowledgeable about the sport or activity you are teaching or coaching. This process (analysis of a sport or activity into expert knowledge structures) requires the translation of knowledge acquired as a student or athlete into knowledge that is appropriate for presentation to others (Module 1).
2. You must become knowledgeable about the environment in which you will be teaching or coaching (Module 2).
3. You must become knowledgeable about the students and athletes you will be working with (Module 3).
4. You must know how to organize the knowledge you have gained about the sport, the teaching and coaching environment, and the students into a scope and sequence of skills, strategies, and concepts (Module 4).
5. Once the skills, strategies, and concepts have been identified in a scope-and-sequence format, you need to design or select the objectives appropriate for the students and the situation you are in (Module 5).
6. You must make a decision about the type of evaluation to use (Module 6).
7. You then must select or design the learning activities that will best achieve the objectives and evaluation strategy you have set out (Module 7).
8. There are a number of vehicles to organize and deliver the knowledge identified. The main vehicles for teaching and coaching are the lesson and practice plan, the unit and season plan, the year plan, the developmental program used in coaching, individualized programs, as well as computer applications (Module 8).

This is a continual process that requires ongoing study, revision, and evaluation of self,

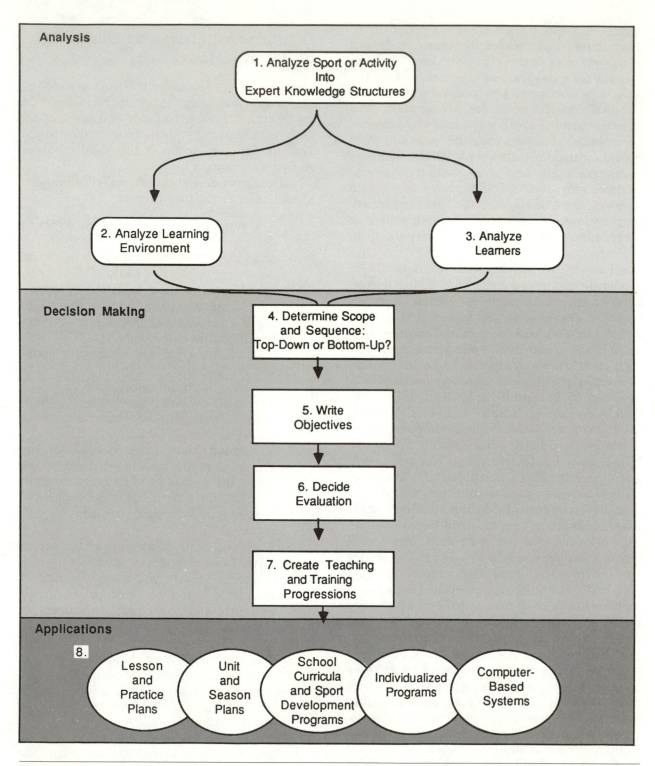

Figure 1.1 Instructional design model utilizing expert knowledge structures. *Note.* This instructional design model has appeared in earlier forms (Vickers, 1983; Vickers & Brecht, 1987).

others, and the programs you are presenting. In this chapter we begin by defining the terms *curriculum* and *instruction* and explaining their roles in instructional design. Following this, you will be introduced to the difference between knowledge-based and process-based models of instructional design. You will also examine the foundations of the KS Model, as supplied by the work of Bruner (1966), Glaser (1984), Shulman (1986b), and the literature from cognitive psychology, the sport sciences, and expert systems development. At the conclusion of the chapter, we look at teaching and coaching in physical education and discover that we are a field in which there are over a dozen distinct curriculum and instruction models currently in use, with an overall emphasis upon process-based models rather than knowledge-based ones.

The KS Model is then presented as a knowledge-based model in which physical activity is of primary importance. Because of its unique combination of knowledge within physical activity, the KS Model must draw on a number of foundations that are new to our field. In the chapters to follow, you will be introduced to the process of knowledge acquisition and semantic representation for the purpose of teaching and coaching. This is discussed within the cognitive framework of a hierarchical knowledge structure. The question of what is knowledge in sport and physical activity settings is addressed within the context of a cross-disciplinary model of sport studies (Lawson & Morford, 1979; Morford & Lawson, 1978; Morford, Lawson, & Hutton, 1981). And the question of how sport knowledge is best planned and delivered in teaching and coaching settings is answered by applying principles of instructional design to the structures of knowledge derived for specific sports. These are the foundations of the KS Model.

Curriculum and Instruction Defined

The KS Model provides a framework within which both curriculum and instruction decisions about sport and physical education teaching and coaching can be made. The term *curriculum* refers to subject matter: what is to be taught, why it is being taught, and what the learning outcomes will be. Curriculum also refers to the underlying values that a society feels should be reflected, taught, or emphasized in a course or program of study. The term *instruction* refers to the techniques, methods, or processes that are used in

planning and delivering lessons and units, in managing the classroom environment, in implementing techniques of evaluation, in discipline, and so on.

Instructional design is a relatively new field, having evolved over only the past fifteen years. Textbooks such as *Instructional Design Theories and Models* by Reigeluth (1983) and *Models of Teaching* by Joyce and Weil (1980) present many of the models used in instructional design today. These models may be categorized as being either process-based or knowledge-based models. *Process-based models* place an emphasis upon the strategies and methods associated with planning and delivering instruction. Instructional design models of this type (Gagné, 1977; Merrill, 1983; Reigeluth, 1983; Tyler, 1949) make an assumption about the subject matter of an area and concentrate upon the "hows" of design and delivery: instructional conditions, instructional methods, instructional outcomes, organizational strategies, delivery strategies, designing and setting objectives, determining evaluation, designing learning activities, managing the learning environment, and so on.

Knowledge-based models, in contrast, do not assume that subject matter has been determined, nor do they assume that instruction can be planned effectively without considering the inherent nature of subject matter at each step in the design process. These models advocate the first step in a design process being an analysis of subject matter for the purposes of teaching, followed by an integration of subject matter with the methods and processes of instruction. Bruner (1966), Glaser (1976, 1984), Shulman (1986b), and Clancey (1987) have all contributed models that recognize that subject matter itself has an informative structure that affects how teachers and coaches think, plan, set objectives and evaluation, and determine other instructional tasks.

In *Toward a Theory of Instruction*, Bruner (1966) explains the role of a structure of knowledge in teaching as follows:

A theory of instruction must specify the ways in which a body of knowledge should be structured so that it can be readily grasped by the learner. "Optimal structure" refers to a set of propositions from which a larger body of knowledge can be generated, and it is characteristic that the formulation of such a structure depends on the state of advance of a particular field of knowledge. (p. 41)

Bruner continues by defining a structure of knowledge as a medium for *"simplifying information, for generating new propositions, and for increasing the manipulability of a body of knowledge"* (Bruner, 1966, p. 41). The creation of a knowledge structure as described in Module 1 (see examples for badminton, golf, and ice hockey in Appendices A through C) follows principles that are the same for all sports and activities. These principles are covered in depth in the chapters to follow, but first let's look at why a knowledge-based approach is being advocated. We begin with cognitive psychology and expert systems development.

Cognitive Science and Its Contribution to Educational Thought and Instructional Design

Cognition is the science that looks at "how we gain information of the world, how such information is represented (in the brain) and transformed as knowledge, how it is stored, and how that knowledge is used to direct our attention and behavior" (Solso, 1979, p. 1). A typical textbook in cognitive psychology includes chapters on sensation and perception, attention, memory structure and models, semantic representation, imagery, language, concept formation, problem solving, thinking, cognitive development, artificial intelligence, and expert systems.

One of the main research goals of scientists working in the early years of cognitive psychology was to identify generic information-processing abilities that underlie all thought and behavior. Foremost in this research was an assumption that complex mental processes such as problem solving, creativity, thinking, and reasoning could be acquired independent of specific subject matter or content. This was a powerful and tremendously attractive assumption that emerged during the late fifties and early sixties and still dominates educational thought today.

Under this assumption, a learner is viewed as someone who can develop (or be taught) sophisticated thought processes that are independent of subject matter, context, and change. In this scenario, a learner is one who perceives, attends, develops a memory system, forms concepts, solves problems, reasons, develops intellectual and physical skills, and has the capacity to think and be creative independent of specific domain

knowledge; generic information processing or mental skills can and should be developed as an end in themselves. Early research in cognition seemed to support this idea (Bourne, Dominowski, & Loftus, 1979). For example, one of the most exciting early research findings stated that the capacity of short-term memory was seven, plus or minus two pieces of information (Miller, 1956). This research appeared to establish a real limit on our ability to process information. However, as explained by Gardner (1985), this type of research and much of what was to follow was content blind.

Other lines of investigation bear in a critical way on the classical information processing model of the 1950's and 1960's. That model was essentially content-blind: the assumption was that information of any sort is processed in essentially the same manner. Thus, if short-term memory holds seven slots, these slots are equally capacious for any kind of information, be it verbal, pictorial, or musical, be it dross or gold. By the same token, if a search takes a certain period of time per item and is exhaustive rather than self-terminating, these processes obtain irrespective of what is being searched for and of who is doing the searching.

These assumptions, which were made by all the pioneering cognitivists on both sides of the Atlantic, served as simplifying beginning points. They also reflected the computer model and information-theoretical origins of modern cognitive psychology: with such mechanisms, it is relatively easy to set up experiments so that actual contents are irrelevant. After all, information theory and computers are deliberately constituted to be content blind. (p. 128)

The Growth of Process-Based Approaches in Education

Now, let's back up in time and consider the impact of this early "content free" type of research in cognition upon educational thought and practice. Out of this research grew *process models of instruction.* The logic ran as follows. If the human mind processes all information in essentially the same way, then content or subject matter is irrelevant. What is most important is the development of information processing skills. Of greatest importance in education is the development of programs that teach sophisticated cognitive skills. These skills, once learned, can then be applied to any type of content or subject area. This type of thinking was and still is an appealing and powerful approach. It suggested that the "hard slogging" often associated with learning specific content was no longer necessary. It also meant that in education we should be teaching children how to solve problems, be creative, think, reason, and master other cognitive skills; concerns about subject matter could and should be left to later.

A Critical Analysis of Process Models and Approaches

Glaser (1984) provides a critical analysis of process models of instruction. *Process-oriented programs* teach metacognitive and other reasoning skills and suggest the application of these skills to all subject areas. These programs assume knowledge proficiency in students and deduce that any problems encountered are due to deficiencies in setting goals, analyzing the problem space, impulsive acting out, and trial-and-error thinking, not to deficiencies in the students' knowledge base. A closer scrutiny of these approaches points out, however, that their effectiveness is found in the context of everyday events such as planning a holiday, choosing a career, or buying a house. There is little evidence to show their effectiveness beyond this, especially in areas where the knowledge base is complex.

A second type of process-based approaches teaches *problem-solving heuristics*, strategies for well-structured domains. These programs were originally developed for subject areas such as mathematics, physics, and engineering and stress the learning of problem-solving skills such as problem decomposition, working backwards, indirect proofs, and other strategies. The work of Polya (1957), Newell and Simon (1972), and Wicklegren (1979) are examples of this approach. Difficulties arise when these same strategies are applied to content areas that do not inherently have apparent mathematical structures. Glaser (1984) summarizes the overall success and applicability of process models as follows:

The programs that I have described are based on early theories of human cognition

. . . on concepts of divergent thinking in older theories of problem solving. Others derive from early information processing theory that explored knowledge-lean problems and that concentrated on early information-processing capabilities humans employ when they behave more or less intelligently in situations where they lack the focus of domain specificity because of their wide applicability and generality . . . this research used relatively knowledge-free problems, and as such offered limited insight into learning and thinking that require domain-specific knowledge. (From "Education and Thinking: The Role of Knowledge" by R. Glaser, 1984, *American Psychologist*, **39**[1], pp. 96-97. Reprinted by permission.)

Glaser goes on to explain that in the past decade a different understanding has emerged about the power of generic information-processing abilities and in particular the role of subject matter and domain-specific knowledge in human thought.

In contrast, more recent work on problem solving done in knowledge-rich domains shows strong interactions between structures of knowledge and cognitive processes. The results of this newer research and theory force us to consider the teaching of thinking not only in terms of general processes, but also in terms of knowledge structure–process interactions. (From "Education and Thinking: The Role of Knowledge" by R. Glaser, 1984, *American Psychologist*, **39**[1], p. 97. Reprinted by permission.)

Expert Children and Novice Adults

Further evidence for the inherent power of knowledge in human thought and performance is supplied by research comparing expert children and novice adults. Why is it that a 10-year-old child can play chess as well as an adult (Chi, 1978)? If the work of early "knowledge-free" theories is accepted, adults should possess more sophisticated problem-solving and thinking abilities than do children and therefore should be able to play the game at a higher level than children. Chi et al. compared the chess-playing abilities of elite children with beginner adults and showed that it was the knowledge base of the player in chess that determined the ability level, not maturation or age.

Glaser (1984) concludes the following:

> Our interpretation is that the problem-solving difficulty of novices can be attributed largely to inadequacies in their knowledge bases and not the inability to use problem-solving heuristics. Novices show effective heuristics; however, the limitation of their thinking derive from their inability to infer further knowledge from the literal cues in the problem statement. In contrast, these inferences are necessarily generated in the context of the knowledge structure that the experts have acquired.
>
> Current studies of high levels of competence support the recommendation that a significant focus for understanding expert thinking and problem solving and its development is investigation of the characteristics and influence of organized knowledge structures that are acquired over long periods of time. (From "Education and Thinking: The Role of Knowledge" by R. Glaser, 1984, *American Psychologist*, **39**[1], p. 99. Reprinted by permission.)

Glaser's Competency Model of Instructional Design

The KS Model, with its eight modules, shows you how you can create a structured cross-disciplinary body of knowledge for a specific sport or physical activity and then use this as the basis for designing instruction for either a coaching, a teaching, or a recreational setting. The design process shown in the eight modules of the KS Model is derived from a number of sources, one being Glaser's Competency Model of Instruction (1976, 1984). Glaser's model includes four components.

1. The designer first carries out an "analysis of competence," determining what is known about the state of knowledge and the skill to be achieved.
2. Methods are next identified whereby the teacher can gain an understanding and description of the initial state of learning, the apparent level of the students as instruction begins.
3. Methods, conditions, and other strategies are identified that will bring about a change from the initial state to the state of competence identified in Step One.
4. Short- and long-term assessment procedures are identified that determine the effectiveness of the model.

The Emergence of Expert Systems and Their Impact Upon Instructional Design

For four decades the computer has been used as a convincing model of the human mind and its functions. Put simply, a computer programmed to perform complex thought processes is a type of model of how the human mind functions. Early research in artificial intelligence (AI) sought to develop computer programs programmed with generic or fundamental thinking, problem solving, and other complex cognitive abilities. One of the first large-scale attempts to build such a program was the General Problem Solver, developed by Newell and Simon (1972). This program was designed to solve diverse types of problems irrespective of the subject area or complexity of the problem or environment encountered. This project and others like it were eventually abandoned when it was found that they could solve only simple problems or those that were highly structured and predictable in outcome.

It soon became apparent that in order for the computer to solve problems that we humans deal with daily, it was necessary to provide it with a knowledge base that was extensive and specific to the events of daily life and work. Thus the evolution of *expert systems*. An expert system is created by interviewing experts in specific areas (e.g., medicine, law, engineering, psychology), using a variety of question-and-answer processes and other *knowledge-elicitation* techniques. Through this process the computer is provided with the information and rules underlying how experts go about solving problems and making decisions. An expert system therefore is a computer program programmed to think and perform as an expert in a specific domain. Expert systems today are founded upon the careful study of multiple experts and how they go about solving very specific problems.

One of the earliest expert systems developed was MYCIN, a program that helps doctors or nurses recognize and treat infectious diseases. In *Knowledge-Based Tutoring: The Guidon Program*, Clancey (1987) describes how he has taken MYCIN and combined it with GUIDON, a tutorial program. Together the two programs teach student nurses and doctors how to diagnose and treat infectious diseases. The important point here is that it was necessary to combine the knowledge base found in MYCIN with the tutorial and educational program GUIDON in order for MYCIN to be effective as a tutor or teacher.

Similarly, in formulating a model for instructional design, it is necessary to develop a model that combines domain-specific knowledge with effective teaching and coaching practices. In the KS Model an activity-specific knowledge structure is first created in Module 1. Following this, Modules 2 through 8 present the processes needed in order to deliver this knowledge base to learners of different types, in different environments, and with different intended outcomes. As will be shown in the following chapters, the knowledge structures developed in Module 1 become *generative* in nature (Gaines, 1987), that is, they lead to the generation of other knowledge that is instructional in nature and fundamental to successful teaching or coaching.

Shulman's "Missing Paradigm" in Teacher Education

> "He who can, does.
>
> He who cannot, teaches."

I don't know in what fit of pique George Bernard Shaw wrote that infamous aphorism, words that have plagued members of the teaching profession for almost a century. They are found in "Maxims for Revolutionists," an appendix to his play *Man and Superman*. "He who can, does. He who cannot, teaches" is a calamitous insult to our profession, yet one readily repeated even by teachers. More worrisome, its philosophy often appears to underlie the policies concerning the occupation and activities of teaching.

Where did such a demeaning image of the teacher's capacities originate? How long

have we been burdened by assumptions of ignorance and ineptitude within the teaching corps? Is Shaw to be treated as the last word on what teachers know and don't know, or do and can't do? (From "Those Who Understand: Knowledge Growth in Teaching" by L.S. Shulman, 1986, *Educational Researcher*, **15**[2], p. 4. Reprinted by permission.)

Shulman answers his own questions in the following way. He begins by examining the elementary teacher examinations of the 1850s. He concludes that teachers were universally tested in the following 20 knowledge categories: written arithmetic, mental arithmetic, written grammar, oral grammar, geography, history of the United States, theory and practice of teaching, algebra, physiology, natural philosophy (physics), constitution of the United States, school law of the state, penmanship, natural history (biology), composition, reading, orthography, defining word analysis and vocabulary, vocal music, and industrial drawing.

Shulman then contrasts these expectations with those used today in a new wave of accountability and certification found in education.

> Teachers are now tested on "basic spelling, reading and writing" and a cluster of areas entitled "capacity to teach" defined as:
>
> 1. organization in preparing and presenting instructional plans,
> 2. evaluation,
> 3. recognition of individual differences,
> 4. cultural awareness,
> 5. understanding youth,
> 6. management, and
> 7. educational policies and procedures.
>
> As we compare these categories . . . to those of 1875, the contrast is striking. Where did the subject matter go? What happened to the content? Perhaps Shaw was correct. He accurately anticipated the standard for teaching in 1985. He who knows, does. He who cannot, but knows some teaching procedures, teaches. (From "Those Who Understand: Knowledge Growth in Teaching" by L.S. Shulman, 1986, *Educational Researcher*, **15**[2], p. 5. Reprinted by permission.)

Shulman describes the absence of subject matter knowledge in the education of teachers as "the missing paradigm." In identifying reasons for this emphasis, Shulman suggests that "in their necessary simplification of the complexities of classroom teaching, investigators ignored one central aspect of classroom life: the subject matter. . . . No one asked how subject matter was transformed from the knowledge of the teacher into content of instruction" (p. 6). Shulman further defines the "missing paradigm" as

> . . . a blind spot with respect to content that now characterizes most research on teaching and, as a consequence, most of our state level programs of teacher evaluation and certification.
>
> In reading the literature of research on teaching, it is clear that central questions are unasked. The emphasis is on how teachers manage their classrooms, organize activities, allocate time and turns, structure assignments, ascribe praise and blame, formulate the levels of their questions, plan lessons, and judge general student understanding.
>
> What we miss are questions about the *content* of the lesson taught, the questions asked, and the explanations offered. From the perspective of teacher development and teacher education, a host of questions arise. Where do teacher explanations come from? How do teachers decide what to teach, how to represent it, how to question students about it and how to deal with problems of misunderstanding? (From "Those Who Understand: Knowledge Growth in Teaching" by L.S. Shulman, 1986, *Educational Researcher*, **15**[2], pp. 7-8. Reprinted by permission.)[1]

The Impact of Process- and Knowledge-Based Approaches Upon Curriculum and Instruction in Physical Education

Physical education is a relatively new field, with a body of knowledge created through research and development only since the 1950s. Since this time we have seen the emergence of a number of new subdisciplines: exercise physiology, biomechanics, neuro-motor psychology, growth and development, athletic therapy, sport psy-chology, sport sociology, philosophy of sport and history of sport, as well as other areas of inquiry. Paradoxically, at the very time this rich, cross-disciplinary body of knowledge has been emerging in sport and physical activity, the preparation of teachers and coaches and the design of curriculum and instruction have followed the paths of all other educational areas, with an emphasis upon process models, or the how of teaching sport and physical activity. Very little of the knowledge we now possess about the body in action (as informed by exercise physiology, growth and development, motor learning, sport sociology and psychology, biomechanics, and other areas) has been integrated formally into our schools and educational programs as a universally identifiable curricula. Curriculum development in K–12 physical education has not evolved to reflect the richness of the body of knowledge in physical education today. Inherent with this is the fear that a knowledge-based approach will reduce the amount of physical activity children will experience.

In addition to this, the absence of explicit attention to subject matter has also resulted in the growth of the overwhelming number of different models in use today in physical education. Lawson and Placek (1981) have identified five models used in teaching physical education: traditional, fitness, lifetime sports, humanistic, and alternate. Jewett and Bain (1985) identify seven models: developmental, humanistic, fitness, movement education, kinesiological studies, play education, and personal meaning. Seidentop, Mand, and Taggert (1986) define seven models: multiactivity, fitness, sports education, wilderness sports and adventure, social development, conceptually based, and informal curriculum. Allowing for duplication, there appear to be twelve distinctly different models in use today, with the vast majority being process-based ones. Process-based models do not define subject matter, but assume that teachers already possess the necessary knowledge base, and therefore concentrate upon methods and strategies of presentation.

Summary of Assumptions and Goals of the KS Model

Instructional design is a new field emerging in the 1970s that describes how planning can be

---

carried out in the teaching or coaching environment. Instructional design models are many, but all follow one of two basic formats, *process-* or *knowledge-based*. Process models assume that all content or subject matter is processed the same by the human mind. For this reason, these models tend to bypass descriptions of subject matter and concentrate on how information may best be processed by students. There is an emphasis on developing problem-solving skills, thinking strategies, and creativity. The development of these cognitive skills is considered not only prerequisite to subject matter mastery, but facilitative to learning any type of subject matter in the future.

Knowledge-based models, by contrast, do not assume that subject matter can be left out of the instructional design process. Instead, an analysis of subject matter for the purpose of teaching or coaching is viewed as one of the most exciting and rewarding parts of the design process. Mastery of subject matter is considered empowering, *underlying* one's ability to solve problems, to think, or to be creative. The KS Model is a knowledge-based model developed specifically for teaching and coaching sports and physical activities.

The KS Model as presented here encompasses a number of characteristics and assumptions:

1. The KS Model can be applied to all sport and physical activity—team sports, individual sports, dance, combative activities, aquatics, outdoor pursuits, any area where extensive practice is necessary to acquire physical skill.

2. The KS Model contains eight modules. Module 1 requires the development of a knowledge structure, in recognition of the importance of activity subject matter. Modules 2 through 8 identify critical teaching and coaching methodologies and show how they are integrated and applied to the knowledge structure.

3. A knowledge structure reflects a cross-disciplinary framework; that is, it identifies the skills and strategies in a sport and shows how sport science concepts (exercise physiology, neuro-motor psychology, biomechanics, sport psychology, sport history, sport sociology, etc.) have affected their performance, teaching, and coaching.

4. A knowledge structure should be viewed as a personal construct, and the first step in the instructional design process. Once completed, it is used by the individual teacher or coach as the guide to planning. In this way, the KS Model promotes a personalized approach to instructional design, with each student teacher experiencing ownership over a body of knowledge to be taught or coached.

5. The development of a knowledge structure is facilitated by foundational courses in such areas as athletic therapy, neuromotor psychology, biomechanics, exercise physiology, growth and development, historical/cultural foundations of sport and physical activity, sport psychology, and sport sociology. Extensive experience in an activity as an athlete is also beneficial.

6. A knowledge structure is derived using knowledge elicitation techniques, such as text analysis, structured interview, analogical reasoning, and stimulated recall. During its development, a knowledge structure is constantly validated against the appropriate sport science literature.

7. The process of instructional design, as presented in Modules 2 through 8, takes into account different settings, age and ability groups, and motivational levels.

8. The KS Model underlies the instructional design of the Steps to Success Activity Series. This series makes available to both students and teachers the knowledge base of master teachers and coaches and sport scientists in specific activities. This series contains all the components of the KS Model, presented as a series of carefully designed Steps that take both learners and teacher-coaches from novice to expert.

9. The KS Model encourages a *quality versus quantity* approach to teaching and coaching. *All* students should be given the opportunity to learn and practice selected activities in depth. Children and youth should be provided with ongoing instruction and extensive play and competitive experiences beyond the repetitive beginner level. For too long we have reserved the best facilities, space, and time and the expertise of teachers and coaches for highly skilled or gifted students. Teachers of physical education should be given the challenge of teaching in settings beyond the beginner level, in public schools, colleges, and universities. The Steps to Success Activity Series provides the curriculum resources to make this a reality.

Topics

for Chapter 2

- Seeing the big picture
- The generative nature of a knowledge structure
- Three phases of the KS Model
- Overview of the eight modules of the KS Model

    Module 1: Creating a personalized knowledge structure

    Module 2: Analyzing learning environments

    Module 3: Analyzing learners

    Module 4: Developing a scope and sequence

    Module 5: Writing objectives

    Module 6: Determining evaluation

    Module 7: Designing learning activities

    Module 8: Making real-world applications

2

Overview of the KS Model

Seeing the Big Picture

How is it possible to get an overview of the knowledge needed to teach or coach a sport or activity, especially without experience? Let's begin by considering what it is like to see the big picture or the overview of a complex body of information. Think about the experience of getting around in an unfamiliar city. At first the streets and buildings and landmarks have no connection or association. But gradually you connect street A to avenue B, and you remember that building C is on the corner of intersection D, and so on. Getting from one place to the next becomes manageable, and the city seems to shrink in size and complexity. It is obvious that the city did not change, so your knowledge of it must have. What was once an unwieldy and intimidating body of knowledge became familiar

and easy to handle (for more on the importance of real-world maps, see Clancey, 1988).

The same process can happen when you are faced with the body of knowledge needed in teaching or coaching. It can indeed be difficult to see the big picture. Students are often told this can only be achieved through experience in the classroom or gymnasium. But although experience is very important in learning to teach and coach, it is best approached in small doses and when one is prepared. Experience, after all, has been described as "the worst teacher; it gives the test before presenting the lesson" (Law, 1986).

So you can wait and let experience be your teacher, or you can try to get an overview of what you need to know before you go out into the teaching environment. Helping students gain an overview is the goal of the KS Model.

Think of the different types of knowledge important in teaching an activity as analogous to the streets, buildings, and landmarks of a city. In Figure 1.1 you saw the types of knowledge found in the KS Model. What is important beyond simply the types of information identified is an understanding of the relationships among them. It can be difficult at first to see how all the skills, strategies, and concepts in an activity fit together and how best to teach and discipline and manage the learning setting. In fact, the initial strategy of many teachers is to present a different drill, skill, or concept every day, with little cohesion or integration from one lesson to the next. The alternative to this approach is to develop a high-level overview or knowledge structure of the sport or activity and to develop from this a cohesive and comprehensive plan of instruction.

The Generative Nature of a Knowledge Structure

The interrelationship between the eight modules of the KS Model is illustrated in Figure 2.1, in which the generative (Gaines, 1987, 1988) nature of a sport and physical activity knowledge structure is shown. The modules are named across the top, with a brief explanation of each in the column below. The most important part of Figure 2.1 is the circle radiating out from the knowledge structures column. The circle and its rays illustrate the generative and empowering nature of the knowledge structure across all other modules.

Module 1 requires the development of a cross-disciplinary knowledge structure (Lawson & Morford, 1979; Morford & Lawson, 1978; Morford, Lawson, & Hutton, 1981), which is created through study and analysis of a specific activity. A knowledge structure is developed through the use of principles that define the skills, strategies, and sport science concepts considered essential in teaching and coaching. Once in place, this body of knowledge becomes generative, guiding the process of analyzing the teaching and coaching environment, analyzing learners, determining a scope and sequence, setting or designing objectives and evaluation, selecting learning activities, and implementing a variety of teaching and coaching applications (each step in the process corresponding to a module).

Each module is summarized in this chapter, then later presented as a separate chapter, with instructional design exercises at the conclusion of each. Modules 1 to 7 should be viewed collectively as knowledge-acquisition, organization, and decision-making stages. Information about a sport, a dance, or an activity is collected and analyzed, and then organized for purposes of teaching or coaching. Module 8 presents applications to teaching and coaching, the knowledge bases identified in Modules 1 through 7 put into practice as lesson plans, unit plans, individualized instruction, year plans, and so on. Module 8 shows you how to put information drawn from a single knowledge base into use in different ways in order to achieve different ends. These ends depend upon whether you are teaching or coaching, your background in the sport, the age of your students, their ability levels, their backgrounds in the sport, their motivational levels, your own feelings of competence both in the activity and in teaching or coaching, the amount of time you have available, the expectations of others (parents, principals, supervisors) and yourself, and other variables that are typical of all teaching and coaching environments.

Three Phases of the KS Model

The KS Model contains an analysis phase, a decision-making phase, and an applications phase. The analysis phase consists of three modules: analysis of a sport into hierarchical knowledge structures, analysis of learners, and analysis of the teaching or coaching environment. The decision-making phase contains four modules: determining an appropriate scope and sequence, writing objectives, designing an evaluation system, and preparing teaching or training progressions. The applications phase, covered by the final module, introduces the basic planning vehicles used in all teaching and coaching. It teaches skills in lesson and unit planning, year and season plans, complete curricula, developmental programs, and techniques for individualizing instruction. Examples for all of the above are provided in Module 8 of this volume and in the Steps to Success Activity Series.

Overview of the Eight Modules of the KS Model

The remainder of this chapter summarizes the goals of the eight modules of the KS Model.

Module 1	Module 2	Module 3	Module 4	Module 5	Module 6	Module 7	Module 8
Knowledge Structures	Analysis of Environment	Analysis of Learners	Scope and Sequence	Writing Objectives	Determine Evaluation	Select Learning Activites	Real World Applications
Hierarchical analysis of selected cross-disciplinary categories of knowledge	Analysis of environmental conditions and constraints	Analysis of a specific group of learners	Determine a scope and sequence for a unit or season	Determine objectives using the scope and sequence as a guide	Determine overall evaluation scheme for objectives	Determine progressions of learning activities	Design and delivery of lesson and unit plans, practice and season plans
Skills, strategies, and sport science concepts to be taught or coached	Goal is to understand the teaching or coaching environment you have been given.	Determine entry-level characteristics of students.	Given:	For each skill, strategy, and concept identified develop a progression of objectives for:	Develop formative and summative evaluation procedures for the objectives written in Module 5.	Learning activities are selected to help students achieve the objectives and evaluation levels.	The development of the basic vehicles of teaching and coaching:
Knowledge structure is a *generative structure* -	How will the environment affect the instructional or coaching process?	Design and implementation of a pretest of selected skills, strategies and sport science concepts derived from the knowledge structures.	The knowledge structure of activity,	1) The class or group as a whole	Be sensitive to needs of	Selection of drills, activities and individual programs.	1) Lesson plans
This is the foundation from which new knowledge is generated for teaching and coaching in Modules 2-8.	Analysis of: Time Facilities Safety Equipment Costs Management Repairs Security Other	Classify student/athletes as Beginners Intermediates Advanced	The environmental contraints present, The entry level characteristics of students, What is the sequence of skills, strategies and sport science concepts that will be taught?	2) For those who are behind or ahead	Beginners: 1. 2. 3.	Beginners: 1. 2. 3.	2) Practice plans 3) Unit plans 4) Season plans
				Beginners: 1. 2. 3.	Intermediates: 4. 5. 6.	Intermediates: 4. 5. 6.	5) Curriculum plans 6) Developmental programs
				Intermediates: 4. 5. 6.	Advanced: 7. 8. 9.	Advanced: 7. 8. 9.	7) Individualized programs 8) Computer-based learning systems.
				Advanced: 7. 8. 9.			

Figure 2.1   The generative nature of a knowledge structures model of instructional design.

Later each module will be specifically addressed in a separate chapter.

Module 1: Creating a Personalized Knowledge Structure

Module 1 requires the analysis of a sport, a dance, or another activity into declarative knowledge structures. A declarative knowledge structure, as defined in the KS Model, contains categories of information structured to reflect a cross-disciplinary approach to physical activity (Lawson & Morford, 1979; Morford & Lawson, 1978; Morford, Lawson & Hutton, 1981). These categories, in combination, reflect the richness of the knowledge base of a specific activity as elicited from expert teachers and coaches in combination with knowledge about sport and physical activity that has evolved from the sport and other sciences. The following cross-disciplinary categories are included in whole or part in a knowledge structure:

- *Sport-specific background category* includes the purpose of the activity; its rules, safety concerns, and equipment; and historical and contemporary events, personalities, and unique developments.
- *Physiological testing and training category* includes warm-up, testing and training, injury prevention, nutrition, and other areas derived from the exercise physiology and medical sciences literature. This information is of an applied nature and reflects the adaptation of such sciences to the demands and conditions of a specific activity.
- *Psychomotor skills and strategies category* names all the individual skills in an activity and, for each skill, their subskills. For each subskill, selected technical, biomechanical, motor learning, and other teaching and coaching points are presented that describe mature or expert performance. This information is ordered hierarchically, following principles derived from the representation of knowledge, cognition, the sport sciences, and instructional design. Following the identification and analysis of individual skills, the basic strategies of the sport are analyzed. These are also placed in a hierarchical arrangement, in most cases beginning with individual strategies and leading to partner, three-plus, full-game, and special situations.

- *Psychological category* identifies concepts from the sport psychology literature that have been shown to contribute to our understanding of and participation in the activity.
- *Sociocultural category* identifies selected concepts from the sport sociology and leisure studies literature that contribute to a better understanding of how the activity has a social impact upon participants.
- *Philosophical category* identifies selected concepts from the philosophy literature that help learners appreciate the impact of the activity upon themselves and others.
- *Other categories* may be added if they have an origin in a recognized literature base and can be applied in a meaningful way in a teaching or coaching setting.

As discussed in the previous chapter, physical education is a field in which over a dozen curriculum and instruction models have been identified in the literature (Jewett & Bain, 1985; Lawson & Placek, 1981; Seidentop, Mand, & Taggert, 1986). A knowledge structure can be used as a guide in curriculum planning by emphasizing one or more cross-disciplinary categories. If a physical fitness program is desired, then the physiology training and conditioning analysis should be developed thoroughly. If a play or lifetime-sports program is desired, attention should be paid to the background information and beginner levels of psychomotor skills and strategies. If an affective or humanistic program is required, psychological, social, and philosophical analyses should take precedence. If demonstrated knowledge about physical activity is considered an important outcome, then carefully selected physiological, motor learning, biomechanical, psychological, sociological, and philosophical concepts should be identified for each activity, and an instructional program should be built upon this foundation. In this way, curricular models can be selected and a knowledge base identified that reflects and emphasizes the goals of those models.

Module 2: Analyzing Learning Environments

In Module 2 you are shown how to analyze the learning and teaching environment you will be working in. Beginners often underestimate the importance of careful prior planning in this regard, so we begin by looking at the differences between experienced and inexperienced teachers in handling a new teaching situation. Module 2 includes an analysis of the teaching environment in terms of management, safety, facilities, equipment, cost associated with teaching or coaching a unit or season, time factors and their effect on learning, handling an injury, and game modifications. All of these are developed through a series of instructional design exercises for determining personal strategies for the teaching or coaching situation you are in.

Module 3: Analyzing Learners

In Module 3 we look at the different ways you can analyze your students and athletes on selected aspects of the knowledge structures created in Module 1. For the age group that you are teaching, should some skills be omitted partly or entirely because of safety or development concerns? We target pre-assessment techniques, with your first tasks being the design of a pretest that can be implemented in portions of two or three introductory classes or practices. The overall emphasis in Module 3 is toward developing a "plan of discovery," one that incorporates a cross-disciplinary focus and results in a good understanding of the background and ability level of your students. It is this process of development that provides guidance for the next step—development of the overall scope and sequence.

Module 4: Developing a Scope and Sequence

In Module 4 you move from the analysis phase to the decision-making phase of the model. It is now time to make decisions specifically about *what* you will teach and the *order* in which the different skills, strategies, and all other information will be presented. This is called determining the scope and sequence of your program. *Scope* in instructional design is the selection of content that is appropriate for a specified, known group of students or athletes. *Sequence* is the order in which this information is presented. In a knowledge structures approach, scope and sequence decisions are made by referring to the knowledge structures. Content is selected from a knowledge structure in two fundamentally different ways, bottom-up and top-down.

Bottom-Up Sequencing Strategy. In a *bottom-up* sequencing strategy, content is selected from the bottom of the hierarchical structures upward or from the beginning of the structure to the end. This strategy is similar to that used in a task analysis (Gagné, 1977; Singer & Dick, 1980) or a mastery learning system (Block, 1971; Bloom, 1971; Carroll, 1963), where simpler skills and strategies are built one upon the other, more complex material being reached as a result of a linear process. A bottom-up strategy has merit in settings where risk factors are prevalent or where discipline and control factors make it necessary to exercise tight control over the learning environment. Bottom-up approaches may be easier for beginning teachers and coaches to understand and manage because the simple-to-complex ordering of hierarchical information is intuitively appealing and easy to see and comprehend.

Top-Down Sequencing Strategy. *Top-down* sequences are not as easily conceptualized as bottom-up sequences. For this reason they are less apparent in the literature and in practice. A top-down sequence is created by selecting, from the top of the knowledge structures in Module 1, higher level skills, strategies, and concepts, then building by selecting from any part of the structure as needed. The KS Model accommodates a top-down approach through the use of what Ausubel (1968) calls an "advance organizer." An advance organizer is presented to the students at the outset of a unit or practice for the purpose of helping students see the *whole* of a skill, strategy, or concept before they must deal with and understand its parts. The KS Model defines an advance organizer as the smallest strategic component of the activity that captures the purpose and form of the entire game, dance, or event, but with a minimum amount of players, facilities, and equipment. For example, in basketball two-on-two strategies may be identified as the advance organizer. Two-on-two strategies allow the dribble, the pass, shooting, and the execution of the basic offensive and defensive maneuvers within a game-like context. Other advance organizer examples are as follows: in badminton, singles or doubles play; in volleyball, two-on-two or three-on-three strategies; in golf, the full swing; and in swimming, the concept of buoyancy. After the advanced organizer has been identified, then learning steps are designed by drawing upon specific skills and concepts from throughout the structure.

The rules underlying the creation of a top-down sequence cannot be explained by a singular rule such as the simple-to-complex rule used in a bottom-up strategy. Of the two approaches, the easier to learn and apply is the bottom-up strategy. This is because of the adoption of a simple-to-complex rule that follows the path of the hierarchy. Top-down approaches are more difficult to plan because they require seeing the whole activity and having abstract knowledge about how its skills and strategies combine to create whole events. One way to develop an effective top-down sequencing strategy is to develop a knowledge structure, because this requires the identification and organization of all the critical knowledge components. The Steps to Success Activity Series has been designed to help you in this process. Primarily, a top-down sequencing strategy is used, with the sequence of "steps" derived through a knowledge acquisition process with expert teachers and coaches. At every step, the learner is shown how a skill or concept fits into the larger context of game play.

Module 5: Writing Objectives

Objectives are statements of intent that describe what the teacher or coach expects the students to accomplish by the end of a lesson, a course, a unit, or a season. In Module 5, progressions of objectives are written that chart the novice-to-expert transition for each skill, strategy, and concept identified in the scope and sequence plan. Four types of objectives are written that specify the attainment of the following:

Psychomotor Technique. These objectives specify the *quality* of movement or style you want to see exhibited for each skill or subskill, that is, the qualitative biomechanics or elements of mature technique. This information has already been identified in the knowledge structures in Module 1 and needs only to be selected and stated as a technical objective. In the Steps to Success Activity Series, this information is called the "Keys to Success."

Psychomotor Performance. These objectives specify *quantity* and accompany technical objectives. The quantification of a skill specifies such aspects as number of repetitions, degree of ac-

curacy, speed, height, and consistency. Performance objectives encourage students to practice skills in order to attain these and other observable objective indicators of improvement. In the Steps to Success Activity Series, these are called "Success Goals."

Knowledge About. These objectives test learners on factual knowledge, and problem-solving ability, derived from the background, physiology, psychomotor skills and strategies, psychological, sociocultural, and other cross-disciplinary categories of information. At the most basic level, objectives are written that test knowledge about rules, technique, strategies, and any of the other areas where a pencil-and-paper understanding should be exhibited. More advanced types of objectives ask students to undertake projects that require the analysis of skills, and the display of an understanding of more complex concepts. The Steps to Success Activity Series contains banks of questions on these, as well as many innovative project and problem-solving ideas.

Objectives That Stress Personal Development. These objectives specify outcomes related to student self-development and the attainment of goals related to self and society. Traditionally called affective objectives, concepts include self-concept, motivation, teamwork, self-discipline, confidence, empathy, goalsetting, and other categories. Each of these objectives differs from those in the previous group, where some of the objectives assessed the student's knowledge *about* concepts. Objectives in the personal development category are written so as to determine the extent to which individuals are able to exhibit these qualities in everyday life. In the Steps to Success Activity Series, each author has selected one or more personal development concepts and integrated them throughout the texts. For example, mental skills and setting goals are presented in golf (Owens & Bunker, 1989a, 1989b); concentration is presented in tennis (Brown, 1989a, 1989b); fear reduction is presented in swimming (Thomas, 1989a, 1989b); teamwork in volleyball (Viera & Ferguson, 1989a, 1989b); developing confidence in archery (Haywood & Lewis, 1989a, 1989b); anticipation (read and prepare, read and react) in softball (Potter & Brockmeyer, 1989a, 1989b); and mental discipline in bowling (Strickland, 1989a, 1989b).

Module 6: Determining Evaluation

In Module 6, the art and science of skill analysis, evaluation, and correction is presented. You are first introduced to the concept of a skills acquisition knowledge structure. You will see that this knowledge structure is simply an extension of the one created in Module 1, in which you described expert or mature performance. A skills acquisition knowledge structure describes the characteristics of learners (novices and intermediates) en route to expert performance as perceived by master teachers and coaches in the activity.

Evaluation is presented in Module 6 as an individualizing vehicle for providing feedback, as a motivational aid, and as a medium that facilitates communication and discussion between teachers and students about the subject matter of a sport or activity. Both formative and summative approaches are presented. Evaluation is used in order to assess students relative to established criteria or to each other, and to assign final or summative grades. In designing instruction, it is important to consciously decide the type of evaluation you want to use. Deciding to use a formal system is an important decision that will have a significant impact on the learning environment you create.

Module 7: Designing Learning Activities

Once you have determined your objectives and evaluation strategy, the next step is to create interesting and effective learning experiences that will help your students achieve the objectives you have set. In Module 7, you are encouraged to select drills and other exercises only if they will achieve the outcomes you have in mind. Module 7 discourages the common practice of choosing, at random, drills and other activities that simply keep students busy. Such an approach ultimately leads to classes and practices that lack purpose, cohesion, and overall direction and to students who are disinterested and bored. The KS Model is designed to prevent this, to help you teach in an integrated and cohesive way. Drills, progressions, films, posters, software, and other aids should be selected and used only because they contribute to your overall vision or knowledge structure of the sport.

Module 8: Making Real-World Applications

The information identified previously is now used to create different vehicles for teaching or coaching. In the KS Model, the design of teaching and coaching applications, such as lesson and unit plans, is the culmination of a thought process that has identified the following knowledge components:

1. the subject matter of the activity (Module 1);
2. the teaching environment (Module 2);
3. your students (Module 3);
4. the scope and teaching sequence of skills, strategies, and concepts (Module 4);
5. your objectives (Module 5);
6. with evaluation (Module 6); and
7. the design of learning activities (Module 7).

Modules 1 through 7 are pieces of a puzzle that can be combined in different ways to create numerous applications in teaching and coaching. Module 8 puts the pieces together into nine applications:

1. lesson planning;
2. unit planning;
3. curriculum design for a single activity;
4. curriculum design for the multiactivity program;
5. instructional design of the coaching program;
6. individualized programs for teaching or coaching settings;
7. ActionMark, a software program;
8. design of the Steps to Success Activity Series; and
9. the on-campus teaching laboratory.

Part II

Becoming Knowledgeable for Teaching and Coaching

Topics

for Chapter 3

- The elusive nature of expertise
- Knowledge acquisition techniques
- Early research on the nature of expert knowledge
- The process of knowledge acquisition
- Knowledge acquisition techniques used in the KS Model
  1. Text analysis
  2. Structured interview
  3. Stimulated recall
  4. Analogical derivation
- Integration and validation of expert knowledge
- Three cognitive characteristics of experts
  1. Experts "chunk" or group information into larger, cohesive units
  2. Experts display hierarcical organization of knowledge
  3. Experts differ from novices in knowledge organization and decision making
- How a knowledge structure differs from a task analysis

3

Photo by Dac Dang.

Understanding the Nature of Expertise and the Process of Knowledge Acquisition

The essence of becoming an athlete is to make more and more of what you know unconscious and therefore out of reach of description, verbalization, explanation. The essence of becoming a teacher or coach is the reverse. You must find a way of making that which is unconscious, conscious, that which is non-verbal, verbal, and that which defies description, descriptive and easy for others to understand.

In this chapter we look at how knowledge acquired as a student or an athlete is transformed into subject matter for presentation to others in a teaching or coaching setting. We first look at the nature of expert knowledge and the fact that much of what is known by an expert is unconscious, automatic, and not easily subjected to analysis. This is true for all areas of expertise, not just physical skills as exhibited in sports and athletics. Yet it is the process of becoming aware of the intricacies of a domain of knowledge that lies at the heart of becoming a teacher or coach. We look first at the concept of knowledge acquisition and the techniques that may be used to analyze the knowledge of experts found in classes, books, texts, films, and other media. As you become familiar with these techniques, you will also become aware that the type of analyses you carry out is influenced by your own state of knowledge in the activity and the experiences you have had as athlete, student, official, teacher, or coach.

You will also see that when we speak of expert knowledge, we are referring not only to master coaches and teachers but also to the

25

knowledge contributed to a sport by scientists in exercise physiology, biomechanics, psychology, philosophy, history, and other research areas. After reading this chapter, you will also be familiar with the cognitive changes that occur in a knowledge base as a state of expertise is acquired: the hierarchical nature of knowledge, the chunking of knowledge, and some of the important differences in decision making found between novices and experts in all domains.

The Elusive Nature of Expertise

In arriving at a method for representing the knowledge of expert teachers and coaches, we must first deal with the problem of the elusive nature of expertise. With the attainment of a high degree of skill—mental or physical—come both automaticity and unconscious behavior (Hunt, 1982; Lindsay & Norman, 1977; Schneider & Schriffrin, 1977, 1984). It is only by making aspects of a task unconscious that a person is able to do more and more with the same or less expenditure of effort. Wickelgren (1981) describes this cognitive phenomenon, which occurs in all areas of human endeavor, as follows:

> It is clear that as we acquire concepts for ever more complex combinations of simpler ideas, we are not finding it ever more difficult to think with these concepts. The new higher-level concept nodes allow us to think about complex subject matter just about as easily and as efficiently as we could previously think about simpler subject matter using lower-level concepts. This is a remarkable accomplishment. It is surely an important reason for the seemingly boundless potential of the human mind to understand ever more about anything. (p. 28)

In recent years, researchers have developed the methods and tools whereby we can understand how experts in different areas function. You will find that to develop structures like those shown in the appendices, you require a different type of thinking, one that is not commonly known as "normal science." Normal science requires the use of the following steps in investigating a problem or carrying out research: formulation of hypotheses, design of investigation, accumulation of data, classification of data, development of generalizations, and verification of results. The development of a knowledge

structure draws upon an array of other tools. In order to develop an understanding of the different type of inquiry you will be involved in when developing a knowledge structure, consider how the following problem was investigated and the solution derived.

The night is stormy and the wind heels the craft to 45 degrees. It maintains a steady, relentless course due east. The sky is totally black, with neither the moon nor the stars to act as a guide. The warm wind has a steady howl that drives the hull of the boat into the sea. The man at the tiller is calm and still and glances steadily to his left and right from time to time. He is alert and restful all at once. There will not be landfall of any kind possible for at least a week. The boat is seven meters long; it has no form of power or communication except the sail and the wind. It is in the midst of an expanse of water that stretches almost unbroken for a thousand miles.

The man at the tiller is not lost; he knows exactly where he is and what he is doing. He is a seafarer raised from birth in the ways of long sea travel. He navigates by holding a picture of the sea world in his mind. He places himself at the center of this world and expects the world to pass by him in a predictable way as he sails. At certain times he sees a star or an island or senses the presence of sea messages carried in a current or the tide, by the color of the water, by the swells, winds, and seabirds. If the weather occludes his view, then he extrapolates in his mind the passage of one set of references points to another, and adjusts the points if blown off course. The man has developed an exceptionally complex knowledge structure for long sea navigation that works flawlessly. [Story written by author, after reading Hutchins (1983, pp. 191-225).]

The preceding passage suggests the challenge facing researchers who have as their goal the explanation of exceptional human skill. For decades Western scientists have tried to unravel the mystery of the South Seas navigators. The

Caroline Island seafarers have maintained their traditional skills to this day and routinely travel out of sight of land without navigational aids of any kind. In a thousand years of such travel, there have been only a few accounts of boats lost at sea. What makes the navigators so successful? A beginning solution to the problem is provided by the work of Hutchins (1983), who studied the navigational skills of the Micronesians of the Caroline Islands by traveling with them, interviewing them, and using a number of methods collectively known as *knowledge acquisition techniques.*

> Western researchers travelling with these people have found that at any time during the voyage the navigators can accurately indicate the bearings of the port of departure, the goal island, and other islands off to the side of the course steered even though all of these may be over the horizon out of sight of the navigator. These navigators are also able to tack upwind to an unseen target keeping mental track of its changing bearing, something that is simply impossible for a Western navigator without instruments. (pp. 191-192)

In carrying out his study of the Micronesian seafarers, Hutchins (1983) found that much of the work of earlier Western researchers was inaccurate. He attributed this to the exclusive use of usual Western scientific procedures that blocked an understanding of the seafarers' skills.

> In our tradition, the operations of observation, computation, and interpretation are each a different sort of activity and they are executed serially. The Micronesian's tool box is in his mind. . . . The interpretation of the result (bearing of the reference island, for example) is embedded in the computation (construction of the horizon image) which is itself embedded in the observation (time of day). The Micronesian technique is elegant and effective. It is organized in a way that allows the navigator to solve in his head problems that a western navigator would not attempt without substantial technological supports. (p. 223)

Knowledge Acquisition Techniques

In understanding how knowledge is represented and used by those involved in complex areas such as navigation or teaching and coaching, it is necessary to use methods of research and data collection that move beyond the limits imposed by a strict scientific method. The knowledge structures created in Module 1 (and those in the appendices) were created using techniques collectively called knowledge acquisition techniques (Boose & Gaines, 1988; Gaines & Boose, 1988; Shaw & Gaines, 1988). The term *knowledge acquisition* is derived from the fields of cognition and expert systems development and is defined as the process of eliciting knowledge from experts in specialized areas using techniques such as text analysis, protocol analysis, structured interviewing, stimulated recall, and analogical derivation. Each of these methods is used in the KS Model and is explained in detail later. But first it is important to know something about the underlying characteristics of expert knowledge.

Early Research on the Nature of Expert Knowledge

Over the past decade, a considerable amount of work has been carried out in the study of expertise. One of the first projects was carried out by Johnson (Hunt, 1982) who studied doctors, engineers, stockbrokers, lawyers, and other experts as they performed the everyday tasks of their professions. As you read his account below, think about how he studied the individuals involved and about which principles and techniques allowed him to derive his conclusions.

> The most striking feature of expertise in these less-than-orderly fields is that the experts, though they are faster and better at problem solving than novices, have trouble explaining how they do it. "What did you do?" we'd say. "I don't know," they'd say, "Why don't you watch me and see?" Or they'll say, "It just comes to me."
>
> . . . the expert also has a high altitude overview—the hierarchical structure Reif talks about. Highly expert people have an enormously efficient picture of what they are trying to do—they see things in perspective, so they know just what additional information they need. The less expert individual collects a great deal of unnecessary data because he doesn't know what he needs to know.

... the expert has a whole bunch of specifically tailored tricks to make the problem manageable—quick little associations, based on a lot of experience, linking one or two scraps of information with the heart of the problem—pointers, crosslinks in the knowledge network. . . .

And the paradox of expertise is that the expert can't tell you how he does what he does. As he was growing proficient, he had to think about what he was doing, then he went through a phase where he was practicing those hook-ups, and finally he got to the stage of automaticity, where all that stuff is filed away, out of sight. So when I ask, "How did you know? What did you do?" he says, "You can't reduce diagnosis to rules. It's an art—I just do it." (From *The Universe Within: A New Science Explores the Human Mind*, [pp. 264-265] by M. Hunt, 1982, Brighton, England: Harvester Press.)

The Process of Knowledge Acquisition

Knowledge acquisition techniques have evolved over the years and, as described by Gaines (1987), have undergone two stages of development. Figure 3.1 shows the earliest model of knowledge acquisition, involving a single researcher (called a knowledge engineer) and a single expert. A knowledge engineer is a scientist trained in the techniques of knowledge acquisition, typically with a background in cognition, expert systems development, and computing science. This model was the approach used by Johnson in the studies reported earlier and was also used in initially developing MYCIN, the expert system already described for diagnosing and treating cardiorespiratory disease.

Because of the limitation of relying on only one expert and one knowledge engineer, the earlier approach has been replaced by the model shown in Figure 3.2. Here we see that a knowledge base is derived from a number of experts and a number of knowledge engineers. Modern-day expert systems elicit knowledge from many experts, often using the computer as a knowledge acquisition device. Complex knowledge bases are encoded and made available to a variety of clients or marketed as expert system shells,

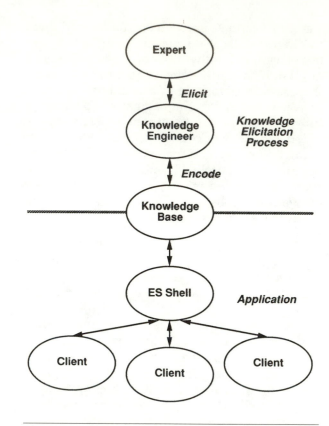

Figure 3.1. Basic model of manual knowledge acquisition. *Note.* From "Advanced Expert System Support Environments" by B.R. Gaines. In *Proceedings of the 2nd Knowledge Acquisition for Knowledge-Based Systems Workshop* (p. 8.2) by B.R. Gaines and J. Boose (Eds.), 1987, Banff, AB: American Association of Artificial Intelligence. Copyright 1987 by B.R. Gaines and J. Boose. Reprinted by permission.

empty programs into which domain experts and engineers may enter their knowledge. Also, newer expert systems do not strive for consensus or agreement between experts, but provide alternate approaches to problems and guidance in arriving at appropriate solutions.

Knowledge Acquisition Techniques Used in the KS Model

The KS Model adopts the procedures conceptually shown in Figure 3.2 in the following ways. Put yourself in the position of knowledge engineer, with the experts being the collective of coaches, teachers, courses, books, teams, and other resources and experiences you have had as student, player, coach, or official. Your task

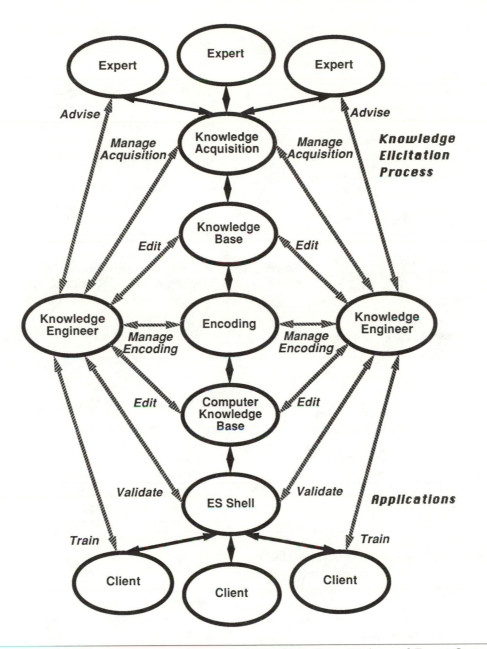

Figure 3.2. Recent model of knowledge acquisition techniques. *Note.* From "Advanced Expert System Support Environments" by B.R. Gaines. In *Proceedings of the 2nd Knowledge Acquisition for Knowledge-Based Systems Workshop* (p. 8.3) by B.R. Gaines and J. Boose (Eds.), 1987, Banff, AB: American Association of Artificial Intelligence. Copyright 1987 by B.R. Gaines and J. Boose. Reprinted by permission.

is to create a knowledge structure for a specific sport using acquisition techniques that help you gain insight into how experts in an activity think and act.

The knowledge acquisition techniques identified by Gaines (1987) and used in the KS Model are text analysis, structured interview, stimulated recall, and analogical derivation (see Figure 3.3).

Text Analysis

In text analysis, materials created by experts (books, manuals, films, videos, software) are analyzed and represented following guidelines of knowledge representation. The task you face as a beginning professional is to understand the many sources of information available in every sport and physical activity. It can seem over-

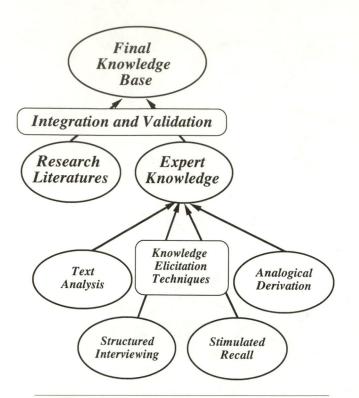

Figure 3.3 Knowledge acquisition approaches. *Note.* From "Advanced Expert System Support Environments" by B.R. Gaines. In *Proceedings of the 2nd Knowledge Acquisition for Knowledge Based Systems Workshop* (p. 8.10) by B.R. Gaines and J. Boose (Eds.), 1987, Banff, AB: American Association of Artificial Intelligence. Copyright 1987 by B.R. Gaines and J. Boose. Reprinted by permission.

whelming because the approaches suggested by experts appear limitless. And in a multiactivity setting the problem is compounded as you move from one activity to the next. In the next two chapters, you will be introduced to both general and specific guidelines to help you analyze the material available in every sport, dance, or physical activity. The guidelines, principles, and rules of analysis are the same for all activities, with accommodations for different ages and ability levels and for different environmental contexts.

Structured Interview

In a structured interview, a coach, teacher, or researcher is asked a series of preplanned questions. The responses are recorded on an audiotape, coded, and analyzed. Also called *protocol analysis*, this technique has as its goal the definition of the underlying knowledge structures and rules that the expert uses to solve problems.

It is also possible to carry out a structured interview using a graphic format, a process developed and used extensively in creating the knowledge structures shown in this book and the Steps to Success Activity Series. This process is illustrated in a sample interview with an expert soccer coach, presented at the end of Module 1.

Stimulated Recall

In stimulated recall, experts are videotaped as they teach or coach and then review the tapes and analyze their own performances. A stimulated recall procedure involves posing questions that are similar to those in a structured interview, but with the added stimulation of the individual reacting to and elaborating upon his or her own teaching and coaching behaviors. Stimulated recall is used widely in research, education, and other areas. It is a procedure you may want to try, but it requires the willingness of an expert to be videotaped and interviewed.

Analogical Derivation

Analogical derivation involves the use of an example or ideal prototype from which new cases are derived. The KS Model makes extensive use of this method, called *reasoning by analogy;* sample knowledge structures in badminton, golf, and ice hockey are provided in the appendices as prototypes or examples. It is not intended that you copy them verbatim, but that you use them "by analogy," that is, as examples from which you may generate your own knowledge structures. Remember that a knowledge structure, by definition, is a personal construct that portrays the subject matter *you* wish to teach in a sport or physical activity.

Integration and Validation of Expert Knowledge

The final step in the creation of a knowledge structure is *knowledge integration and validation.* This final phase validates, or determines the veracity of, the knowledge you have selected and portrayed in the knowledge structure (Shaw & Woodward, 1988). This process of validation is carried out continuously by you—the teacher or coach—and is an exciting and challenging process. There are three steps in the validation process.

1. *Consult scientific authorities*. The first line of validation is through scientific authorities, for example, in the course work you are taking as a student in physical education. Your studies in exercise physiology, biomechanics, motor learning, growth and development, sport psychology, sport sociology, and other areas should lend support to the structures you have created.

2. *Do not expect complete consensus among expert coaches and teachers*. To what extent do experts agree on the material you have assembled in your structure? Check sources in addition to those you used and solicit the opinions of other experts by showing them the representation you have created.

Again, do not expect or strive for complete consensus. There are aspects in every expert system and every sport where experts present differing opinions. These areas of nonconsensus create a personal challenge for you, because you must work your way through these conflicting situations and arrive at your own personal position and reasons for following a certain approach.

3. *Strive for self-validation in the world of professional practice*. This final level of validation for a teacher or coach is one of self-validation and is arrived through your own use of the knowledge structure in designing instruction. Find a situation where you can achieve a real-world experience teaching or coaching (as in Module 8) and ask yourself the following questions:

- Did the knowledge structure help me understand the overall organization of the subject matter in this activity?
- Did I use the structure to help me organize the material for my classes or practices, from Day 1 through the end of the unit?
- Did the structure help me set objectives and make evaluation decisions?
- Did the structure increase my level of confidence as a coach or teacher?

Three Cognitive Characteristics of Experts

A considerable amount of research has evolved over the past 15 years as a result of the preceding techniques' being used. There are well-documented differences between experts and novices in fields as diverse as chess, physics,

mathematics, piloting, radiology, notetaking, teaching, clinical psychology, and computer programming. In addition, cognitive differences have been documented between expert and novice athletes and coaches in basketball, volleyball, gymnastics, badminton, ice hockey, and many other sports. In this section, we look at this research and discuss three important characteristics that underlie the attainment of a state of expertise: chunking, hierarchical organization, and expert-novice difference in knowledge organization and decision making.

Experts "Chunk," or Group, Information Into Large, Cohesive Units

Cognitive research on expert-novice differences in many respects began with a study by Chase and Simon (1973) comparing the ability of experts and novice chess players to reconstruct the arrangement of pieces on chessboards after a few seconds of study. When the pieces were organized in a meaningful way, the experts could reconstruct the boards and the novices could not. However, when the boards were set in a random organization, neither the experts nor the novices could recall the boards. This study showed that the expert players had developed a memory structure that recognized the different chess openings, endings, defenses, and offenses. The novice, in contrast, tried to remember the surface details of the board, an impossible task.

This study has been replicated in a number of sport settings. Allard and Burnett (1985) described a number of studies in which set-play situations were shown to novice and expert athletes. Expert players could reconstruct the plays and other tactical maneuvers with only brief glimpses of slides showing different phases of a play. Novices, in contrast, did not have this ability. However, when game information was shown that lacked tactical sense (as in the chess study), there was not difference between the groups.

These studies show that as expertise is acquired, the expert develops a memory structure made up of large "chunks" of information (Miller, 1956) that have numerous associations and relationships. The expert also develops a global overview, so that seeing one small piece of information primes the larger network of concepts, ideas, skills, and subskills. The novice's knowledge structure, in contrast, is not as extensive, is fragmented and incomplete, and lacks the links between skills and concepts that permit rapid decision making, precision, and ease in thought and action.

The development of a knowledge structure for a sport involves chunking information for purposes of teaching and coaching. To illustrate, turn to the ice hockey knowledge structure in Appendix C. On the first page or map structure, find the individual skills technique category. There are only four major skills named: skating, puck control, checking, and goaltending. Now leaf through the pages of the structure until you come to the first individual skill, skating. Displayed here in hierarchical form are all the skills and subskills for skating identified by the experts involved. This organization of skating information is chunked, or organized in a meaningful way for teaching and coaching. Furthermore, as we move on to the explanation of the KS Model in Modules 2 through 8, you will see that each of the skills and subskills named in the knowledge structure is linked to progressions of objectives, evaluation techniques, teaching progressions, drills, learning activities, and other information proven effective in practice. This information is also part of the memory structure, the chunk, of skating information.

Experts Display a Hierarchical Organization of Knowledge

A hierarchy is defined as an organization of elements, concepts, motor units, or other entities arranged in such a way that there are successive components in a tree or other structure with branching elements. Another way to view a hierarchy is as a set of progressively smaller cups, each fitting neatly within the previous. When they are fully fit together, you see only the largest cup, which in reality is holding many others. Similarly, if you look at the structures shown in Appendices A through C, you will see that the map structure (the first page of each) contains only a few skills, strategies, or concepts. When you look further into the structure, however, you will see that each has a rich knowledge structure made up of numerous interrelated components.

The early literature defined a hierarchy as a rigid structure. That is, if you activated the top element of the hierarchy (the executive or high-level command, the information on the first page, the map structure), then all of the bottom or lower units were enslaved to or entrained to this one command. Today, the hierarchical

model has been revised to allow any element in the structure to be dominant (Charniak & McDermott, 1985). Dominance is dependent upon training, context, and numerous other variables (Anderson, 1983; Gardner, 1985; Johnson-Laird, 1988; Pew, 1974). In the field of motor skills, Pew reflected this view early on, as he described the hierarchical organization of physical skills as follows:

A hierarchically organized system is one in which the distinction among levels is diffuse and in which there is a rich interplay among the various processes that the individual calls upon to complete a task. The relative importance of each level depends on the environmental constraints, the criteria with respect to which performance is to be optimized, and the level of experience the performer brings to the activity. (p. 3)

Hierarchical Organization in the KS Model. A knowledge structure, as defined in Module 1, shows how the skills and strategies in an activity relate to one another in a hierarchy for purposes of teaching or coaching. The identification of skills and concepts as illustrated does *not* necessarily imply that you will teach each skill separately, nor does it mean that the components are taught in a step-by-step, linear manner. Decisions about whether to include an element in the sequence of instruction is a separate question and is procedural in nature. Approaches to these questions are covered in Modules 2 through 8.

Experts Differ from Novices in Knowledge Organization and Decision Making

Housner (1981) investigated the knowledge structures that underlie expert and novice play in badminton. He defined a knowledge structure as "domain specific content residing in long term memory" and cognitive processes as "procedures employed for performing a sequence of actions with the content" (Chi & Glaser, 1980).

Two knowledge acquisition techniques were used. Using a protocol analysis approach (much like a structured interview), an expert and a novice player were asked to explain the strategies they used while playing and provide reasons for why they chose one approach over another before and after play. Each subject competed in a number of games. During each game, structured interviews were carried out at the beginning of the match and at every 20 minutes during play. The players were asked to explain what they were doing on the previous point and what they would try to do on the next serve. At the completion of play, they were asked to reflect back over the entire game. Figures 3.4 and 3.5 show the different knowledge structures of the novice and expert players.

As is evident, the hierarchical natures of the expert and the novice player differ, with the differences being similar to those discussed earlier. Experts chunk information into larger units and possess more chunks of information organized into a hierarchical structure. Housner (1981) interprets Figures 3.4 and 3.5 as follows:

The expert was found to have more strategic concepts, more production systems and more interconnections among concepts within his strategic knowledge structures than did the novice. In addition, the expert was found to employ an information gathering solution strategy characterized by the chunking of game events into probability or summary statements and the use of evaluative and

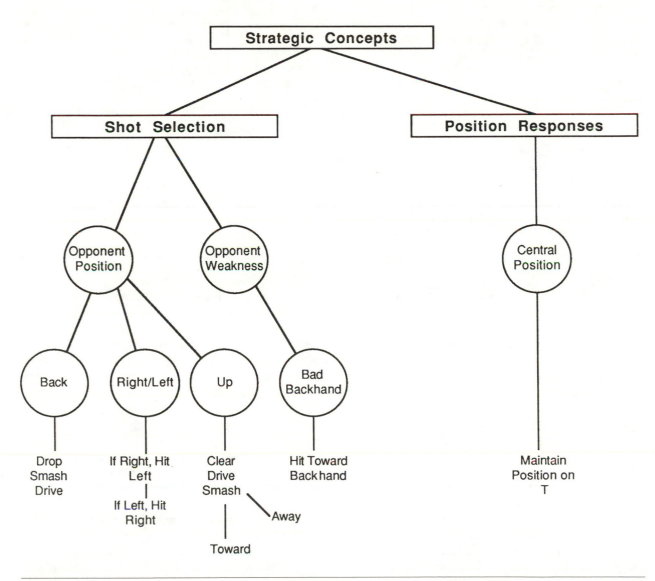

Figure 3.4. Knowledge structure of a novice badminton player. *Note.* From *Skill in Badminton* by L.D. Housner, 1981, unpublished manuscript. Reprinted by permission.

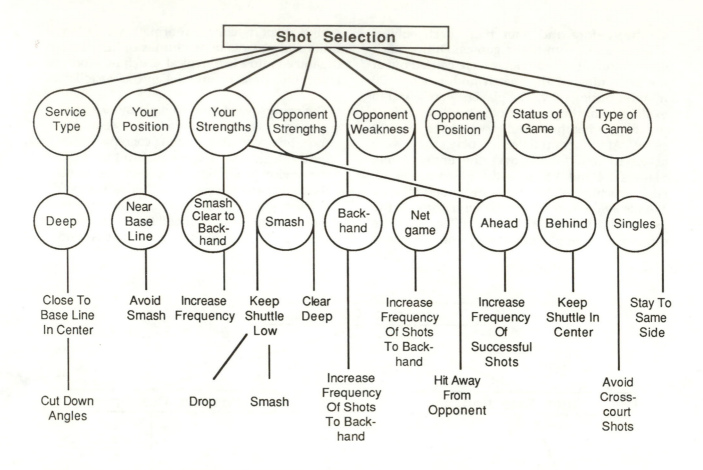

Figure 3.5. Knowledge structure of an expert badminton player. *Note*. From *Skill in Badminton* by L.D. Housner, 1981, unpublished manuscript. Reprinted by permission.

shot selection statements as a mode of semantically analyzing the flow of action during the game. The novice, however, was not found to employ these solution strategies, but rather relied on a straight forward application of a small number of stored strategic concepts. (p. 16)

Housner and Griffey (1985) extended the preceding work to look specifically at differences in planning strategies of expert and novice teachers. Eight expert and eight novice teachers were compared on their planning strategies in teaching physical education classes. The teachers were audiotaped as they planned their lessons in a thinking-aloud procedure, then videotaped while teaching. They were then asked to analyze their own teaching as they viewed the tapes

in a stimulated recall–knowledge acquisition technique.

During the planning phase, it was found that relative to the novices, the expert teachers actively collected more information, asked more questions (almost double), and were different in asking about the background of the students, the equipment available, the materials, and the nature of the facilities in which the lessons were to be taught. In addition, the experienced teachers made more planning decisions, had a greater repertoire of ideas, and initiated more interactions and feedback sessions with the students.

During the teaching of the lessons and the self-analyses afterward, the experienced teachers emphasized subject matter and teaching specific motor skills more, and directed their attention to the individual students and to providing feedback on the activities and tasks at hand. The novices, in contrast, were influenced by what Housner and Griffey (1985) call "student interest cues." The students were able to influence the direction of the class by displaying interest or enjoyment in what was being taught. The novices often changed their lessons in response to this type of student input, whereas the experts were not as easily diverted from their original objectives.

Many of the characteristics identified earlier by Chase and Simon (1973), Hunt (1982), and others are prevalent in athletes, teachers, and coaches of physical skills. As you pursue your career, expect to develop a hierarchical overview for each activity you teach, one that contains rich chunks of information interconnected by links and decision rules that become more intricate, more automatic, and easier each year.

How a Knowledge Structure Differs From a Task Analysis

At first glance, a knowledge structure may appear to be the same as a task analysis. However, there are distinctive differences between the two concepts, differences that change how instructional design is thought about and implemented. The concept of a task analysis, as used in instructional design, was founded by Robert Gagné (1974, 1977). Gagné identified a number of different types of learning as part of attaining intellectual ability, with simpler or lower types of stimulus-response learning being prerequisite to more complex or higher learning. A cumulative learning hierarchy was developed, with the simplest type of learning being stimulus-response learning (associations and chains), followed by discrimination, concepts, rule learning, and finally the highest form, problem solving. For any task, learners were thought to pass through linear, simple-to-complex steps that were captured in a hierarchy of learning objectives.

In suggesting the use of a knowledge structure as the basis for instructional design, it is important to be aware of fundamental differences and similarities between it and task analysis.

Glaser (1976) describes task analysis as a useful technique that potentially could (a) provide an analytical description of what is to be learned, (b) describe what a competent performer in a subject matter domain has learned that distinguishes him or her from a novice, (c) provide an analysis of the content of instruction, and (d) define the properties of a certain class of performance.

However, upon closer scrutiny, there are relationships that logically exist in a structure of knowledge that are not "caught" by a rational task analysis procedure and its assumptions. Consider the following:

1. *In a task analysis approach to instructional design, the first step is to state the end objectives, and second to select content that will attain the objectives.* This approach is exactly opposite the one used in a knowledge structures approach to instructional design. In developing a knowledge structure, it is the nature of the content that informs structure, and it is from this base that objectives are then derived for specific learners and situations. In a task analysis approach, the origin of objectives is not explained. In reality, though, we know they are derived from the combination of the teacher's knowledge of the subject area and knowledge about how children learn that subject. However, this aspect of instructional design is not handled in a direct way but becomes an assumption upon which the planning process is placed. Secondly, the teacher, after stating an objective, is then asked to select subject matter that will achieve the objective. This type of planning hides the inherent structure of subject matter knowledge and prevents the teacher and students from seeing the interrelationships between skills, strategies, and concepts.

2. *A task analysis approach recommends the orderly presentation of content from simple to complex through a set progression of objectives.* The task analysis approach as founded by Gagné (1977) ordered objectives according to a cumulative learning hierarchy, the simplest types of learning followed by more complex types and finally by problem solving. For any task, learners were thought to pass through linear, simple-to-complex steps that were operationalized in a lockstep manner.

In the KS Model, this approach to instructional design is included as one of two approaches you may use and is called a *bottom-up scope and sequencing strategy*. In learning sport skills, however, the learning of simpler tasks may not always occur before complex ones can be learned. To restrict instructional design to this one approach is to put restrictions upon students and teachers that are both unnecessary and inappropriate.

Consider a two-on-two situation in basketball. Students can learn the rudiments of strategies that accompany this maneuver (give and go, screen to, post play) at the same time or even before they have mastered the intricacies of the prerequisite individual skills (dribble, pass, shoot). In addition, students often learn these skills independent of one another and not in a set, simple-to-complex progression. It is not unusual to be adept in what is considered a complex skill (e.g., shooting), but deficient in what is often considered an underlying or simpler skill (e.g., footwork). Requiring learners to move in a lockstep manner from one simple skill to the next can be a debilitating design strategy when used exclusively.

For this reason the KS Model advocates two different types of sequencing content for purposes of teaching, bottom-up and top-down. A bottom-up strategy is similar to the task analysis approach; a top-down strategy, however, begins with concepts that are nearer the top of the knowledge structure—in particular, strategic concepts and selected content from the structure—in order to achieve the higher level type of knowledge. The basis of this selection is not as straightforward as the bottom-up strategy and appears to reside with expert teachers and coaches. This is one of the main reasons the KS Model advocates the use of the knowledge acquisition techniques described earlier in this chapter.

3. *In a knowledge structure, subskills themselves may be hierarchically related to one another, constituting a sequenced progression leading to intratask transfer across the hierarchy.* This lateral type of transfer of knowledge and skill is not recognized as a factor in task analysis (Bergan, 1980; Glaser, 1984), where relationships are considered to be vertical and not within families or categories. Lateral or intratask transfer describes how subskills and concepts combine to constitute whole skills and is related to the literature on transfer of training (Magill, 1989; Singer, 1980). If you look at the analysis of individual skills in the knowledge structures in the appendices, you will see numerous examples of intratask transfer derived from a study of expert knowledge.

4. *In analyzing the performance of students in many areas, Glaser points out that many learners have the ability to identify efficient solution routines that are quicker and intuitively more intelligent than the simple-to-complex process of task analysis.* Learners do not always have to work their way through each prerequisite step to a solution; more often than not, they make intuitive leaps over what can be cumbersome and unnecessary intervening steps. The Steps to Success Activity Series primarily presents the top-down sequencing approach as a major focus. For example, golf instruction begins with the full swing and badminton with the singles or doubles game. In each activity there is an early integration of skills into play and game situations.

A knowledge structure shows the simple-to-complex relationship between skills and the instances of lateral transfer between skills. It also reflects the insights of expert teachers and coaches. It does not, however, lock you into a simple-to-complex or bottom-up type of sequencing strategy. Instead, you have a choice of either the bottom-up approach or a top-down approach. Decisions of this type are explained in Module 4 of the KS Model, discussing scope and sequence, as well as in Modules 5 through 7, where progressions of objectives and learning activities are designed that follow the scope and sequence you have selected. There is a tendency for master instructors to teach in a top-down fashion. This occurs because they possess a rich knowledge structure for their sport, in which they have come to understand the relationships between multiple skills and between skills and strategic maneuvers.

5. *A task analysis approach is context dependent, that is, it is necessary to state an objective and create a different task analysis for every context or condition encountered. A knowledge structures approach, in contrast, identifies a declarative body of knowledge that is stable and used in all contexts.* A declarative knowledge structure provides a structured overview for a domain that is created only once, with revisions as warranted. When preparing to teach or coach in a particular context, one selects information from the structure, in whole or part, as required. In contrast, a task analysis approach requires a distinctive set of objectives with accompanying task analyses for each situation encountered. Because the number of con-

texts is limited only by the number of learners to be taught, so is the number of objectives with their task analyses. The never-ending aspect of this type of planning does not equate with what we know about how experts function. Experts establish a stable knowledge base from which they extract, devise, and create multiple strategies.

Topics

for Chapter 4

- A knowledge structure recognizes specificity
- A knowledge structure provides a role for expert knowledge
- Knowledge used in teaching and coaching is categorized as declarative or procedural
- A cross-disciplinary approach defines declarative knowledge in Module 1
- Procedural knowledge is defined in Modules 2 through 8
- The cross-disciplinary categories selected vary to reflect curriculum goals and resources
- A declarative knowledge structure displays ''cognitive economy''
- A declarative knowledge structure employs hierarchical representation
- A declarative knowledge structure permits the flexible sequencing of content
- Developing a knowledge structure promotes three qualities important in teaching and coaching

4

Another powerful strategy exploited by intelligent human beings . . . is to break up a complex problem into more tractable sub-problems; it is a strategy of divide and conquer.

—Douglas Lenat

Photo by Kimberlie Henris.

Ten Guidelines for Developing a Knowledge Structure

In this chapter we look at 10 general guidelines that underlie the development of a knowledge structure. A strategy of "divide and conquer" is advocated to help you deal with the complexity in the knowledge base of all sports and activities today.

But such a strategy does not recommend a part method of instruction—quite the opposite. Your goal is to gain an overview of the whole body of knowledge of a sport or activity in order to better make decisions that fulfill the needs of all your students. Of special importance are the distinction between declarative and procedural knowledge and the contribution of the cross-disciplinary model of sport studies. Cross-disciplinary categories of knowledge are defined,

with knowledge in each represented in a hierarchy. Relationships between content nodes are shown graphically to reveal those that affect teaching and coaching. Also, since the analysis procedures are the same for all sports and activities, it is easy to apply them to other activities and to interpret the work of anyone who is using a similar approach.

1. A Knowledge Structure Recognizes Specificity

A knowledge structure recognizes the specificity of information used in teaching and coaching sports and physical activities. The KS Model begins in Module 1 by asking you to select as the subject of your first analysis, a specific sport or activity that you are familiar with as athlete, student, teacher, official, or coach. Any sport or activity may be selected—a team sport, individual sport, dance, aquatics, combative or outdoor pursuits, or fitness.

In choosing a specific sport or activity as a beginning point, the KS Model accepts that teaching and coaching are best understood within the context of a specific sport or activity. This approach to instructional design is in contrast to other models that first identify general concepts to which sport-specific information is then fitted. For example, concept curricula (Jewett & Bain, 1987) identify 22 key purpose concepts and 7 movement processes to which specific activity knowledge is then applied. Movement education programs adopt Laban analysis principles as the core of teaching elementary and secondary physical education (Logsdon et al., 1977; Stanley, 1977) with dance, games, gymnastics, and other activities presented within this framework. Humanistic programs (Hellison, 1978, 1985) adopt Maslow's hierarchy of self-actualization as the basis of instruction in all sports and activities, and they select sport information that leads to the attainment of Maslow's levels.

All of these models begin with large concepts to which specific sport knowledge is then applied. The KS Model reverses this practice and requires that you begin with specific sport knowledge (skills, subskills, strategies, rules) and then show how concepts and principles derived from a cross-disciplinary knowledge base (biomechanics, exercise physiology, motor learning, sport psychology, and so on) are applied and used in teaching and coaching. In this process you are first asked to develop a cross-disciplinary knowledge structure for a specific sport or activity, and then to apply instructional design and other strategies in Modules 2 through 8.

2. A Knowledge Structure Provides a Role for Expert Knowledge

The development of a knowledge structure begins with the analysis of current resources in an activity. These books, technical manuals, films, posters, research papers, courses of study (such as your degree program), coaching certification programs, videotapes, and interviews with experts in the field are collectively called expert sources. In addition, you are encouraged to draw upon your experiences in the activity as student, player, teacher, or coach. Developing a knowledge structure for a specific activity should be viewed as a process that helps you make the transition from knowledge acquired as student, athlete, or observer to that used in teaching and coaching.

Begin becoming knowledgeable about an activity by scanning through the materials you have collected. Check the tables of contents and indexes of your sources and write down the differences and commonalties you find across them. You may find that over time some of the skills, strategies, and concepts have changed in name and number. The knowledge base in specific sports and activities evolves, just as do all forms of knowledge. For this reason, it is important that you use a variety of current resources. Begin your study and analysis with the most recent materials and work backward in time.

3. Knowledge Used in Teaching and Coaching Is Categorized as Declarative or Procedural

The KS Model categorizes all knowledge used in teaching and coaching as being either declarative or procedural. The knowledge structures created in Module 1 are declarative structures. A *declarative structure*, as defined by the KS Model, is one that identifies and displays the subject matter of a sport or activity for purposes of teaching or coaching. Examples of declarative structures in badminton, golf, and ice hockey are shown in Appendices A through C. The subject matter of a sport is defined within these structures and uses the cross-disciplinary model of sport studies (Lawson & Morford, 1979; Morford & Lawson, 1978; Morford, Lawson, & Hutton, 1981) to define the major categories of information represented.

Procedural knowledge is derived from the literature in instructional design, cognition, growth and development, motor learning, and other areas that inform us about teaching and coaching methodology. As shown in Figure 4.1, this includes the analysis of environment, analysis of learners, scope and sequence strategies, designing and setting objectives, evaluation,

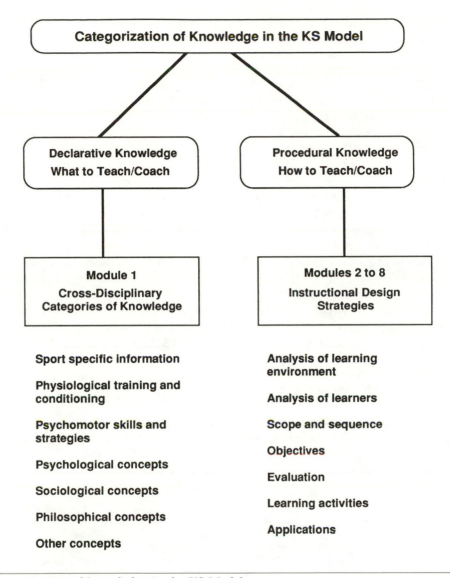

Figure 4.1. Categorization of knowledge in the KS Model.

designing progressions for teaching or coaching, and planning specific applications, such as lesson and practice planning, units, year plans, and seasons of play.

Understanding the Difference Between Declarative and Procedural Knowledge

Knowledge represented in long-term memory has been classified as declarative and procedural (Anderson, 1980, 1982, 1983; Chi & Glaser, 1980; Clancey, 1987; Winograd, 1975). These terms, having evolved from cognition and computer science, classify knowledge as declarative when the facts, the subject matter of a domain, are stored and represented in long-term memory.

Knowledge is classified as procedural when a process, or procedure, for using declarative knowledge is stored. Procedural knowledge is viewed as a type of knowledge that acts upon declarative knowledge (Johnson-Laird, 1988).

The philosophical origin of the term *declarative knowledge* is "knowing that," for *procedural knowledge* "knowing how" (Ryle, 1949). "Knowing that" implies that intelligence is composed of specific facts that describe a domain of knowledge. "Knowing how" means that both general and specific procedures are developed for manipulating declarative knowledge in carrying out tasks. For example, numbers are stored as facts in mathematics, and we develop procedures for adding, subtracting, and dividing them. We store the names and characteristics of places as facts and develop plans that get us from one place to another.

But how would you classify the knowledge developed when we perform complex physical skills? Furthermore, how would you classify the knowledge we use when we teach and coach complex physical skills? Consider the following example from the perspective of both a performer and a coach of baseball. Hitting a baseball is acknowledged as one of the most difficult skills one can perform. At the very least, it requires knowing the components of the movement: the stance, reading the speed of the ball and its changes of direction, timing the stride and the swing, knowing how to hit to different parts of the field, knowing what to do after a hit, and so on. In addition to this, it can mean knowing how to analyze your own and others' performance, knowing how to provide corrective feedback, and knowing how to practice and handle difficult situations. Would you classify this information as athlete knowledge, as teacher-coach knowledge, as scientific knowledge, as declarative knowledge, or as procedural knowledge?

It becomes apparent that information useful to a batter may be different when considered from the perspective of the player, the coach, the researcher, and others involved in the sport.

The declarative-procedural classification, as it has evolved from cognitive science, however, treats all the information about physical skills as procedural. Baseball skills are classified as actions that are procedural in nature and are viewed as being unconscious, and beyond overt description or declaration. Strict adherence to this point of view suggests that there is no declarative knowledge in sport and physical activity beyond the statement of rules, historical facts, equipment characteristics, and other factual types of information. This is a problem that has been debated within the field of physical education for decades (Bressan & Pieter, 1985; Greendorfer, 1987; Henry, 1964).

The KS Model handles this problem by defining declarative and procedural knowledge as one form when possessed by the teacher or coach, another form when possessed by the athlete or performer, and still another when possessed by the researcher or scientist (see Figure 4.2).

The Researcher or Scientist: Declarative Knowledge

Declarative knowledge as possessed by the researcher or scientist in sport and physical activity exists as a number of distinct subdisciplines as shown in Figure 4.2. Shown is only a partial

	Researcher or Scientist	Teacher or Coach	Learner or Athlete
Declarative Knowledge	Knowledge of sport and physical activity defined within a subdiscipline. Such as exercise physiology motor learning, biomechanics, sport psychology, sport sociology, sport history, sport philosophy	Knowledge of skills, strategies, and cross-disciplinary sport science concepts, integrated, structured, and sequenced so as to facilitate teaching and coaching (Module 1)	Knowledge of skills, strategies, and sport science concepts exhibited through modelling, verbalization, and other overt displays of knowing
Procedural Knowledge	Knowledge of the practice of science, displayed through teaching, research, and publication. Such as Level 1, Level 2, and Level 3 forms of research as defined by Christina (1987)	Knowledge of methods or how to teach and coach with a sensitivity to age, ability, and individual differences. The planning and and delivery of instruction (Modules 2 through 8)	Unconscious, automatic form of knowledge, displayed through performance of complex physical skills and strategies. Verbalization difficult, level of automaticity high

Figure 4.2. Declarative and procedural knowledge defined for the researcher or scientist, the teacher or coach, and the athlete.

list of the areas of research and study that have evolved, some quite recently. Each area has a distinctive body of literature that contributes to our understanding of the phenomenon of movement in general and serves as applied research to specific sports.

The Researcher or Scientist: Procedural Knowledge

Science can be practiced in a number of different ways. Christina (1987) has differentiated three levels of research carried out in motor learning. His classification system can be applied to all sport science areas and informs us about the assumptions and procedures of researchers and scientists. The goal of "Level 1" research is to develop a theoretical understanding of how skill is acquired and/or controlled that can be applied to all types of movements. Level 1 research is carried out under tightly controlled conditions in the laboratory, where subjects perform simple movement tasks in which they have had no previous experience, such as linear positioning, tracking, or tapping. For example, Pew (1966) used a key pressing task to reveal the hierarchical nature of control. His results are now generalized to all motor skills. The goal of "Level 2" research is the same as Level 1, but with an important difference. In all cases the subject performs a real-world task, and it is important to use tasks that are familiar to the subjects, and to introduce and control difficult variables such as previous experience, skill level, and performance conditions. For example, the role of vision in baseball batting has been researched by Bahill and LaRitz (1984) and Hubbard and Seng (1954). The goal of "Level 3" research is to find practical solutions to performance problems. "Level 3" research is carried out in real-world situations, and it is not unusual to discover an approach that is effective, without fully understanding the underlying reasons why.

As is evident, procedural knowledge possessed by the researcher or scientist describes how to conduct research, and this can vary from theoretical to applied approaches. Christina (1987) does not make a value judgment about which type of research is more effective or valuable. Instead, he encourages us to understand the assumptions, goals, strengths, and limitations of each approach, and to apply these to our own needs and situations.

The Teacher or Coach: Declarative Knowlege

Learning to teach and coach physical skills requires the evolution of a new form of movement knowledge, one that requires bringing to consciousness that which is often unconscious: an understanding of complex physical skills, their strategic relationships, their precise biomechanical, physiological, motor, psychological, and other characteristics. This type of knowledge comes to us through contributions from multiple sources: from being an athlete, from formal study, from observing and talking with others, from practical experience and self-instruction. This type of knowledge is present when the teacher or coach (a) is consciously aware of the skills, strategies, and concepts that make up a sport or physical activity, (b) is able to verbalize about this information to others, (c) is able to analyze skills and strategies correctly, and (d) can provide corrective feedback and instruction. Module 1 of the KS Model defines the declarative knowledge of the teacher or coach.

The Teacher or Coach: Procedural Knowledge

Procedural knowledge as possessed by the teacher or coach describes the methods, strategies, and processes used in presenting subject matter. This information is defined in Modules 2 through 8 and describes strategies on how to analyze the learning environment and the learners, how to design a scope and sequence, how to set objectives and carry out evaluations, and how to design and deliver progressions of learning experiences, lesson plans, practice plans, units, seasons of play, and complete curricula.

The Athlete: Declarative Knowledge

Athletes display declarative knowledge when they are able to verbally describe or model physical skills or strategies. Declarative knowledge is exhibited by the athlete in situations where description, explanation, modeling, teaching, or coaching behaviors are possible or appropriate.

The Athlete: Procedural Knowledge

Procedural knowledge underlies the performance of complex physical skills. We know little about the procedural knowledge possessed by athletes. As skill is achieved, more and more of what an athlete knows becomes automated. Skills come to be performed automatically in dynamic, action-oriented settings. Athletes exhibit little conscious awareness of what underlies performance and typically are unable to describe or verbalize the factors underlying their performances. And the more skill that is achieved, the more automatic and indescribable it may become. Such procedural knowledge is exhibited among all individuals who achieve high levels of competence in physical tasks, be they pilots, surgeons, concert pianists, or artists (see the research by Johnson discussed in chapter 3). Performers must automatize their knowledge to function at higher levels of competence.

4. A Cross-Disciplinary Approach Defines Declarative Knowledge in Module 1

The KS Model uses the cross-disciplinary model of sport studies (Lawson & Morford, 1979; Morford & Lawson, 1978; Morford, Lawson & Hutton, 1981) as a framework within which to define and describe the declarative knowledge of a sport or activity used in teaching and coaching. Figure 4.3 shows the underlying foundations of the cross-disciplinary approach. Specific sport knowledge is made up of a cross section of knowledge (light shaded areas—exercise physiology, biomechanics, kinesiology, motor learning, sport psychology, sport sociology,

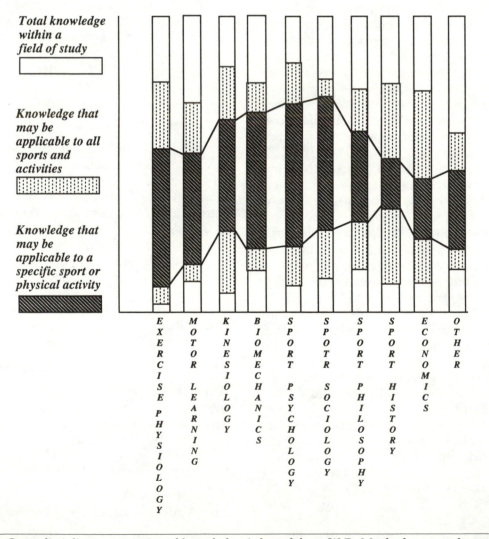

Figure 4.3. Cross-disciplinary categories of knowledge (adapted from W.R. Morford, personal communication, 1980).

sport philosophy, management, music, and others) contributed by a variety of subdisciplines. Each has evolved over time and been applied in a unique way to each sport and physical activity (dark shaded areas). Carefully developed, discrete portions of information are drawn from several subdisciplines, providing a cross-disciplinary framework that constitutes the subject matter of modern-day sport and physical activity.

In the KS Model, the concept of a cross-disciplinary approach is used to define the knowledge base of sport, dance, or physical activities through the identification of common categories of knowledge defined as follows:

1. *Sport-specific information* is unique to each sport or activity and states the purpose of the activity, its rules, safety, current events, records, equipment, and other basic types of information that must be known in order to teach or coach.
2. *Physiological training and conditioning* category defines the knowledge about physical fitness and training as it is applied to a particular sport or activity and includes concepts and principles from the medical sciences, exercise physiology, medical therapy, and nutrition.
3. *Psychomotor skills and strategies* category names all the individual skills and selected strategies of the sport or activity, incorporating motor learning, biomechanical, and physiological concepts.
4. *Psychological category* identifies concepts derived from both the social and cognitive psychology literatures as applied to the activity.
5. *Sociological and cultural concepts* are derived from literature in sport sociology and are of an applied nature.
6. *Philosophical/historical concepts* are derived from sport philosophy, history, and other literatures that have impact on the sport or activity.
7. *Other concepts* may be derived from other relevant literature and applied to a specific sport or activity.

A cross-disciplinary approach defines the knowledge base of sport and physical activity as one defined by *both* the unique nature of the sport (purpose, rules, skills, strategies), and an applied one derived from sport science subdisciplines. Teaching and coaching modern sport and physical activity has this integration. It is recommended that student teachers and coaches concentrate first on developing a cross-disciplinary knowledge structure for one activity (preferably a familiar one), then expand their design strategies to other activities as they become more and more familiar with the concepts underlying the function of the KS Model.

5. Procedural Knowledge Is Defined in Modules 2 Through 8

As mentioned previously, procedural knowledge is defined in Modules 2 through 8, and is defined by the methods and practices of instructional design, cognition, growth and development, and other areas that inform us about how to teach or coach. A number of critical design strategies are presented in depth in Modules 2 through 8. Strategies are presented for analyzing the learning environment, analyzing of learners, developing a scope and sequence, setting objectives, designing and carrying out evaluation, designing teaching progressions, and designing and implementing many applications such as lesson plans, unit plans, individualized programs, and computer applications. Each of these strategies is generated from and linked to the knowledge structures created in Module 1.

Strengths and Weaknesses of Designing Instruction With an Emphasis Upon Declarative Knowledge

What are the advantages of creating a knowledge structure as described in Module 1, and as shown in the Appendices A-C? Winograd (1975) has identified a number of strengths and weaknesses associated with using declarative and procedural knowledge in the design of computer systems. In the following section, we apply his points to the design of instruction.

Declarative Knowledge Is Easier to Understand and Learn Than Procedural Knowlege. A declarative knowledge structure is a set of interdependent skills, strategies, and concepts that can be changed and adapted more easily than can procedural types of knowledge, which are context- and learner-dependent. Declarative knowledge is also a relatively stable type of knowledge, with changes occurring only occasionally. In sport, new knowledge is added as athletes and coaches create new and better ways to perform, and as researchers reveal more about a skill. For example, the forearm pass, or the bump, was added to volleyball by the Japanese in the early sixties; the skating stride was added to cross-country skiing in the early eighties; the Bergofer underwater start was added to the backstroke in the late eighties. Each of these rare developments is within the declarative knowledge base of the sport and has far reaching effects on the procedural knowledge of the sport or how the activity is taught and coached.

Declarative Knowledge Is More Accessible and Easier to Communicate Than Procedural Knowledge. Winograd (1975) states that "much of what we know is most easily stateable as a set of declaratives. Natural language is primarily declarative, and the usual way to give information to another person is to break it into statements" (p. 189). Shulman (1986a) further states that the basis of communication between teachers and students is the content or declarative subject matter, that "the teacher interacts with the student in and through the content and the student interacts with the teacher in the same way" (p. 8). The knowledge structures in Appendices A through C are surprisingly easy to develop; for beginning teachers and coaches they offer a body of knowledge that is easier to identify and that they feel a need to set in place before they can apply procedural knowledges effectively. Developing structures of this type provides a map that can guide teaching and coaching.

A Declarative Knowledge Structure Leads to Flexibility and Economy In Teaching. The information identified in a knowledge structure can be tailored to accommodate all age and ability groups. In terms of instructional design, this is both a flexible and an economical approach, because subject matter becomes a constant and, once identified, is applicable to different situations and learners. For example, the information shown in the knowledge structures in Appendices A through C may be used, in whole and in part, with beginners, experts, young, and old and in recreational, competitive, and educational settings. Procedural knowledge, in contrast, is context dependent and must change to be effective with different learners and in different settings. In the KS Model declarative knowledge displays qualities of permanence and invariability, whereas procedural knowl-

edge (Modules 2 through 8) provides the vital media needed for change and adaptation.

Procedural Knowledge Provides Context-Dependent Solutions That May Not Generalize to Other Settings. The strongest argument in support of a procedural approach in instructional design is that it provides immediate solutions to immediate problems. Procedural knowledge is prescriptive, context dependent, and quickly leads to actions and outcomes. Procedural knowledge is necessary for handling specific settings and individuals. This point was also covered in chapter 1, where teachers, coaches, and students were advised to follow a procedural focus if they must meet a class or team of students immediately, with little time available for in-depth study, analysis, or planning. The weakness of procedural knowledge is, however, its narrow focus and lack of generalizability, and its ineffectiveness outside the narrow confines where it is typically used.

6. The Cross-Disciplinary Categories Selected Vary to Reflect Curriculum Goals and Resources

The development of a knowledge structure begins with the selection of the cross-disciplinary categories most suited to the environment you will be teaching and coaching in. You may include all the cross-disciplinary categories listed earlier, or you may tailor the number and type to reflect specific curriculum goals as set out by state and provincial curriculum guides, school planning groups, department heads, or individual teachers. In practice, the number of categories selected tends to be influenced by (a) whether you are developing the structure for a teaching, coaching, or recreational setting, (b) by the numbers of students to be taught, (c) by the amount of time available, and (d) by the space and facility resources.

7. A Declarative Knowledge Structure Displays "Cognitive Economy"

Information is identified and represented in a knowledge structure for purposes of teaching or coaching. It is not included to serve as a study aid for the designer. Use of this rule leads to extensive decision making by the teacher or coach at the analysis stage and structures that exhibit a quality called "cognitive economy" (Rosch, 1975). Cognitive economy is seen when the individual teacher or coach selects, from a vast amount of material, information that is relevant and appropriate for the teaching and coaching situations to be encountered. This is a vital planning skill encouraged and fostered through the process of creating a declarative knowledge structure. A skill, strategy, or concept is also represented only once in a knowledge structure. It is assumed, however, that each piece of information may be accessed and used in different ways, depending upon student, situational, and other variables (procedural knowledge). A skill or concept, once represented, may be revised, modified, updated, or deleted; it is, however, never repeated.

8. A Declarative Knowledge Structure Employs Hierarchical Representation

In a knowledge structure, relationships between content nodes are shown graphically and reveal flexible relationships between content items that advise teaching and coaching practice. A number of different approaches have evolved showing how knowledge can be represented as concepts (Rumelhart et al., 1972); schemes, schema, and schemata (Bartlett, 1932; Rumelhart & Ortony, 1976); scripts (Shank & Abelson, 1977); networks (Lindsay & Norman, 1977); frames (Minsky, 1975); and hierarchies (Gallistel, 1980; Glencross, 1978; McClelland et al., 1986; Pew, 1974; Rumelhart et al., 1986).

The knowledge structures created in Module 1 employ hierarchical representation techniques with sequence, time, and the inheritance of properties dominant (Charniak & McDermott, 1985). Sequence sets out a general order of introduction of skills, strategies, and concepts as advised by expert teachers and coaches in the field, and as additionally supported by motor learning, biomechanical and other principles. Time is displayed in the hierarchy laterally for each skill and recognizes that subskills should be introduced gradually and in a preferred sequence. Again, the origin of this material is from expert sources, and as supported by biomechanical, motor learning and other areas. The inheritance of properties is best explained

through Figures 4.4a–c, in which the knowledge structure for teaching the three overhand forehand strokes in badminton is shown. The basic forehand defensive clear is presented first. Following the defensive clear are two additional subskills, attack, and around-the-head clear. Each of these subskills inherits properties from the forehand clear. Next is the forehand overhead drop, with basic, and around-the-head subskills. Again, the foundation for each of these subskills is the forehand overhead clear. Finally, the smash is presented, with its three subskills basic, off-speed, and around-the head. Each has inherited properties from the basic clear and the drop. Numerous other examples of this property of inheritance are presented in Appendices A through C.

9. A Declarative Knowledge Structure Permits the Flexible Sequencing of Content

The hierarchical and graphic nature of a completed knowledge structure informs one about teaching or coaching, but *does not dictate* a set order. The dominance of one knowledge component over another is instead set in Module 4, "Developing a Scope and Sequence," and is determined by your decision to present a bottom-up or a top-down learning experience. In making this decision, you take into account the nature of the teaching or coaching environment, the ability levels of your students, and the time constraints under which you are working. In no way does the knowledge structure advocate a lock-step or exclusive part method.

10. Developing a Knowledge Structure Promotes Three Qualities Important in Teaching and Coaching

Developing a knowledge structure requires independent study, analytical thought, and extensive decision making. As a consequence of this process, three qualities recognized as important in teaching and coaching are fostered: (a) achieving a high level overview of the subject matter, (b) curriculum pacing, and (c) a sense of self-efficacy (Harrison, 1987).

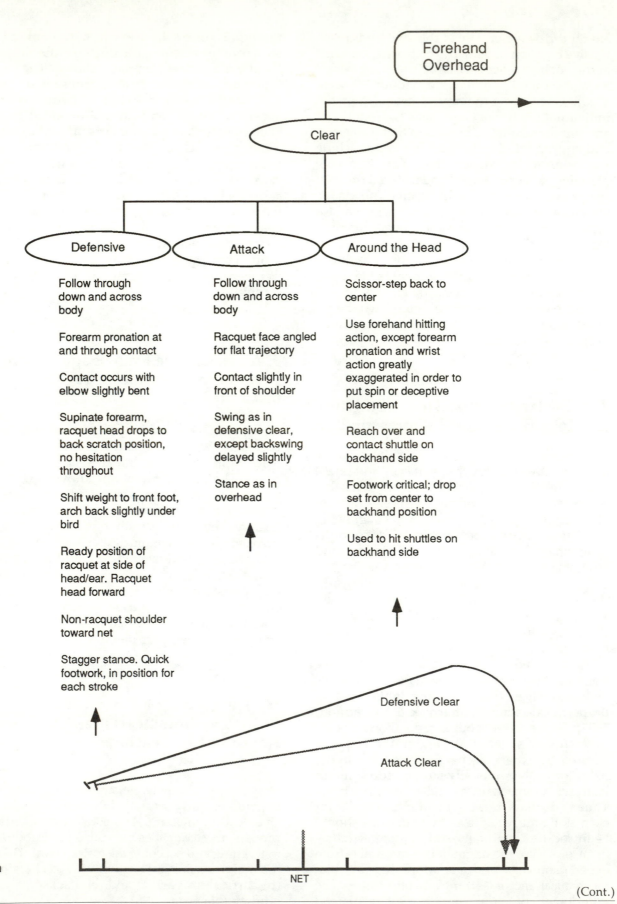

Figure 4.4. The knowledge structure for the overhand forehand strokes, showing the inheritance of movement properties from the overhand clear (a) to the drop (b) and smash (c).

(Cont.)

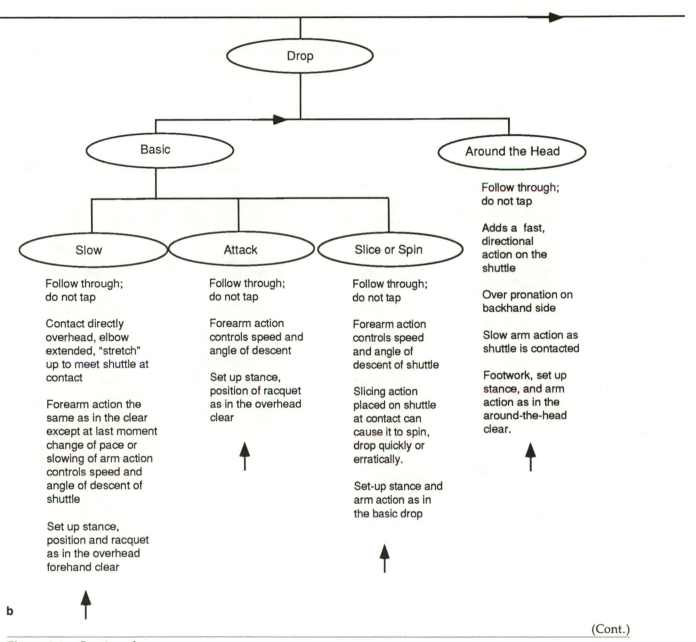

Figure 4.4.   Continued.

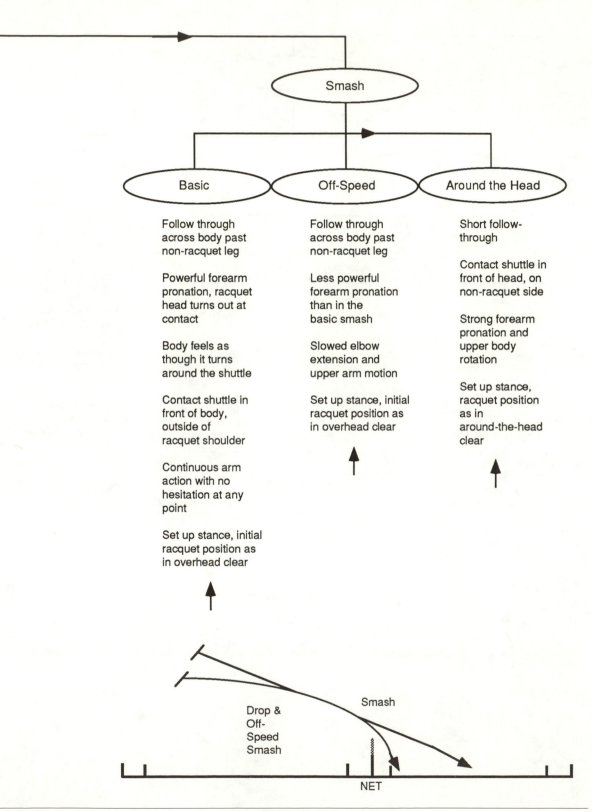

Figure 4.4.   Continued.

Achieving a high-level overview of the subject matter of a domain is a characteristic of master teachers and coaches (Donald, 1980, 1987; Harrison, 1987). Sport and physical activity has a *holistic* quality, meaning that all of its components may occur at once in play or competition. All the skills and strategies are potentially present, as are the underlying necessities of fitness, psychological well-being, and so on. As a teacher or coach, you need to be able to see, as soon as possible, how all of these components fit together and interact. The development of a knowledge structure, with its cross-disciplinary foundations, helps to accomplish this, and in a much shorter space of time than learning through experience only, without an analytical strategy as offered by the KS Model.

Curriculum pacing is defined as the ability of teachers to "select material at an appropriate level of difficulty for their students and move the students through it at a rapid pace" (Harrison, 1987, p. 44). In order to deliver instruction so that curriculum pacing occurs, you need to know how the subject is inherently structured. You also need to be able to select and deliver experiences that are sensitive to student needs and accelerate their passage through the material. The KS Model promotes curriculum pacing by providing, through the knowledge structures, an overview of the content and how it can be economically structured. Curriculum pacing is also fostered in Modules 2 through 8, where the information identified in the structures is further developed and organized for teaching.

Self-efficacy is defined as knowing that you can bring about a desired or intended outcome in your students and athletes. The act of creating a knowledge structure, then using this as a means of guiding instructional planning, helps you to develop a feeling of empowerment and self-confidence. In particular, you feel that you understand the activity and that you have something worthwhile to teach. In addition to this comes a can-do attitude that begins with an enhanced feeling about your own abilities that is communicated to your students and athletes. You view your students as being able to learn and perform at levels that are often beyond their own expectations.

Part III

Photo by Lisa Davis. Courtesy of *The Daily Illini*, University of Illinois.

Implementing the KS Model of Instructional Design

Modules in Part III

Topics

for Module 1

- Applying techniques of knowledge acquisition
- Developing the map or overview structure
- Developing the psychomotor skills knowledge structure
- Developing the strategies knowledge structure
- Developing the knowledge structures for background, physiological, psychological, sociological, and philosophical concepts
- Exercise 1: Develop an individual skills knowledge structure
- Exercise 2: Define the underlying principles at work
- Exercise 3: Develop a strategies knowledge structure
- Exercise 4: Develop a knowledge structure for psychological, sociological, or philosophical concepts
- Exercise 5: Develop a knowledge structure using a structured interview technique
- An example of a structured interview

All learning has an emotional base.

—Plato

Photo by Marcie Bright. Courtesy of *The Daily Illini*, University of Illinois.

Creating a Personalized Knowledge Structure

In Module 1 you look at the steps in developing a personalized knowledge structure, the one you will use in your teaching and coaching. You first review the knowledge acquisition techniques used in developing a knowledge structure, followed by a number of instructional design questions that help you begin thinking about sport and physical activity subject matter and how it can be analyzed for teaching or coaching. Following this I introduce the development of the map or overview structure, which requires selecting the cross-disciplinary categories and identifying the skills, strategies, and concepts to be included in each. This information is then arrayed in a hierarchical map or overview structure. Each element in the map structure is analyzed in turn, beginning with the individual skills and strategies and followed by physiological, psychological, sociological, and philosophical concepts. The chapter concludes

with a number of exercises to help you design your own knowledge structure.

Applying Techniques of Knowledge Acquisition

In this chapter, you will see how the four techniques of knowledge acquisition introduced in chapter 3—text analysis, structured interview, stimulated recall, and analogical derivation (see Figure 3.1)—are used to analyze and structure the skills, strategies, and concepts of an activity for teaching and coaching. Let's review each briefly. In text analysis, materials created by experts in a sport or activity (books, manuals, films, videos, software) are analyzed and represented following hierarchical principles of knowledge representation. In a structured interview, a coach, teacher, or researcher is interviewed using a series of preplanned questions. In stimulated recall, experts are filmed as they teach or coach and then review the tapes and analyze their own performances following a preplanned protocol. Analogical derivation involves using a sample or ideal prototype from which new cases are derived. The sample knowledge structures for badminton, golf, and ice hockey in Appendices A through C are presented as prototypes from which you may generate your own knowledge structures.

Module 1 emphasizes text analysis and analogical derivation because they can be undertaken independently by student teachers with resources that are readily available. Techniques of structured interviewing are also presented, but require arranging an interview with a master teacher or coach. Stimulated recall is not covered because of the need for video equipment, subjects to be filmed, releases, and considerable time.

By the end of this module, you should be able to answer the following instructional design questions:

1. What is the subject matter of the sport or activity?
2. How can I identify its most important skills, subskills, and concepts?
3. For each of the skills and subskills, what are the most important technical, biomechanical, motor learning, or other points to be stressed?
4. What are the essential strategies of the activity?
5. How can I organize this information to illustrate the interrelationships between the skills, subskills, and strategies for purposes of teaching and coaching?
6. Is there a best order or sequence for presenting the information?
7. How can I introduce sport science and other types of knowledge? To what extent should I include this kind of subject matter in my instruction? Will this affect activity time?
8. Is there some way to extract a simpler overview while still analyzing all the pertinent information in an activity?
9. How can I become more comfortable about teaching activities I haven't participated in or really learned?

Developing the Map or Overview Structure

You begin the text analysis process by collecting a variety of resources in an activity, such as books, videos, coaching certification information, and sport science research, classifying the information in each as declarative or procedural. (Remember that declarative knowledge defines the subject matter of the sport or activity, including its skills, strategies, and applied sport science concepts, while procedural knowledge refers to the methods of teaching or coaching an activity, including analyzing the learning environment and learners, developing a scope and sequence, writing objectives, carrying out evaluations, designing learning activities, and doing lesson, unit, and yearly planning.)

The map or overview structure defines the first level of declarative knowledge in an activity; samples appear in Figures M1.1 (badminton), M1.2 (golf), M1.3 (ice hockey), and M1.4 (jazz dance). The map or overview structure identifies the cross-disciplinary categories of information—the major skills, strategies, and concepts that you expect to teach. The cross-disciplinary categories are

- physiological training and conditioning,
- sport-specific or background information,
- philosophical and historical concepts,
- psychomotor skills and strategies,
- psychological concepts,
- sociological and cultural concepts, and
- other concepts.

For example, the badminton, golf, and jazz dance structures (see Figures M1.1, M1.2, and M1.4) all contain four cross-disciplinary categories: physiological training and conditioning, sport-specific information (background information), psychomotor skills and strategies, and other concepts (i.e., psychosocial or artistic concepts). The ice hockey structure (Figure M1.3) contains five: background knowledge, philosophy of the game, physiological training and conditioning, psychomotor skills and strategies, and psychological concepts. (For examples of other map structures, see Appendix A of each instructor's guide within the Steps to Success Activity Series.)

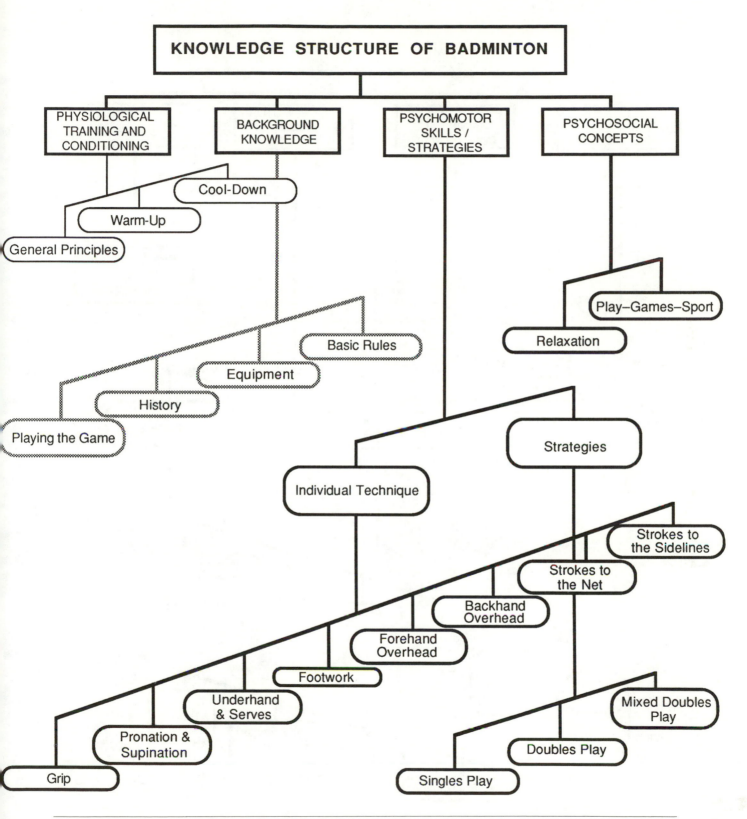

Figure M1.1. A map or overview structure for badminton.

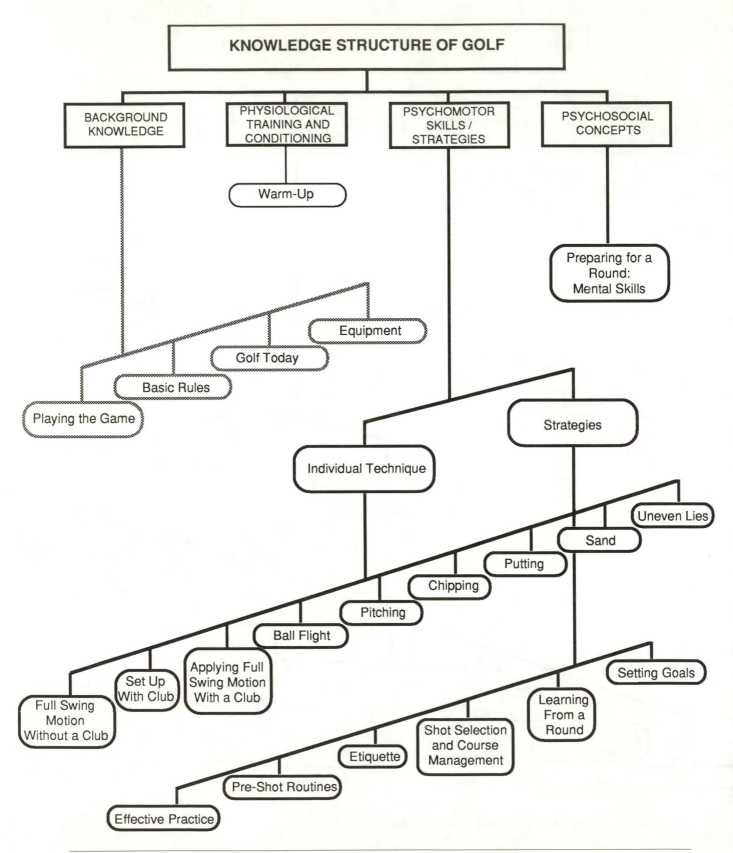

Figure M1.2. A map or overview structure for golf (Owens & Bunker, 1989b). Reprinted by permission.

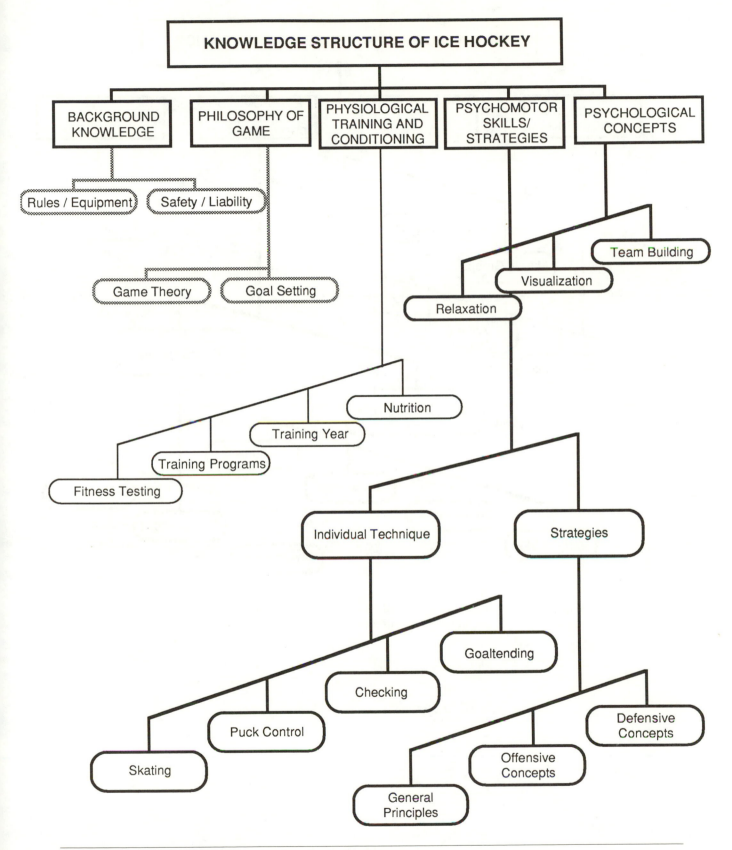

Figure M1.3. A map or overview structure for ice hockey.

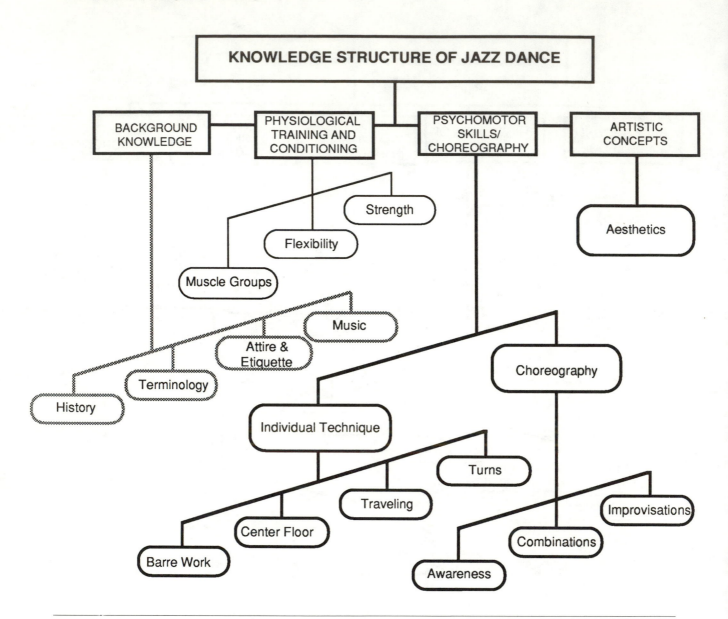

Figure M1.4.   A map or overview structure for jazz dance. *Note.* From *Instructional Design in Jazz Dance* by J. Currie and L. Dusterhoft, 1988, unpublished manuscript. Reprinted by permission.

Determining the Cross-Disciplinary Categories

The number and type of cross-disciplinary categories and their order is decided by considering

- whether you are creating the structure for a teaching, coaching, or recreational setting;
- safety, liability, and risk factors;
- the inherent nature of the subject matter (such as its complexity);
- curriculum goals of state, provincial, and other bodies;
- ease of teaching and understanding; and
- the amount of time you and your students have available for instruction and practice.

Teaching. In the teaching setting, you are usually required to design a unit of instruction (a sequence of lessons taught to a single group of students). The emphasis is on learning, self-development, recreation, and competition, in that order. In such situations, include the following cross-disciplinary categories: activity-specific knowledge (purpose of the activity, safety and liability concerns, basic rules, equipment), physiological training and conditioning (warm-up, cool-down), psychomotor skills and strategies (all individual skills and selected basic strategies), and psychosocial concepts (at least one psychological or sociological concept).

Coaching. In the coaching setting, you emphasize skill acquisition, competitive performance, participation, physiological, and psychological well-being and competence. For coaching include all cross-disciplinary categories: background knowledge, physiological training and conditioning, all psychomotor individual skills, basic and selected advanced strategies, and selected psychological, sociological, philosophical, historical, and other concepts.

Recreation. In the recreation setting, a single unit is taught to a single group of students (often adults) as one course. The emphasis is upon personal development, participation, minimal or as-needed instruction, and different types of competition. Include the following cross-disciplinary categories: background knowledge (purpose of the activity, safety and liability concerns, basic rules, equipment), physiological training and conditioning (minimum warm-up and cool-down, testing and training), all psychomotor individual skills, selected basic strategies, and selected psychological, sociological, or philosophical concepts.

Representing Information in Each Cross-Disciplinary Category

Once you have identified the cross-disciplinary categories, your next step is to define the information in each category and represent it in a hierarchy.

The *physiological training and conditioning* category contains warm-up and cool-down, testing, training, nutrition, and any other physiological or medical information. For example, in ice hockey (Figure M1.3) fitness testing, training programs, training year, and nutrition are included.

The *background knowledge* category lists the purpose of the activity, safety and liability concerns, equipment, and basic rules. For example, golf (Figure M1.2) includes playing the game, basic rules, golf today, and equipment. Jazz dance (Figure M1.4) develops the concepts of history, terminology, attire and etiquette, and music.

The *psychomotor skills and strategies* category, unlike the other categories, is exhaustive because all the individual skills are identified, followed by basic strategies. For example, in badminton (Figure M1.1) the individual skills developed are grip, pronation and supination, underhand clear and serve, footwork, forehand overhead strokes, backhand overhead strokes, strokes to the net, and strokes to the sidelines. In jazz dance (Figure M1.4), individual skills are analyzed in barre work, center floor, traveling, and turns. One strategy in jazz dance is the process of choreography, including awareness, combinations, and improvisation.

The *psychosocial concepts* are selected from the sport psychology and sociology literature; they may be taught to student athletes as separate lectures or integrated throughout a unit or season. For example, in the Steps to Success Activity Series books, different key concepts have been identified by the authors as especially important in their activity: mental skills and setting goals in golf (Owens & Bunker, 1989a, 1989b); concentration in tennis (Brown 1989a, 1989b); fear reduction in swimming (Thomas, 1989a, 1989b); teamwork in volleyball (Viera & Ferguson, 1989a, 1989b); developing confidence in archery (Haywood & Lewis, 1989a, 1989b); anticipation in softball (Potter & Brockmeyer, 1989a, 1989b); and mental discipline in bowling (Strickland, 1989a, 1989b).

Other concepts is an open category that permits the identification of information not included in any of the above. For example, in jazz dance (see Figure M1.4 on p. 60) aesthetics is presented; in backpacking (see Figure M1.12 on p. 77) environmental awareness is presented.

Organizing the Map Structure

Array the above categorical information on a single sheet of 8-1/2 by 11-inch paper to prepare a map as illustrated in the badminton, golf, ice hockey, and jazz structures. Use a hierarchical arrangement, with the cross-disciplinary categories (which are larger and more inclusive and abstract) at the top of the page and the more specific, concrete skills, strategies, and concepts farther down. Use a sloping line and/or arrow to indicate a preferred order of introduction (one sensitive to safety and liability concerns, subject matter complexity, ease of understanding, and sport science principles important in teaching and coaching). A horizontal line and no arrow indicates a free order of introduction; meaning that material can be taught in any order determined by the instructor.

As you work through each cross-disciplinary category in more detail, you will find yourself changing your map structure. This is a normal result of changes in your knowledge base. You may make changes in your map structure weeks, months, and even years after you first devise it—it represents a body of knowledge that develops and grows as your level of expertise increases. So even if you feel a little shaky at this point and question the depth of your knowledge, it is important to take a stab at developing your first structure. Expect it to change, for it is a barometer of your level of teaching knowledge.

Developing the Psychomotor Skills Knowledge Structure

In developing a psychomotor skills knowledge structure, your goals are

1. to name all the individual skills and subskills in the activity or sport;
2. to identify their biomechanical, motor learning, and technical qualities, as reflected in expert performance and as advised by master teachers and coaches and the sport science literature; and
3. to arrange this information in a hierarchy showing the interrelationships between

skills and subskills for purposes of teaching or coaching.

Levels of Analysis for the Individual Skills Structure

There are eight levels of analysis for individual skills:

- Level 1 names the activity in which the knowledge structure is being created.
- Level 2 identifies the cross-disciplinary categories being developed.
- Level 3 shows the psychomotor skills and strategies analyses, with two subcategories: individual skills and strategies.
- Level 4 shows each of the major individual skills. (Note that Levels 1 through 4 are included in the map structure.)
- Level 5 shows the first level of subskills.
- Level 6 shows a second level of subskills (if necessary).
- Level 7 shows a third level of subskills (if necessary).
- Level 8 (or the last level) shows the technical analysis of each subskill for purposes of teaching or coaching, skill analysis, and correction. This information is called the Keys to Success in the Steps to Success Activity Series. It is also the information used in writing technical objectives in Module 5.

For example, the map structure for badminton shown in Figure M1.1 contains eight individual skills: grip, supination and pronation, underhand clear and serve, footwork, forehand overhead strokes, backhand overhead strokes, strokes to the net, and strokes to the sideline. In Figure M1.5 the map structure for badminton is reduced and placed in the upper-left corner of the page. Each of the skills in the structure is selected and analyzed in turn, resulting in a hierarchical analysis of seven or more levels, as follows:

- Level 1: The activity in which the knowledge structure is being created is badminton.
- Level 2: The cross-disciplinary categories are physiological training and conditioning, background knowledge, psychomotor skills and strategies, and psychosocial concepts.
- Level 3: The psychomotor skills and strategies analyses show two subcategories, individual technique (grip, pronation and

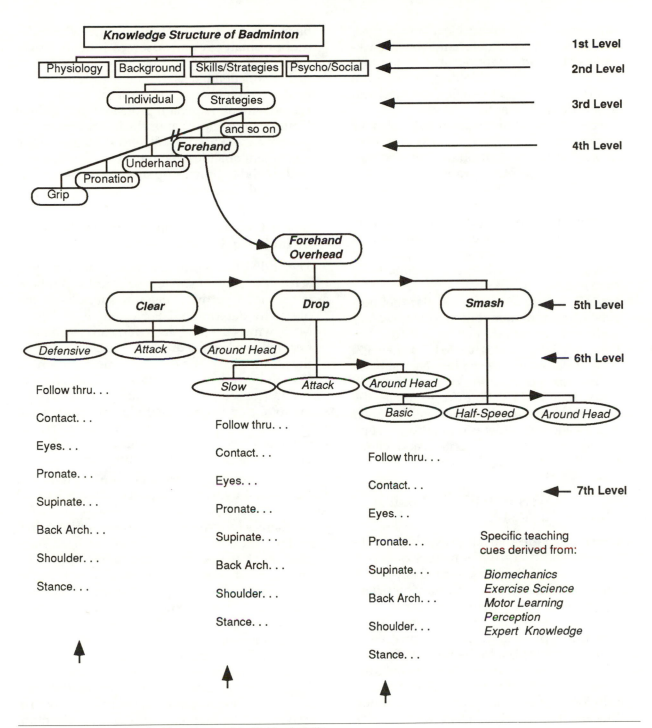

Figure M1.5. The levels of analysis of individual skills.

supination, underhand clear and serves, footwork, forehand overhand clears, backhand overhand clears, strokes to the net, and strokes to the sidelines) (see Figure M1.1), and strategies (singles, doubles, and mixed doubles play).

- Level 4: Each of the major individual skills (for example, forehand strokes) is shown. (Note that Levels 1 through 4 were identified in the map structure.)
- Level 5: The first level of subskills is the clear, drop, and smash.
- Level 6: The second level of subskills (if necessary) are the defensive, attack, and around head clears; slow, attack, around head drops; and basic, half-speed, around head smashes.
- Level 7: A third level of subskills is not necessary for badminton, but may be necessary with other activities.
- Level 8: (shown in Figure M1.5 as Level 7) A technical analysis is made of each subskill for purposes of teaching or coaching, skill analysis, and correction (for example, the teaching points for the defensive clear refer to the stance, shoulder turn, back arch, supination, pronation, eyes, contact, and follow-through).

Technical Analysis of Individual Skills (the Keys to Success)

The final level of the analysis presents the technical points that characterize mature or expert performance. Described here are the key points that underlie teaching for technically proficient performance. This information is derived from multiple sources: biomechanics, kinesiology, motor learning, perception, observational learning, and expert sources. In the Steps to Success Activity Series this information is called the Keys to Success. This information is also used in writing technical objectives in Module 5 and underlies the ability to analyze skills and provide corrective feedback.

Being able to analyze the skills of a sport or activity in this way requires proficiency in what I will call *cognitive biomechanics*, which, as the term suggests, integrates cognition (the science that studies sensation, perception, attention, memory, knowledge representation, comprehension, problem solving, and creativity) with

biomechanics ("the interdiscipline which describes, analyzes and assesses human movement," Winter, 1979). Cognitive biomechanics is therefore defined as the ability to perceive, attend to, comprehend, and verbalize about physical movement. A person proficient in cognitive biomechanics understands the function and purpose of each skill, subskill, and strategy and the movement qualities that must be perceived and understood to provide optimal instruction, feedback, and assistance.

Seven Guidelines Underlying Analysis of Individual Skills

The individual skills are named and arrayed across the page in clusters or chunks. But how is the order of the skills and subskills in the hierarchy determined? For example, in Figure M1.5, why is the forehand overhead clear shown first, followed by the drop and the smash; within the clear, why is the defensive clear presented first, followed by the attack and around the head? The sequencing of skills is done according to one or more of the following guidelines, which are unique to the field of human movement and further define cognitive biomechanics and its role in effective teaching or coaching.

1. The Relationships Between Skills Are Supported by Kinesiological or Biomechanical Principles. Courses in kinesiology and biomechanics introduce the concepts foundational to the study of human action, such as summation of forces, pronation and supination, center of mass, range of motion, conservation of momentum, and angular velocity. However, this is only partial knowledge for the future teacher or coach—the next step requires that these concepts be applied specifically to each sport and meaningfully to learners.

Figure M1.6 illustrates how a kinesiological or biomechanical principle is incorporated in a knowledge structure, using the concepts of pronation and supination as applied in badminton. These concepts are used extensively in helping athletes understand the source of power and control in all strokes. Figure M1.6 defines pronation and supination as movements of the forearm either toward or away from the midline of the body, and then describes how each occurs in the forehand (overhead and underhand); the backhand (overhead and underhand), and the

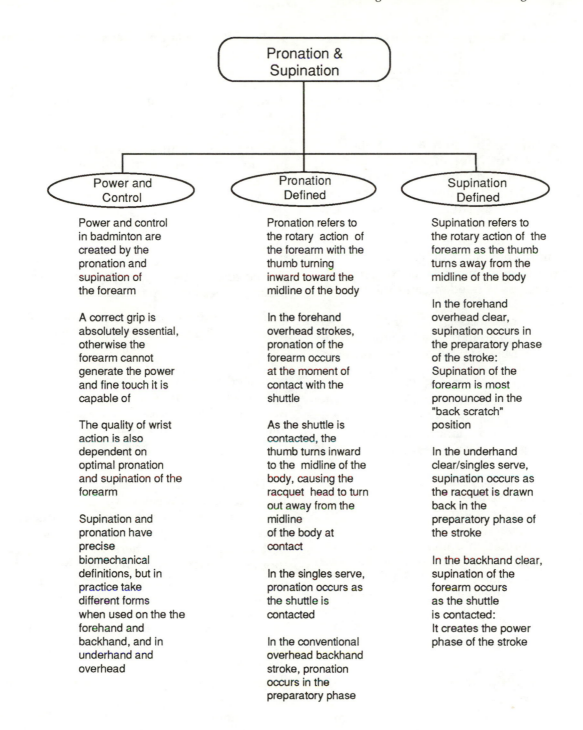

Figure M1.6. Pronation and supination in badminton.

serve (long). As is evident, the actual application of pronation and supination in badminton is a complex process; these concepts appear quite differently when applied on the forehand, on the backhand, in the overhead, and on the underhand.

2. The Relationships Between Skills Are Supported by Principles of Motor Learning, Skill Acquisition, and Control.

The principles reflected here have been drawn from the literature of motor learning and skill acquisition. Examples of concepts helpful in developing an individual skills knowledge structure are transfer of learning, knowledge of results, hierarchical structure of movements, executive control, concept of degrees of freedom, and automaticity (for others see Magill, 1989).

Let's look at one concept, transfer of learning, as it has been applied in the badminton knowledge structure. Magill (1989) defines transfer as ''the influence of a previously practiced skill on the learning of a new skill'' (p. 368). This principle, used extensively in developing a knowledge structure, is referred to as the *inheritance of properties* in the artificial intelligence and expert systems literature: Knowledge acquired and used in one setting is found to be effective in understanding ideas, concepts, and skills in a new setting. For example, in Figures M1.7a and b, intratask transfer is shown to occur between the underhand defensive clear and the singles serve. The information underlying instruction (and performance) of the underhand defensive clear facilitates teaching (and performance) of the singles serve and the basic doubles serve. Similarly, the backhand basic underhand clear is shown to transfer to teaching (and performing) the backhand or front-of-body short serve.

3. The Relationships Between Skills Are Grounded by Physiological or Medical Principles.

Fitness prerequisites of strength, endurance, and flexibility are kept in the forefront when analyzing the skills and strategies of a sport or activity. Skills are ordered with attention to physiological prerequisites such as flexibility, aerobic and anaerobic power, muscular strength and endurance, and body composition. For example, in badminton, the smash is introduced midunit to give students a chance to build a biomechanical base for the stroke from the clear and drop and to allow them to physically condition their arms for this explosive stroke.

4. The Relationships Between Skills Are Grounded by Safety and Liability Concerns.

In all sports and activities, skills must be introduced so as to minimize risk, increase confidence, and create a secure, safe environment for both students and instructors. This is true in all activities but is especially pertinent to gymnastic, target, combative, aquatic, outdoor, and high-risk activities. Safety and liability concerns are acknowledged in the knowledge structures by the order of presentation of cross-disciplinary categories, skills, subskills, and concepts. For example, a gymnastics knowledge structure shows the floor events first, followed by the apparatus. Basic skills are practiced first at floor level, then moved to progressively higher and more challenging pieces of apparatus.

5. The Relationships Between Skills Allow for Mastery of Fear.

Hand in hand with safety is the need for mastery of fear. A knowledge structure shows how skills can be introduced and combined to reduce fear or anxiety. Figure M1.8 shows the swimming structure of the Steps to Success Activity Series. The concepts of buoyancy, floating, and fear reduction are presented first in order to increase confidence in and around the water.

6. The Relationships Between Skills Are Derived From a Consensus of Expert Opinion.

My experience in developing knowledge structures has revealed greater consensus among expert coaches and teachers than is generally thought to exist. Although complete consensus cannot be expected, I have found a high degree of agreement among experts, especially in analyzing written sources (text analysis) and in the categories of background knowledge, physiological training and conditioning, and individual psychomotor skills.

7. When Consensus Cannot Be Established, the Merits of the Competing Approaches Should Be Weighed.

All sports and activities have areas of controversy concerning how best to analyze and teach skills, strategies, and concepts. In chapter 3 a similar situation in expert systems development was described; it was solved by providing users with options in the data base and help in making decisions about competing approaches. You too will encounter controversy about how best to structure or present certain skills, strategies, or concepts. You must then weigh the merits of each approach and select the one most appropriate for your situation.

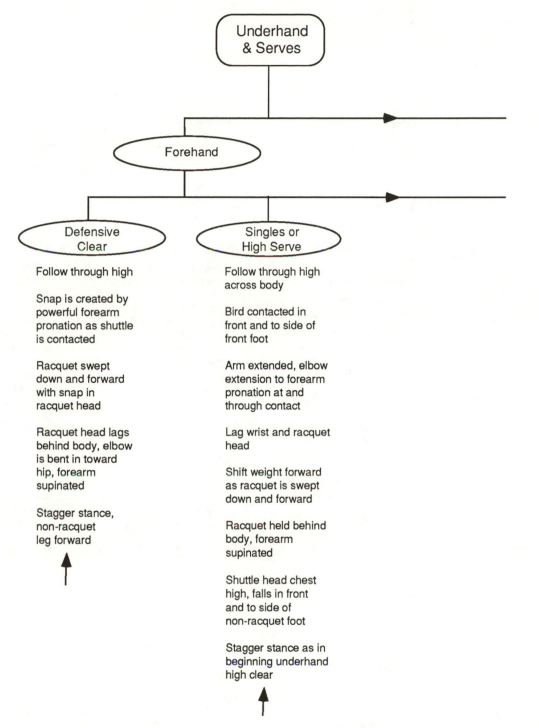

Underhand
& Serves

Forehand

Defensive
Clear

Follow through high

Snap is created by
powerful forearm
pronation as shuttle
is contacted

Racquet swept
down and forward
with snap in
racquet head

Racquet head lags
behind body, elbow
is bent in toward
hip, forearm
supinated

Stagger stance,
non-racquet
leg forward

Singles or
High Serve

Follow through high
across body

Bird contacted in
front and to side of
front foot

Arm extended, elbow
extension to forearm
pronation at and
through contact

Lag wrist and racquet
head

Shift weight forward
as racquet is swept
down and forward

Racquet held behind
body, forearm
supinated

Shuttle head chest
high, falls in front
and to side of
non-racquet foot

Stagger stance as in
beginning underhand
high clear

a

(Cont.)

Figure M1.7.   Intratask transfer as shown from the underhand defensive clear to the serves.

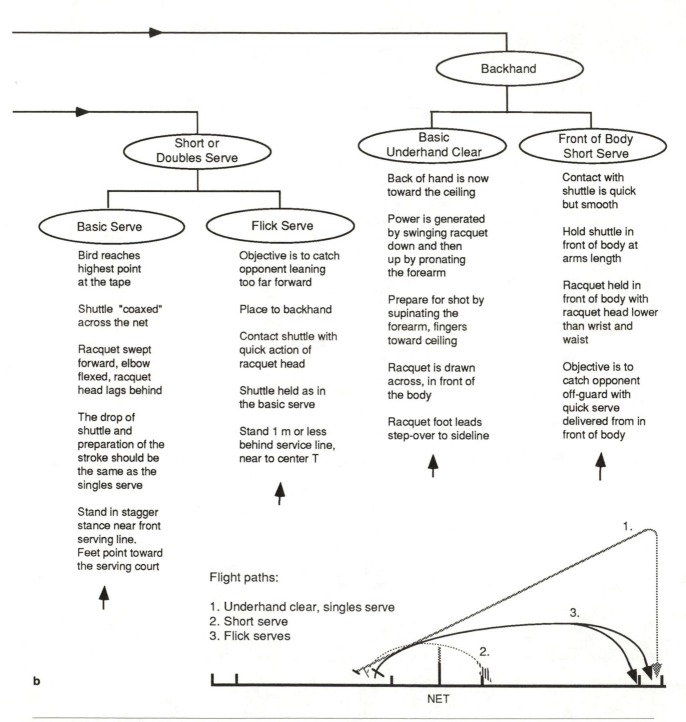

Backhand

Basic Underhand Clear

Back of hand is now toward the ceiling

Power is generated by swinging racquet down and then up by pronating the forearm

Prepare for shot by supinating the forearm, fingers toward ceiling

Racquet is drawn across, in front of the body

Racquet foot leads step-over to sideline

Front of Body Short Serve

Contact with shuttle is quick but smooth

Hold shuttle in front of body at arms length

Racquet held in front of body with racquet head lower than wrist and waist

Objective is to catch opponent off-guard with quick serve delivered from in front of body

Short or Doubles Serve

Basic Serve

Bird reaches highest point at the tape

Shuttle "coaxed" across the net

Racquet swept forward, elbow flexed, racquet head lags behind

The drop of shuttle and preparation of the stroke should be the same as the singles serve

Stand in stagger stance near front serving line. Feet point toward the serving court

Flick Serve

Objective is to catch opponent leaning too far forward

Place to backhand

Contact shuttle with quick action of racquet head

Shuttle held as in the basic serve

Stand 1 m or less behind service line, near to center T

Flight paths:

1. Underhand clear, singles serve
2. Short serve
3. Flick serves

NET

b

Figure M1.7. Continued.

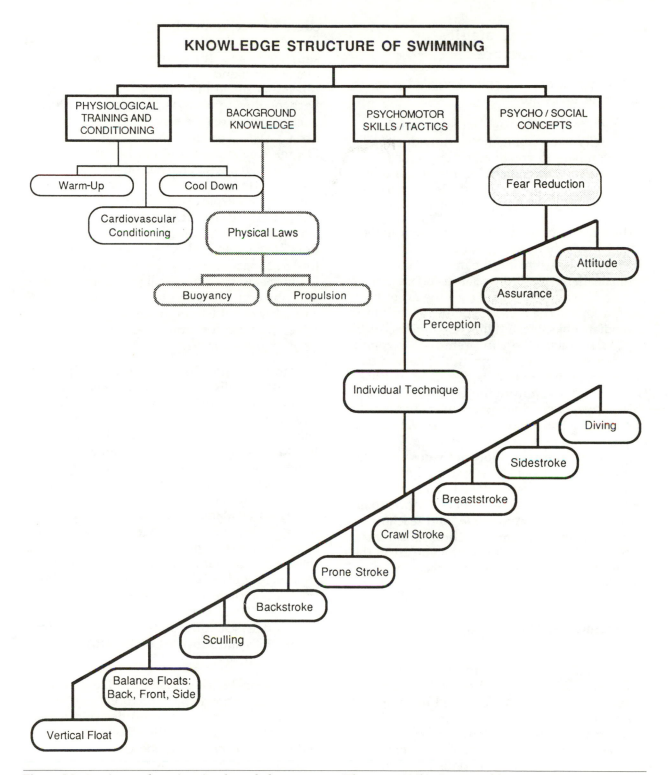

Figure M1.8. A sample swimming knowledge structure (Thomas, 1989b). Reprinted by permission.

Developing the Strategies Knowledge Structure

In developing the strategies knowledge structure, your goals are

1. to identify the basic strategies of the activity, describing how individual skills combine to create advantages; and
2. to describe the decision-making or thinking skills required for students to understand how these strategies are executed.

The terms *tactics* and *strategies* are often applied interchangeably in sport and physical activity, but they have distinctive meanings. Tactics was originally defined as ''the science and art of military and naval evolutions, esp. the art of handling troops in the presence of the enemy or for immediate objectives'' (Funk & Wagnalls, 1978, p. 1363). Tactical ability referred to one's prowess in handling troops in the heat of battle. Strategy, in contrast, is described by Reber (1985) ''as derived from the Greek for generalship, a plan of conduct or action, a consciously arrived-at set of operations for solving some problem or achieving some goal'' (p. 736). Of the two terms, *strategy* more aptly describes the analytical process of developing a knowledge structure. The analysis is done before any teaching or coaching, and your aim is to develop an overall plan of action to guide your teaching or coaching over an extended period. In contrast, tactical decisions are made when you are in the midst of a game, competition, class, or other situation.

Guidelines for Developing the Strategies Structure

In the KS Model, the principles underlying the individual skills analyses have led to relatively stable procedures easily adopted by students, teachers, coaches, and designers. The steps in creating a strategic knowledge structure, however, are not as definitive. Indeed, we know little about strategic thinking as defined by master teachers and coaches or as researched by sport science authorities. However, we have discovered some useful principles through accessing the literature in motor learning, cognition, curriculum, and instruction and through conducting the knowledge acquisition process with master teachers and coaches.

In developing a strategies knowledge structure, you encounter two new types of knowledge: (a) decision-making skills that describe how the athlete gains an advantage in specified situations, and (b) optimal combinations of players with and against an opponent (how to physically move in combination with others). Each of these points is illustrated in the ice hockey structure (see Figure M1.3 and Appendix C). This structure was elicited from Dr. George Kingston and Robin Laycock, using a combination of text analysis, analogical derivation, structured interview, and stimulated recall. George is an expert in international ice hockey and an elite coach at the university, national team (Canada and Norway), and NHL levels. Robin is an elite ice hockey player who played for Dr. Kingston for 5 years and professionally in Europe. Robin is also an instructional designer and physical education teacher. Following are a number of guidelines for developing a knowledge structure for strategies, with ice hockey used as the example.

1. The Strategies Structure Is Built Upon the Individual Skills Analysis.   Strategic ability demands strong individual skills. An analysis of strategies describes how individual skills and subskills combine to create strategic advantages. In a knowledge structure for strategies, the individual skills are not repeated or reanalyzed, but are assumed to be inherited or transferred, as described earlier. An analysis of strategies describes how individual skills are combined to create strategic advantages. The ice hockey structure, for example (Figure M1.3), shows that there are only four major individual skills (skating, puck control, checking, and goaltending), but the complete analysis (Appendix C) identifies over 100 different subskills. The strategic knowledge structure shows how these individual skills and subskills combine to create strategic advantages.

2. Decision-Making Skills Are Defined First.   A strategies knowledge structure identifies two new types of knowledge: (a) decision-making skills that describe how the athlete gains an advantage in specified situations and (b) optimal combinations of players with and against an opponent (how to physically move in combination with others). Of the two, you need to define the decision-making skills first. This point is illustrated in the ice hockey structures shown in Figures M1.3 and M1.9. Figure M1.3 identifies three major strategic concepts: general principles, offensive concepts, and defensive concepts. Figure M1.9 shows the underlying concepts of each, which reflect the type of decision making that the athlete must be capable of. Six general principles are presented: the overall concept of the game, initiative, activity, possession, time and space, and cooperative team play. Seven offensive concepts are taught: recurring spatial situations, support, finishing attack, pressure, puck control, movement, and transition. Five defensive concepts are taught: concentration of defense, support, patience and restraint, angling, and transition. The overall goal of the strategies structure is to identify a progression of principles that underlie strategic thinking ability. Each of the principles identified is analyzed into subprinciples that provide more detail and direction for teaching, coaching, and performance (see Appendix C for the complete analysis).

3. A Strategies Hierarchy Reflects Increasing Numbers of Athletes and Complexity in Game or Environmental Conditions.

The strategies structure describes the optimal combinations of players that can function with and against an opponent (how to physically move in combination with others). Given that it is important for an athlete to possess the decision-making skills shown in Figure M1.9, you can now identify the specific movement combinations that lead to their attainment.

As the number of teammates who work together increases, so does the information load on each athlete. A strategies structure therefore reflects that the athlete will experience greater success in communicating in small units, with the number and size of units increasing as strategic skills develop. A strategies analysis often exhibits the following progression of interactions, with the first number in each combination being the offensive player:

- 1 vs. 0, 0 vs. 1, 1 vs. 1
- 2 vs. 0, 2 vs. 1, 2 vs. 2, 1 vs. 2
- 3 vs. 0, 3 vs. 1, 3 vs. 2, 3 vs. 3, 0 vs. 3, 1 vs. 3, 2 vs. 3
- and so on

An alternate but related rule is sensitive to the degree of opposition encountered:

- No opposition: 1 vs. 0, 2 vs. 0, 3 vs. 0
- Advantage: 2 vs. 1, 2 vs. 2, 3 vs. 1, 3 vs. 2
- Equal: 1 vs. 1, 2 vs. 2, 3 vs. 3
- Disadvantage: 1 vs. 2, 2 vs. 3

The technique of analyzing a sport by considering the number of players interacting with and against one other is not new; it has been developed by a number of theorists, each con-

tributing valuable guidance in implementing this concept. For example, Jewett and Bain (1987) has defined three movement process categories, hierarchically arranged as generic movement, ordinative movement, and creative movement. Generic movements are simple movements, whereas creative movements involve the upper limit in interactions and environmental conditions. Sinclair (1986) has applied Jewett and Bain's principles to practice organization in a team sport through successive stages from individual skills through to full game play. Rink (1985) has developed a four-stage model of skill acquisition (control of object, control of object with skills combined, simple offensive and defensive roles, full game experiences for the development of game skills), with three nested principles called extension, refinement, and application operating at each of the four stages of development. These models illustrate the practice of analyzing an activity into progressive levels based on the numbers of competing athletes. Each model also recognized the need to define environmental constraints and to take these into consideration progressively as you design instruction.

4. Relationships Between Skills and Concepts in the Strategies Analysis Adhere to Many of the Same Cross-Disciplinary Guidelines That Underlie the Individual Skills Analysis.

Many of the same principles that were given to explain the relationships found between individual skills also apply to the development of strategic knowledge structures. Of particular importance are the following:

- Biomechanical principles—The movement of players relative to one another often is explained by principles and concepts derived from kinesiology and biomechanics. For example, in the ice hockey structure, strategies are explained on concepts of time, space, and angling.
- Skill acquisition and control principles—Interactions between athletes and groups of athletes are often explained and refined through the use of a motor learning and control principle. In ice hockey the principle of read-and-react reflects the literature on cue identification and anticipatory timing.
- Physiological or medical principles—Fitness prerequisites need to be kept in the forefront when defining the strategies of a sport or activity. Skills and strategies continue to be ordered with attention to physiological prerequisites such as aerobic and anaerobic

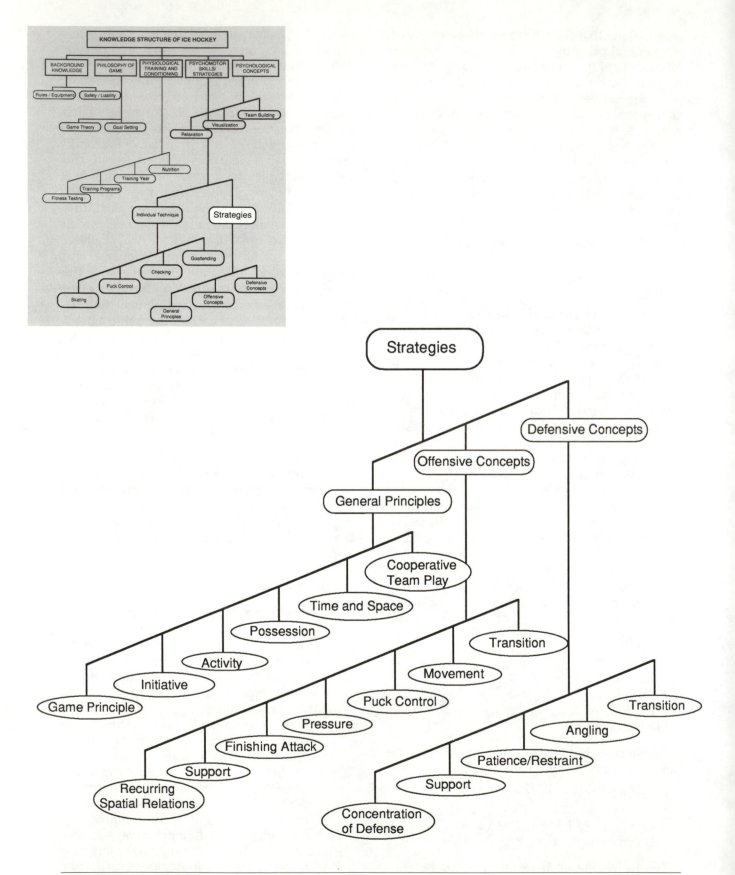

Figure M1.9.   Overview of ice hockey strategies.

power, muscular strength and endurance, flexibility, body composition, and weight control.

- Psychological concepts—The impact of research in sport psychology is especially evident in the strategies structure. For example, the ice hockey structure includes the principles of initiative, cooperative team play, support, and patience and restraint.

- Safety and liability concerns—In all sports and activities, it is mandatory that strategies be introduced to minimize risk, increase confidence, and create a secure, safe environment for both students and instructors. Small units (1 vs. 1, 2 vs. 1) better prepare players for situations that could be dangerous.

- Mastery of fear—Strategies can be introduced and combined in order to reduce anxiety or fear and increase confidence. For example, modulating different and increasing levels of competition can help players become more confident.

5. A Strategies Structure Can Be Developed for Individual Sports. It is relatively easy to see how a strategies structure can be developed in a team sport. But what about individual activities, such as archery, golf, jazz dance, or swimming? A knowledge structure in an individual or expressive activity should also include an analysis of strategic thinking and should be sensitive to numbers of participants and to changes and variability in the environment. Consider the following questions as they relate to decision making and optimum combinations of players in individual activities:

1. Does the activity require decision-making skills related to different events? (For example, in track the strategies for sprinting differ from those for middle-distance or long-distance events.)

2. Does the activity have a team event? (For example, swimming and track have team relays; and golf and tennis stage a number of different team competitions.)

3. Does the activity involve choreography (expressive strategic thinking)?

4. Does the activity impose differing environmental demands? (For example, in golf, playing the ball in different lies requires critical observation and decision-making skills.)

Developing the Knowledge Structures for Background, Physiological, Psychological, Sociological, and Philosophical Concepts

As is evident in the psychomotor skills and strategies structures, concepts derived from motor learning, biomechanics, exercise physiology, sports psychology, and other cross-disciplinary areas are integrated within the skills and strategies analyses. Why is it additionally necessary to identify background, physiological, psychological, sociological, and philosophical concepts in a knowledge structure? The influence of these disciplines on coaching and teaching has become pronounced over the last several decades. They have come to play a critical role in the knowledge base of teaching and coaching.

Concepts Selected Are Derived From Recognized Literature Bases

Concepts should be derived from research journals, textbooks, or other sources that have achieved favorable peer review (meaning that other professionals have scrutinized the work and found it sound). Concepts identified are analyzed to show how they can be applied to teaching and coaching. For example, Figure M1.10 shows one component, aerobic endurance, of the structure for physiological training and conditioning in ice hockey. This structure was derived from the work of Howie Wenger (1986), an exercise physiologist specializing in ice hockey, as well as from Physical Best, the new AAHPERD approach to physical fitness assessment and training (McSwegin et al., 1989). The physical testing analysis addresses anthropometric measures, flexibility, muscular strength and endurance, aerobic endurance, and anaerobic endurance. The physiological training and conditioning category provides developmental programs for off-ice and on-ice conditioning.

Concepts Are Identified and Analyzed as a Hierarchy That Portrays a Recommended Order of Introduction

Figure M1.11 (p. 76) shows an analysis of the sociocultural concept of play–games–sport and illustrates the changes that occur when an activity is approached as play, as a game, or as

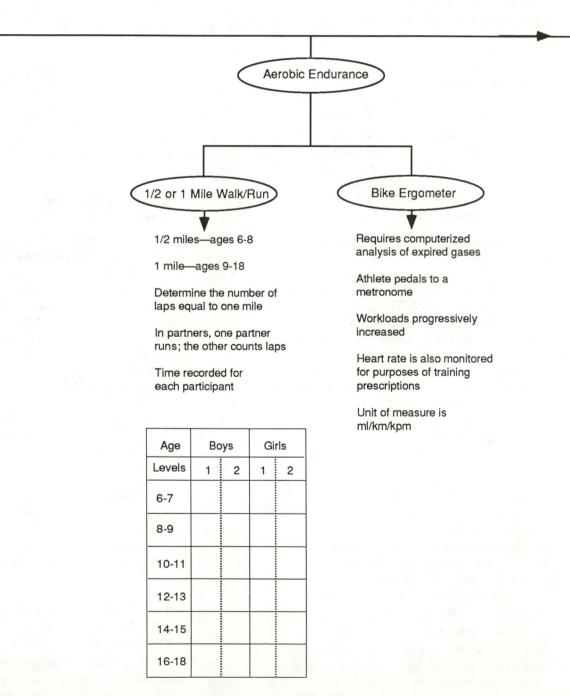

Figure M1.10. One component of the knowledge structure for physiological training and conditioning in ice hockey (see Appendix C for complete knowledge structure).

sport (Lawson & Placek, 1981). This concept is taught as part of a university course in badminton. Students are introduced to badminton first as play, then as a game or recreational activity, and finally as a competitive sport. The students plan and enact the different forms in a class of their own design. At the conclusion, they discuss the strengths and weaknesses of the three approaches. This concept is integrated as part of the course and places a different theme on each of three play/competitive days. It is the first opportunity for many students to gauge the impact of a social/competitive structure on their own and others' behavior and on their interaction with others' assumptions and values. As future teachers and coaches, they also become aware of the impact the play–games–sport concept has on students and their own role as a teacher.

**Concepts May Be Taught
in Lecture/Discussion or During
"Teachable Moments" as an Activity
Is Performed**

Figure M1.12 (p. 77) shows the analysis of a number of environmental concepts taught in backpacking (Vickers, Rodney, & Rodney, 1984). Outdoor specialists Doug and Wendy Rodney teach these concepts both as planned lectures/talks and in the outdoor environment as appropriate opportunities arise.

 **EXERCISE 1**

**Develop an Individual Skills
Knowledge Structure**

Module 1 described the specific procedure for developing a knowledge structure using primarily text analysis and analogical derivation. Develop an individual skills knowledge structure in a sport or activity of your choice, including the following components:

a. Name all the major individual offensive and defensive skills.
b. Break down each basic skill into subskills.
c. For each subskill, describe in point form the ideal, mature, or expert technique ("Keys to Success") you want your student to achieve. This information will be derived from many sources: biomechanics, motor learning, your experience. Write the actual words you use

when you teach. Consistently order this information for all subskills.

 **EXERCISE 2**

**Define the Underlying
Principles at Work**

As reflected in the analysis in Exercise 1, identify and present examples of any *three* of the following situations:

a. Relationship dictated by a biomechanical principle
b. Relationship dictated by a skill acquisition or control principle
c. Relationship dictated by a physiological principle
d. Relationship dictated by a safety or liability concern
e. Relationship dictated by mastery of fear
f. Relationship dictated by expert opinion and experience
g. No relationship established; disagreement exists among experts on how best to proceed

 **EXERCISE 3**

**Develop a Strategies
Knowledge Structure**

Develop a basic strategies knowledge structure for the activity. Identify first the decision-making skills that describe how the athlete gains an advantage in specified situations and then optimal combinations of players with and against an opponent (how to physically move in combination with others). Present selected parts on overheads or handouts to your classmates. Be prepared to identify and defend your sources and the content of your structure; have at hand arguments to support the interrelationships between skills and strategies that you have mapped.

 **EXERCISE 4**

**Develop a Knowledge Structure
for Psychological, Sociological,
or Philosophical Concepts**

Choose one psychological, sociological, philosophical, or other sport science concept that you will use directly in your coaching or teaching.

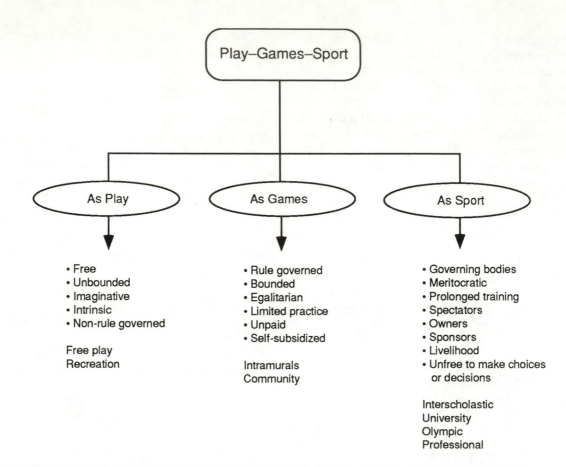

Figure M1.11. Analysis of play–games–sport.

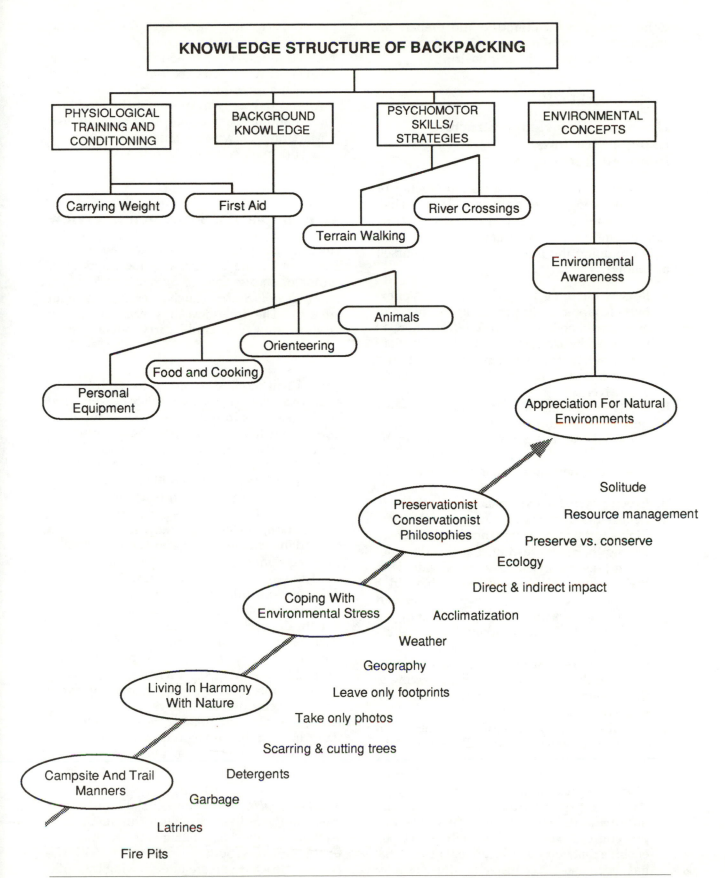

Figure M1.12. Analysis of environmental concepts (map overview). *Note.* From *Instructional Design Series: Introduction to Backpacking* by J.N. Vickers, D. Rodney, and W. Rodney, 1984, unpublished manuscript. Reprinted by permission.

Collect the relevant literature and prepare an analysis that identifies the major components and principles you will emphasize.

EXERCISE 5

Develop a Knowledge Structure Using a Structured Interview Technique

Your task is to interview a master teacher or coach following a set protocol. Figure M1.13 presents a template that you may use to structure the information you gather.

Before doing the interview prepare yourself as follows:

a. Review the underlying characteristics of experts (chapter 3). In particular, be aware of an expert's ability to chunk information, to use hierarchical arrangements of information, to interrelate time with spatial elements and content, and to use sport science concepts extensively.

b. Study any books or other materials the expert has developed before the interview. Otherwise, review a number of books on the activity.

c. Expect sureness and certainty in the expert's answers.

d. Expect physical demonstrations and modeling.

e. Realize that expert coaches and teachers exhibit a certain imperviousness to differences among their athletes but that this does not mean they are insensitive to individuals in their actual teaching and coaching. In a knowledge elicitation session, an expert easily separates the content or subject matter of an activity from the many ways it is exhibited and acquired by learners.

f. Use the template structure (see Figure M1.13) to orient the expert you are interviewing to the cross-disciplinary categories of information you wish to develop.

g. Initially be very specific and somewhat narrow with your questions. The scope of the interview will widen naturally as you work through the structure and discuss the cross-disciplinary categories.

h. Paraphrase to the expert the answers and information given to you. This counseling procedure, developed by Carl Rogers (1980), ensures that you have accurately heard what has been said, confirms to the coach or teacher that you understand and that you can

keep pace, and encourages the person to continue.

i. Limit an interview to 45 minutes or less. It is very easy for you to become overwhelmed with the amount of information provided.

j. After a day or two, draw out the structure (by hand or using a computer program like MacDraw, Canvas, etc.); use this as the basis of your next session.

An Example of a Structured Interview

The example given below was derived from an interview by the author with Joe Luxbacher, author of *Soccer: Steps to Success* and *Teaching Soccer: Steps to Success* (Luxbacher, in press-a, in press-b). The interview has been reworded to show how you could carry out a similar interview.

You. I will soon be going out to teach [coach] at the [*name the age group you will be working with*] level, and I would like to ask you a few questions about how you prepare before teaching [coaching] your class [team].

Shown on this template [Figure M1.13] are four major categories that will help me identify the information you use in teaching or coaching soccer. The first category, sport-specific information, includes all the necessary background information in the sport, such as safety, rules, equipment, historical information, and so on. The second, physiological training and conditioning, includes warm-up and cool-down, training, nutrition, sports medicine, and so on. The third, psychomotor skills and strategies, includes individual skills and strategies. Finally, the last category identifies the psychological, sociological, or other sport science concepts that you build into your teaching or coaching every day or teach on specific days through discussions, question and answer, lectures, films, or day trips. I'd like to begin now with my questions. When you first meet a new group of students [athletes], which category do you begin with?

Teacher/Coach. Psychomotor skills and strategies and the individual skills technique. [Note: At this point you begin filling in the components of the structure by hand. Share this with the coach or teacher you are interviewing by working side by side at a table. I have included the

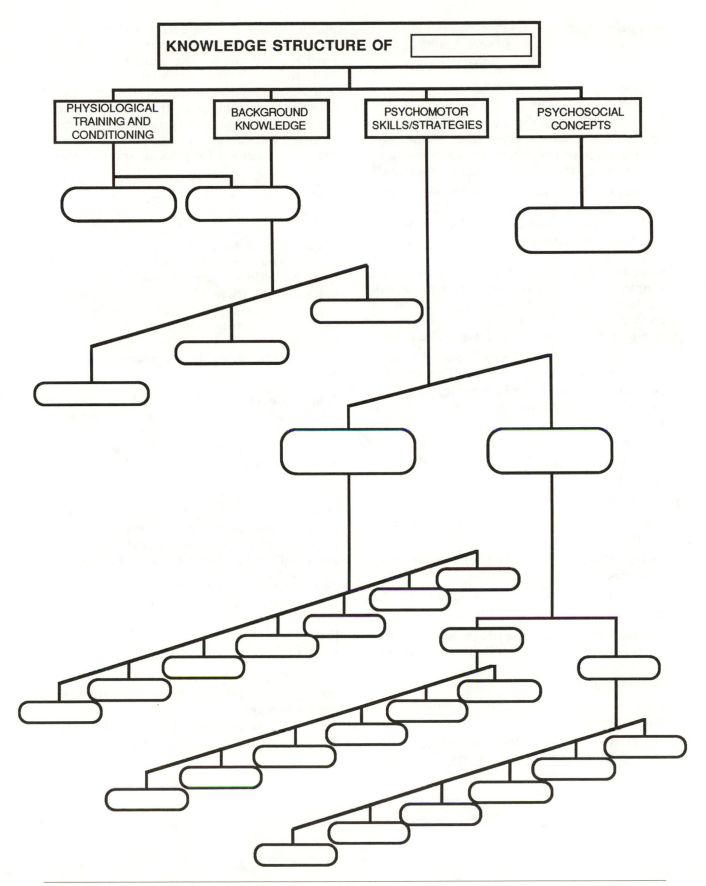

Figure M1.13. Template for a knowledge elicitation interview.

first page of my session (see Figure M1.14) to show you an example of what results.]

You.   What is the first individual skill you teach?

Teacher/Coach.   Passing and receiving, with an emphasis on efficiency.

You.   Let's develop these two skills in their entirety. That is, let's analyze them completely, even though you probably do not teach all of them at once. What do you mean by "efficiency"?

Teacher/Coach.   There is a technically correct and efficient way to perform each skill. Although each student may exhibit an individual way to execute a skill, there are certain underlying principles I want them all to understand. I stress basic technique, no extraneous movements, simple and direct lines—actually a lot of biomechanics. Passing skills are taught first on the ground, and later lofted. After each passing skill is taught, the reciprocal receiving skill is taught.

You.   OK. You begin with individual skills with a concept of efficiency stressed. The first skill you teach is passing and receiving, first passing on the ground and then lofted. Which do you begin with?

Teacher/Coach.   Passing ground skills.

You.   Do you start with a specific ground passing skill?

Teacher/Coach.   Inside foot.

You.   Inside foot. Do you teach right only or both?

Teacher/Coach.   All skills are taught on both sides from Day 1.

You.   So you teach passing skills, on the ground, both right and left foot.

Teacher/Coach.   Yes, the progression for passing skills is inside foot pass (left and right), outside foot pass (left and right), and instep pass (left and right).

You.   So there are just three ground passing skills taught?

Teacher/Coach.   Yes. Next, receiving on the ground is taught, and there are three skills presented here: absorption or giving with the ball, receiving with the inside of the foot, and receiving with the outside of the foot. We then move to lofted passes as follows: short chip (left and right), long chip (left and right), lofted receiving, receiving with the instep (left and right), receiving with the thigh (left and right), chest (concave and convex), and receiving with the head. That's it for passing and receiving.

You.   OK, let's see if I have this structured correctly. *Passing* and *receiving* with efficiency are first, with two subcategories each, on the *ground* and *lofted*. Under *passing ground* there are three subskills (inside foot, outside foot, instep); under *passing lofted* there are two subskills (short chip, long chip). Under *receiving ground*, efficiency is still stressed. There are three subskills or concepts (absorption, inside foot, outside foot); under *lofted receiving* there are four (instep, thigh, chest, head). One of these, *chest receiving*, is also further subdivided into *concave* and *convex* receiving.

Teacher/Coach.   Right. I should also mention that I teach the individual skills as they relate to the layout and strategic use of the playing field. Students are told from the start that passing skills operate in the midfield, dribbling-shielding skills at the top of the offensive zone, heading skills as you get nearer the net, and shooting skills at the goal. This is the order the skills are introduced in, and they are taught through drills that are set up and practiced on an actual field and in each of these zones.

You.   So you see the field as having sections in which individual skills are taught, but with a strategic emphasis at the same time. Like so? [You draw a picture of the field as he or she explains.]

Teacher/Coach.   Yes, always; the kids have to see where the skills fit into the game right from the beginning.

[We then move on to dribble-shielding skills, with an emphasis on the top of the offensive zone.]

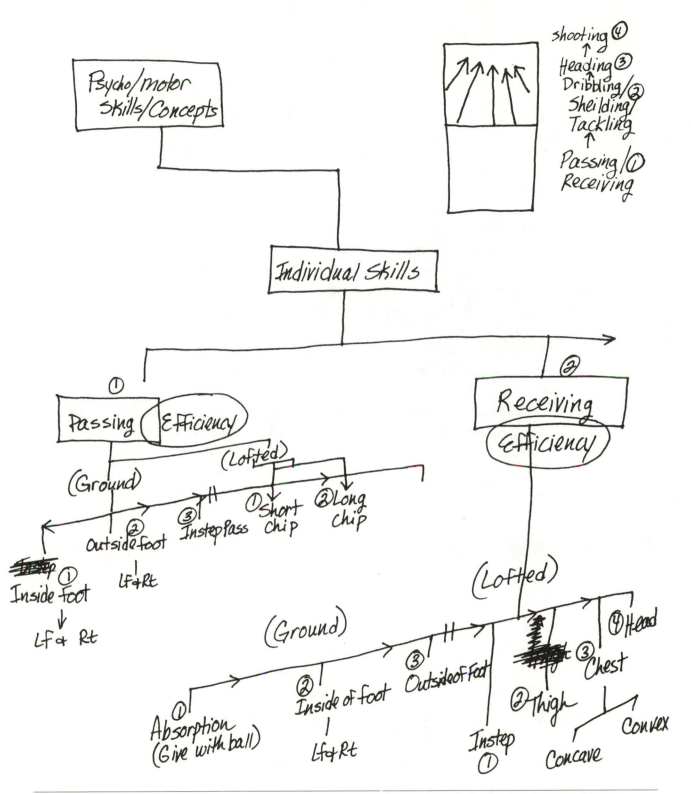

Figure M1.14. Knowledge structure in soccer (initial structured interview) (J. Luxbacher, in press-b).

Topics

for Module 2

- Expert-novice differences in analyzing the teaching or coaching environment
- Managing facilities and equipment
- Exercise 1: Planning the teaching space without a class in attendance
- Exercise 2: Managing equipment
- Exercise 3: Planning the teaching space with a class in attendance
- Exercise 4: Developing a mini-lesson plan for the management of equipment
- Safety and Liability
- Exercise 5: Handling a minor injury
- Exercise 6: Handling a major injury
- Modifying facilities, equipment, and games
- Exercise 7: Planning game, facility, and equipment modifications

I must create a system or be enslaved by another man's.

—William Blake

Photo by Joan Vickers.

Analyzing Learning Environments

This introductory quote by Blake may appear to be dramatic, but there is a ring of truth in it when planning to teach or coach. Especially when first meeting a class or a team, you are the only one empowered or given the responsibility for creating an environment where learning, growth, and personal development can occur. Over time, your students can become facilitators of this, but at the outset it is your responsibility to create a "system" that will permit you and others to be successful.

In Module 2, we cover questions about understanding and managing the learning environment. We begin by looking at how master teachers differ from novices in handling new teaching situations. Much of what characterizes good teaching or coaching is fostered by *actively gaining information* about the environment in which you will be teaching or coaching. In this regard, we cover expert-novice differences, safety, equipment, and management of people and equipment. It is important as well that you

think out in advance the steps needed to handle an injury (a certain occurrence) and a serious emergency (hopefully a nonoccurrence). Finally, principles of game modification are covered. All of these are developed as a series of instructional design exercises to help you determine personal strategies for the teaching or coaching situation you will be in.

Expert-Novice Differences in Analyzing the Teaching or Coaching Environment

Two groups of teachers are asked to design two lessons to be presented to public school students ages 7 to 9 who will arrive in about an hour. The lessons are to be in either soccer or basketball. The teachers are asked to plan the lessons by thinking out loud into a tape recorder. They have 30 minutes to do this, after which they meet their students and deliver the lessons they have designed. Each actual class will be 30 minutes long, and the entire session is video-taped. After the lesson is complete, the teachers are shown their own tapes individually and asked to explain why they taught as they did (a stimulated recall procedure).

How do you think they will differ, if at all, if one group is made up of master teachers in physical education and the other of student teachers? This study was carried out by Housner and Griffey (1985), who found the following results. In the planning session, experienced teachers made an average of 53 requests (in 30 minutes) for information, whereas the novice teachers made 37. The master teachers wanted to know about the number of students, their age and sex, their ability levels in the activity, and their previous experience and background in the activity. They also asked questions about equipment, teaching materials, and resources available, and they asked to see the physical layout and the equipment available. Many asked to walk about the actual space. This unabashed attention to detail and overt questioning is characteristic of experienced teachers and coaches.

Quite often, novice teachers are shy about asking questions or underestimate the importance of knowing details about the physical environment. Experienced teachers and coaches have learned that time is of the essence and that what appears to be a small detail (for example, being unable to find pinnies, cones, or a power outlet) can eat away valuable class time and result in disciplinary problems. Also, compared to classroom teachers, teachers of sport and physical activities must manage very large spaces. Physical education students are not assigned to a constant location, a desk, or a single workspace, but are mobile. In a typical 40-minute class in physical education, there is an average of 14 transitions, or changes in location of students (Siedentop, Herkowitz, & Rink, 1984). There is only one individual who can orchestrate all of this, and that is you, the teacher or coach. So Module 2, more than anything else, encourages you to be very much in charge and to think of the gymnasium or playing field or classroom as *your space.*

Following are some typical instructional design questions you should ask at the outset about your teaching or coaching environment:

1. What is the physical environment in which I am required to teach or coach?

2. How large is the instructional space?
3. How many students can be comfortably accommodated?
4. If the facility is undersize, what are some strategies to maintain a high activity ratio? Are auxiliary classrooms, stage space, or hall space available?
5. Will all of the instruction be given in the one facility, or will classrooms, the library, or outside areas be needed? If teaching out-of-doors, what will I do if it rains? (It will.)
6. Are some of the areas high-risk areas?
7. What type of equipment is necessary to teach the unit?
8. Is the equipment available? If not, how can I obtain what is needed?
9. Is the equipment of good quality and in good repair?
10. What are the change rooms like? Are they well equipped with lockers and showers, and is there adequate security in the form of individual locks and door security? How far are the change rooms from the gymnasium, and how long do students need to change and move to and from the locker area?
11. If I subtract change time from the total time available, how much time do I have to teach the unit? How long in minutes is each lesson or practice? How many sessions are there? How many hours in total have been allocated?
12. Given the possible range of skill levels I will encounter, will it be necessary to modify the facilities and equipment in order to individualize learning? How can this be done? Where can I find resources on game modifications?
13. In managing the instructional environment, will I need the help of others—caretakers, peer tutors, audiovisual assistants, librarians, teaching aides, parents, or outside resource people?
14. Given all of the preceding, what must be booked or arranged early? What can be left to the last minute?
15. How would I handle an injury or an emergency in this setting?
16. Is the space visually pleasant? Are there posters, charts, pictures of sequences of movements, artwork, an overview of the program, and other materials on the walls that are recent and reflective of my teaching?

Managing Facilities and Equipment

In planning the physical environment, facility management and safety should be your first considerations. Be sure to visit where you will be teaching or coaching at least 2 weeks before you meet your students. You need this time in case equipment is missing or damaged or there are problems with the space. Walk about the facility and look into every nook and cranny. Check for cleanliness and for areas that are in need of repair. In particular, look for protruding hooks or obstructions on the walls or around the sidelines. Have equipment you do not need put in storage. Check the floor for broken boards or tiles that are loose. Check the locker rooms for whether the showers work, the personal security system for each student (locks, baskets), and whether you can lock the whole area during class or practice time. Check the equipment room and be prepared to spend quite a few minutes there. Is the equipment organized and arranged so that items can be taken in and out easily? Are there carts to transport equipment, or will you have to find a way to get the equipment out piece by piece? Are all spaces clean and pleasant places for students? If not think about how conditions can be improved.

Student Uniforms and Their Management

If you are teaching or coaching in a situation where a uniform policy has been put in place, then it is necessary for you to ask your supervising teacher or the head coach what his or her policy is. What constitutes a full uniform? How do they handle uniform check? What do they do if a student has forgotten his or her uniform?

If you are in a new situation, you must devise your own policy. Although it may seem strange to be asked to concentrate on this, you will find that the daily task of administering a uniform policy can be unduly time consuming unless you have thought it through and manage it with care. Some suggestions:

1. Require a uniform, if possible. Inquire first about the policy for your district, because some areas forbid requiring uniforms. If that is the case, find out why the policy exists and whether it is possible to begin a uniform purchase program in your school. If not, adopt the policy of the district.

2. If you will have a school uniform, research the available suppliers carefully and ask for bids; involve students and other teachers in the decision. Look for an attractive, high-quality uniform with a top, a bottom (shorts or warmups), and socks. You should be able to get a complete uniform for about half of retail cost.

3. Try to make arrangements whereby students who are unable to pay can do work for the physical education department in exchange for their uniforms (for example, organizing the equipment room, helping at practices, or interscholastic games).

4. Set up a system of rotating peer uniform checks, with students administering the uniform policy.

5. Do not penalize students when uniforms are missing. Wearing a uniform should not be tied to academic grades.

6. When students forget uniforms, have extras in the equipment room that you can lend them for a nominal sum, refundable when the uniform is returned after laundry.

7. If any students claim illness at the beginning of class, be understanding, but have them change anyway, with permission to sit out strenuous portions; once dressed, most forget their problems.

8. Do not have students change if the class has no physical activity.

EXERCISE 1

Planning the Teaching Space Without a Class in Attendance

During your first visit, take with you a clipboard and diagram the environment. Also make a list of what needs to be done. Figure M2.1 presents a physical layout planning sheet that will help you formulate a plan of action.

Draw the following to scale:

1. All entrances and exits
2. Locker room locations
3. Paths of students to and from locker room areas and gymnasium
4. Courts and spaces to be used
5. Equipment room, arrangement of equipment
6. Emergency exits, those used to evacuate the space as well as those through which an injured student would be taken

7. Location of fire alarms, phones, fire extinguishers, first aid kits, and water
8. Any dangerous wall fittings, problems with the floor, and other potential problems

After completing the diagram, make a list of what needs to be done. List and prioritize the resources that you need to carry out each item on your list.

 **EXERCISE 2**

Managing Equipment

Equipment, or the lack of it, can make or break your teaching and coaching, so you need to be especially attentive to this item. Consider the activity you will be teaching and the number of students in each class. Before your first visit, make a list of what you would feel would be the ideal type and amount of equipment needed, and then check this against what is actually available. Consider the following: balls, nets, goals, standards, racquets, shuttles, pinnies or colored jerseys, cones, whistles, stop watches, scoresheets, first aid equipment.

On your visit to the school, first itemize all the equipment present, then use a 3-point classification system as to condition: 1 = usable; 2 = usable if repaired; 3 = unusable and needs to be replaced. Follow up on how the repairs are to be carried out. Visit the appropriate administrator in your school to find out how to purchase new equipment.

If you find yourself in a situation where there is not enough equipment and it is impossible to secure new equipment by the time you have to teach, do not panic. *This occurs often* and is simply a signal to you that you must devise alternate types of equipment, teaching methods, groups, stations, and other procedural types of knowledge that will temporarily get you around the problem. You should view this as a temporary problem only. Devise a long-term scheme for getting the equipment you need and do so, even if your stay at the school will be a short one. Submit a written budget with a rationale for each item. As part of your plan, look into money-raising schemes that students can lead and manage, look at the possibility of corporate donors and sponsors, and so on. Pass your list on to the administrator in charge of this; others will gain from your foresight.

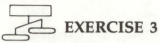 **EXERCISE 3**

Planning the Teaching Space With a Class in Attendance

After you have finished planning your equipment, now imagine a class in attendance. On the second diagram, position the following:

1. Show where your class will gather for roll call, announcement, and uniform check. Also show your location.
2. Show where you will teach when you need to use a blackboard or an audiovisual aid that requires power or a screen.
3. Show the location(s) of the warm-up.
4. Show the location(s) of instruction to the group.
5. Show the location of practice activities or station(s).
6. Sketch what you feel will be your supervision and skill analysis walking pattern during the class.
7. Show where students will sit out if necessary for project work, injury, or discipline.
8. Show the cool-down and after-class-question location.

EXERCISE 4

Developing a Mini-Lesson Plan for the Management of Equipment

Teach the management of equipment as a skill, and introduce this aspect of your teaching thoroughly (just as you would teach the class how to perform a physical skill). For each activity that you teach, develop a portion of a lesson or of lessons to teach students how to get out equipment, set up courts and other playing space, and take down and put equipment away. Do *not* undertake the task of putting up or taking down equipment yourself. Instead, delegate by teaching your students carefully how this is to be done automatically, with confidence, and without being asked before and at the end of each class. For example, if teaching badminton, spend a few minutes at the beginning of each unit thoroughly teaching the following: (a) how to set up the courts, especially how to tie knots that are minimal in number but maximum in tautness and ease of release; (b) how to take down the nets, fold hand over hand, roll, and store in the space designated; (c) how to return posts to holders and replace floor caps; (d) how

Organizing the Physical Layout

Teaching space without a class in attendance

1. Draw gymnasium layout. Show all entrances and exits.
2. Show location of locker rooms.
3. Draw in courts to be used.
4. Show equipment room.
5. Show location of equipment at beginning of class.
6. Show emergency exits.
7. Show location of fire alarm, phone, fire extinguisher, first aid kit, water.
8. Identify potential environmental hazards.

Teaching space with a class in attendance

1. Show where class begins for roll call, announcements, uniforms.
2. Show blackboard or audiovisual center, power outlets.
3. Show warm-up location(s).
4. Show location(s) for group instruction.
5. Show location of activity stations.
6. Show your walking pattern as class progresses.
7. Show where students will sit out if working on projects, injuries, discipline.
8. Show cool-down location(s).

Figure M2.1. Organizing the physical layout.

to put good shuttles back in rounds and leave damaged ones out for discard; (e) how to replace racquets in storage and leave out racquets that have broken strings and so on for repair. Do not try to teach all of this each class, but spread it over two or three lessons.

Safety and Liability

Despite the fact you have thought out the physical environment and anticipated how your students can move safely about the space, there will be injuries and mishaps that you must learn to deal with in advance of their occurrence. This, too, is a reality of teaching sport and physical activity that is rarely encountered in classroom teaching. It is necessary that you think out how you will handle minor and major injuries.

Teachers and coaches of physical education and sport should have formal training and, preferably, certification in handling injuries. In the following section, a thinking process is presented only. Think out what you will do in the event of a minor, than a major, injury. If you find it difficult to answer the following questions, then you should enroll in first aid or other courses.

EXERCISE 5

Handling a Minor Injury
(Sprain, Minor Cut, Bruise)

During a gymnastics class, a student performing a vault on the low horse has landed awkwardly and is sitting on the mat in pain, holding her ankle.

1. At the moment the injury occurs, what do you do?
2. What are your instructions to the rest of the class? How do you allocate your attention?
3. What procedures should you use in order to determine the severity of the injury?
4. How do you make the injured person comfortable?
5. How do you obtain or request the first aid kit or water? How do you obtain assistance from the main office, the school nurse, or the trainer?

6. What procedures are best for moving the injured person to the side of the gymnasium?
7. Do you continue the class after the injured person has been treated?
8. What procedures should you follow in filing an injury report? To whom does the report go?
9. The student returns to class the following day limping. In what ways can you include her in your class?

EXERCISE 6

Handling a Major Injury
(Cessation of Breathing, Injury
to the Back or the Head, Severe Bleeding,
Broken Bone)

During a gymnastics class, a student performing on the rings has slipped and landed on his head and is unconscious on the mat. Itemize your course of action:

1. At the moment the injury occurs, what should you do?
2. What instructions do you give to the rest of the class? How should you allocate your attention?
3. How do you get help immediately from the main office, the school nurse, or the trainer?
4. How do you make the injured person comfortable?
5. How do you determine the severity of the injury? What steps must be taken if there is a cessation of breathing?
6. What emergency treatment is warranted? What would be irresponsible?
7. What procedures are mandatory for moving the injured person?
8. Do you continue the class after the injured person has been taken for treatment? Should you go with the student to the hospital?
9. Who is responsible for calling the student's parents or guardian?
10. What procedures should you follow in filing an injury report? To whom does the report go?
11. The student returns to class after observation and release from the doctor. How do you welcome him back? In what ways do you include him in your class?

Modifying Facilities, Equipment, and Games

All sports have modified forms that facilitate full game play for those who are younger or smaller, or do not have the time available or the motivation to play the contest in its full form. Game modifications are made by

- altering the size of the playing space, most often making it smaller for smaller students;
- modifying the equipment by reducing its size, height, and weight;
- reducing the number of people on a team, thus increasing the number of contacts each person has with the ball, puck, or other object; or
- modifying the rules to guarantee maximum involvement and success in terms of goals scored, and time on the field of play.

For example, minivolleyball can be played three against three on a badminton court. Use the badminton nets and volleyball standards; lower the net for young and inexperienced students. This modification works very well, even for students in high school and college, because it places an emphasis on three hits, receipt of a soft serve, the set, the attack, and the basic elements of defense. After extensive three-on-three practice, it is easy to move the units to the larger regulation volleyball court.

In soccer, field hockey, and ice hockey, two or more small surfaces can be created by reducing the number of players per side and going from side to side rather than end to end. In many sports, grids divide playing surfaces into small game-like sections that permit maximum play. You can also modify the rules for safety reasons. For example, in ice hockey, special rules prevent contact before a certain age is reached.

 **EXERCISE 7**

Planning Game, Facility, and Equipment Modifications

In this exercise, think about the activity you analyzed in Module 1. Consult the sources you used in developing your knowledge structure. Are modifications described? Would they improve your teaching or coaching? How can you implement them? Using the physical layout form and a modified games approach, rethink Exercises 1 and 2. Develop and describe two modifications. Present them to others in your class.

Topics

for Module 3

- Understanding entry-level skills and knowledge levels
- A knowledge structure is an ''ordering mechanism'' for analyzing learners
- Exercise 1: The plan of discovery
- Exercise 2: Designing the pretest as part of the total course of instruction

People only see what they are prepared to see.

—Ralph Waldo Emerson

Photo © Cleo Photography.

Analyzing Learners

I have introduced this chapter with Emerson's quote because Module 3 is concerned with learning how to be an astute observer of your students. It is not enough to meet your class or team on Day 1 with a plan that involves casual observation or "eyeballing." Instead, you should have a thorough *plan of discovery* and one that gives your students a fair chance to show their strengths. In Module 3 we look at the different ways you can analyze your student athletes on selected aspects of the knowledge structures created in Module 1. First we target preassessment techniques, with your first tasks being the design of a pretest that can be implemented in a portion of two or three introductory classes (the equivalent of this in coaching is the structured tryout). You will also see that this pretest is part of the posttest and so ties the beginning and end of your instructional unit together.

The KS Model advocates the use of *criterion-based formative evaluation* as an approach for understanding student entry- and exit-level skills. This approach is introduced through two

vehicles. The Steps to Success participant's books are designed with checklists that permit students to check off their technique progress for all basic skills. The second vehicle is a computer program called ActionMark, designed specifically to help teachers and coaches select pretest items and administer them to their students. ActionMark keeps track of student progress not only on the pretest items but also allows the instructor to select other skills, strategies, and concepts to be included in a complete unit of instruction. ActionMark is introduced and explained in Module 8 (Real-World Applications).

Understanding Entry-Level Skills and Knowledge Levels

What is your view of the needs, characteristics, and problems of your students? What is your role as a teacher in meeting needs and helping students solve their problems? Could students be expected to become physically educated without your professional interventions? These questions and your answers to them lead the way to your view of, or assumptions about, your students. Put differently, they uncover your views of human nature. (Lawson & Placek, 1981, p. 30)

How can you come to understand your student's entry-level skills and knowledge? In the world of practice, you will find that there is little formal evaluation of this (Carre & Lashuk, 1986; Lashuk, 1984; Lawson & Placek, 1981). There are many reasons for this, but probably the main one is the time-consuming nature of skills and fitness assessment. Unlike pencil-and-paper tests, where a whole class of students can be tested at once on a battery of items in a set period of time, skills and fitness testing requires that each individual student be observed while performing each skill or test. The problem can be appreciated through two examples.

First, let's consider a typical class of 30 students in which the teacher designs a pretest of only five skills. Let's assume the teacher needs only 2 minutes in order to evaluate each student on each skill. Simple arithmetic shows how time consuming this can be if each student is observed individually: 30 students × 5 skills × 2 min./skill = 300 minutes. The result? Five 60-minute classes would be required. Since a unit of instruction may average only 8 to 12 classes, it is difficult to justify using one half to one third of the available time in this way.

A second example is in fitness testing. We have available accurate, well-developed fitness tests that should be used routinely as an aspect of all teaching and coaching. However, administering fitness tests can be very time consuming, with the added problem of interpreting each student's score according to established norms or other means. This can require a considerable amount of time outside of class and is often too cumbersome for most teachers and coaches to apply. Beginning teachers are caught by surprise by the difficulties associated with skills and fitness testing; in the majority of cases, they cease to evaluate at entry and at exit points (Carre & Lashuk, 1986; Lashuk, 1984).

In Module 3 you are asked to approach each teaching or coaching situation with a plan of discovery that makes you an information gatherer and an astute observer of *each* of your students.

Begin by answering the instructional design questions below as they apply to the teaching or coaching situation you will soon be in.

1. Who are you teaching or coaching?
2. How old are they? Boys? Girls? Coed?
3. What experiences have they had in performing the skills, strategies, and concepts identified in the knowledge structure you created in Module 1?
4. Would you classify your student athletes as beginners, intermediates, or advanced? Are they mixed in ability level?
5. Did you objectively determine this through a testing procedure of some type, or did you determine this subjectively by simply observing them in classes or tryouts?
6. Are there safety precautions that must be taken with this group of learners? Why? Should there be age or ability restrictions? Why?
7. Have you been able to locate literature, films, books, or other resources that describe the type of student athletes you have?
8. Do students generally go through recognizable stages or steps as they become more skilled or knowledgeable in the activity you will be teaching or coaching? If so, what are these steps? On what literature, research, or other sources do you base your answer?

A Knowledge Structure Is an "Ordering Mechanism" for Analyzing Learners

Lawson and Placek (1981) recommend that new professionals in physical education develop "an ordering mechanism," or a means whereby they can apply their body of knowledge to their everyday work. They additionally state that this body of knowledge should

. . . be drawn in no small part from the knowledge base of the profession and as such cannot be tapped haphazardly. If it is to serve as a blueprint for day to day operations, it must be structured to facilitate its application. (p. 28)

The KS Model provides a "knowledge ordering mechanism" in the form of the knowledge structures created in Module 1. It is now time to use this knowledge structure as the basis for analyzing your students.

In previous chapters we found that a knowledge structure is comprised of the following cross-disciplinary categories of knowledge: (1) activity-specific background information, (2) psychomotor skills and strategies, (3) physiological training and conditioning, (4) psychological concepts, (5) sociocultural concepts, (6) philosophical and historical concepts, and (7) other concepts. Your task now is to develop an understanding of your students relative to each of these cross-disciplinary categories of information. Consider each of the following statements as they apply to your own situation and student athletes.

Background Knowledge

What do my students already know about the rules, equipment, history, and other categories of information I have identified in the background knowledge category? How can I find out what they know? Are there approved tests or other vehicles already developed that will help me assess their level of knowledge on the categories identified? What type of evaluation skills do I need as a teacher or coach in order to assess individuals on this type of information? Of what use will the results be in helping me teach or coach each individual and the group as a whole?

Physiological Training and Conditioning

What is the fitness level of each of my students in this activity? Are there approved tests for determining levels of fitness? Do these tests have criterion levels that inform students about their overall fitness level? If so, are there training programs recommended for this age group? What type of evaluation skills do I need as a teacher or coach in order to assess individuals on this type of information? Of what use will the results be in helping me teach or coach each individual and the group as a whole?

Psychomotor Skills and Strategies

Given the skills and strategies identified, what is the skill level of my students on selected items? Do skills or strategies tests already exist that assess ability levels in a valid, reliable way? What type of evaluation skills do I need as a

teacher or coach in order to assess individuals on this type of information? Of what use will the results be in helping me teach or coach each individual and the group as a whole?

Psychological, Sociological, Philosophical, and Other Concepts

How aware are my students of the psychological, sociological, and philosophical concepts identified in the knowledge structure? Are there tests or approaches that have already been developed that will help me gain an understanding of my students' knowledge on these concepts? What type of evaluation skills do I need as a teacher or coach in order to assess individuals on this type of information? Of what use will the results be in helping me teach or coach each individual and the group as a whole?

Assessing What You Know About Your Students

Were you able to provide answers to these questions, or were you constantly saying, "I don't know"? Do not feel bad, because this is a typical problem for everyone when first beginning teaching and meeting a new group of students. Remember, in the last chapter we looked at the planning strategies of expert and novice teachers (Housner & Griffey, 1985) and found that the experts were constantly asking questions and actively trying to understand their students and the environment in which they will be teaching. Similarly, it is now necessary here to go on a "fact-finding mission," with the objective being to develop an increased understanding of your students' skills and abilities relative to the knowledge structure.

 **EXERCISE 1**

The Plan of Discovery

Instructional design Exercise 1 requires the development of a comprehensive pretest or plan of discovery that will take up a portion of the first two or three class periods you have with each class or group of athletes. Your objective is to create a pretest for selected items from the knowledge structures you created in Module 1. Scan through the knowledge structures for each of the cross-disciplinary categories and determine the *most important* skills, tactics, psychological, and other concepts present there. Use the following rules to guide your decision:

Rule 1: In each category, choose the *minimum* number of skills, strategies, or concepts that will provide you with the *maximum* amount of information about each student. For all sports and activities, there are key skills, strategies, and concepts that are the foundation of many others within that activity. You identified these as a consequence of creating the hierarchical knowledge structures. They are usually, but not always, the first components identified in each category. For example, the first individual skills identified in badminton are grip, pronation and supination, underhand clear, serve, and forehand overhead clear.

Rule 2: For each skill or concept identified, seek out a recommended test from current resources and determine whether or not it is feasible to use the test in the time and space you have available. Consult tests and measurement books for this, as well as the expert sources you have collected. It is important to remember the context under which you are using the test in order to understand the skill and knowledge levels of your students. It is not unusual to find tests used within the research environment to be too time consuming for use in the instructional environment.

Rule 3: If appropriate tests do not exist or they are too time-consuming to administer, then create one of your own. This is not as difficult as it sounds, but does require a thorough knowledge of the technical aspects of the skill (you identified these in developing your knowledge structure in module 1). Also, use the Steps to Success Activity Series, because each book includes dozens of drills and learning activities that can be adapted and used as pretest items.

Rule 4: Try to create a balanced pretest, one with a selection of items from the cross-disciplinary categories, to communicate to students that you are interested in their achievements in a number of areas. This is especially meaningful to students with low skill or who are disabled in some way, because they are provided with alternate ways to excel. It is also important for students who are new to an activity and need the opportunity to see its many dimensions.

Figure M3.1 presents a form to help you plan the pretest. Summarize the items selected and estimate the time required for each student to be evaluated on each item and for the whole class to finish.

 **EXERCISE 2**

Designing the Pretest as Part of the Total Course of Instruction

After selecting items, use the physical layout chart from Module 2 and organize your teaching space to determine how realistic it is to administer the pretest items you have selected. You may find it necessary to modify and refine your test battery. Imagine your students in the gymnasium or classroom. Where will each pretest occur. Will you move from station to station or will students rotate past you? Will you be able to observe each student on each skill? You must organize the test environment to give a fair evaluation to each student. Also consider how you will keep track of scores and report them to students.

Two words of caution about planning your pretest: First, be sure to maintain a high activity level during the test procedure; don't require students to wait in line to be tested. Second, be aware that a few items skillfully administered and communicated to students are far preferable to many items administered poorly.

It is easiest to explain this concept through an example. Let's say you are teaching a 10th-grade badminton class; you have a 12-lesson unit with 50 minutes of active time available. Your students are in a school setting and have variable skill levels. You have court space for six doubles games. Having consulted your knowledge structure for badminton (or the one in Appendix A), you have decided to include in your pretest these items: basic rules of doubles and etiquette from the background knowledge category; grip, forehand overhead clear, and doubles play from psychomotor skills and strategies; and reading your opponent from the psychological category.

Prior to the first class, place all the pretest items on a form similar to the one in Figure M3.2, which includes the pretest items as well as the final skills, strategies, and concepts that you will evaluate students on in the course. You may want to use separate formats, one for the pretest and another for the complete program, but from a class management point of view, it is easier to give the students a single program evaluation sheet from the outset. For each skill or concept listed, a technical or performance objective is stated with four progress levels shown. Written tests are also given on rules, etiquette, and strategies.

Pre-Test Items	Number of Students	Time/ Student	Total Time

(Select no more than three items from the knowledge structures for each of the following cross-disciplinary categories)

Background Information

1.

2.

3.

Psychomotor Skills and Strategies

1.

2.

3.

Physical Fitness Testing and Training

1.

2.

3.

Psychosocial and Other

1.

2.

3.

Total time estimated to carry out pre-test: —————————————— .

Figure M3.1. Designing the pretest from the cross-disciplinary categories.

INDIVIDUAL COURSE IN ___Badminton___

STUDENT'S NAME ___

GRADE/COURSE SECTION ___

STUDENT ID # ___

SKILLS/CONCEPTS	TECHNIQUE AND PERFORMANCE OBJECTIVES	WT*	POINT PROGRESS** 1 D	2 C	3 B	4 A	FINAL SCORE***
1 Grip	*Technique:* V to opposite shoulder; fingers elongated; mobility forehand to backhand; show consistency from forehand to backhand.	8					
2 Forehand overhead clear	*Technique:* Stagger-stance position with shoulder turn; back scratch throwing action; weight shift; elbow extension; forearm pronation. No hesitation in back swing.	8					
	Performance: Cooperative consistent hitting from just in front of back alley; no lunge attempts; forehand to forehand. Each contact counts one.	8	5	8	10	15	
3 Backhand overhead clear	*Technique:* Set up with back to net; racquet drawn across body; elbow high; forearm pronation; elbow extension to follow through up; explosive.	8					
	Performance: Cooperative consistent hitting down the alley. Feeder sets shuttle high on backhand; each clear must be beyond center court and down alley.	8	5	8	10	15	
4 Doubles play	*Performance:* Demonstrate correct position when, 1) serving; 2) receiving; 3) playing sides strategy; 4) up and back strategy.	8					
5 Short serve	*Technique:* Stagger-step position; racquet back; shuttle coaxed across net; legal contact and follow through.	8					
	Performance: Number out of 4 serves to fall in within one racquet length of short service line; 2 right, 2 left court, anywhere along double service line.	8	1	2	3	4	
6 Forehand drop	*Technique:* Shoulder turn; full throwing action; forearm pronation showing wrist control; follow through; cut through the bird; Do Not Tap.	8					
	Performance: Continuous drops from in front of the back service alley. Feeder places shuttle high on the forehand. Count only drop shots. Errors in feeding do not stop count.	8	5	8	10	15	
7 Written tests	Pretest on doubles rules and etiquette (5%); Final test on rules, technique, and strategies (15%).	20	/5	/15			/20

Total value = 100   Final score = ___

Figure M3.2. A formative program in badminton showing both pretest and posttest items.

In Lesson 1, give each student a personalized copy of the program as shown in Figure M3.2. Explain that you will be doing a preassessment during the first three classes on the basic rules of doubles, etiquette, the grip, the forehand overhead clear, doubles play, and reading the opponent. The preassessment of skills and doubles play will be done while students play recreational doubles games, and a short written test will be given on etiquette, doubles rules, and reading your opponent. Also explain that the marks are not final marks, but only a beginning. They have the rest of the unit to improve their skills, so they should not worry if they are just beginning or have an off day; the marks they receive can improve.

The program shown in Figure M3.2 is a criterion-referenced, formative design. This means that specific objectives are named with set progress levels. Encourage students to work on their own in and out of class to improve and explain that they will have many opportunities to be evaluated. A full explanation of this type of program design is given in Module 6, and sample programs for a variety of other activities can be found in the Steps to Success Activity Series instructor's guides. Each program is designed to be modified and adjusted to your own circumstances. The computer program Action-Mark has also been developed to facilitate management of the whole concept.

Following an explanation of the pretest, show your students a video of a doubles game. Stop and start it at selected points to review the fundamental concepts of the game and basic rules of doubles. Then place four volunteers on a court and review the court dimensions and basic scoring procedures. Strategically, ask your students to play sides, with the forehand player taking the middle shots (for mixed-handed partners, an additional decision needs to be made). Students who understand the up-and-back alignment may also use that system. All of this should take 20 minutes, leaving 30 minutes for game play and evaluation. Students then choose partners and play recreational doubles games, rotating every 5 minutes. If there are not enough courts, students who are waiting should continue watching the video. Once the games are underway, begin your evaluations by walking from court to court and assessing each student's technique on the grip, forehand overhead clear, and doubles serve. Students should have placed their program sheets at the side of the court near

the standards, so you can record your evaluations. Answer any individual queries about rules and scoring.

In Lesson 2, students continue to play 5-minute recreational games (for 40 minutes). Before play begins, however, introduce four points of etiquette: Do not walk behind the courts while play is in progress; pick up the bird after play on your side and return it to the server; do not lean on the nets; call the score if you are serving. Then move from court to court and continue your evaluations. Some students will be very tired by the conclusion of this class, as a result of playing approximately eight doubles games.

In Lesson 3, continue recreational doubles play for 25 minutes and complete your preassessment of all students. Use about 15 minutes to give students a two-page test in which they label the doubles court, answer five multiple-choice questions about etiquette and doubles scoring, and, in a section called reading your opponent, diagram "if-then" scenarios on an empty court (for example, *if* the serve is low to the outside corner, *then* the best return is _____). If possible use the last 10 minutes of class to have students mark each others' tests as you go over the answers, or carry out this process in Lesson 4.

Beginning with Lesson 4, again explain to students the purpose of their individual programs (Figure M3.2). Explain again the concept of formative evaluation. Stress that students have the rest of the unit to improve on the skills and knowledge tests listed in their programs. In the remaining classes proceed to teach all of the skills, strategies, and concepts listed on their programs, leaving half of each class for competitive or recreational play. During all practice and play times, have students leave their programs sheets by the court standards as they play. You then can go from court to court and individually teach and evaluate using the format in Figure M3.2.

The pretest is clearly an integral part of the complete unit or program of study. It should be designed to communicate to your students the overall tone of the class and to launch them into the complete unit. The pretest should also communicate that there are ample opportunities to excel, but that students must apply themselves on the many cross-disciplinary dimensions of the course in order to be successful. This concept is explained in greater detail in Module 6 (Determining Evaluation) and Module 8 (Making Real-World Applications).

Topics

for Module 4

- Scope and sequence defined
- Scope and sequence format
- The "step" as a planning unit
- Bottom-up and top-down sequencing of knowledge

  Using a knowledge structure to create a bottom-up scope and sequence

  Using a knowledge structure to create a top-down scope and sequence

- Exercise 1: Developing a unit plan for a teaching situation
- Exercise 2: Developing a season plan for a coaching situation

Knowledge advances by steps and not by leaps.
—**Lord Macauley**

The art of progress is to preserve order amid change, and to preserve change amid order.
—**Alfred North Whitehead**

Photo © Cleo Photography.

Developing a Scope and Sequence

In Module 4 your task is to develop a scope and sequence that will take your students or athletes through planned learning experiences to the end of a unit or season. In some respects you have already had a beginning to this in the development of the pretest and introduction to the formative evaluation format in Module 3, the analysis of learners. In Module 4 we now go into this concept in depth and enter a phase that requires you to make final decisions about what your student athletes will be taught and required to do over a set period of time. In both the teaching and coaching setting, a scope and sequence is developed by using the knowledge structure in Module 1 both as a content source and as a

sequencing guide. In Module 4 you are also introduced to the bottom-up and top-down approaches to developing a scope and sequence. Before we begin, though, consider the following instructional design questions as they apply to scope and sequence decision making:

1. Given the knowledge in the activity, as identified in the knowledge structures, what should you teach to your student athletes?

2. Given the learning environment—the number of students, number of classes or practices, availability of facilities—what can be covered in the time available?

3. Given the nature of your student athletes and their prior knowledge and skill levels as assessed in Module 3, where should instruction begin?
4. In what order should this information be presented? Should instruction begin with individual skills, team or group strategies, or one of the sport science categories? Why?
5. As a teacher or coach, do you feel it is most important to start with the presentation of the basics (for example, individual skills), or are you more comfortable presenting a holistic approach that includes strategies of play and sport science concepts?
6. Do you feel that new subject matter should be taught every day of a unit?
7. How do you plan to teach information that has a lower level of physical activity, such as the concepts identified in the psychological or other cross-disciplinary categories? Will you present this as an independent series of classes taught in a separate classroom, or will you integrate this information within the activity component of each class?

Scope and Sequence Defined

In instructional design the term *scope* refers to the selection of content to be included in a lesson, a practice, a unit, or another instructional event. In the KS Model, content is selected from the knowledge structures analyzed in Module 1. The term *sequence* refers to the order in which content is to be presented. In all teaching settings, scope and sequence decisions are made for lesson plans, unit plans, and curriculum plans (series of units in a single activity). In coaching, the planning units are the practice, a season of play, and two or more seasons of play in a single sport. Figure M4.1 shows the interrelationships between these three planning units. A lesson or practice plan is put into action on a single occasion and may be anywhere from 5 minutes to 2 or more hours in length. A unit or season plan is a series of lessons or practices, with content sequenced across separate lessons or lectures. A curriculum or season plan is a series of unit or season plans sequenced across a number of years, grades, seasons, or courses of study. Figure M4.1, for example, shows three

units of 8 lessons each, a total of 24 instructional lessons in a single activity spread across 3 years, grades, courses, or seasons.

Scope and Sequence Format

Figure M4.2 presents the scope and sequence format adapted for the Steps to Success Activity Series. Scope and sequence formats show the order of introduction of content (scope) across units of time (sequence). Figure M4.2 shows there is room for 25 skills, strategies, or concepts (scope or steps) to be scheduled across 30 sessions or lessons. In addition, a scope and sequence chart shows how class time relative to that content item is to be used. Figure M4.2 provides for the introduction of new content (N = New); the review of content (R = Review); the continuation of instruction in the same skill, strategy, or concept (C = Continue); and time allocated for skills, strategies, or concepts to be practiced (P = Student Directed Practice).

The "Step" as a Planning Unit

The *step* is the planning unit developed specifically for the Steps to Success Activity Series. A step, which is created by drawing information from all eight modules of the KS Model, provides a wealth of information about *both* learning and teaching a skill, strategy, or concept. Think of a step as being similar to a lesson plan, but with one major difference: A step is more expansive and includes information important to both the student learning the skill and the instructor teaching it. Several lesson plans may be needed to teach certain steps.

Figure M4.3 shows how the concept of a step is included in a scope and sequence chart, as developed for golf by Owens and Bunker (1989b) for the Steps to Success Activity Series. There are 17 steps listed, beginning with introduction and full swing motion and ending with learning from a round of golf and setting goals. The 17 steps are taught in 28 separate 50-minute lessons or sessions, meaning that some steps require more than one session to be taught effectively. For example, in Step 4 full swing with clubs, four sessions are scheduled before introducing the next step. In Session 1, full swing

Scope and Sequence Planning Units

A Single Lesson Plan

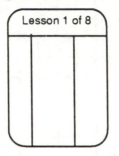

A Unit Plan of 8 Lessons

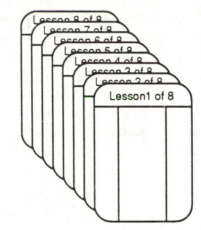

A Series of 3 Units: A Curriculum in a Single Activity

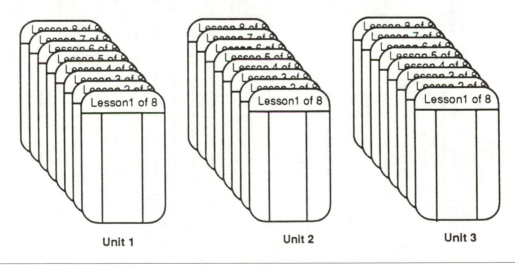

Unit 1   Unit 2   Unit 3

Figure M4.1.   Scope and sequence planning units: lesson, unit, curriculum plan for a single activity.

Scope and Teaching Sequence

Figure M4.2. A scope and sequence planning chart. *Note.* From *Badminton: A Structures of Knowledge Approach* (p. 99) by J.N. Vickers and D. Brecht, 1987, Calgary, AB: University Printing Services. Copyright 1987 by Joan N. Vickers. Adapted by permission.

Sample Scope and Teaching Sequence

NAME OF ACTIVITY Golf

LEVEL OF LEARNER _____

Legend: New [N]   Review [R]   Continue [C]   Student Directed Practice** [P]

Steps	Session	1	2	3	4	5	6	7	8	9	10	11	12	13	14	15	16	17	18	19	20	21	22	23	24	25	26	27	28	29	30
1	Introduction*	N																													
1	Full swing motion	N	R	R	R	R	R	R	R	R	R	R	R	R	R	R	R	R	P	P	P	P	P	P	P	P	P	P			
2	Setup		N	R	R	R	R	R	R	R	R	R	R	R	R	R	R	R	P	P	P	P	P	P	P	P	P	P			
3	Full swing with clubs			N	C	R	R	R	R	R	R	R	R	R	R	R	R	R	P	P	P	P	P	P	P	P	P	P			
4	Ball flight						N	R	R	R	R	R	R	R	R	R	R	R	P	P	P	P	P	P	P	P	P	P			
5	Pitching								N	R	R	R	R	R	R	R	R	R	P	P	P	P	P	P	P	P	P	P			
6	Chipping											N	C	R	R	R	R	R	P	P	P	P	P	P	P	P	P	P			
7	Putting													N	C	R	R	R													
8	Sand shots															N	P	R													
9	Uneven lies																N	P	R	R											
10	Effective practice														N	R	R	R	R	R	R	P	P	P	P	P	P	P			
11	Routines														N	R	C	R	R	R	R	P	P	P	P	P	P	P			
12	Mental skills																N	R	N	R	R	R	P	P	P	P	P	P			
13	Etiquette			N															R	C	R	P	P	P	P	P	P	P			
14	Course management																		N	R	C	R	P	P	P	P	P	P			
15	Learning from round																			N	N	R	N	P	P	P	P	P			
16	Setting goals																					N	N	P	P	P	P	P			
17	Quiz		▓	▓																											
18	Exam																												N		
19																															
20																															
21																															
22																															
23																															
24																															

RAINY DAY FROM DAY 4 - 27

Notes: *Warmups done every day.
        **Students have directed practice on their own in stations each day.

Figure M4.3. A scope and sequence for golf (Owens & Bunker, 1989b). Reprinted by permission.

motion without clubs is introduced (N); in Session 2, the full swing motion without clubs is reviewed (R), and the setup and the full swing with clubs is introduced (W); in session 3, the full swing motion and the setup are reviewed, and instruction on how to use the full swing with clubs continues (C); in Sessions 4 and 5, instructor-supervised review occurs (R). (For a more complete explanation of a step, see "Designing a Step" in Module 8, Making Real-World Applications.)

Bottom-Up and Top-Down Sequencing of Knowledge

Upon what basis do you make scope and sequence decisions? Are there underlying rules or principles that guide the process of selecting and ordering content? To what extent do the knowledge structures guide this process? Look at Figure M4.1 again. Shown here are 8 lessons to be presented in a single activity over 3 years, grades, or courses, a total of 24 lessons. The terms *bottom-up* and *top-down* offer two different *conceptual* approaches you may use in sequencing content across these 24 lessons. Both terms have their origins in cognitive psychology (Gardner, 1985; Lindsay & Norman, 1977; Solso, 1979).

Bottom-Up Approach

The term *bottom-up* implies that we construct our world from many separate pieces that are put together by our cognitive system in a one-step, two-step process. Our perceptual and cognitive systems first encode the features or data found in an object, a movement, a scene, or an event. Then these features or data are combined by our information processing system into percepts or whole objects: movements, events, landscapes, a piece of music, a picture of a face, a sequence of actions, and so forth.

This idea, when adopted as an instructional design strategy, implies that we need to break content down into its separate components in order to enable learners to understand and reconstruct the whole. A bottom-up scope and sequencing approach, therefore, implies that we need to break down an activity into its many subcomponents (as we did in the knowledge structures), then reconstruct the activity for the student by using a simple to complex rule. This

is a strategy widely used in education in all subject areas (Block, 1971; Gagné, 1977; Merrill, 1983; Reigeluth, 1983), including sport and physical education (Singer & Dick, 1980).

A partial example of a bottom-up sequence applied to the teaching of badminton is shown in Figure M4.4. The skills and concepts to be taught are listed down the left-hand side (the scope of unit) and allocated across 12 classes (the sequence of the unit). Instruction begins with the grip, pronation and supination, and so on. If you refer to the complete knowledge structures for badminton in Appendix A, you will see that the order of the skills follows the hierarchical path shown there.

Advantages and Disadvantages of a Bottom-Up Sequencing Strategy. A bottom-up approach pays close attention to teaching individual skills, and there is extensive use of drill and practice of discrete skills. There is, however, reduced instruction in strategic game concepts because they are thought to be too advanced for most learners. Game play is often omitted, left to the end of class, or treated as play or recreation time.

However, bottom-up strategy may be best in some settings. Beginning teachers and coaches who are unfamiliar with an activity may find it easier to organize instruction using this approach because the simple-to-complex rule is easy to understand and apply. Also, in some settings where control, discipline, or an exceptionally thorough pace is warranted, bottom-up scope and sequence strategies may work best.

Top-Down Approach

The concept of top-down processing has also evolved from cognitive psychology (Gardner, 1985; Lindsay & Norman, 1977) and states that the compilation of features into whole objects, movements, or events is unnecessary and perhaps unnatural. Humans are able to instantly perceive the whole without needing intervening feature analysis. A top-down approach, when adopted as an instructional design strategy, accepts that learners are able to understand complex principles and concepts underlying the execution of skills, strategies, and full activities. When used as an instructional design strategy, a top-down approach calls for the provision of planned experiences that help students see the whole or achieve an overview of the subject. Ausubel (1968) called the provision of such as an experience an "advance organizer."

	SCOPE AND SEQUENCE												
NEW [N] REVIEW [R] CONTINUE [C]	ACTIVITY __Badminton__ LEVEL OF LEARNER __Beginner__												
LESSON NUMBER	1	2	3	4	5	6	7	8	9	10	11	12
Grip	N											
Pronation and supination	N											
Underhand clear		N										
Singles serve		N										
Forehand clear		N										
Forehand drop shot			N									
Forehand smash			N									
Backhand clear			C									
Backhand drop				N								
Net shot				N								
Footwork				C								
Doubles serve and reception					N							
Drive					N							
Drop net continuity drills					N							
The net game						N						
Doubles tournament						N	C					
Doubles tournament								C				
Doubles tournament									C			
Doubles tournament										C	C	
Skills test												C

Bottom-Up Example

Figure M4.4. Bottom-up scope and sequence: partial example applied to badminton.

An advance organizer involves the use of appropriately relevant . . . introductory materials (organizers) that are maximally clear and stable. These organizers are introduced in advance of the learning material itself and are also presented at a higher level of abstraction, generality, and inconclusiveness. The function of the organizer is to provide ideational scaffolding for the stable incorporation and retention of the more detailed and differentiated material that follows. (p. 148)

With this definition in mind, the KS Model defines an *advance organizer* as a *complex strategy, skill, or concept that captures the maximum purpose and form of the whole game, dance, or event, but with a minimum number of players, facilities, and equipment.* An advance organizer, therefore, should be presented to the students at the outset of a unit or class for the purpose of helping them see the whole before they must deal with or understand the parts.

Figure M4.5 shows a top-down scope and sequence for badminton. In this partial example, instruction begins in Lesson 1 with the following advance organizers: (a) seeing a video of an international singles match, (b) being given the individual development program for the whole unit (as shown in Figure M3.2), and (c) continuous play in 5-minute games. These activities are all designed to introduce students to the complete game as quickly as possible, but under conditions that are possible for them to handle. Notice that as the unit progresses, there is instruction in individual skills, but these are always taught within the context of the advance organizers, which in Figure M4.5 is play in singles games and progress on their individual programs.

For basketball the advance organizer could be 2-on-2 play in a modified court situation (1-on-1 is inadequate since the passing game is impossible). A 2-on-2 teaching strategy permits the introduction of all the individual skills of the full game (dribble, pass, shoot, rebound, and so on), offensive concepts (give and go, screens, post, rebounding), defensive concepts (player-to-player, simple zone, switching, rebounding, blocking out), and modified and competitive play as desired. The 2-on-2 advance organizer can also be used as practice units or as competitive units, and they can also easily be transferred into 3-on-3 and 5-on-5 half- and full-court situations when desired.

Advantages and Disadvantages of a Top-Down Scope and Sequence Strategy. Top-down strategies allow for high activity ratios as well as teaching environments that keep motivation levels high. This strategy encourages rapid skill development because students are in small groups, each with a court or space in which to practice and perform. For this reason, it is often necessary to modify facilities and equipment and pay close attention to how students are grouped. One of the key elements operating in a top-down sequence is the provision of small group learning experiences that are game-like, and provide extensive on-task activity without constant teacher supervision. Top-down scope and sequence plans are, however, more difficult to conceptualize than bottom-up because they require an overview of the complete game or activity.

Using a Knowledge Structure to Create a Bottom-Up Scope and Sequence

A knowledge structure accommodates both bottom-up and top-down approaches. For a bottom-up scope and sequence, begin by selecting content from the bottom of the knowledge structure and proceeding from left to right through the structure. Bottom-up strategies assume that simpler skills and factual information must be taught before more complex conceptual and strategic movements are introduced.

Using a Knowledge Structure to Create a Top-Down Scope and Sequence

Scan the knowledge structures and select a key strategy or concept that captures the fullness of the contest or play. Next, select and sequence the subskills and other content that this advance organizer is comprised of. Introduce and teach each subskill thoroughly and incorporate this through learning activity into a realistic play situation. Top-down approaches tend to be used by master teachers and coaches as a consequence of their greater knowledge and experience. If a top-down approach appeals to you, there are two strategies you can use to hasten your ability to design this type of learning experience. First, develop a knowledge structure for each activity you teach because this process facilitates an overview of the activity. Second, study how master teachers and coaches sequence content in order to discern the principles and rules they are working with. The books within the Steps

SCOPE AND SEQUENCE

NEW [N]   REVIEW [R]   CONTINUE [C]   ACTIVITY LEVEL OF LEARNER — Badminton / Beginner

LESSON NUMBER	1	2	3	4	5	6	7	8	9	10	11	12
Video and basic rules—singles	N											
Introduction to individual program: 3 pretest items	N	C	C									
Play in singles games/5 min/rotation/pretest	N	C	C	C	C	C						
Grip, underhand clear, individual program		N	C	C	C	C	C	C	C	C	C	C
Long or singles serve		N										
Forehand clear			N									
Forehand drop			N									
Net shots				N								
Backhand clear				N								
Backhand drop				N								
Short serve and reception, doubles video and play					N	N						
Footwork					N							
Net play/the short game					N							
Tournament/doubles or singles (student choice)							C	C	C	C	C	C
Drop continuity drill						N						
Flick serve/reception						N						
Forehand smash							N					
Drives							N					
Final for individual programs								C	C	C	C	C
Final for individual programs								C	C	C	C	C

Top-Down Example

Figure M4.5. Top-down scope and sequence: partial example applied to badminton.

to Success Activity Series primarily use a top-down approach. Each instructor's guide contains a top-down scope and sequence similar to that shown in Figure M4.3.

EXERCISE 1

Developing a Unit Plan for a Teaching Situation

Develop a scope and sequence for a unit of approximately eight lessons using the knowledge structures created in Module 1. Remember to take into account the environment in which you are teaching (Module 2) and your students' pretest results (Module 3). Design either a bottom-up or a top-down unit of eight lessons. Use the template scope and sequence planning sheet shown in Figure M4.6 if you wish, or develop your own format. Present your scope and sequence to your classmates, asking them to identify the type being presented.

EXERCISE 2

Developing a Season Plan for a Coaching Situation

Repeat the preceding exercise, but develop a scope and sequence for a coaching season of interscholastic play. Determine the number of practices and games, then develop your plan according to preseason, midseason, late season, and play-off cycles. Use the template shown in Figure M4.2, or develop your own format. Present your scope and sequence to your classmates, asking them to identify the type being presented.

	SCOPE AND SEQUENCE												
NEW ☐ REVIEW ☐	ACTIVITY _____												
CONTINUE ☐	LEVEL OF LEARNER _____												
	LESSON NUMBER	1	2	3	4	5	6	7	8	9	10	11	12

Figure M4.6. A template scope and sequence planning sheet.

Topics

for Module 5

- The traditional role of objectives in instructional design
- Research on teachers' planning
- Characteristics of teachers in high- and low-achieving schools
- Seven guidelines for writing objectives
- How to write objectives
- Exercise 1: Writing objectives for psychomotor skills
- Exercise 2: Writing objectives for psychomotor strategies
- Exercise 3: Writing objectives to assess factual, conceptual, and analytical knowledge
- Exercise 4: Writing psychosocial (affective) objectives

An objective is a description of performance you want learners to be able to exhibit before you consider them competent. An objective describes an intended result of instruction, rather than the process of instruction itself.

—Robert Mager

Photo by Claudio Gratton. Courtesy of *The Daily Illini*, University of Illinois.

Writing Objectives

Objectives are statements that capture the teacher's or coach's goals and intentions. Objectives describe what you feel can be taught and your students can accomplish, given the subject matter and constraints present in the learning environment. Objectives therefore are *mature* statements that reveal the extent to which you feel you can bring about change in your students. Writing objectives in the KS Model is presented as an advanced instructional design skill and one that is undertaken only after four things are known: knowledge of subject matter, knowledge of the teaching environment, knowledge of learners, and decisions about scope and sequence.

In this chapter you are asked to make a decision about the *extent* to which you will design and set objectives for your students, both grouped and as individuals. We begin by reviewing the history of objectives-based instructional design. We then look at research in two new areas, (a) research on teachers' planning and the evolution of the natural or intuitive planning model of instruction (Clark & Peterson, 1986), followed by (b) research comparing low-achieving and high-achieving schools. You will find that the KS Model encourages setting objectives and implementing a thorough evaluation system for all students. However, the extent to which you adopt this approach is a decision that requires three commitments. First, you must be willing to set standards and to maintain these in the face of student surprise and some initial opposition. Second, you must be willing to engage in extensive, daily communication with students about the objectives you have set and what they must do to accomplish them. And third, you must have *patience* and the belief that your students can and will acquire the complex physical skills, strategies, and concepts you have assigned. The conclusion of this chapter describes how objectives are written, with instructional design exercises.

The Traditional Role of Objectives in Instructional Design

For some time, instructional design models have begun with statements of objectives or instructional goals with accompanying task analyses (Joyce & Weil, 1980; Reigeluth, 1983). These models, also known as the ''university planning'' or ''rational models,'' have been prevalent in all subject areas (Goc-Karp & Zakrajsek, 1987; May, 1986). The university planning model, which traces its beginnings to Tyler (1949), is a linear model of four sequential steps: Formulate learning objectives, select content and appropriate learning experiences, organize the learning environment, and determine evaluation. Goc-Karp and Zakrajsek (1987) comment that this approach has also been used extensively in physical education, as witnessed by the work of Bucher and Koenig (1978), Daugherty and Lewis (1979), Mosston (1981), Siedentop (1976), and Singer and Dick (1980).

We found in Part 1, chapter 1, that the difficulty in beginning the instructional design process with a statement of objectives is that the underlying origins of objectives are never defined. Teachers and coaches are asked to set objectives, but one is left wondering upon what basis the objectives were set in the first place. A scrutiny of the writings of those who originated or promoted the objectives movement indicates they assumed that objectives were written by teachers and coaches who possessed two qualities: mastery of subject matter and an understanding of individual students (Mager, 1975).

In practice, however, as the ''state your objectives first'' approach grew in popularity, it often became the only avenue whereby new teachers were introduced to subject matter (Davies, 1976; May 1986). The merits of proceeding with this approach have been questioned by many, with May summarizing the problem as follows:

> Objectives writing places sophisticated demands upon teachers (especially upon beginners) who have little understanding of either subject matter as applied in teaching or of their students. Students lack the sophisticated knowledge base in subject matter, pedagogy, and understanding particular pupils essential to using the Tyler approach to planning effectively. The probability is next to nil that students in teacher education programs have mastered the nuances of any one discipline, developed a pedagogical repertoire, or spent any meaningful length of time with any one group of pupils in their field experiences. (p. 7)

The KS Model, through its first four modules, has been designed to alleviate such concerns. Module 1 is a vehicle for understanding subject matter, Module 2 is a vehicle for understanding specific learning environments, and Module 3 is a vehicle for understanding your students or athletes and their level of knowledge and skill relative to the subject matter identified in the knowledge structures. Module 4 asked you to develop an overall scope and sequence, or master plan for instruction, extending across a series of lessons or practices. Module 5 now asks you to write specific objectives for the skills, strategies, and concepts identified in your scope and sequence plan. However, before we move on to describe how objectives are written and implemented, it must be mentioned that recent research in the ''teachers' planning'' area places the role of objectives in teaching in a controversial position. Although educators have promoted the use of objectives for decades, their use in the real world of teaching and coaching is limited. In the following section, we look at this problem.

Research on Teachers' Planning

Research on teachers' planning involves the extensive study of experienced teachers as they plan and deliver lessons. In some cases, teachers have been observed and analyzed over a complete year, with profiles of some of their planning characteristics emerging. Clark and

Peterson (1986) have summarized the results of these eight studies.

a. Planning early in the school year focused on establishing the physical environment and social system of the classroom (Clark & Elmore, 1981).

b. Early in the year the teachers worked to adapt curriculum materials to their knowledge and priorities. Teachers learned the structure and content of new curricula. They then developed a practical schedule for instruction (Clark & Elmore, 1981).

c. Eight types of planning were identified: weekly, daily, unit, long range, short range, yearly term, with three types of planning most prevalent—unit, weekly, daily (Clark & Yinger, 1979).

d. Most teacher planning is done mentally and not necessarily put on paper. Teachers prepare a "mental image" of a lesson that often takes the form of a list of topics that will be covered each in turn (Morine-Dershimer, 1978-1979).

From the above and other studies has evolved the "intuitive" or "natural planning model" of instruction (Clark & Peterson, 1986). Teachers stress establishing the learning environment, the social system in the classroom. They adapt the curriculum to accommodate their own state of knowledge, and they pragmatically develop plans that span the week, the unit, and the year. Most planning is done mentally with an absence of objectives as targets or goals of the planning process.

Goc-Karp and Zakrajsek (1987) extended the Clark and Peterson (1986) research to physical education and found that the same characteristics are present. They compared the curricula and instruction models used by college professors in physical education with those used by junior high teachers of physical education. As in the research found in other subject areas, their data indicate that two different planning models were operative, one a theoretical model taught in university courses and the other an actual model used by teachers in the field.

Professors of instructional design taught an *ends-means planning process* that identified and sequenced objectives, selected content, identified delivery methods, and set evaluation. Teachers in the field, on the other hand, approached planning from an activity or content focus. Once the activity and the day's skills were set, the teachers concentrated on organizing time, equipment, and facilities, arranging these so that the students actively participated. Little attention was directed toward determining entry skill levels, specifying learning objectives, or selecting teaching methods. Objectives as defined by the university planning models were only casually integrated into the lesson. Evaluation was something that happened at the end of the unit; it was not predetermined according to specific objectives.

Characteristics of Teachers in High- and Low-Achieving Schools

Research on teachers' planning appears to place the use of learning objectives in doubt, yet the picture is not complete without looking at the research showing the characteristics of teachers in low-achieving and high-achieving schools. Teachers in high-achievement schools (Brookover et al., 1979) use *objectives as the vehicle for portraying to their students their high expectations and confidence in their abilities.* Table M5.1 presents the results of a study by Brookover et al. (1979) that compared the characteristics of teachers in four schools classified as high- or low-achieving (Good & Brophy, 1986). Two schools seen as having a high degree of achievement were compared to two schools in which there was a persistence of little achievement. All four schools were located in low-SES (low-socioeconomic) communities.

Observed Differences

The differences in the approach of teachers in the low- and high-achieving schools were pronounced. Teachers in high-achievement schools spent 80-90% of the class time on teaching and actively instructing students. Few students in these schools were viewed as "write-offs," or were judged to be unteachable. Teacher expectations were very high for *all* students. Clear objectives were stated. Students were expected to complete assignments, with pretests used to classify, reclassify, and group students so that they could receive the help they needed. Rewards and reinforcements were given appropriately, and only when work was completed satisfactorily.

Table M5.1 Highlights of Four Case Studies: What Makes a Difference in Predominantly Black and Predominantly White High- and Low-Achieving Schools in Low-SES School Districts

	High-Achieving White School	Low-Achieving White School	High-Achieving Black School	Low-Achieving Black School
Time	Most of class time spent on instruction except for one teacher—80-90% of time used.	Time spent on instruction varied between classrooms. In several classrooms only 10% of time spent on instruction. Several teachers had managerial problems. Many teachers who did not used low-level work to keep students involved.	Teachers did much teaching. While students were working the teachers were available for clarification and reteaching as necessary.	Most teachers attempted to keep students busy but not a lot of productive task-relevant work was achieved. Very little academic interaction with students.
Write-Offs	Few students seen as destined to fail, as hopeless cases; no remedial programs.	Usually 2-3 students per class remained outside of learning process. However, most of "slower" students were less involved in work and interactions with teachers.	Teachers felt vast majority of students were capable of mastering assigned materials. Only a very few students were seen as unlikely to make it. When one strategy didn't work, teachers were willing to try other strategies.	Teachers appeared to write off large numbers of children; large numbers of students were required to attend remedial classes and such classes were seen as "dumping grounds."
Teacher Expectations	Teachers expected students to work at grade level.	Expectations for student achievement were low in general but especially for students in slow reading tracks. Grade-level achievement not seen as a realistic goal for many students.	Teachers generally reported that they expected at least 75% of their students to master assigned work and that 75% would complete high school.	Teachers generally held low performance expectations for students and teachers were unwilling to assume responsibility for student learning.
Reinforcement Practices	Appropriate reward.	Teachers varied. Some teachers used appropriate reinforcement practices but several teachers were observed to use confusing and/or totally inappropriate reinforcement practices most of the time.	Teachers tended to use reinforcement patterns that were likely to encourage higher achievement.	Many teachers in the regular classrooms used reinforcement inappropriately, often telling students they had done well when, in fact, they had not.

Grouping Procedures	No homogeneous grouping after third grade. Grouping to classrooms basically random.	Students grouped 1-6 for reading instruction. Only two groups per class—high and low. Mobility between groups very limited.	Extensive use of grouping, however, did not encourage advancing students to join higher groups and appeared to be more of a management than an instructional tool. Also, there was extensive assignment of "slow" students to remedial classes. The extensive grouping and regrouping appeared to be disruptive.
Teaching Games	Reflected high expectations of teacher and appropriate reinforcement—emphasized team rather than individual learning.	No mention.	Teaching games seldom used in regular classes—used much in remedial classes, but tended to be individual games and not used in a way likely to stimulate achievement gain.
Principal's Role	Heavily involved in instructional issues. Provided instructional leadership. Assumed measure of responsibility for the educational functions of the school. Visited classrooms frequently.	Time shared between two buildings. Seemed to be a part-time administrator-part-time disciplinarian. Seldom visited classrooms; did not function as an educational leader. Often expressed low performance expectations for students.	Principal at this school was mainly an administrator and disciplinarian. Although the principal talked about the importance of student achievement, there was little pressure brought to bear by the principal on teachers to improve classroom performance.
Commitment	Commitment to high achievement—willing to make public announcements to one another and to parents that students could learn.	Considerable interest in providing students with high-quality education. Much warmth directed toward individual students.	Teachers' behavior suggested that there was little they could do to increase student achievement.

Note. Reprinted with permission of Macmillan Publishing Co., a division of Macmillan Inc., from "School Effects" by T.L. Good, and J.E. Brophy. In *Handbook of Research on Teaching* (3rd ed.) (pp. 576–577), by M.C. Wittrock (Ed.). © 1985 by the American Educational Research Association.

In contrast, teachers in low-achieving schools spent inconsistent amounts of time on instruction (in some cases as low as 10%; they essentially stopped teaching). There were no clear-cut goals or objectives. Students were often classified as unable to learn and were routinely "left outside of the learning process." Expectations for students were universally low, with grade-level achievement seen as an unrealistic goal. Reward and reinforcement procedures were erratic and often inappropriate. Students were rigidly classified, with few tests given that allowed the teachers to revise their stratification of students into high- and low-ability groups.

Making a Decision

The sections presented on teachers' planning and on the characteristics of teachers in high- and low-achieving schools have shown that research on the use of objectives and evaluation in teaching indeed presents a controversial picture. Research on teachers' planning indicates that teachers prefer to focus first on content and activities to be taught, then on the physical and social environment of the classroom. These teachers downplayed the use of objectives and evaluation, stating that there was not enough time for students to learn the skills or achieve the outcomes stated in objectives. In contrast, research on teachers in high-achieving schools show that they routinely use objectives as vehicles for communicating to students their high expectations and their confidence that students can and will achieve what is asked of them.

In making your decision of whether to use objectives or not, realize that implementing an objectives-based learning environment requires extra resources as well as a personal commitment to be extensively involved with each student's learning. Extensive preparation, management skills encompassing both the group and the individual, and creative learning materials, such as task cards, individual programs, and other learning aids will be required.

University and professional groups (supervisors, curriculum planners, university professors) encourage the use of objectives and evaluation. The KS Model also emphasizes and encourages the use of objectives, because of the rewards associated with learning, teaching, and coaching in this way. However, remember that writing and implementing objectives is an *advanced instructional design skill*, and one that should be adopted only after important prerequisites are in place. Four of these prerequisites are included in the KS Model as Modules 1 to 4, with analyses of subject matter, environment, and learners and scope and sequence strategies being carried out before objectives are written.

If you chose to use objectives, the Steps to Success Activity Series has been designed to help you with the area of resources. Each pair of activity books contains a wealth of technical (keys to success) and performance (success goals) objectives that you can use or modify for your own situation. In addition, the books contain hundreds of visual aids, drills, self-learning activities, task cards, test questions, skill analyses, and correction activities that illustrate the technical, performance, and other requirements of each sport or activity. In the following sections, specific guidelines are given for writing objectives for the different categories of knowledge identified in the knowledge structures.

Seven Guidelines for Writing Objectives

In Module 4 you developed a scope and sequence chart in which you listed the skills, strategies, and concepts to teach in a unit or over a number of lessons. In developing a scope and sequence, you selected content from the knowledge structures following a bottom-up or a top-down strategy. For each skill, strategy, or concept listed it is now necessary to write specific learning objectives.

1. Determining the Sequence of Objectives

The sequence of writing objectives follows the scope and sequence charts created in Module 4. Now consider what you want your students *to do, or say, or write*, that will be indicative of their knowing or mastering a skill, strategy, or concept. In the sections to follow you will see that objectives may be written in a number of different ways, depending upon whether you want your students to physically perform a skill or strategy, or display their knowledge about a skill, strategy, or concept.

2. Writing Objectives for Psychomotor Skills and Strategies

Objectives for skills and strategies are of two types: technical (qualitative) and performance (quantitative) (Haywood, 1986). For each skill or strategy identified in the scope and sequence chart, two types of objectives may be written. *Technical or qualitative* objectives encourage students to strive for a sound biomechanical base for each movement. *Performance or quantitative objectives*, on the other hand, stress the production of observable results such as consistency, distance, accuracy, and so on (Haywood, 1986).

In the regular classroom, it is not unusual to find some students who can achieve sound style or technique, but find it almost impossible to perform at a high level. Let's use the high jump as an example. Some students who have grown rapidly can clear the bar easily. Other students may be slow to mature and find jumping high physically impossible. The slow or late maturers should be encouraged to develop sound technique, for whatever height of jumping they can achieve, and be rewarded through your evaluation scheme.

3. Writing Technical, or Qualitative Objectives (Keys to Success)

The information needed to write technical objectives or *keys to success* in the Steps to Success Activity Series has already been identified and is found in the last level of the knowledge structures. Technical, or qualitative objectives, specify the criteria underlying mature technique or style (Haywood, 1986). For each skill or strategy, the criteria that constitutes technical objectives has already been identified in the knowledge structures. Turn again to Figure M1.4 and/or to the example structures in Appendices A through C. In the hierarchical analysis of skills into their subskills, the last level of the analysis shows the technical components of each skill, subskill, and strategy as derived from expert and sport science sources.

This information was earlier defined as a combination of biomechanics, kinesiology, motor learning, perception, observational learning, and expert sources. The term *cognitive biomechanics* describes the declarative nature of the information at this last level of the knowledge structure, which is age-independent and describes what the master teachers or coaches have defined as

characteristic of a mature or expert level of performance. The qualities described here can often be achieved by both adults and children and is most dependent upon training and practice. Technical objectives are used to assess the *quality of a performance against some standard of expert, or mature performance*. Evaluation is subjective and dependent upon the ability of the observer to compare the skill to some internally held representative prototype.

Example: Badminton Overhead Clear

Preparation Phase: Set up stagger stance, opposite shoulder to the net; stage racquet at the ear; racquet head forward.

Execution Phase: Draw the racquet back to the back-scratch position (supination) and then forward in one continuous motion. Contact the shuttle with elbow slightly bent; power is generated as the forearm pronates. The racquet head turns out from body at contact.

Follow-Through Phase: The racquet continues down and across the body to the non-racquet side.

Example: Golf Putt

Preparation Phase: Grip in palm; shoulder-width stance, weight even; ball on target side; blade square.

Execution Phase: Arms, hands, and putter move as a unit; shoulders still, hips still. Backswing to 1, 2, or 3. Blade stays on target line; upper and lower body still.

Follow-Through Phase: Arms, hands, putter stay as unit; blade remains square; swing length 1, 2, or 3. (Owens & Bunker, 1989a, pp. 90-91)

4. Writing Performance, Quantitative Objectives (Success Goals)

The information needed to write performance or quantitative objectives, or success goals as they are called in the Steps to Success Activity Series, can be found in (a) established tests designed specifically for the activity, (b) can be derived from expert sources (such as the Steps to Success Activity Series), or (c) can be original and created to suit your students and your situation. A quantitative or performance objective, specifies the *product* of skill development (Haywood, 1986). Such objectives differ from qualitative objectives in that they are measurable in some concrete way. The product of skill performance is specified by the number of times the skill is to be performed, how consistent the learners should strive to be, how accurate they are, how high they can jump, how fast they can run, or how many contests they have won and so on. These objectives may be evaluated by observer peers who record scores or otherwise note objective scores.

Example: Badminton Overhead Clear

Quantitative objective [for formative evaluation] = Hit cooperatively with a partner, from midcourt to midcourt, consecutive overhead clears without a miss. Partners keep independent scores. Use the following grade equivalences:

20 or more contacts (A grade)

15 contacts (B grade)

10 contacts (C grade)

5 contacts (D grade)

Your grade [at this point in the unit] =

_____ A (20 or more contacts)

_____ B (15 to 19 contacts)

_____ C (10 to 14 contacts)

_____ D (5 to 9 contacts)

Example: Golf Putt

Quantitative objective [for success goal] = 60 total putt attempts from 1-6 feet away from hole

10 putts from 1 foot

10 putts from 2 feet

10 putts from 3 feet

10 putts from 4 feet

10 putts from 5 feet

10 putts from 6 feet

Your score =

(#) _____ putts from 1 foot

(#) _____ putts from 2 feet

(#) _____ putts from 3 feet

(#) _____ putts from 4 feet

(#) _____ putts from 5 feet

(#) _____ putts from 6 feet

5. Performance Objectives Accommodate Age and Ability Differences

Performance objectives are age and ability *dependent* and are written as progressions ordered

novice to expert. Performance objectives not only specify quantitative measures of skill attainment but also show progressive levels of improvement that are sensitive to motivational level, experience, environment, and so on. Performance objectives explain what the teacher or coach expects learners to be able to do in a measurable way. Another way to view these objectives is as *challenges* that help individual students gain an understanding of how competent they are in the activity. Performance objectives are written so that learners can achieve a sense of their own progress without the presence of an instructor. Performance objectives may also be written to reflect skill developmental differences for young children, or novice adults, intermediate performers, and advanced performers. An example of a progression of performance objectives for novice, intermediate, and advanced players in the overhead forehand clear in badminton follows.

Example: Badminton Forehand Overhead Clear

Novice

1. From the midcourt area, hit a bird served high to you by a partner 5, 10, 15, 20 or more times without an error.
2. From the midcourt area, hit cooperatively with a partner 5, 10, 15, 20 or more times without a miss or a break in technique. Use a relaxed style, with no lunging attempts.
3. Play a singles game and concentrate on placing a defensive overhead clear deep to your opponent's forehand.

Intermediate

4. From just in front of the back service alley, hit cooperatively with a partner 5, 10, 15, 20 or more times. Use a relaxed style, with no lunging attempts.
5. Hit cooperatively with a partner, placing the bird deep to his or her backhand.
6. Hit competitively with a partner, varying the placement of the bird deep and to the corners of the court.

Advanced

7. From within the back doubles serving alley, hit cooperatively with a partner 5, 10,

20, 30 or more times. Use a relaxed style, with no lunging attempts.

8. Hit with a partner in continuity drills combining the forehand clear with other strokes in combinations. Vary the placement of the bird deep, to the net, and to the corners of the court.

Example: Ice Hockey Shooting; Forehand to Snap Shots Progression (Vickers & Kelm, 1984).

Novice

1. Perform stationary shooting at a target placed on boards 3 feet above the ice. Record the number of successful shots out of 20. (D = 7-10; C = 11-13; B = 14-16; A = 17-20).

2. Perform stationary shooting to a partner's stick presented as a low target. Record the number of successful shots out of 20. (D = 7-10; C = 11-13; B = 14-16; A = 17-20).

3. Shoot at targets suspended at the four corners of the goal. Record the number of successful shots in rotation, five shots taken at each target, for a total of 20 shots. (D = 7-10; C = 11-13; B = 14-16; A = 17-20).

Intermediate

4. Shoot at four goal targets while skating straight toward goal at slow to average speed. Record the number of successful shots out of 20. (D = 7-10; C = 11-13; B = 14-16; A = 17-20).

5. Shoot at four goal targets while skating straight on at fast speeds. Record the number of successful shots out of 20. (D = 7-10; C = 11-13; B = 14-16; A = 17-20).

6. Shoot at goal targets while skating toward goal with one defense player (dummy defense). Record the number of successful shots out of 20. (D = 7-10; C = 11-13; B = 14-16; A = 17-20).

Advanced

7. While skating toward goal with partner, shoot at goal targets against one defensive player (normal defense), 20 attempts each player. Record the number of successful shots out of 20. (D = 7-10; C = 11-13; B = 14-16; A = 17-20).

All Levels at Any Time

8. Take the Canadian Amateur Hockey Association skills test for shooting accuracy. Record your performance as a percentile against national norms. (D = above 60th percentile; C = above 70th percentile; B = above 80th percentile; A = above 90th percentile.)

6. Writing Objectives to Assess Factual, Conceptual, and Analytical Knowledge

Objectives are written for the background knowledge, physiological testing and conditioning, psychomotor skills and strategies, psychosocial, and other categories that assess the student's factual, conceptual, and analytical abilities. These objectives are normally administered through paper-and-pencil tests, as projects, in computer-assisted learning environments, or as lab exercises requiring the collection of data and formal analysis. Each of the Steps to Success instructor's guides comes with a test bank of questions as well as projects that require students to supply factual information, solve problems, acquire, and use information effectively. For example, Figure M5.1 shows a progression of paper-and-pencil exercises designed to help students manage a complete round of golf. The procedures for writing these objectives are covered in the following section.

7. Writing Psychosocial or Affective Objectives

Objectives that stress personal development are written for each of the categories of knowledge identified in the psychosocial category. These objectives have traditionally been called affective objectives and have long been stressed in physical education teaching and coaching. The KS Model provides for the writing of affective objectives, but ties their design to the identification of concepts derived from sport psychology or sociology or other relevant literatures. This process began in the creation of the knowledge structures when you were asked to identify key concepts shown to have an impact upon participation and practice of the activity. These objectives specify outcomes related to student self-development and the attainment of goals related

3. Listing Strengths and Weaknesses

Given the sample of three golf holes below, identify the strengths and weaknesses of the holes. Write a brief description of each and mark their locations on the diagram. Mark each hole's strengths as s1, s2 and s3; indicate the locations of the weaknesses as w1, w2, w3 (see example hole).

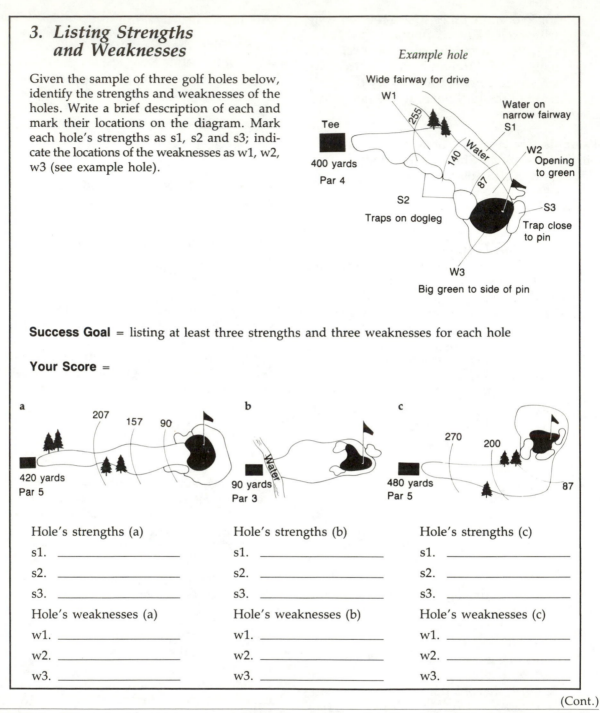

Example hole

Success Goal = listing at least three strengths and three weaknesses for each hole

Your Score =

Hole's strengths (a)	Hole's strengths (b)	Hole's strengths (c)
s1. _____	s1. _____	s1. _____
s2. _____	s2. _____	s2. _____
s3. _____	s3. _____	s3. _____
Hole's weaknesses (a)	Hole's weaknesses (b)	Hole's weaknesses (c)
w1. _____	w1. _____	w1. _____
w2. _____	w2. _____	w2. _____
w3. _____	w3. _____	w3. _____

(Cont.)

Figure M5.1. Progression of course management exercises (numbers 3 to 5) and checklist of objectives (Owens and Bunker, 1989a, pp. 183-188). Reprinted by permission.

4. Managing an Entire Hole

When you decide to plot a strategy for a given hole, you must match your strengths as a golfer with the weaknesses of the hole. Identify your preferred landing area for each shot by marking an X over the spot. Indicate the club you should use to hit the ball from that location by placing a symbol adjacent to the X (e.g., 4i = 4-iron; 3w = 3-wood; pw = pitching wedge). See the example hole below.

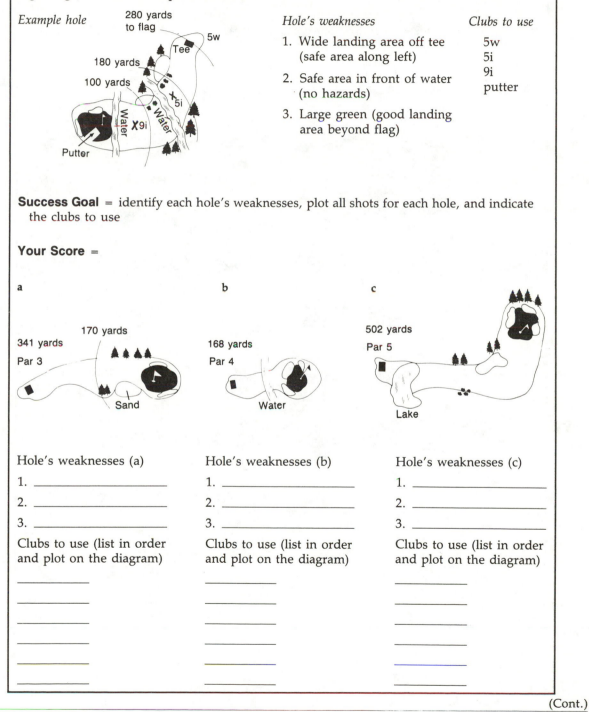

Example hole

Hole's weaknesses

1. Wide landing area off tee (safe area along left)

2. Safe area in front of water (no hazards)

3. Large green (good landing area beyond flag)

Clubs to use

5w
5i
9i
putter

Success Goal = identify each hole's weaknesses, plot all shots for each hole, and indicate the clubs to use

Your Score =

a

341 yards

Par 3

170 yards

Sand

b

168 yards

Par 4

Water

c

502 yards

Par 5

Lake

Hole's weaknesses (a)

1. _____
2. _____
3. _____

Clubs to use (list in order and plot on the diagram)

_____
_____
_____
_____
_____
_____

Hole's weaknesses (b)

1. _____
2. _____
3. _____

Clubs to use (list in order and plot on the diagram)

_____
_____
_____
_____
_____
_____

Hole's weaknesses (c)

1. _____
2. _____
3. _____

Clubs to use (list in order and plot on the diagram)

_____
_____
_____
_____
_____
_____

(Cont.)

Figure M5.1. Continued.

5. Managing a Round

Ultimately, the task in golf is to plot your strategy for a round of golf. Given an entire 18-hole course layout, determine how you would ideally play each hole, given your strengths and weaknesses. Lay out the shots you would make on each hole. Mark an X on the landing area and indicate the *club* you should hit from each location.

Success Goal = plot your course management for each of 18 holes

Your Score =

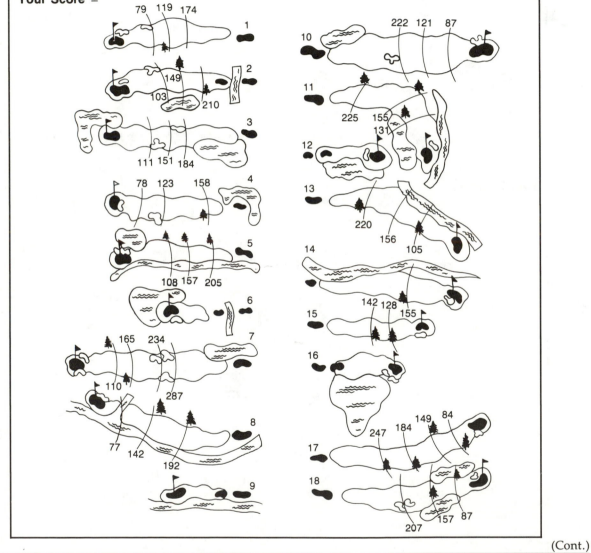

(Cont.)

Figure M5.1. Continued.

Course Management
Keys to Success Checklist

In determining your ability to match your skills (strengths) against the weaknesses of a golf hole, you may wish to refer to this checklist. Place a check on the line for each element you consider when you attempt to determine your strategy for each hole.

Preparation Phase

Analyzing Your Own Strengths

____ Distance you hit each club

____ Any biases regarding shot direction (push, straight, pull)

____ Any biases regarding curvature of shots (slices or hooks)

____ Typical shot trajectory with each club

Psychological characteristics

____ Concern for hazards rather than landing areas

____ Tension

____ Attentional control

Execution Phase

Selecting a Route

____ Locate safe landing areas, as opposed to hazards or other trouble

____ Locate out-of-bounds areas

____ Consider width of fairway as narrow (tight) or wide (open)

____ Find opening to green (free of hazards)

____ Consider location and height of rough

Selecting a Club

____ Lie of ball

____ Trajectory of desired shot

____ Distance ball must travel

Follow-Up Phase

Keeping Track of Performance

____ Review decisions regarding hole's weaknesses

____ Review decisions regarding selecting route

____ Review decisions regarding selection of club

____ Make mental note for future reference

Figure M5.1. Continued.

to self and society, such as self-concept, motivation, teamwork, self-discipline, confidence, empathy, and goal setting.

As an example, Figure M5.2 presents a progression of exercises, with Success Goals, for developing confidence in archery, including mental rehearsal, imagery, and thought stopping. The exercises are designed to help performers gain control over negative thought processes, replacing them with positive images and goals conducive to success. Other examples in the Steps to Success Series are *developing mental skills and setting goals* in golf (Owens & Bunker, 1989a, 1989b); *concentration* in tennis (Brown, 1989a, 1989b); *fear reduction* in swimming (Thomas, 1989a; 1989b); *teamwork* in volleyball (Viera & Ferguson, 1989a; 1989b), *anticipation* in softball (Potter & Brockmeyer, 1989a, 1989b; and *mental discipline* in bowling (Strickland, 1989a; 1989b).

How to Write Objectives

The writing of objectives may be thought of as an equation with four factors:

Action + Content + Qualification +
Any special conditions = An objective

Whether you write objectives for lesson plans, practices, unit plans, season plans, year plans, or complete curricula, you may follow the basic format that Kemp (1977, p. 31) outlined in four steps.

Step One

Start with an action verb that describes a specific behavior or activity by the learner. Here is a selection of action verbs taken from Kemp (1977).

analyze	demonstrate	examine
apply	describe	execute
appraise	design	experiment
argue	differentiate	explain
arrange	discriminate	express
assemble	discuss	formulate
calculate	distinguish	identify
choose	dramatize	illustrate
criticize	employ	indicate
defend	estimate	interpret
define	evaluate	judge

label	predict	schedule
list	prepare	select
locate	propose	set up
manage	question	sketch
memorize	rate	solve
name	recall	support
operate	relate	tell
order	repeat	test
organize	report	translate
perform	reproduce	use
plan	restate	value
practice	review	write

Step Two

Follow the action verb with the content reference, that is, specify the content being derived from the scope and sequence chart. For example:

- Execute a crossover dribble.
- Perform a badminton overhead forehand clear (technique).
- Perform a badminton overhead clear (performance).
- Write a report on the most recent Winter Olympics.

Step Three

If the objective identified by the verb and content reference lends itself to some quantification, add a performance standard that indicates either the minimum acceptable accomplishment in measurable terms or a continuum of performance standards to be achieved across time. For example:

- Execute a crossover dribble continuously for twenty seconds.
- Perform a badminton overhead forehand clear (technique) with four criteria present: stagger stance setup, backscratch supination, powerful forearm pronation, and no hesitation.
- Perform a badminton overhead forehand clear (performance) with a partner, hitting the bird continuously 5, 10, 15, 20 or more times.
- Write a report on the most recent Winter Olympics valued at 20% of your grade.

Step Four

As necessary for student understanding and in order to set evaluation requirements, add any

Confidence Drills

1. Mental Rehearsal

At a regular practice session, shoot as you normally do. After any shot you consider a mistake, mentally rehearse the feel of a good shot and see the arrow hitting the bull's-eye before taking your next shot.

Success Goal = to mentally rehearse 12 shots

Your Score = (#) _____ shots mentally rehearsed

2. Imagery Practice

Sit quietly with your eyes closed. Practice imaging by trying to see every detail of a close friend's face. Make the image as vivid as possible, almost as though you were seeing this friend on television. When you can do this well, image your bow, including every detail possible. Then image yourself performing with the bow. See every detail and hear the sounds that accompany shooting. Feel your muscles as they tense or relax. Note that you can image your performance either from the "outside" as if you were seeing yourself on television, or from the "inside" as it actually feels to perform.

Success Goal = to image for 4 minutes

Your Score = (#) _____ minutes imaging

3. Thought Stopping

Below you will find several examples of negative statements about archery performance. Write a positive counterpart to each. Speak these statements aloud. Then write several negative statements you find yourself saying and their positive counterparts. Speak the positive ones aloud several times.

Success Goal = to write 6 positive statements about archery performance

You Change =

a. From "It is so windy I cannot keep the arrows on the target" to

b. From "I can't shoot well from 40 yards" to

c. From "I'm afraid I'll miss the whole target" to

Your additional negative statements:

d. _____
   _____ to

e. _____
   _____ to

f. _____
   _____ to

Your Positive Statements

_____

_____

_____

_____

_____

_____

Figure M5.2. Building confidence in archery shooting with success goal objectives (Haywood & Lewis, 1989a, pp. 149-150). Reprinted by permission.

criteria or conditions under which the learning must take place. For example:

- Execute a crossover dribble between cones for 20 seconds, counting the number of cones passed. (D = 1-5; C = 6-10; B = 11-15; A = 16-20).
- Perform a badminton overhead forehand clear (technique) with a partner, hitting the bird continuously and showing the following technical abilities: setup with stagger stance, opposite shoulder to the net; step under the bird with a slight bend in back; racquet arm supination (back scratch position) to pronation (power hit) without hesitation; and follow through down opposite side.
- At midcourt, perform a badminton overhead forehand clear (performance) with a partner hitting the bird continuously and progressing over the next ten classes (D = 1-5; C = 6-10; B = 11-15; A = 16-20 or more hits). You are encouraged to practice this skill as many times as you wish both in and out of class time. Initial each other's progress up to and including a B level. An instructor must observe an A performance, which may be attempted as many times as time permits.
- Write a 5-page report on the most recent Winter Olympics valued at 20% of your grade, concentrating on one of the following events: biathlon, luge, or ski jumping. Begin with a description of the event, draw a diagram of a typical facility, describe the skills involved in the event and how they should be performed, and provide a profile on one athlete.

EXERCISE 1

Writing Objectives for Psychomotor Skills

Following the guidelines in this chapter, write technical and performance objectives for the *sequence of individual skills* identified in your scope and sequence charts as created in Module 4. Keep in mind the characteristics of your students and environmental conditions and constraints. See Figure M5.3 for an example of a 1-page format for writing technical and performance objectives for all skill levels.

EXERCISE 2

Writing Objectives for Psychomotor Strategies

Following the guidelines in this chapter, write technical and performance objectives for the sequence of strategies identified in your scope and sequence charts as created in Module 4. Keep in mind the characteristics of your students and environmental conditions and constraints.

EXERCISE 3

Writing Objectives to Assess Factual, Conceptual, and Analytical Knowledge

Following the guidelines in this chapter, write objectives for the background knowledge, physiological, or other concepts in the scope and sequence charts. Begin by writing objectives that stress knowledge of facts, then develop objectives that require problem solving and analytical skills. The example presented here is taken from Step 19, Learning by Watching, in *Tennis: Steps to Success* (1989b), and in *Teaching Tennis: Steps to Success* (1989a). Although formal objectives have not been written to reflect what is to be accomplished, the description of the purpose of the step contains the following objectives:

- Using the Postmatch Scouting Form (see Figure M5.4a), complete an analysis of an opponent by observing and commenting on the following: forehand, backhand, first serve, second serve, forehand volley, backhand volley, smash, best shot, weakest shot, speed, strength, quickness, endurance, style of play, handedness, honesty on call, and final comments.
- Using the Error Chart (see Figure M5.4b), carry out an observational analysis of an opponent and determine the errors committed during first serve, second serve, forehand serve return, backhand serve return, forehand groundstroke, backhand groundstroke, forehand volley, backhand volley, lob, smash, and drop shot.
- Using the Winning Shot Chart (see Figure M5.4c), carry out an observational analysis of an opponent and determine the winning shots they execute from first serve, second

Badminton Overhead Clear
Technical and Performance Objectives

Technical Objectives	Performance Objectives
(All Skill Levels)	(Progression of Novice to Expert)

Technical Objectives (All Skill Levels)

Preparation:

1. Set up stagger stance.
2. Point opposite shoulder to the net.
3. Stage racquet at the ear, racquet head forward.
4. Arch back slightly under the shuttle.

Execution:

1. Draw the racquet back to the back-scratch position (supination).
2. Make forward action in one continuous motion with no hesitation.
3. Contact the shuttle with elbow bent slightly (pronation).
4. Power is generated as the forearm pronates; the racquet head turns out from body at contact.

Follow-through:

1. Down and across the body to the nonracquet side.

Performance Objectives (Progression of Novice to Expert)

Novice

1. Hit a shuttle served high by your partner in the midcourt area: 5, 10, 15, 20 times.
2. Hit with a partner from midcourt 5, 10, 15, 20 times without a miss or a break in technique. No lunging attempts.
3. Play a singles game; concentrate on placing a defensive overhead clear deep to your opponent's backhand.

Intermediate

4. Hit with a partner from just in front of the back service alley: 5, 10, 15, 20 times.
5. Hit cooperatively with a left-handed player and place the shuttle deep to his or her backhand.
6. Hit with a partner, varying the placement of the bird deep and to the corners of the court.

Advanced

7. Hit with a partner from within the back doubles serving alley 5, 10, 20, 30 times.
8. Hit with a partner in continuity drills, combining the forehand clear with other strokes; vary the placement of the bird deep, to the net, and to the corners of the court.

Figure M5.3. Technical and performance objectives for the overhead forehand clear in badminton (novice to expert).

serve, forehand serve return, backhand serve return, forehand groundstroke, backhand groundstroke, forehand volley, backhand volley, lob, smash, and drop shot.

EXERCISE 4

Writing Psychosocial (Affective) Objectives

Following the guidelines in this chapter, write personal development objectives that show how the psychosocial concepts identified in the scope and sequence charts can be achieved. Keep in mind the characteristics of your students and the environmental conditions and constraints. As necessary review the archery examples in Figure M5.2.

Postmatch Scouting Form

Directions: Play a set or a match, then complete this form.

Name of opponent _____ Date of match _____

Results of match: _____ Won, _____ Lost; Score _____

Type of court _____ Weather _____

WRITE ONE OBSERVATION IN EACH CATEGORY ABOUT YOUR OPPONENT

Forehand _____

Backhand _____

First serve _____

Second serve _____

Forehand volley _____

Backhand volley _____

Smash _____

Best shot _____

Weakest shot _____

Speed _____

Strength _____

Quickness _____

Endurance _____

Style of play _____

Right-handed/left-handed _____

Honesty on calls _____

Comments _____

a

(Cont.)

Figure M5.4a-c. Observational analysis charts for tennis (Brown, 1989a, 1989b). Reprinted by permission.

Error Chart

Directions: Tally errors made in each game on the strokes listed in the left column. For example, if the first serve fails to go into the proper court three times in the first game, mark "III" in that box.

Game

Stroke	1	2	3	4	5	6	7	8	9
1st serve									
2nd serve									
FH serve return									
BH serve return									
FH groundstroke									
BH groundstroke									
Forehand volley									
Backhand volley									
Lob									
Smash									
Drop shot									

b

Winning Shot Chart

Directions: Tally winning shots during each game for the strokes listed in the left column.

Game

Stroke	1	2	3	4	5	6	7	8	9
1st serve									
2nd serve									
FH serve return									
BH serve return									
FH groundstroke									
BH groundstroke									
Forehand volley									
Backhand volley									
Lob									
Smash									
Drop shot									

c

Figure M5.4a-c. Continued.

Topics

for Module 6

- Skill analysis, evaluation, and correction
- The art and science of qualitative evaluation
- Skills acquisition knowledge structure
- Norm-referenced and criterion-referenced evaluation
- Formative and summative evaluation
- Exercise 1: Creating a skills acquisition knowledge structure
- Exercise 2: Setting the overall distribution of evaluation for a unit

You can observe a lot by just watching.
—Yogi Berra

The eye sees only what the mind is prepared to comprehend.
—Robertson Davies

Photo by Dac Dang.

Determining Evaluation

In this chapter we look at the analysis, evaluation, and correction of physical skills. We begin by reviewing both technical (qualitative) and performance (quantitative) objectives as presented in Module 5. We then concentrate on technical objectives and their qualitative and subjective nature. The knowledge structures created in Module 1 can be used to generate a *skills acquisition knowledge structure*. This structure describes the characteristics of individuals as they make the transition from novice to intermediate to elite performance. It is this knowledge that underlies one's ability to analyze skills and strategies, and provide corrective feedback. The term *cognitive biomechanics* describes this ability to evaluate the technical qualities present in a performance, to make decisions about what is correct and what is incorrect, and to provide diagnostic feedback.

Following this, we look at two systems for setting the levels of attainment found in objectives. *Criterion-referenced* evaluation uses standards set according to some ideal model derived from the inherent nature of the skill, strategy, concept, or the conditions present in the learning environment. *Norm-referenced* systems, involve comparing a score against standards or norms derived from research on large populations. In addition to determining a norm-referenced or criterion-referenced approach, it is also important to decide whether to administer or manage the evaluation using a *formative* or a *summative* strategy.

Formative systems call for ongoing evaluation, whereas summative systems use a single, final test at the conclusion of a unit of instruction.

Skill Analysis, Evaluation, and Correction

In Module 1 the knowledge structures described the characteristics of each skill, strategy, or concept as performed or understood at the mature or expert level. In terms of formal research, we know very little about the transition that occurs in an individual progressing from novice to intermediate to advanced in a skill (Haywood, 1986). Research from the field of growth and development describes the behavior of youngsters performing basic locomotor, throwing, catching, striking, kicking, and other fundamental skills. This research provides a valuable beginning; however, it does not answer the question of how students learn specific skills, strategies, or concepts and move from novice to expert.

In arriving at a process for assessing learners in sports and activities, Haywood (1986) describes two different approaches, ones quantitative and the other qualitative, which were covered in Module 5. In quantitative assessment, the *product* of skill development is recorded: how many, how high, how fast, how consistent, how accurate. In qualitative assessment, the performer's *technique or style* is assessed. Haywood (1986) states that we know a relatively great deal about quantitative evaluation, but very little about qualitative. This is because quantitative skill assessment techniques have been easier to develop, are more objective, and use measurement devices that are easily available, such as stopwatches and measuring tapes. In contrast, research in qualitative assessment is limited because it requires sophisticated technology, such as high-speed filming and analysis techniques. Qualitative assessment is subjective and requires the presence of a skilled observer. The irony of the situation is that there is a greater need for qualitative than quantitative assessment. In the everyday world of teaching and coaching, 99% of assessment is qualitative and is done subjectively by teachers and coaches as they observe student athletes perform.

The Art and Science of Qualitative Evaluation

The act of teaching or coaching involves verbalizaton, observation, skill analysis, and correction. We talk to learners about the technical aspects of their performance, and as instructors we learn how to observe each skill and combination of skills. But what is the nature of the knowledge underlying this ability? Earlier the term *cognitive biomechanics* was introduced to describe the ability to analyze a sport and provide corrective feedback. *Cognitive* means to perceive, attend to, have knowledge about, problem solve, put to language, comprehend, create, and so on. *Biomechanics* is "the interdiscipline which describes, analyzes and assesses human movement" (Winter, 1979, p. 1). Cognitive biomechanics was therefore defined as the ability to perceive, attend to, understand, and verbalize about physical movement.

The concept of cognitive biomechanics may logically be applied to three distinct groups. What does the *athlete* perceive, attend to, comprehend, and understand about his or her own performance? Some answers may be found in observational learning studies (Carroll & Bandura, 1982, 1985, 1987) and eye movement studies (Petrakis, 1986; Vickers, 1988). What does the *scientific researcher* understand about the movement of the athlete? For this we look primarily to quantitative biomechanics (Norman, 1976; Winter, 1979; Hay, 1985). Finally, what does the *teacher/coach* understand about the movements of their student athletes? Answers to this question may be found in pedagogical kinesiology (Hoffman, 1977; Hoffman, 1983), and in expert-novice studies of teachers and coaches (Housner & Griffey, 1985; Imwold & Hoffman, 1983). In the following section, a skills acquisition structure is introduced as a method of defining knowledge used by the *teacher and coach* in skill analysis and correction.

Skills Acquisition Knowledge Structure

A skills acquisition knowledge structure describes the characteristics of learners as they make the transition from novice to intermediate to elite levels of performance. In Module 1, you were introduced to the concept of a knowledge structure, in which all the skills and strategies in a sport or activity are named and analzyed. A completed analysis described how each skill or strategy is performed in an ideal or proto-typical sense. A skills acquisition knowledge structure is a conceptual extension of the knowledge structures created in Module 1.

To demonstrate, Figure M6.1 shows a skills acquisition knowledge structure for the badminton forehand overhead clear. The left-hand column contains the mature or elite level of analysis and was derived from the original knowledge structure (see Appendix A). How-ever, the middle and right columns are gener-ated from and describe the characteristics of individuals at the novice and intermediate levels. This analysis was derived from a combination of badminton sources and from the developmen-tal literature in throwing (Haywood, 1986; Mosher & Schutz, 1980).

I recommend the following procedures for creating a skills acquisition structure:

- Develop the skills acquisition structure after the Module 1 structures are complete. The resources for describing mature or proto-typical performances are more plentiful and easier to locate. Also, the mature structure should be put in place mentally first, as it is the template against which you judge novice and intermediate performances.
- For each skill, subskill, or strategy, derive information that explains how these skills are *typically* performed by novices and in-termediates. Order this as in Figure M6.1. Notice the parallel procedures used. For ex-ample, in the badminton overhand clear the mature performer uses a stagger stance, the intermediate typically shows a variable stance (especially when fatigued); and the novice often has an ipsilateral stance.
- Use the same knowledge acquisition methods as you did in developing the struc-tures in Module 1: text analysis, structured interview, analogical derivation, stimulated recall.
- Validate your skills acquisition structure against the available research in the sport sciences, in particular growth and develop-ment, medical research on injuries, exer-cise physiology, biomechanics, and motor learning.
- Consult coaching and teaching materials in specific sports, and note the sections on typical errors and how to correct them. For example, the Steps to Success Activity Series devotes a large section of each book to error identification and correction.

Norm-Referenced and Criterion-Referenced Evaluation

In writing objectives and setting levels of achievement, there are two different approaches that you can take. In *criterion-referenced* evalua-tion, you set desired achievement levels accord-ing to standards based on the inherent nature of the task and to accommodate local or class conditions. Glaser (1971) defines criterion referencing as follows:

Criterion levels can be established at any point in instruction where it is necessary to obtain information as to the adequacy of an individual's performance. . . . Measures which assess student achievement in terms of criterion standard thus provide informa-tion as to the degree of competence attained by a particular student which is independent of reference to the performance of others. (pp. 7-8)

Criterion-referencing procedures therefore do not involve comparing a student's achievement to that of others, but instead to idealistic stan-dards based on the nature of the skill, strategy, or concept, or to the conditions found in the learning environment.

In contrast, *norm-referencing* procedures in-volve comparing a student's score to a national standard or norm table. These external standards are almost always set through an extensive period of test construction and development, in which validity measures (the test assesses what it says it does) and reliability measures (the test is stable and performs the same way each time it is used) have been established. In sport and physical activity norm-referenced standards are probably best known in fitness testing. For ex-ample, the AAHPERD fitness tests were ad-ministered in a norm-referenced way until

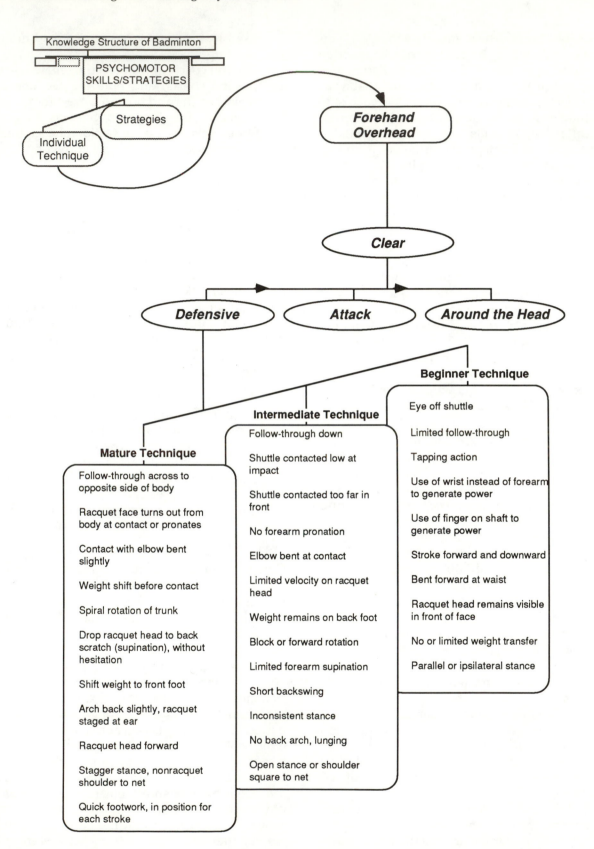

Figure M6.1. A skills acquisition knowledge structure for the badminton forehand overhead clear.

recently, when a shift was made to a new program called Physical Best (McSwegin, Pemberton, Petray, & Going, 1989). Children ages 6 to 18 are assessed on sit-ups, pull-ups, mile and half-mile walk-runs, percent body fat, and the sit-and-reach. In norm-referenced fitness procedures, a child's score is compared to a set of national norms. For example, if a 9-year-old boy performs 3 pull-ups, then he is placed at the 75th percentile level, meaning that only 25% of the national population of 9-year-old boys can perform more pull-ups than he can. In Physical Best, percentile rankings are no longer used; a child is classified simply as being within an optimal health standard or not. This is a more "forgiving" approach that takes into account test and individual variability.

Criterion-referenced tests are used more extensively that norm-referenced tests, especially for skills evaluation. They are less formal, constructed to suit environmental conditions, and less time-consuming to adminster. Instructors often develop their own criterion-referencing systems to facilitate skill achievement, to motivate students, and to provide fun and encouragement. The progression of badminton and golf objectives shown in Module 5 illustrates criterion-referenced tests; the levels of progress can be varied depending on the setting, the number of courts, the ages of the students, and practice time available. The progress levels may be set after the class is pretested and you get a sense of the range of abilities. Further tailoring can be carried out to accommodate individual students ahead of or behind the class pace. The Steps to Success Activity Series contains a wealth of criterion-referenced learning objectives developed by the authors as a result of their many years of teaching and coaching.

Formative and Summative Evaluation

In developing an evaluation system, you should also decide whether you want to administer the evaluation using a *summative* or a *formative* approach. Summative evaluation occurs on one occasion at the conclusion of a class, a lesson, a unit, or a year; it sums up the student's progress on a particular aspect of the course. Think of the final exams you have had, where you had to perform your best on single occasions. In contrast, formative evaluation occurs continuously, with ongoing testing opportunities made available. For example, the mastery learning system as devised by Carroll (1963) and Bloom (1971) is based on a formative evaluation system. Students are encouraged and expected to achieve a high success level on each objective. This is achieved primarily by your making available adequate amounts of time and by providing an atmosphere that provides help and encouragement. Students are expected to progress continuously through a series of well-designed, formative objectives.

There is a need for both formative and summative evaluation in teaching and coaching physical activities. In order to create a situation where students can realistically achieve the objectives you have set, you must give them ample time to practice and must set conditions where they can receive feedback and encouragement from you and others as they practice. This requires a formative system. It is also necessary to set a summative evaluation experience near the conclusion of the unit to give everyone a final chance on objectives they have not yet completed.

 **EXERCISE 1**

Creating a Skills Acquisition Knowledge Structure

Select a single skill from the knowledge structure you created in Module 1. Create a skills acquisition structure showing typical novice, intermediate, and mature characteristics. Show these as an addition to the analysis of expert performance you carried out earlier. Place all three (expert, intermediate, novice) on a single overhead and present them to the other members of your class. Be sure to reference all sources and be prepared to defend your analyses (see Figure M6.1 for an example).

 **EXERCISE 2**

Setting the Overall Distribution of Evaluation for a Unit

Listed in Figure M6.2 are a number of areas to which a percentage of a total grade may be allocated. Assume that the complete unit has a

Setting the Overall Evaluation Scheme for a Unit

For each unit, a final grade will be derived as follows:

Background knowledge

Knowledge of rules, equipment, history　　　　　　　　＿＿＿＿＿＿＿

Physiological testing and training

Physical fitness　　　　　　　　＿＿＿＿＿＿＿

Psychomotor skills and strategies

Individual skills program　　　　　　　　＿＿＿＿＿＿＿

Strategic skill　　　　　　　　＿＿＿＿＿＿＿

Psychosocial concepts

Project　　　　　　　　＿＿＿＿＿＿＿

Other　　　　　　　　＿＿＿＿＿＿＿

Total　　　　　　　　＿＿＿＿＿＿＿ **(100%)**

Figure M6.2. Organizing the overall evaluation scheme for a unit.

value of 100%. Look back at the scope and sequence chart you created in Module 4 and at the objectives you have designed. Allocate a percentage for each of the cross-disciplinary areas. Make an overhead of your overall evaluation scheme and defend your decisions to your class, including the following:

- What percentage of the total mark will be for *individual skill development*?
- What percentage of the total mark will be for *strategic skill*?

- What percentage of the total mark will be allocated to *written tests* on skills and strategies, rules, equipment, and so forth?
- What percentage of the total mark will be for *physiological training and conditioning*?
- What percentage of the total mark will be allocated for the *psychological and sociological* categories?
- Are you assigning a percentage for *participation*? If so, list the criteria underlying this decision?

Topics

for Module 7

- The art and science of designing learning activities
- Implications of research in motor skill acquisition for instructional design
- Principles in designing effective learning activities
- Good teaching is good coaching and vice versa: John Wooden
- Exercise 1: Design a progression of learning activities (individual skills objective)
- Exercise 2: Design a progression of learning activities (strategies objective)
- Exercise 3: Design a progression of learning activities (physiological testing and training objective)
- Exercise 4: Design a progression of learning activities (psychological objective)

Photo by Alex Tziortzis. Courtesy of *The Daily Illini*, University of Illinois.

Designing Learning Activities

Learning activities are drills, projects, questions, demonstrations, modeling, problem-solving exercises, videos, individual programs, and other events planned by the teacher or coach to help the student achieve the stated objectives. You can better understand how to design learning activities by reading, taking courses, and being a performer in the sport activity. Most important of all, the design of learning activities comes from your imagination, and a central core of knowledge that serves as a critical foundation. In the KS Model the design of learning activities is the culmination of a thought process that takes into consideration the following core components:

1. the *subject matter* of the activity (Module 1),
2. the teaching *environment* (Module 2),
3. your *students* (Module 3),
4. the *scope and teaching sequence* of skills, strategies, and concepts (Module 4),
5. your *objectives* (Module 5), and
6. *evaluation* (Module 6).

As you can see, the design of learning activities brings to bear diverse types of knowledge and requires a creative energy that is one of the joys of teaching and coaching. This is the aspect of teaching and coaching that is always changing and should continually fascinate and challenge you. Perhaps this is because it is a risky business: You never really know whether something will work with your students until you have tried it out.

Let me give you an example. Two student teachers were asked to prepare and deliver a 15-minute lesson on badminton equipment. They did the necessary work, researching the subject, setting objectives, and developing a lesson plan. They ran into serious difficulty, however, because their learning activities consisted solely of arranging the students in a semicircle and discussing each piece of equipment in turn. The lesson was not what they had intended, and to their dismay it was over in a few minutes. Why? What did they do wrong? They forgot to design learning activities that were challenging, were fun, and involved the students personally and actively.

They were given a second chance to present the lesson, and the difference was dramatic. They began with an introduction of the different types of racquets and stringing (wood, metal, graphite, composition; tight or loose stringing) by having the students rotate in groups of four through a series of stations and play with a different type of racquet at each. They then introduced different types of shuttles, first explaining the rule on flight characteristics (the shuttle should land in the back alley when hit with an underhand clear from the back of the court), and the effects of altitude and materials. The students tested high- and low-altitude feather and synthetic shuttles. Different types of court shoes were introduced by having the students sit in a circle with *their* shoes as the basis of discussion. They discussed the merits of one type of shoe over another, their cost and wear characteristics, and the rules relative to attire and competition. This second lesson was creative, using activities that stimulated students and involved them in trying, testing, discussing, and comparing.

It is through the skillful design of learning activities that you get your students' attention and absorb them in the lesson or the practice. This is done through introductory explanation, drills, discussions, modeling, playing, problem solving, and other events collectively called learning activities. In this chapter, we begin with a number of instructional design questions related to the design of learning activities. Following this, the phases of skill acquisition that learners typically go through are discussed, and why the designer of learning activities should always keep these in mind. Of special importance is attention to the characteristics of beginners because the vast majority of students in sport and physical activity are at a beginning level. As part of this discussion, five principles used in designing effective learning activities are presented and examples are drawn from the Steps to Success Activity Series. Each book in the series has dozens of learning activities tried and tested by the authors of each activity. We next look at a study by Tharp and Gallimore (1976) on John Wooden, the legendary former coach of the UCLA men's basketball team. We see through his example that good teaching is good coaching and vice versa, and that there is a need to combine compassion for your students with a positive demand for learning. Instructional design exercises complete the chapter.

By the end of this module, you should be able to answer the following instructional design questions:

1. What progression of learning activities would facilitate the achievement of the objectives you have identified?
2. Consider the background knowledge objectives. What types of learning activities will help your students grasp the content outlined by the objectives?
3. Consider the physiological training and conditioning objectives. What learning activities can you use to accomplish the objectives you have set out?
4. Consider the psychomotor skills and strategies objectives. Are there recognized progressions of drills that facilitate or enable the acquisition of the objectives?
5. Consider the psychosocial objectives. What types of learning activities will help your students grasp the ideas contained here? Are there readings, field trips, films, experiences, role models, guest speakers, projects, debates, or other activities that will facilitate the achievement of the objectives?
6. For each of the categories set out, are there established learning activities that you can locate and use, or will you need to create your own?
7. When all the categories are thought of in total, will the learning activities you have in mind achieve your overall objectives?
8. For those students who are behind or ahead of the rest of the class, do you have a selection of special learning activities suited to their levels of achievement? Elaborate on these for each of the background, physiological, psychomotor, and psychosocial categories.
9. Do you feel that your selection of learning activities will adequately and fairly enable your students to achieve the objectives you have set out?

The Art and Science of Designing Learning Activities

The overall goal of Module 7 is for you to design creative learning activities that will help your students achieve the objectives you have set for them. Module 7 requires a combination of art and science. The art is being able to integrate all the information you have about subject matter, the teaching environment, your students, scope and sequence, and specific objectives (with evaluation) into a comprehensive set of learning activities. The science emerges from a number of areas that give us insight into the process of skill acquisition and from research on factors that underlie the design of effective learning activities.

Characteristics of Beginners

Cognitive psychology tells us that the amount of information a learner can attend to, and the effort required to absorb it, is limited and variable, depending on skill level (Kahneman, 1973). Learning activities design must therefore take into account the conditions under which an optimal amount of information can be presented so that it can be absorbed and used by a student learning a new physical skill or improving an existing one. Singer (1982) identifies nine characteristics of beginners that have impact on the design of teaching and coaching progressions. Beginners tend

(1) to be too *attentive* to too *many cues* in a situation. They need to be more selective; to attend to the minimum but most relevant cues in a situation at any given time.

(2) to think and worry too much, about too many things. A state of *relaxed concentration* for learning and performance is the desired goal.

(3) to lack the ability to set *realistic expectations* for themselves in performance—sometimes they are too high, other times too low.

(4) to have difficulties with *too much information* (instructions and directions) given to them at one time. Teachers and coaches are often guilty of providing *information overload*: overloading the minds of learners.

(5) to view each learning experience as truly new. Yet, in reality, new learnings are derived from old learnings. Gross motor patterns,

such as throwing and kicking, serve as the basis of more complex ball sports skills. *Relationships* of already acquired skills to newly introduced ones need to be perceived.

(6) to lack appropriate *strategies* to handle information and situations.

(7) to lack the knowledge of when and how to use available response-produced *feedback*.

(8) to lack the *confidence* and *security* they need for positive experiences.

(9) to expend too much *unnecessary energy*. (pp. 84-85)

Phases of Skill Acquisition

Consider novice basketball players. If you put them in a one-on-one situation, you will observe that most of what they are thinking about are the basic mechanics of the fundamental skills involved. They are probably very concerned with dribbling the ball properly because they do not want to lose it to the opponent. Or they attend to the basic mechanics of shooting a lay-up. These concerns pre-dominate. This is quite different from highly skilled basketball players. Highly skilled performers do not direct attention to the mechanics of dribbling or shooting, since these skills are already mastered. Rather, concentration is centered on how to maneuver around the opponent. They may be watching for specific cues from the opponent's movements that will let them know exactly how to move to make a shot. Since skilled players do not have to concentrate on the dribbling or shooting mechanics of the task they are free to direct attention to other concerns. (Magill, 1989, p. 65)

Magill, in the preceding quote, describes the characteristics of learners as they first begin to acquire a skill and the changes they undergo as they become more skilled. For some time researchers have attempted to define the stages of skill acquisition. One of the first models was provided by Fitts and Posner (1967) who identified a three-stage model. The notion of a three-stage model has been developed and refined over the years by many authors, and Magill (1989) defines the stages as follows. The *cognitive* phase, the initial stage of learning, describes a student's attempts to understand the intent of the activity or the specifics associated with a skill being learned. Learners in this phase commit errors of a gross motor type and display little ability to correct their own errors. In the second phase, the *associative* phase, the learner now knows what needs to be done and is in a practice and training phase of learning the physical components of the skill. Errors tend to be of a fine motor type, and the learner displays an increased ability to correct his or her own errors. Finally, in the *autonomous* stage, the performer is now able to perform the skill with little conscious control necessary. He or she has attentional resources available that can be directed toward the conditions of play, the opponent, and other factors often missed entirely by beginners and intermediates.

Another point merits attention: It is no longer appropriate to call the first stage of skill acquisition the cognitive stage and by inference or omission to infer that the other, more advanced stages are not. Cognition and its many subfields—perception, attention, knowledge representation, problem solving, creativity, and so on—occur in some form in all phases of skill acquisition.

Implications of Research in Motor Skill Acquisition for Instructional Design

For some time it has been debated whether motor learning research has an impact on professional practice, especially on how teachers and coaches carry out their daily work. In this section, I look at four lines of research identified by Magill (1989) that describe changes that occur as skill is acquired. Each of these provides directions for the design of learning activities. Research shows that during motor skill acquisition, changes occur

1. in how learners perceive the spatial, velocity, and acceleration demands of a task (Marteniuk & Romanow, 1983);
2. in error detection abilities (Schmidt & White, 1972);
3. in movement efficiency (Sparrow & Irizarry-Lopez, 1987); and
4. in coordination (Southard & Higgins, 1987).

Knowledge acquired through research must be translated into sound, interesting, and challenging learning activities. I begin by looking at the research just cited and then at sample learning activities derived from the Steps to Success Activity Series that are illustrative of these findings. I discuss each in a framework proposed by Christina (1987), who explains that research in motor learning may be carried out in different ways, ranging from purely theoretical to applied research. Level 1 research is carried out in the laboratory, where subjects perform simple, artificial tasks such as linear positioning, tracking, or tapping. The artificial tasks ensure that the subjects have had no prior experience with the movements. The goal of Level 1 research is to develop an overall theory that describes how physical skills are acquired. Level 2 research, in contrast, is carried out using real-world tasks. The goal of Level 2 research is the same as Level 1, to develop theory. However, conclusions reached are derived from the study of physical skills in real-world settings. Level 3 research is carried out in the field in real-world settings and has as its goal the discovery of results that improve performance. Level 3 research is result-oriented and does attempt to explain the reasons underlying effective performance.

As you read the following studies, identify each as Level 1, Level 2, or Level 3. Furthermore, as you read the sample learning activities from the Steps to Success Activity Series, think about the process the authors went through in developing the learning activity. Would it be correct to classify the development of innovative and effective learning activities as a form of Level 3 research?

1. Changes Occur in How Learners Perceive the Spatial, Velocity, and Acceleration Demands of a Task

We know that with practice, learners become successful at achieving the goal of the skill (as evidenced by baskets scored, targets made, shuttles served accurately, games won). However, it also appears that there are certain dimensions within a task that learners choose to improve before others. Subjects concentrate first on the spatial elements in the task, and after a degree of mastery is achieved, they then show improvements in velocity and acceleration. Evidence for this is supplied by Marteniuk and Romanow (1983). Subjects were required to follow a wave form with a stylus presented on a computer screen, right to left. All subjects performed 800 trials, and it was found that during initial learning they worked at keeping the stylus spatially close to the wave form; after success was achieved at this, they improved measures of velocity (distance traveled in a specified time) and acceleration (the rate at which velocity of a body increases).

Now, let's look at some of the Steps to Success learning materials. In golf (Owens & Bunker, 1989a, 1989b), the first three instructional steps emphasize the full swing motion and especially the spatial elements of club position, such as the distance and angle through which the club should ideally travel. A natural pendulum swing motion is emphasized. In the next two steps, distance considerations are introduced, as are the effects of club acceleration, speed, and velocity. Similarly, in archery, the initial steps emphasize basic form, followed by concerns for accuracy, and then distance (Haywood & Lewis, 1989a, 1989b).

Learning activities should be designed that encourage the attainment of the important spatial elements in the skill, followed by increases in velocity, acceleration, and distance. It was also shown in the Marteniuk and Romanow (1983) study that the subjects chose to practice the whole skill rather than segmenting it into units. Whenever possible, learning activities should be designed that encourage the learner to practice in a holistic way. This principle is followed throughout the Steps to Success Activity Series through the implementation of a top-down sequencing strategy (see Module 4).

2. With the Acquisition of Skill Comes an Increased Ability to Detect and Correct One's Own Errors

With the attainment of skill, we become better able to identify and correct our own movement errors. Evidence for this is provided in a study by Schmidt and White (1972) in which subjects were required to move a lever along a linear track, to a goal 9 inches away in 150 msec. After each trial, the subjects were asked to estimate how far they thought they had moved the lever, and then were told the actual distance. Over trials, they improved steadily in their ability, not only to move the lever to the goal, but also to correctly estimate how accurate they were.

This research shows that in designing learning activities, we should involve learners in experiences that require self-analysis and correction. For example, in archery (Haywood & Lewis, 1989a, 1989b), Step 8 presents a series of three learning activities designed to assist the individual in analyzing and correcting their own performance. Students are shown how to carry out a photographic, videotape, and arrow pattern analysis of their shooting style. In golf (Owens & Bunker, 1989a, 1989b), Step 15 presents a series of learning activities that help students assess their own effectiveness in playing a round of golf.

3. With the Acquisition of Skill Comes Improvement in Movement Efficiency

Magill (1989) defines *efficiency of movement* as a decline in the amount of energy expended in producing a movement. Evidence by Sparrow and Irizarry-Lopez (1987) showed that performers improve mechanical efficiency and at the same time decrease caloric coast (energy expenditure) as skill is acquired. Subjects were required to crawl on a treadmill for 3 minutes per day for 20 days. Mechanical efficiency measures increased by 13.7%, while caloric cost decreased.

This research shows that learning activities should be designed to challenge learners more and more because they become more efficient and, in order to improve, require additional challenges. This is evident in the individual programs created for each of the activities in the Steps to Success Activity series. Through the formative evaluation medium, students are encouraged to achieve higher and higher goals as the course proceeds. For example, the swimming program by Thomas (1989b) shows the distances that swimmers are able to accomplish for each stroke over the course of the program (see Figure M7.1).

4. With Skill Comes Improvement in Coordination

As skill level increases, performers are able to improve the coordination between the limbs involved in the movement (Magill, 1989). Evidence for this is supplied by a study by Southard and Higgins (1987). A racquetball forehand hitting task was performed by naive subjects for

Sample Individual Program

INDIVIDUAL COURSE IN __Swimming__   GRADE/COURSE SECTION __Beginning__

STUDENT'S NAME _____   STUDENT ID # _____

SKILLS/CONCEPTS	TECHNIQUE AND PERFORMANCE OBJECTIVES	WT* ×	POINT PROGRESS**				= FINAL SCORE***
			1	2	3	4	
Back Float	*Technique:* Back fully arched, arms extended overhead. Breathes fully, easily. Relaxed. Scoops and recovers smoothly.	0.5					
Kick and Pull on Back	*Technique:* Recovers arms to top of shoulder. Reaches high and far for catch. Pulls full and level. Long glide. Ankles flex properly. Knees and feet stay under. Relaxed, rhythmical kick.	1.0					
	Performance: Moves well with moderate speed in deep water. Swims 45–150 ft.	1.0	45 ft	90–100 ft	100–125 ft	150+ ft	
Prone Kick, Pull, Breathe	*Technique:* Full reach forward. Catch with high elbow. Elbow bent 90°. Pulls long, one arm at a time. Kicks easily. Flexible ankles. Some knee bend. Breathes easily. One side only. Ear on water.	1.5					
	Performance: Moves smoothly with no distress. Swims 45–150 ft.	1.5	45 ft	60–90 ft	100–125 ft	150+ ft	
Turning Over	*Technique:* Does both rolls and through-vertical turnovers. Does both front-to-back and back-to-front rolls smoothly, head remains up. Tucked legs pass through smoothly on vertical turnovers.	1.0					
Crawl Stroke	*Technique:* Long reach, full pulls. Lifts shoulders for recovery. High elbows. Elbow leads hand on recovery. Fingertips enter before elbows. Steady, relaxed kick. 2, 4, or 6 beats. Breathes low on pull. Flows smoothly. Effortless.	1.75					
	Performance: Breathes every stroke. Swims with relative ease 45 ft to 100 yd.	1.5	45 ft	50 yd	75 yd	100 yd	

		WT	25 yd	50 yd	75 yd	100+ yd
Elementary Backstroke	*Technique:* Smooth arm recovery; high catch; long, full pulls. Long glide. Relaxed. Feet hook as they drop back. Hooked feet turn out. Wide kick with inside of foot/ankle. Streamlined. Toes pointed. Kick, stroke finish together.	1.0				
	Performance: Each stroke covers 6 ft or more. Relaxed long glide of 25–100 yd.	1.0	25 yd	50 yd	75 yd	100+ yd
Breaststroke	*Technique:* Does not pull past shoulders. Hands dig in. Elbow 90°. Coordination is pull-kick-glide. Long glide. Breathes low. Breathes at end of pull. Legal kick. Knees narrow, feet hooked.	1.5				
	Performance: Smooth, at least 8–10 ft per stroke. Swims 25–100 yd.	1.5	25 yd	50 yd	75 yd	100+ yd
Sidestroke	*Technique:* Head down. Arms work in exact opposition. Top arm works exactly with leg. Kick. Top leg forward. Stays exactly on side. Strong kick, long glide, stream-lined. Feet do not pass.	1.0				
	Performance: Smooth. Each stroke equals at least 6 ft. Swims 25–100 yd.	1.0	25 yd	50 yd	75 yd	100+ yd
One-Foot Dive	*Technique:* Forward knee locked. Rear legs straight. Toes hooked over edge. Lifts rear leg to vertical. Vertical entry. Body stretched. Feet together. Knees straight. Toes pointed. Very small splash.	1.0				
Standing Front Dive	*Technique:* Arms circle. Good height. Legs lift together. Toes pointed. Vertical entry. Body stretched, streamlined. Stays in close. Very little splash.	1.5				
	Performance: Achieves 4–10 *consecutive* dives (or 4 in 10 trials) displaying good technique.	1.0	4/10	6/10	8/10	10/10
Exam on Knowledge of Technique	Value = 25%					

*WT = Weighting of an objective's degree of difficulty.

**PROGRESS = Ongoing success, which may be expressed in terms of (a) accumulated points (1, 2, 3, 4); (b) grades (D, C, B, A); (c) symbols (merit, bronze, silver, gold); (d) unsatisfactory/satisfactory; and others as desired.

***FINAL SCORE equals WT times PROGRESS.

Figure M7.1.   Sample individual program in swimming (Thomas, 1989b). Reprinted by permission.

10 minutes a day for 10 days. Changes in coordination would be evident if the angle between the upper arm, the forearm, and the wrist-hand-racquet—as well as the overall velocity of each limb segment—changed as a result of practice. During the pretest phase, it was found that the subjects brought the arm forward to contact as a single unit. After 10 days practice a noticeable lag in the wrist-hand-racquet and an increased angle at the elbow was found. Velocity changes in the upper arm relative to the forearm were dramatic (a pretest score of 23.5 degrees per second compared to a posttest of 320.7 degrees per second). The change in forearm relative to the wrist-hand-racquet was pretest, 34.5 degrees per second compared to 596.5 degrees per second. This change from a unitary arm action to a segmented control is referred to as "segment specific control" (Magill, 1989, p. 74).

This study shows that increases in coordination can occur in a relatively short space of time, and with large improvements in performance, if adequate practice opportunities are provided. For this reason, learning activities should be provided that motivate learners to practice extensively on their own. All of the Steps to Success Activity Series books provide extensive "perfect practice" exercises designed to help learners achieve maximum gains in minimum time. In addition, each instructor's guide in the series identifies factors that can be manipulated to either increase or decrease each drill's difficulty level to better fit students' initial skill levels. Drill modifications enhance individualization and time-on-task because students are motivated to practice at their particular skill levels.

Principles in Designing Effective Learning Activities

Learning activities in sport and physical activity take the form of drills, small group practice, projects, modeling, observation activities, modified games, and so on. A number of principles underlie the design of effective learning activities. As you read this section, think of designing your own drills, instead of always relying on those created by others. Why? As a teacher or coach you identify the skills, strategies, and concepts that you want your student athletes to achieve. You organize these into a scope and sequence and set realistic objectives. Next it is time to provide activities that will help your students learn this material. If you rely exclusively on drills and learning activities developed by others, you will find they are often limited in helping students achieve what you have in mind. Indeed, they sometimes can throw you completely off track, and the plan you made for your students is lost. The design of learning activities is a creative endeavor that is fun, challenging, risky (they may not work), and personal. As a teacher or coach, you should always be looking for different ways to get the same material across, always trying to find innovative ways to help individual students. Four principles for designing effective learning activities follow.

1. *Initially, control the amount and type of information made available to the learner, as well as the number of variables he or she must manipulate when performing a skill or sequence of skills.*

When designing a progression of drills, control the number of variables the beginner must initially handle. Variables to consider within the learning environment are (a) the number of participants, (b) the number of pieces of equipment, (c) the number of sequential skills to be learned and performed, (d) the type of opposition: modeled, cooperative, reduced, real, or event-like; and (e) the expectations of observers. The following progression shows how each of these can be gradually introduced into learning activities, allowing the learner to accommodate the increasing complexity.

   a. One person, modeling a single skill without equipment (e.g., a serve; a throw; a kick; a pass).

   b. One person with one piece of equipment performing a single skill alone to self or against a wall or practice surface of some type (e.g., serve; pass; kick against a wall).

   c. Two persons working as cooperative partners on one skill with one piece of equipment. One partner "feeds" the other in a modified way, from a toss or in as helpful a manner as possible. It is especially beneficial if one of the partners is the instructor.

   d. Two persons working together in a game-like environment executing a single skill (e.g., serve; throw; kick; or pass on a court, or on a field of play in a position that simulates a realistic game or activity situation).

   e. Two persons with equipment working

cooperatively, together modeling two or more skills, without opposition (e.g., shoot off the dribble; give and go; set and spike; serve and receive).

f. Two persons with equipment working cooperatively, together performing two or more skills with reduced opposition (e.g., shoot off the dribble with "dummy" defense; give and go with one opponent who offers no resistance; set and spike with one blocker who offers limited resistance).

g. Two persons with equipment performing two or more skills with realistic opposition (e.g., give and go with one opponent who offers resistance; two opponents with game-like opposition).

h. Additional levels include the following:

- adding additional teammates (three-plus to full game);
- increasing the number of skills in a sequence;
- adding equipment or apparatus that represents a greater degree of difficulty; and
- adding officials, coaches, spectators and other conditions that are game- or event-like.

2. *As part of a teaching progression, provide a visual model that shows the skill or strategy performed by a skilled individual.*

Verbally interpret the movement to your students. A visual model should be used and may be a student in the class, a videotape, a filmstrip, a poster, a picture in a book, or your own demonstration. Do not feel obligated to use yourself as a model, especially if you have not seen a video of your own performance; it is surprisingly easy to say one thing and do another. It is often best to use someone else's performance as the model; you can see clearly the dynamics of the skill and explain it more easily than if you try to do the demonstration, too.

Why is it so important to incorporate a visual model, and a skillful one, into a teaching progression? The importance of observation in physical skill acquisition has been shown in observational learning and modeling studies. Skill attainment has been shown to be greater under conditions of observation followed by physical practice, rather than under conditions of physical or observational practice alone (Carroll & Ban-

dura, 1982, 1985, 1987; Gould & Roberts, 1982; Magill, 1989; Martens, Burwitz, & Zuckerman, 1976). An important factor in acquiring a complex physical skill is the ability to observe how the skill is performed and to extract the cues that will benefit one's own performance. Beginners may make perceptual errors when first introduced to a skill; for this reason highly skilled models should be provided, and students should be helped to carefully analyze what is involved in a performance. Instructors should ask questions and encourage learners to verbalize about what they feel is involved in performing a skill.

In addition, eye movement studies have found that skilled and unskilled athletes differ in what they attend to in basketball (Bard & Fleury, 1976; Ripoll et al., 1986), ice hockey (Bard & Fleury, 1981), gymnastics (Vickers, 1988), and pistol shooting (Ripoll et al., 1985). For example, Vickers (1988) found differences in the eye movements of three groups of female gymnasts (N = 30; average age 13.4) differentiated by skill level: elite (international level), intermediate (regional), or novice. The groups viewed slide presentations of six basic gymnastic sequences representing the four events of women's gymnastics. Differences between the three groups were recorded in how they viewed each sequence: The elite gymnasts viewed the mid- and lower body regions, while the intermediates attended to the shoulders and the head. This occurred even though both groups were the same age and had practiced in the same club under the guidance of the same coaching staff. The novices differed from both the intermediates and elites, dividing their attention between the lower and the upper body.

These studies indicate that learners, depending on skills level, are drawn to observe certain parts of a performance and may miss other parts entirely. Learning activities should be designed so that skills and strategies are clearly shown and interpreted for the learner. As a movement is shown, draw the students' attention to the key technical, biomechanical, and other aspects underlying a successful performance.

3. *Learning activities should contain the three elements of repetition, contextual relevance, and spatial orientation (Sinclair, 1979).*

Once your progression of learning activities has been thought out, with attention to the number of variables and the provision of clear and concise demonstrations, you must give the learner optimal practice conditions. Sinclair (1979) has identified three conditions that underlie optimal practice:

Repetition. The central element in practice is repetition, because the game situation provides little opportunity for repeated attempts of either individual game skills or group skills. Time motion analysis of team games such as basketball, soccer, field hockey, and rugby reveal that the actual average "ball contact time" experienced during a full game can be equalled in eight minutes by providing one ball for a group of four players. Obviously, then, "playing the game" provides neither the structure nor the opportunities for skill acquisition.

Contextual relevance. All situations should be "gamelike," that is, they should be experienced in a context that is relevant to the actual game requirements. There should be as little difference as possible between practice and playing behavior so that each practice element is actually a small element of the actual game with only the modifications being that various numbers of the other players are temporarily removed from the immediate act.

Spatial orientation. Definition of the working area is crucial and the directional element must be stressed. The strategic awareness associated with various portions of the playing area should be developed within these exact portions or within work areas or sections of the same size and design (goal provided, boundaries defined, critical lines provided). This acts as a guide to a player's positional relationship with his/her teammates as well as with his/her opponents, and it is essential to the whole framework of skilled response in a game. (pp. 24-25)

Good Teaching Is Good Coaching and Vice Versa: John Wooden

In this book a distinction has *not* been made between good teaching and good coaching. This is because there is far greater similarity between the two than dissimilarity. To more fully appreciate this idea, consider the following study on a master teacher and coach, John Wooden, the legendary former basketball coach of the UCLA Bruins. For one season two educational psychologists, Roland Tharp and Ronald Gallimore (1976), sat on the sidelines and watched Wooden run his practices (up to 1976, his teams had won 10 of the past 12 NCAA championships). The researchers objectively recorded courtside data and recorded Wooden's qualities as follows. First, Wooden separated his role as his players' "father figure" from that as their coach by beginning practices in a business-like and demanding way every day. Practices were for practice and not for socializing or working out problems not immediately associated with basketball performance. Second, Wooden taught constantly about the basic fundamentals of play; 50.3% of all his on-court time was spent in giving verbal instructions, 5.4% in modeling skills, and 8.0% in scolding and reinstruction. Indeed, Wooden's characteristics were very similar to those of the teachers in the high-achievement schools (see Table M5.1).

 **EXERCISE 1**

Design a Progression of Learning Activities (Individual Skills Objective)

Select an objective with evaluation that you have designed for a single skill. Design a progression of learning activities that will help *all* your students (beginning, intermediate, and advanced) accomplish this objective.

EXERCISE 2

Design a Progression of Learning Activities (Strategies Objective)

Select an objective you have designed for a specific strategy. Design a progression of learning activities that will help *all* your students accomplish this objective.

EXERCISE 3

Design a Progression of Learning Activities (Physiological Testing and Training Objective)

Select an objective you have written for the physiological testing and training category. Design a progression of learning activities that will help *all* your students accomplish this objective.

EXERCISE 4

Design a Progression of Learning Activities (Psychological Objective)

Select an objective you have written for a psychological concept. Design a progression of learning activities that will help *all* your students accomplish this objective.

Topics

for Module 8

- Application 1: Lesson planning
- Application 2: Unit Planning
- Application 3: Curriculum design for a single activity
- Application 4: Curriculum design for a multiactivity program
- Application 5: Instructional design in coaching
- Application 6: Individualized instruction for teaching or coaching
- Application 7: The ActionMark software program
- Application 8: Design of the Steps to Success Activity Series
- Application 9: The on-campus teaching laboratory
- Conclusion

MODULE
8

Photo by Sandee Greatrex.

Making Real-World Applications

Module 8 is concerned with doing—putting into practice the knowledge identified in Modules 1 through 7. The design of teaching and coaching applications, such as lesson and unit plans, practice and season plans, is the culmination of a thought process that has identified the following knowledge components:

1. The subject matter of the activity (Module 1)
2. The teaching environment (Module 2)
3. The students (Module 3)
4. The scope and teaching sequence of skills, strategies, and concepts (Module 4)
5. The objectives (Module 5)
6. Evaluation (Module 6)
7. The design of learning activities (Module 7)

The purpose of Module 8, the last step, is to show how these components can be combined to create numerous applications in teaching and coaching. You will see how to create daily, weekly, unit, year, and curriculum plans for the teaching setting and practice, season, and developmental programs for the coaching setting. All of these are created from the same knowledge bases, with the basic building blocks being the lesson plan (teaching) and the practice plan (coaching). Three additional applications are derived from the same knowledge bases: individualized programs, a software program called ActionMark, and the concept of a step, as designed for the Steps to Success Activity Series. These applications, which are only a few of the many applications that can be derived from the knowledge bases identified in Modules 1 through 8, show how flexible and powerful knowledge-based instructional design is. I encourage you to experiment and develop applications of your own.

151

The final application presented is the on-campus teaching laboratory. Having been introduced to the different components of the KS Model, you must now plan and deliver a complete unit of instruction, including individual and group evaluation. The goal of this lab is to introduce you to just enough of the real world of teaching that you can learn and adjust from week to week. It has been thought by many that the only way to develop teaching skills is to go immediately into the schools, with experience being the best and only teacher. But a review of research on student teaching experiences (Berliner, 1985) has shown that this practice is often destructive and serves only to facilitate the adoption of coping skills that are often inadequate and do not facilitate sound teaching practices. New teachers and coaches need a clear vision of what they can and should achieve, as well as a sense of possessing the tools they need to attain their goals. As a student teacher you need opportunities to plan, teach, experiment, discuss, study, revise, observe, and reflect, all in an atmosphere where you can become a better judge of your role as a teacher or coach.

By the end of Module 8 you should be able to answer the following questions:

1. How can you arrange the information in Modules 1 through 7 into a *lesson plan*?
2. How can the material developed in Modules 1 through 7 be further organized to create a series of lesson plans, or a *unit*?
3. Could a series of unit plans be planned over a number of grades or years, thus providing a *complete curriculum* for your students in a single activity? That is, could a series of unit plans be sequenced and administered from grades 4-12, 7-12, or 9-12, so that students could progress continuously from unit to unit, year to year, or grade to grade?
4. Could the same planning process be *applied to coaching*? In what ways must the coaching planning units differ from those used in teaching?
5. Can you use the information in Modules 1 through 7 to develop *individual programs* that would permit students to progress within a unit at their own pace? And from year to year?
6. Could you use the same approach in developing individual training programs for athletes in a coaching context?

Application 1: Lesson Planning

A lesson plan is delivered on a single occasion and may be anywhere from 5 minutes to 3 or more hours long. The lesson plan is the building block of more extensive planning units and therefore should receive careful attention. It is a personal document designed by you, the teacher, that helps you feel organized and guards against your forgetting critical elements, something that is surprisingly easy to do once a class begins. Figure M8.1 presents a blank lesson plan form. You may use this format as is or design one of your own. Regardless of the layout, however, all lesson plans should possess the following characteristics and information.

1. The lesson plan is a personal document created to *assist you as you actively teach, therefore* the plan should be easy to read, with just enough information to guide you through the lesson.
2. The lesson plan should be constructed so the chronology of events is evident.
3. The following are the types of information found in a sport and physical activity lesson plan:
   • Class-specific information: Name of activity, grade or class number, number of lessons in total unit, beginning and ending time
   • Objectives of the lesson
   • List of equipment and other resources needed
   • Introductory events, such as procedures for setting up equipment; self-directed warm-up, or conditioning, or skills practice; announcements; roll call; and uniform check
   • Group warm-up and conditioning exercises
   • Review of old material
   • Instruction in new material
   • Modified or full game play
   • Cool-down and question/answer period
   • Post-class announcements
   • Notes to self for next time
   • Time line (optional)

The Components of the Lesson Plan

Figure M8.2 shows the components of the lesson plan and the origin of the material as defined by the KS Model.

LESSON PLAN _____ OF _____	OBJECTIVES _____
ACTIVITY _____	_____
CLASS _____	_____
REMINDERS _____	_____

SEQUENCE OF SKILLS AND CONCEPTS	LEARNING ACTIVITIES	TEACHING POINTS	Time

Figure M8.1. A lesson plan format.

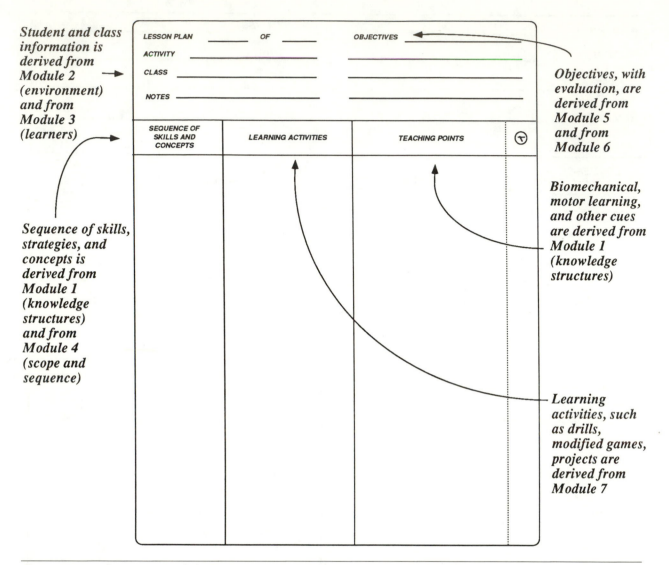

Student and class information is derived from Module 2 (environment) and from Module 3 (learners) →

Sequence of skills, strategies, and concepts is derived from Module 1 (knowledge structures) and from Module 4 (scope and sequence)

Objectives, with evaluation, are derived from Module 5 and from Module 6

Biomechanical, motor learning, and other cues are derived from Module 1 (knowledge structures)

Learning activities, such as drills, modified games, projects are derived from Module 7

LESSON PLAN _____ OF _____   OBJECTIVES _____

ACTIVITY _____

CLASS _____

NOTES _____

SEQUENCE OF SKILLS AND CONCEPTS	LEARNING ACTIVITIES	TEACHING POINTS	⏱

Figure M8.2. Components of the lesson plan and their origin in the KS Model.

Down the left-hand column is listed the *scope and sequence of skills* and concepts and basic events to be presented in the lesson. This material was derived from the knowledge structures created in Module 1 and the scope and sequence plan derived in Module 4. These are organized to reflect the passage of time in the lesson: (a) warm-up, (b) review of material if necessary, (c) instruction of new material, (d) practice, modified, or full game play, and (e) cool-down, with closing questions and announcements.

At the top of the plan are listed the *objectives* for the lesson. These were derived from Modules 5 and 6, objectives and evaluation, respectively, and are called Keys to Success and Success Goals in the Steps to Success Activity Series.

Objectives state what you expect the students to accomplish relative to each of the skills, strategies, or events listed, with evaluation goals specified.

In the middle column are presented the *learning activities* that accompany each of the skills and concepts taught. These are derived from Module 7 and are presented as drills and projects in the Steps to Success Activity Series. Shown here are the drills and other learning activities that students practice to accomplish the objectives you set. *Use diagrams generously in this section.*

In the third column are listed the *key teaching points* that accompany each skill and concept. This material is drawn from the knowledge structures in Module 1, and the Keys to Success in the Steps to Success Activity Series. Also jotted here as a reminder are the key points relative to the attainment of objectives (Module 5) and evaluation goals (Module 6). You may wonder why you should write this information down. It is important to create this list of critical points because it is very easy to overlook or forget to teach a crucial point. We also know that students can take in only a few pieces of information at one time, especially if the material is new; therefore, these points should be carefully selected, and meaningfully presented.

A time line is optional. Some teachers and coaches always use one, whereas others feel there is no need to plan with a time line.

Shown in Figure M8.3 is a sample lesson in badminton illustrating the components just described. This lesson shows how the top-down sequencing format would be planned and carried out. Lesson 3 calls for new instruction in the grip, pronation and supination, underhand clear, and singles serve, and a continuation of singles play.

Managing the Intensity of a Class or Practice

Before explaining each of these components, it is also important to point out that all sport and physical activity lessons or practices should have an intensity line, as shown in Figure M8.4. Each class or practice should begin gradually, with the physical intensity of the activity increasing to a maximum at about two-thirds or 75% of the way through the session. The final 5 to 8 minutes involves a tapering off, with the final 2 minutes being a cool-down. This is also an ideal time for you to ask your students or athletes questions about the class or practice, to query their understanding of what has happened in the class, and to indicate to them what will be occurring in the next session. *Do not send your students to their next class in an exhausted or hyperactive state.*

How Much Detail Is Necessary?

Lesson and practice plans should have *just enough* information so that you may consult them from time to time during the session and be reminded about the events and information you want to present. A lesson plan should be readable at a glance and therefore should not have too much detail. Point form is recommended,

as are brief statements that are meaningful to you. It may also be helpful to develop a color system for the various components (such as red for objectives, blue for learning activities) to make them easily identifiable in the bustle and activity that is common in teaching and coaching sport and physical activity.

Should You Carry Your Lesson Plan With You as You Teach?

This is a point of contention; student teachers in physical education are often advised to teach from memory, without referring to their lesson plans at any time. Trying to commit a whole lesson to memory, though, may cause you to design simplistic lessons, with an overall reduced contribution by yourself. On the other hand, carrying a clipboard about can be a nuisance when freedom of movement is essential. For this reason, many teachers and coaches set up a "teaching center" where the lesson is left and occasionally consulted as the class proceeds. This location has a table or a shelf, a bulletin board, outlets for A-V and musical equipment, and other aids to teaching. This leaves the instructor's hands free to handle equipment, demonstrate, spot, and so on. Student teachers should, however, be encouraged to plan thorough lessons, to consult them openly while the lesson is in progress, and to do so without feeling self-conscious in any way.

Are Lesson Plans Necessary Even When You Become Experienced and Can Remember What You Want to Teach or Coach?

Surprisingly, yes. Ask experienced coaches whether they still plan their practice sessions. In most cases, they will say they reserve 1 or 2 hours *per day* planning each session. Experienced teachers will respond in a similar but somewhat different way. They keep their lessons in a folder or file from year to year and plan each new unit by reading and revising old plans. They do not see this as an onerous task but as a creative time for continually changing their plans, updating and incorporating new knowledge, objectives, approaches to evaluation, and learning activities. Classroom teachers also often plan a week of lessons at one time (Clark & Peterson, 1986), thus making the task a weekly event instead of a daily one.

LESSON PLAN 3 ***OF*** 8

ACTIVITY Badminton

CLASS Grade 8, 9:00 - 10:00

NOTES
- 1 shuttle per student needed
- Students must take turns to play
- While waiting practice grip in hitting target drill against wall - 20X.

OBJECTIVES
1. To demonstrate the forehand and backhand grip
2. To pick up shuttles from floor -10X- forehand and backhand, using pronation and supination
3. To demonstrate underhand forehand clear while hitting to self, 20X
4. To demonstrate long serve on court, to partner
5. To play in 5-min. singles games, using grip and serve in a competitive situation

SEQUENCE OF SKILLS AND CONCEPTS	***LEARNING ACTIVITIES***	***TEACHING POINTS***
Warm-up	4 laps of gymnasium Footwork to net with lunge - 4X Hit to self - upward 40X Hit with partner - till class begins	Aerobic component in jogging Flexibility, prevents injuries, increases mobility Hitting for skill development on court in partners
Grip	Explain todays progression - grip to underhand clear to singles serve to singles game	Grip is foundation for both power and control Draw non-racquet hand down shaft to handshake position V to opposite shoulder Relaxed fingers elongated, pistol grip Partner check, recheck
Pronation/ Supination	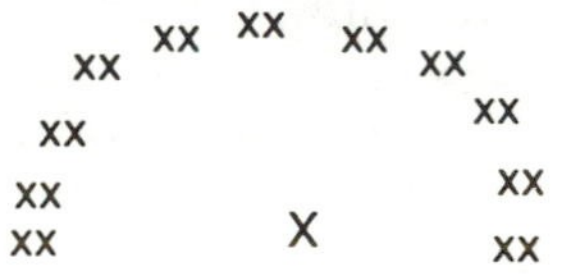 Pick - up drill. Pick up shuttle from floor- 5X forehand and 5X backhand	
Underhand Forehand Clear	Find space on floor Hit to self on forehand only Begin by tapping Add distance to backswing Add slight knee lift Try to hit ceiling	Underhand clear to singles serve: Stress stagger stance, non-racquet foot forward; racquet back; elbow in, fingers to ceiling; Contact shuttle in front, to side, not in front of body; lag on racquet head, use knees slightly lifting up during hit Forearm is source of both power and control, not the wrist Supination in backswing, so that thumb and fingers points up toward ceiling Pronation occurs during downswing at contact Elbow in, lag racquet head
Singles Serve	Move to court with partner Hit to each other from serving position using same movement, both courts 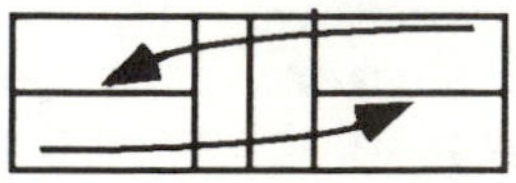	Serving position 1-2 meters back Perform exactly as in underhand forehand clear to self, except now high and deep to opponent. Feet may not move but weight shift to front foot very important
Singles Play	Put grip, and singles serve into game play	Stress use in competition

Figure M8.3. A sample lesson in badminton.

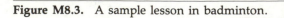

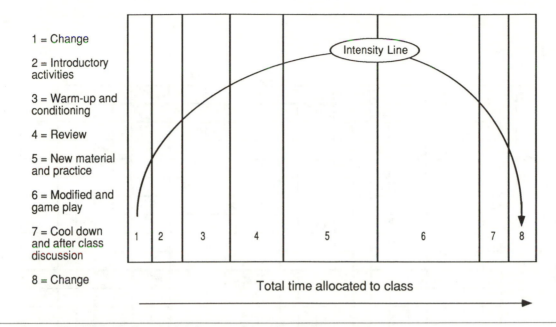

1 = Change

2 = Introductory activities

3 = Warm-up and conditioning

4 = Review

5 = New material and practice

6 = Modified and game play

7 = Cool down and after class discussion

8 = Change

Total time allocated to class

Figure M8.4. The intensity line as implemented in a lesson or a practice.

Lesson Planning Prevents Discipline Problems and Teacher and Student Burnout

The lesson plan is your number one vehicle for discouraging discipline problems and preventing burnout. A well-organized teacher engages students in interesting and stimulating activities every day. Students feel challenged because they know they are progressing daily; for those students who are potential discipline problems, lesson planning keeps them busy and keeps their minds off of ways of acting up.

Lesson planning also prevents burnout, which is characterized by a lack of interest in what you are doing and feelings that are increasingly more negative than positive. Lesson planning provides a time for you to become more knowledgeable, for you to research new areas and to translate this knowledge into exciting and rewarding experiences for students. Remember, too, that students also become burned out, tired and bored with school. Your efforts in lesson planning can make all the difference in their daily lives and experiences.

Application 2: Unit Planning

A unit plan is a series of lessons, ranging from two to many, sequenced to present a comprehensive program of instruction. In the unit plan, the same group of student athletes are taught over an extended period of time. When design-

ing a unit plan, scope and sequence decisions are made that show how skills, strategies, and concepts are to be presented across a predetermined number of lessons. As an example, consider the scope and sequence plan for archery shown in Figure M8.5 (Haywood & Lewis, 1989b). This plan was developed following the procedures for scope and sequencing presented in Module 4.

Eighteen skills, strategies, and concepts make up the *scope* of the archery plan, with 30 sessions or lessons making a complete *sequence* of instruction. This plan was developed for a university or college setting with a one-semester course of 30 continuous classes. But what if you wanted to adopt this program for a public school setting, for example, a junior or senior high with Grades 7-9 and 10-12? It now becomes necessary to break up this scope and sequence into separate unit *plans* that would take your students through a series of courses that, in total, comprise the complete archery program. Figure M8.6 shows that a *single unit* in archery has been made up of 10 lessons. The first 10 sessions in Figure M8.5 cover Step 1 (Fitting Equipment) to Step 7 (Using a Bowsight).

Application 3: Curriculum Design for a Single Activity

In Application 2 we looked at the design of a unit plan in a single activity spanning one time

Sample Scope and Teaching Sequence

Legend: N = New, R = Review, C = Continue, P = Student Directed Practice

NAME OF ACTIVITY: Archery
LEVEL OF LEARNER: Beginning

Steps	Session	1	2	3	4	5	6	7	8	9	10	11	12	13	14	15	16	17	18	19	20	21	22	23	24	25	26	27	28	29	30
1	Fitting equipment	N																													
2	Safety	N	R																												
3	Mimicking		N	R																											
4	Shooting form		N	P	P																										
5	Improving accuracy				N	P	P																								
6	Adding accessories							N																							
7	Using a bowsight							N	P	P																					
8	Correcting errors											N	C	C																	
9	Varying stance														N	R															
10	Bow hand position															N	R														
11	Anchor position																N	R													
12	Mental checklist																	N	P	P											
13	Scoring																		N	R											
14	Tournament shooting																				N	C	C	C	C	C					
15	Mental approach																							N	R	P	P				
16	Tuning equipment																											N	R		
17	Maintaining equipment																													N	R
18	Upgrading equipment																														N
19																															
20																															
21																															
22																															
23																															
24																															
25																															

Figure M8.5. Sample scope and sequence for archery (Haywood & Lewis, 1989b). Reprinted by permission.

Development of the Unit Plan

A Single Lesson Plan (Archery)

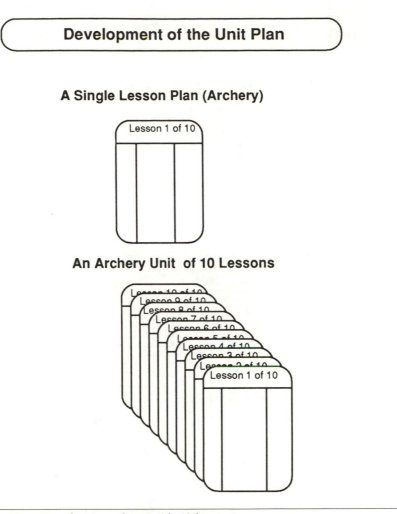

An Archery Unit of 10 Lessons

Figure M8.6. An introductory unit plan in archery with 10 lessons.

frame, with the same group of student athletes involved from beginning to end. Now we'll look at the design of a complete course of study that spans two or more units, years, or grades, with the possibility of different students enrolling each year, using the KS Model and the Steps to Success Activity Series.

The curriculum for a single activity should be designed so that new material is presented in each unit, with the expectation that students will progress and be promoted from one unit or grade to the next. Figure M8.7 shows a complete curriculum in archery (three units of 10 lessons each), as derived from the archery program in Figure M8.5 (Haywood & Lewis, 1989b). The first or introductory unit covers Step 1 (Fitting Basic Equipment) to Step 7 (Using a Bowsight), and requires ten 50-minute lessons. The second unit covers Step 8 (Correcting Errors) to Step 14 (Two Days of Tournament Shooting), and requires ten lessons. The third unit continues

Tournament Shooting and covers Step 15 (Mental Approach) to Step 18 (Upgrading Equipment) and also requires ten lessons.

Determining Student Achievement

In developing a curriculum in a single activity, it is important to determine how students will be promoted from one unit to the next. Let's use the archery program, as presented in Figures M8.5–M8.7, again as an example. If you set up your program in this way, you must decide how students will progress from one level to the next. Consider the following questions:

1. How will students be evaluated? Will they complete the Keys to Success and Success Goals set out in the archery Steps to Success program, or will you devise another method of evaluation?

2. How will students be promoted from one level to the next? Must students have the

Development of the Curriculum in a Single Activity (Archery)

A Single Lesson Plan (Archery)

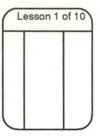

Lesson 1 of 10

An Archery Unit of 10 Sequential Lessons

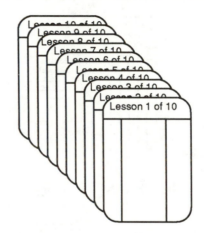

Three Archery Units of 30 Sequential Lessons

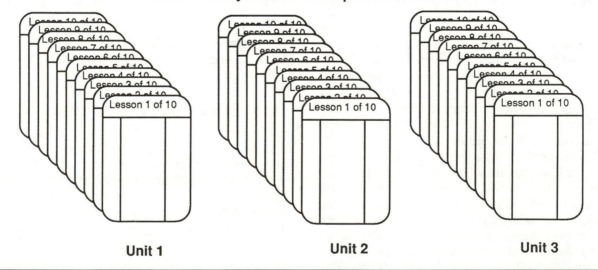

Unit 1   Unit 2   Unit 3

Figure M8.7. A complete curriculum of 30 lessons in archery sequenced across three grades, years, courses, or other sequence.

first program completed before they can move to the next?

3. What will you call the units?
   - Grade 7, 8, 9 archery?
   - Beginner, intermediate, and advanced archery?
   - Bronze, silver, gold archery program?
   - Other?

4. How will progress in the program be administered and reported? (Formative or summative? To the student? To the parents? To administrators?)

5. Will the program be compulsory or optional?

Application 4: Curriculum Design for a Multiactivity Program

You can design a complete curriculum for a physical education program by using the KS Model as a theoretical framework, with the Steps to Success participant's books providing textbooks for students and the instructor's books as your curriculum guides. Consider them resources that you can use to conceptualize and structure your own curriculum.

Let's review why it is possible to use the KS Model and the Steps to Success Series in this way.

1. The Steps to Success Activity Series is activity specific, which means that activities are the primary building blocks of your curriculum.

2. Each activity book has been designed from a knowledge-based perspective that reflects a cross-disciplinary framework; that is, it identifies the skills and strategies in the sport and shows how sport science concepts from exercise physiology, motor learning, biomechanics, sport psychology, sport history, sport sociology, and other areas have affected performance, teaching, and coaching.

3. The knowledge structures were created by eliciting knowledge from master teachers and coaches, using knowledge elicitation techniques such as structured interview, text analysis, analogical derivation, and stimulated recall. During their development, the knowledge structures were constantly validated against the appropriate sport science authorities.

4. Each activity book shows how the knowledge structure should be taught or coached. This methodology is reflected as a series of steps; by sequencing the steps across grades, or by using a competency approach, you offer students new material and help them grow every year.

5. A top-down sequencing approach has been primarily adopted for the Steps to Success Activity Series for two reasons: First, it places the learning of skills and strategies into the context of game play as soon as possible, and second, it is the approach used by most of the master teachers and coaches.

6. Because each Steps to Success Activity Series book highlights one or more of the sport science concepts, a curriculum that encompasses a number of activities should provide good coverage of these concepts across a total program. For example, mental skills and goal setting are presented in golf (Owens & Bunker, 1989a, 1989b); concentration is discussed in tennis (Brown, 1989a, 1989b); fear reduction in swimming (Thomas, 1989a, 1989b); teamwork in volleyball (Viera & Ferguson, 1989a, 1989b); developing confidence in archery (Haywood & Lewis, 1989a, 1989b); anticipation in softball (Potter & Brockmeyer, 1989a, 1989b); and mental discipline in bowling (Strickland, 1989a, 1989b).

Figure M8.8 depicts a multiactivity curriculum for six activities (tennis, badminton, volleyball, swimming, jazz dance, and golf). Both activities and the number of lessons are arbitrary examples. Activity decisions may be made by state, provincial, or district curriculum committees, by members of the department of physical education, or by you.

Questions for Curriculum Developers

In designing a complete curriculum using the KS Model and the Steps to Success Activity Series, you must make a number of important decisions. The following are some important considerations:

- What grade, age, or developmental framework are you developing the curriculum for? Determine the number of years, or grades over which the curriculum or developmental program is to be created. For example, is the

Development of the Multi-Activity* Curriculum (grades 7-9 **)

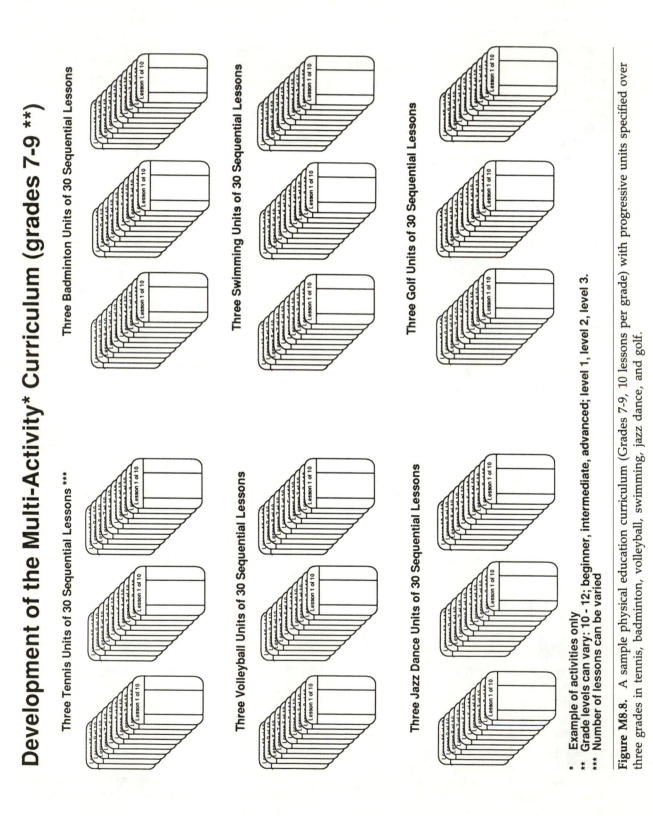

Three Tennis Units of 30 Sequential Lessons ***

Three Badminton Units of 30 Sequential Lessons

Three Volleyball Units of 30 Sequential Lessons

Three Swimming Units of 30 Sequential Lessons

Three Jazz Dance Units of 30 Sequential Lessons

Three Golf Units of 30 Sequential Lessons

*   Example of activities only
**   Grade levels can vary: 10 - 12; beginner, intermediate, advanced; level 1, level 2, level 3.
*** Number of lessons can be varied

Figure M8.8. A sample physical education curriculum (Grades 7-9, 10 lessons per grade) with progressive units specified over three grades in tennis, badminton, volleyball, swimming, jazz dance, and golf.

curriculum to be developed for Grades 7–9, 9–12, 4–12; or Levels 1, 2, 3,; or beginner, intermediate, advanced levels of achievement; or some other continuous organizational scheme?

- What activities should be part of the school physical education experience?
- Should activities be categorized (for example, team sports, individual sports, dance, aquatics, outdoor pursuits, combative, fitness)?
- Should some activities be classified as core activities and therefore compulsory and others as optional?
- How many lessons and steps will be allocated for each activity selected per year? Or, per unit?
- How can you create an overall scope and sequence chart for each activity that reflects the decisions made above?
- What sport science concepts should be emphasized? How are they to be sequenced and offered?
- How will evaluation and promotion occur? Will progress be made within a grade structure or in courses of study with prerequisites required to advance to a new level?
- Will you require textbooks?
- Will parents be informed of the overall program and given an opportunity to play a role in evaluation?
- Will certification, peer teaching opportunities, or some other credential or recommendation be possible for students who complete all the steps in an activity?

Application 5: Instructional Design in Coaching

The instructional design planning units in teaching are the lesson plan, the unit plan, and the curriculum (single or multiactivity). In coaching, the equivalent units are the practice plan, the season plan, and the developmental coaching program.

The Practice Plan

Knowing how to plan effective and interesting practices is a constant challenge for coaches. Not only do you have a smaller group of athletes to keep motivated and challenged, but you also have many more sessions to plan and deliver. Many of the design components of a lesson plan are applicable to a practice plan. Practice plans should include team and individual objectives, warm-up and conditioning exercises, review and instruction in new skills and strategies, a variety of challenging and meaningful learning activities, extensive use of modified and full-game practice, cool-downs, a question-and-answer period, and an optional time line. A practice plan is also a personalized document, with just enough information that you can consult during practice as a reminder about the events and information to be presented. A practice plan should be readable at a glance, using brief statements that are meaningful to you. The lesson plan format in Figure M8.1 can easily be adapted and used in coaching.

Despite the numerous similarities between lesson and practice planning, there are some important differences.

- Practices are normally longer, averaging a minimum of 1 hour to 3 or more.
- You are planning for fewer and more specialized athletes in each session. Even in sports with many athletes, such as football, there are practice plans for specialized groups.
- Practice plans often involve assistant coaches, with separate plans developed and delivered by teams of coaches.
- Practice plans differ according to the time in the playing season (preseason, tryouts, the beginning season, mid-, late, and play-off cycles) because of the unique needs of athletes at each point.
- Practice plans also vary according to a between-game or weekly cycle. The plan the day before a game is different from the midweek plan. The approach taken varies with each coach, but generally, early and midweek are devoted to preparing for the next opponent, emphasizing teaching and learning, with intensity and execution stressed. The practice just before a game is more relaxed, with a tapering effect planned in preparation for competition.
- Practice planning emphasizes physiological training and conditioning more strongly than teaching does.
- Practice planning emphasizes work with special teams, small groups, and individuals.

The Season Plan

A season plan is made up of a series of practices. Your goal is to develop a comprehensive coaching program for your team from the beginning of the season to the end. Imagine that you are coaching in junior high (grades 7 to 9). Your season is 3 months long and you practice 3 times a week. Begin by calculating total practices and total games—in this case, about 36 (a season of 3 months and 3 practices per week)—and develop a master timetable with the dates and locations of games and practices. Next, divide the season into miniseasons as follows: preseason, tryouts, early season (first 25% of matches), midseason (middle 50% of matches), late season (last 25% of matches), play-offs/championships, and the off-season.

Each miniseason requires a different type of thinking and emphasis. During the preseason you are concerned with providing play and recreational opportunities (if permitted by league rules) and with fitness testing and conditioning. During the tryout period you need a means of objectively evaluating each athlete. Once the team has been selected you devote the early season to careful and thorough teaching of individual skills and establishing the offensive and defensive strategies to be used. In the mid- and late seasons you concentrate on developing individual skills, refining offensive and defensive systems, and adding options and variations to gain advantages over specific opponents. In the late season you refine individual skills and set plays and activities that prevent mental and physical fatigue. In the play-off season, only rarely do you introduce radical changes; you will usually consolidate and reinforce what your team has been doing well all season.

Let's use the volleyball scope and sequence shown in Figure M8.9 to illustrate how the KS Model and the Steps to Success volleyball books can be used for coaching. Figure M8.9 shows an instructional program of 24 steps, to be presented in 30 lessons or 50-minute sessions. The program progresses from movement patterns in Step 1 to game play choices in Step 24. It can easily be adapted to the coaching setting.

To develop your season plan, list the miniseasons on one or more blank scope and sequence charts, writing in all game times as well as meetings. Now consult the participant's book and instructor's guide for volleyball and think about what you will teach and coach in each miniseason. Look at the map in Figure M8.10 from *Teaching Volleyball: Steps to Success* for an overview of the complete game as structured by Viera and Ferguson (1989a). Pay special attention to the tryouts, when you must assess the strengths and weaknesses of your players and begin to solidify your overall coaching strategy. Use Modules 2 and 3 (analysis of the learning environment and analysis of learners) as references to help you set up and conduct your tryouts.

Your overall season plan will be based on your evaluation of athletes during the first few weeks of the season. A completed season plan for junior high coaching would probably be very similar to Figure M8.9 in the way that individual skills are taught and incorporated into combinations of three, four, and five skills. It would probably differ in that you would need to select and teach the offense and defense earlier and train your athletes to be proficient in both as a team before your first competitions. A specific season plan depends on the strengths and weaknesses of your players, their experience in volleyball, and your experience coaching them. Athletes at the junior high level are developing, and they need to be taught how to do a few things well. By following Viera and Ferguson's Steps 1–24, you stress the overall game concept, individual skill development, sound execution of basic defensive and offensive fundamentals, and the concept of teamwork.

The Developmental Program

The developmental program in coaching extends across multiple years and is applicable to a range of age and ability groups. The example season plan just described was limited to accommodate the needs of athletes ages 12 to 15 in the school setting. Now let's consider how to develop a multiyear program that athletes of all ages and ability levels can follow from novice to elite.

In designing the coaching developmental program, it is common to find that age classification systems have been established and are enforced by sport governing bodies. They often define competitive groups that are deemed safe for children to compete within, which are derived from a combination of age, weight, and height. For example, children are often grouped into categories, such as mitey mites, novices, peewees, midgets and so on, that specify the ages of children permitted to compete against one another. The developmental program for each sport must be sensitive to any such classification system.

Sample Scope and Teaching Sequence

NAME OF ACTIVITY Volleyball

LEVEL OF LEARNER Beginner-intermediate

| N | New | | R | Review | | C | Continue |

Steps	Session Number	1	2	3	4	5	6	7	8	9	10	11	12	13	14	15	16	17	18	19	20	21	22	23	24	25	26	27	28	29	30
	Introduction/Orientation	N																													
1	Movement Patterns	N	R	C																											
2	Forearm Pass	N	R	C	C	C	C	C	C	C	C	C	C	C	C	C	C	C	C	C	C	C	C	C	C	C	C	C	C	C	C
3	Serve		N	R	R	C	C	C	C	C	C	C	C	C	C	C	C	C	C	C	C	C	C	C	C	C	C	C	C	C	C
4	Two-Skill Combination			N	R	C																									
5	Overhead Pass				N	R	C	C	C	C	C	C	C	C	C	C	C	C	C	C	C	C	C	C	C	C	C	C	C	C	C
6	Set					N	R	C	C	C	C	C	C	C	C	C	C	C	C	C	C	C	C	C	C	C	C	C	C	C	C
7	Three-Skill Combination						N	R																							
8	Attack							N	R	C	C	C	C	C	C	C	C	C	C	C	C	C	C	C	C	C	C	C	C	C	C
9	Four-Skill								N	R																					
10	Dig									N	R	C	C	C	C	C	C	C	C	C	C	C	C	C	C	C	C	C	C	C	C
11	Five-Skill										N	R																			
12	Spike											N	R	C	C	C	C	C	C	C	C	C	C	C	C	C	C	C	C	C	C
13	Block												N	R	C	C	C	C	C	C	C	C	C	C	C	C	C	C	C	C	C
14	Six-Skill													N	R																
15	Advanced Serves														N	R	R	C	C	C	C	C	C	C	C	C	C	C	C	C	C
16	Individual Defense															N	R	C	C	C	C	C	C	C	C	C	C	C	C	C	C
17	4-2 Offense																N	N	R	R				C	C	C	C	C	C	C	C
18	2-1-3 Defense																	N	N	R	R			C	C	C	C	C	C	C	C
19	International 4-2																				N	N	N			C	C	C	C	C	C
20	6-2 Offense																								N	R	R		C	C	C
21	2-4 Defense																						N	N	N	N	R	R	C	C	C
22	5-1 Offense																											N	N	R	C
23	Game Situations																											N	N	R	C
24	Game Play Choices																											N	N	R	C

Notes:

Figure M8.9. Sample scope and sequence for teaching volleyball (Viera & Ferguson, 1989a). Reprinted by permission.

Knowledge Structure of Volleyball (Overview)

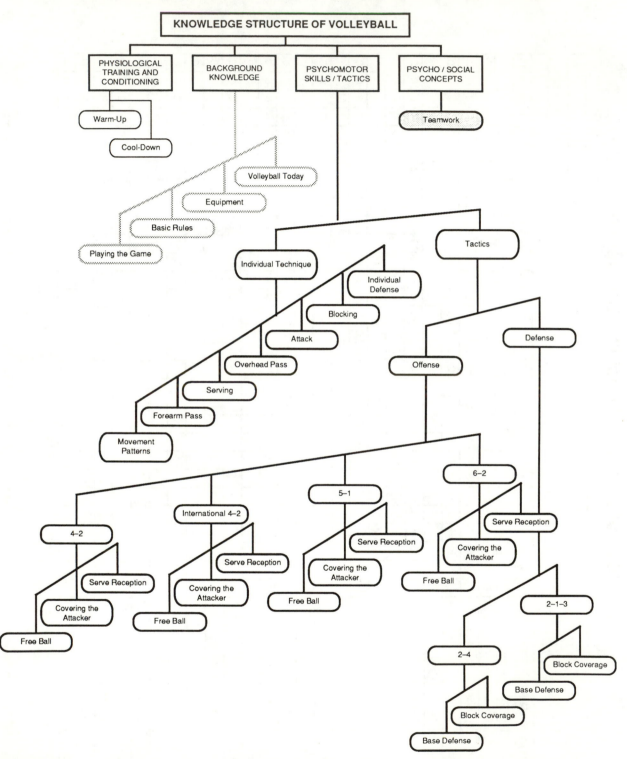

Figure M8.10. Volleyball knowledge structure overview (Viera & Ferguson, 1989a). Reprinted by permission.

The principles used in setting up the developmental program are more extensive than those used for the unit or season plan because one must understand when children and adults are capable of performing the skills, strategies, and concepts of a sport. To conceptualize a program of this magnitude, you should work through all the modules of the KS Model. If you have not already done so, begin by developing a knowledge structure for the activity as described in Module 1, so that you are familiar with the entire range of skills, strategies, and major concepts of the activity. Then analyze the coaching environment (Module 2) and different types of learners (Modules 3 and 6 [see skill acquisition analyses]), consider alternate scope and sequence strategies (Module 4), consult the Steps to Success Activity Series for examples of a top-down sequencing strategy, design progressions of objectives (Module 5), develop evaluation and feedback procedures (Module 6), and identify the learning activities, drills, projects that facilitate skill acquisition and performance (Module 7). A coaching developmental program is an extensive undertaking, but rewarding for anyone pursuing a career in coaching.

Application 6: Individualized Instruction for Teaching or Coaching

Individualized instruction involves designing programs of study tailored to the individual capabilities and needs of students. The merits of individualized instruction are many; they vary depending on the setting. In the *school setting*, one faces tremendous diversity, often in the same grade, in the skill levels of children. Some children have had experiences outside of school that put them far ahead of others who are meeting an activity for the first time. Still others may find an activity difficult because of motivational problems, physical handicaps, or mental disabilities.

In the *coaching setting*, it is common for coaches to develop an individual training program for each athlete to improve performance, maintain performance levels, and counter weaknesses. In the *private club and recreational setting*, individual programs are needed for participants involved in fitness and weight training activities, racquet games, swimming, gymnastics, and many other areas. All age and interest levels are involved, increasing the need for personalized programs.

Figure M8.11 presents a template that can be used to design individual programs for any sport, dance, or activity. This form also appears in each of the Steps to Success instructor's guides. Figures M8.12 (pp. 170-1) and M8.13 (172-3) present sample individual programs for archery (Haywood & Lewis , 1989b) and golf (Owens & Bunker, 1989b). These programs may be adopted as is or adapted to the setting you are in, or you may wish to create your own program from scratch.

Design Concepts Used in Developing Individualized Programs

In creating individual programs, the following instructional design concepts and principles were used.

1. The purpose of an individual program is to emphasize the development of specific skills, strategies, and concepts by providing formative or ongoing evaluation. Students are thoroughly taught the items on the program, and then given the opportunity to work both in and out of class on their programs.
2. Individual programs should accompany lesson or coaching plans. The list of items on the individual program should be in the same chronological order or sequence as when taught.
3. In the left-hand column of the program are listed the names of the skills, strategies, and concepts to be evaluated. These were identified in the knowledge structure and in the scope and sequence charts and are aspects of the course on which you expect a student to work and be evaluated.
4. The middle section sets out the specific technical (Keys to Success) and performance (Success Goals) objectives for each of the skills, strategies, and concepts identified. All objectives should be written so that they can be reasonably achieved within a preplanned time span.
5. The third column weights each component in the program, indicating the degree of difficulty of each. The degree of difficulty may be due to the inherent nature of the skill, and is influenced by the amount of time the students are given to work on the skills.
6. The final column presents the formative evaluation criteria for each objective. A number of different approaches may be used

Individual Program

INDIVIDUAL COURSE IN _____

GRADE/COURSE SECTION _____

STUDENT'S NAME _____

STUDENT ID # _____

SKILLS/CONCEPTS	TECHNIQUE AND PERFORMANCE OBJECTIVES	WT* ×	POINT PROGRESS**				= FINAL SCORE***
			1	2	3	4	

*WT = Weighting of an objective's degree of difficulty.

**PROGRESS = Ongoing success, which may be expressed in terms of (a) accumulated points (1, 2, 3, 4); (b) grades (D, C, B, A); (c) symbols (merit, bronze, silver, gold); (d) unsatisfactory/satisfactory; and others as desired.

***FINAL SCORE equals WT times PROGRESS.

Figure M8.11. A template for developing an individual program.

depending on the learner, the setting, and the overall intent of the unit (for example, D to A, beginner to advanced; 1 to 4 points; gold, bronze, silver, and so on).

7. The number of progress levels is flexible, but usually varies from 2 to 6.

Implementing Individualized Programs

The following suggestions are helpful for individualizing your instruction:

- Use the individual program sheets as the basis of the pretest (as in Module 3, Figure M3.2), from the first or second class onward, and every day if possible.
- Skills defined as *technical* should be evaluated, as soon as possible after they are taught, by you or someone who understands the technical components (cognitive biomechanics) of the skill and can communicate corrections. You might let students who receive A's in a skill become evaluators of that skill.
- Skills defined as *performance* can be evaluated by student peers. The quantitative nature of performance objectives makes evaluation by peers effective. One way to prevent problems in recording scores is to permit peer evaluation up to and including a B, with final A grades observed by you.
- Bring each student's program to class each day. Provide the student with a second copy to take home.
- Let students pick up their sheets as soon as they come to class and begin practice, or use the individual program sheets to take attendance.
- Make the formative evaluation system ongoing, meaning that a student can be marked at any time.
- Permit unlimited testing opportunities to condition students to your presence and to facilitate their confidence and concentration (continual assessment and feedback increases motivation, reduces discipline problems, and also appears to alleviate nervousness about being evaluated).
- Implement a formal summative evaluation during the last few classes. Tell students at the beginning of the unit that this will be given as the last evaluation opportunity. Some students will have completed their programs and can be given the option of playing in games or helping you with the final testing.

Individual Programs: Their Design and Management in the Public School Setting

The following strategies are helpful in using individualized programs in the public school setting.

- Because class sizes are usually large, facilities limited, and the number of instructors few, design the program to include only *four to six* objectives per grade or year.
- When selecting the skills and concepts for evaluation, include four to six *different* objectives each year, so that over the course of junior high experience, for example Grades 7 through 9, the student has worked on 18 or more objectives for *each* activity.
- Select performance objectives that can be practiced *outside* of the normal physical education class, in intramural or club settings, as a part of a team, at home, or in the community center. Performance objectives should permit self-testing and can involve friends, teammates, parents, brothers, or sisters.

Individual Programs: Their Design and Use in the Coaching Setting

The format and procedure is similar to that explained above except that

- the program should be designed after a thorough analysis of each athlete by the coaching staff;
- the athlete should be involved in the planning and setting up of the program;
- each program should contain a few items, with goals to be attained in a manageable amount of time; and
- you should design programs that can be practiced outside of regular training times.

Application 7: The ActionMark Software Program

ActionMark is a software program derived from the eight modules of the KS Model. It is presented to show how knowledge-based instructional design can be applied to the medium of computer and videodisc technology. ActionMark is designed to assist teachers and coaches in school, club, and university settings by using the

Sample Individual Program

INDIVIDUAL COURSE IN Archery

GRADE/COURSE SECTION Beginning

STUDENT'S NAME

STUDENT ID #

SKILLS/CONCEPTS	TECHNIQUE AND PERFORMANCE OBJECTIVES	WT* ×	POINT PROGRESS** 1	2	3	4	FINAL SCORE*** =
1 Stance Technique	Straddles line; weight even, consistent position; aligned with target; body erect	1.0					
2 Nocking Technique	Arrow oriented correctly, against nock locator	1.0					
3 Bow Hand and Arm Technique	Consistent hand placement; handle in V of hand; hand relaxed; elbow rotated	1.0					
4 Draw Technique	3-finger hook; back of draw hand flat, relaxed; elbow back first; elbow at shoulder level; shoulders level, aligned to target	1.5					
5 Anchor Technique	Positioned properly; consistent; teeth together; kisser button positioned	1.0					
6 Aim Technique	Bow level; correct eye used; string aligned; archer settles and holds	1.0					
7 Release Technique	By relaxing hook; head steady; bow hand and arm steady	1.5					
8 Follow-Through Technique	Head steady; bow arm up and toward target; draw hand over rear shoulder	1.5					
9 Basic Shooting Form Performance (Step 4)	Number out of 18 arrows landing on 2 ft × 2 ft paper from 10 yds (without sight)	1.0	6	10	14	18	
10 Improved Shooting Form Performance (Step 5)	Score for 4 six-arrow ends at 80-cm 10-ring target from 10 yds (without sight)	1.0	48	96	144	192	

#	Objective	Description	WT				
11	Sight Shooting Performance (Step 7)	Score for 4 six-arrow ends at 80-cm 10-ring target from 20 yds (with sight)	1.0	48	96	144	192
12	Individualized Form Performance (Step 11)	Score for 4 six-arrow ends shot at 80-cm 10-ring target from each distance: 30, 20, 10 yds	1.5	144	288	432	576
13	Tournament Shooting Performance (Step 14)	Modified Metric 900 Round (Step 14, Drill 1)	1.5	180	360	540	720
14	Tournament Shooting Performance (Step 14)	Modified Interscholastic Metric Round (Step 14, Drill 2)	1.5	144	288	432	576
15	Error Analysis Technique	Identification of likely errors through arrow pattern analysis	1.5				
16	Mental Approach	Concentrates; maintains relaxation	1.0				
17	Goal Setting	Ability to set realistic goals; confident of attaining goals	1.0				
18	Written Exam	Value = 20%					

TOTAL = 100%

*WT = Weighting of an objective's degree of difficulty.

**PROGRESS = Ongoing success, which may be expressed in terms of (a) accumulated points (1, 2, 3, 4); (b) grades (D, C, B, A); (c) symbols (merit, bronze, silver, gold); (d) unsatisfactory/satisfactory; and others as desired.

***FINAL SCORE equals WT times PROGRESS.

Figure M8.12. Sample individual program for archery (Haywood & Lewis, 1989b). Reprinted by permission.

Sample Individual Program

INDIVIDUAL COURSE IN Golf

STUDENT'S NAME

GRADE/COURSE SECTION Beginning

STUDENT ID #

I. DEMONSTRATED BY PHYSICAL SKILLS

Skill	TECHNIQUE AND PERFORMANCE OBJECTIVES	WT* ×	POINT PROGRESS**				= FINAL SCORE***
			1	2	3	4	
Full Swing	*Technique:* Number out of 10 demonstrating 75% or more of the items on the checklist.	10%	3	4	5	6+	
	Performance: Number out of 10 hit from a tee with an iron of choice. A minimum of 125 yards in length with a maximum of 25 yards off target at final resting point.	10%	3	4	5	6+	
Pitch	*Technique:* Number out of 10 demonstrating 75% or more items on checklist.	5%	3	4	5	6+	
	Performance: Number out of 10 hit from 40 yards away into an area with 6 yard radius using a 9-iron, PW, or SW.	5%	3	4	5	6+	
Chip	*Technique:* Number out of 10 demonstrating 80% or more items on checklist.	5%	5	6	7	8+	
	Performance: Number out of 10 hit from 20 yards into an area with 4 yard radius with a 7-, 8-, or 9-iron.	5%	4	5	6	7+	
Putt	*Technique:* Number out of 10 demonstrating 80% or more items on checklist.	5%	5	6	7	8+	
	Performance: Number out of 10 hit into cup from 3 feet away.	5%	4	5	6	7+	
Sand Shot	*Technique:* Number out of 10 demonstrating 75% or more items on checklist.	2%	3	4	5	6+	
	Performance: Number out of 10 hit out of sand from 35 yards away into an area with a 10 yard radius with a SW.	2%	3	4	5	6+	
Uneven Lies	*Technique:* Number out of 10 demonstrating 75% or more items on checklist.	2%	3	4	5	6+	
	Performance: Select 1 of 4 uneven lies. Number out of 10 hit in the direction of the target.	2%	3	4	5	6+	

Shot Selection and Course Management	*Technique:* Effectively plan 80% of shots for 4 holes on a golf course.	1.5%	5	6	7	8+
Use of Routine	*Technique:* Number out of 10 demonstrating routine in order of items on checklist.	2.5%	5	6	7	8+
	Performance: Number of routines out of 10 with proper sequence and alignment.	2.5%	5	6	7	8+
Attentional Control	*Technique:* Number out of 10 demonstrating full attention to pre-shot routine and execution.	1.5%	5	6	7	8+

SUBTOTAL PHYSICAL SKILLS = 66%

II. DEMONSTRATED BY COGNITIVE MEANS

Goal Setting	*Performance:* Number out of 10 goals written that meet the checklist criteria.	5%	5	6	7	8+
Etiquette	*Performance:* Number out of 10 correct answers on questions regarding etiquette.	8%	6	7	8	9+
Rules	*Performance:* Number out of 10 correct answers on questions regarding golf rules.	8%	6	7	8	9+
Mental Control	*Performance:* Number out of 10 examples of thought stoppage including self-enhancing statement substitutions.	5%	5	6	7	8+
Mechanics of Golf Swing	*Performance:* Number out of 10 correct answers on questions regarding techniques (mechanics) of golf swing.	8%	5	6	7	8+

SUBTOTAL COGNITIVE = 34%

TOTAL = 100%

*WT = Weighting of an objective's degree of difficulty.

**PROGRESS = Ongoing success, which may be expressed in terms of (a) accumulated points (1, 2, 3, 4); (b) grades (D, C, B, A); (c) symbols (merit, bronze, silver, gold); (d) unsatisfactory/satisfactory; and others as desired.

***FINAL SCORE equals WT times PROGRESS.

Figure M8.13.   Sample individual program for golf (Owens & Bunker, 1989b). Reprinted by permission.

computer as a vehicle for (a) presenting a comprehensive knowledge base in the activity as derived from the KS Model, (b) letting coaches and teachers select from this knowledge base to develop a unit or course in a sport or physical activity for a specific class or team, (c) communicating to students what is to be taught, and (d) facilitating evaluation and feedback. The ActionMark design, derived from the eight modules of the KS Model, shows how knowledge-based instructional design can be applied to the medium of computer and videodisc technology. ActionMark runs on a Macintosh computer; it has been tested in badminton, ice hockey, and physical fitness.

ActionMark Functions

ActionMark has a wide range of functions:

- It comes complete with a knowledge structure for each sport or activity as identified in Modules 1 through 7.
- Skills, strategies, and concepts are derived from a hierarchical knowledge structure developed for each sport or activity.
- The knowledge structure is presented as a list, permitting the user to scroll through the components and set a scope and sequence for a pretest, course, unit, training program, season plan or to meet individual needs.
- Each skill, strategy, and concept identified in the knowledge structure has associated with it a progression of objectives, listed from novice to elite, with evaluation levels recommended for each objective.
- The instructor may accept the objectives as presented or tailor instruction by varying the weight of an objective or setting performance standards more appropriate for the context and the student athletes.
- The student interface has been designed to function in a gymnasium or other facility where instruction, practice, and/or play is occurring. Only one computer is necessary for a class of 20 students.
- Students input their own scores, as earned in the performance and technical objectives.
- Improvement in each skill, strategy, or concept is facilitated through a formative evaluation system. Improvement is communicated to each student, as is his or her progress in the program relative to the class.

- ActionMark comes with banks of questions for designing tests in rules, techniques, and/or strategies. These questions are designed to be answered in the gymnasium environment.
- ActionMark maintains a record of all scores and provides printouts for students, teachers, and parents.
- A videodisc interface can be included with the program, making it possible to show visual examples of selected skills, strategies, and concepts.
- The user can add components to the knowledge base and change those included as desired.

ActionMark allows you to design a unit or course of instruction to reflect skill level and available time. It also encourages the development of technical skill as it creates a dialogue between you and your students on the technical, biomechanical, and performance aspects of each skill. ActionMark lets you easily incorporate tests into your daily teaching and can foster individualized teaching, with students soon involved in practicing different skills and strategies according to personal need. If a videodisc in the activity is available, then you and your students can consult visual examples of skills, strategies, and learning activities.

Setting Up the Knowledge Base

Figure M8.14 shows the computer screen used by a course designer to input the knowledge base for a specific activity into ActionMark. The example shown is from badminton. In the scroll box entitled "Knowledge Structure (List Format)" are listed the components for badminton as shown in Appendix A, but in scrolling format. Any number of skills, strategies, and concepts may be entered, with each being input through the box entitled "Knowledge Structure (List Format)."

Technical and performance objectives are entered next. The weight of each objective may be set to reflect the degree of difficulty. In addition, the number of competence or performance levels may be set. Finally, at the top right of the screen is the "Videodisc Sequence" box. If a videodisc is available for the activity, frame numbers may be entered, enabling students to view clips ac-

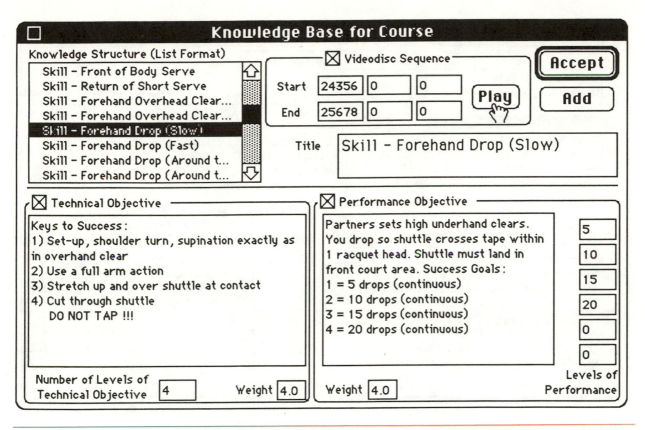

Figure M8.14. Entering the knowledge base into ActionMark.

companying the skills, strategies, and concepts entered.

Entering Student Names and Designing a Course

The computer screen shown in Figure M8.15 is designed to be used by a teacher or coach who is ready to design a learning experience for one or more students. This screen has three functions. First, you can list student names, ID numbers, and other information as shown. Second, you can design specific courses, units, or training programs for students by scrolling through the knowledge base and selecting appropriate objectives. To select an objective, double-click beside it. A selection is highlighted and prefaced by a bullet (•) symbol. Next, activate or deactivate objectives by clicking the "Use Technical Objective" and "Use Performance Objective" boxes at the bottom of the screen. This allows you to enter or delete specific items for particular students to work on. An empty histo-

gram/bar graph also appears, showing each objective activated. The dual histogram displays the student's score (top bar) and the class average (bottom bar). Finally, this screen serves as an Instructor's Preview screen, as it lets you quickly review each student's progress at any time. Progress is indicated by the light and dark bar graphs, with percentage scores also shown (total value). The "Message Box" can be used to communicate information to and from students, to keep attendance records, and to store data about students.

Designing and Taking Tests

ActionMark permits teachers to design and students to take tests in rules, technique, strategies, and "other" (an open category for miscellaneous questions). In most physical education or activity settings, there are occasions when students are waiting, resting, or otherwise taking turns for an activity. Using the ActionMark bank of multiple-choice questions, teachers and coaches

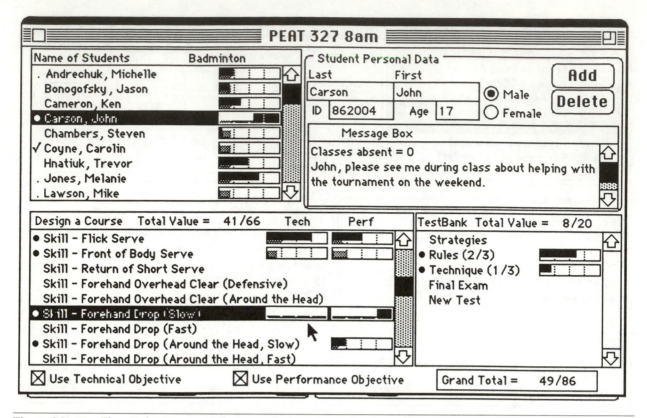

Figure M8.15.   The student name and course design screen for ActionMark.

can set up separate learning stations for testing. The instructor sets the parameters for a test by selecting the type, the number and value of questions, and the number of opportunities a student has to take the test. For example, you may want to set up a station where each student answers five questions from the rules bank. Questions are randomly generated for each student, with questions answered correctly removed from that student's question bank. Students learn their results immediately, and their scores are automatically incorporated into their overall progress reports.

The Student Screen

Figure M8.16 shows the computer screen the student sees. Shown here is the complete program as set by the teacher or coach. All knowledge components with technical and performance objectives are listed, with progress in each shown in the histograms to the right. The top bar shows the student's score and the bottom bar the class average. Described in the

boxes at the bottom of the screen are the specific requirements for each technical and performance objective. The student's progress is recorded by clicking the achievement level on the thermometer (this can be done either by each student or the teacher). At the top is a summary statement summarizing progress to date, both as a raw score and a percentage, and the current class or team average. Notice also the "View" box at the far right; clicking this button will go to a videodisc, thus providing instant visual and auditory learning materials for students.

Application 8: Design of the Steps to Success Activity Series

The planning unit for the Steps to Success Activity Series is the *step*. A step highlights the total presentation of a specific skill, strategy, or concept, from the perspectives of *both* the student athlete and the teacher/coach. For each activity in the series, two books have been

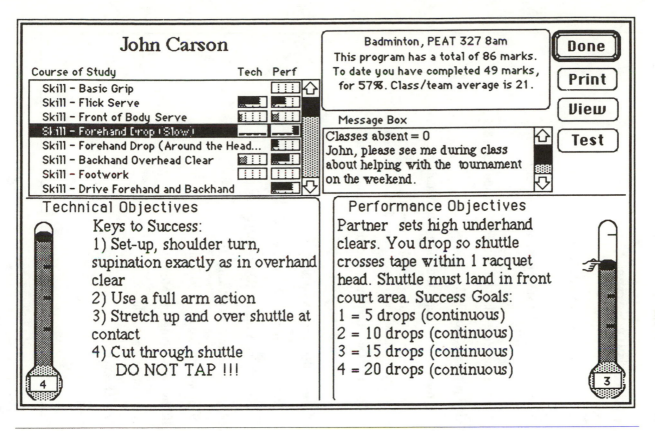

John Carson

Course of Study	Tech	Perf
Skill – Basic Grip		
Skill – Flick Serve		
Skill – Front of Body Serve		
Skill – Forehand Drop (Slow)		
Skill – Forehand Drop (Around the Head...		
Skill – Backhand Overhead Clear		
Skill – Footwork		
Skill – Drive Forehand and Backhand		

Badminton, PEAT 327 8am
This program has a total of 86 marks.
To date you have completed 49 marks,
for 57%. Class/team average is 21.

Message Box

Classes absent = 0
John, please see me during class
about helping with the tournament
on the weekend.

Done   **Print**   **View**   **Test**

Technical Objectives

Keys to Success:
1) Set-up, shoulder turn, supination exactly as in overhand clear
2) Use a full arm action
3) Stretch up and over shuttle at contact
4) Cut through shuttle
   DO NOT TAP !!!

4

Performance Objectives

Partner sets high underhand clears. You drop so shuttle crosses tape within 1 racquet head. Shuttle must land in front court area. Success Goals:
1 = 5 drops (continuous)
2 = 10 drops (continuous)
3 = 15 drops (continuous)
4 = 20 drops (continuous)

3

Figure M8.16. The ActionMark student screen.

written—one for the student learning the sport or activity and the other for the teacher or coach instructing it. Each book is made up of a progression of steps that complement one another. A *step* in the participant's book provides information needed by the student learning the activity; the corresponding step in the instructor's guide provides complementary information vital to the instructor dealing with a group of students. The books are designed to work hand in glove.

The design of the Steps to Success Activity Series resulted from the collaboration of Human Kinetics Publishers, the experts in each of the activities, and the theoretical framework provided by the KS Model. The developmental editor for the series, Dr. Judy Patterson Wright, was instrumental in providing guidelines that facilitated the design of the step. The KS Model provided a theoretical framework that emphasized knowledge-based instructional design, a cross-disciplinary definition for knowledge in teaching sport and physical activity, and the recognition

of the power and effectiveness of expert knowledge. The series authors are all master teachers and coaches who have devoted years to perfecting how best to teach and coach their activities; now they share their knowledge with you.

What Is a Step?

A *step* represents the total presentation of a skill, strategy, or concept from the perspective of both performer and instructor. A progression of *steps* sets out a cohesive plan of instruction. In developing the sequence of steps in each book, knowledge structures were developed for the activities in interviews with the authors. (The specific procedures were similar to those explained in chapters 1 through 4 and Module 1. Then a progression of *steps* was developed following a top-down sequencing strategy (Module 4). Figure M8.17 provides an overview of the design of the participant's book and the instructor's guide.

Design of the Steps to Success Activity Series

Participant's Book

1. The Steps to Success Staircase (Modules 1 through 4)

2. The Game of _____ (Modules 1 and 2)

3. Equipment (Module 2)

4. Preparing Your Body for Success (Module 1)

5. Each Step includes:

   a. Why is the Skill, Strategy, or Concept Important? (Module 1)

   b. How to Execute? (Module 1)

   c. Keys to Success (Module 1)
      • Preparation Phase
      • Execution Phase
      • Follow-Though Phase

   d. Detecting Errors (Module 6)

   e. Drills to Achieve Success (Module 7)

   f. Keys to Success Checklist (Modules 1, 5, and 6)

6. Rating Your Progress (Module 6)

7. Individual Program (Module 8)

Instructor's Guide

1. Implementing The Steps to Success Staircase (Module 2 to 6)

2. Preparing Your Class for Success (Module 2 and 8)

3. Equipment (Module 2)

4. Progression of Steps, with each Step containing:

   a. Criterion for rating beginning level, intermediate level, and advanced level (Module 1 and 6)

   b. Error Detection and Correction (Modules 5 to 7)

   c. Additional Drills (Module 7)

5. Evaluation Ideas (Module 6)

6. Individual Program (Module 6)

7. Knowledge Structure (Overview) (Module 1)

8. Instructional Aids (Module 2)

9. Scope and Sequence (Module 4)

10. Individual Program (Module 8)

11. Lesson Plan (Module 8)

12. References

Figure M8.17.   Instructional design of the participant's book and instructor's guide in the Steps to Success Activity Series.

Participant's Books

The introduction of each participant's book explains the rationale behind the Steps to Success Staircase, in particular that students can learn on their own and progress from step to step through the activity. Each participant's book has a *background knowledge* section that includes the overall purpose of the activity, equipment, rules, a description of the activity today, warm-up and other exercises performed before beginning play, and cool-down as appropriate.

In the participant's books, each *skill, strategy,* or *concept* is introduced by explaining why it is important and how it fits into the context of game play or the whole activity. Following this is a thorough written and graphic description of how each skill, strategy, or concept is to be performed, summarized as a list of technical objectives called Keys to Success and organized into preparation, execution, and follow-through phases. Then comes a section on common errors and how to correct them.

A progression of learning activities follows, designed to help the individual student athlete effectively practice the skill, strategy, or concept. The drills and activities are progressive, with considerable care taken in how they are sequenced and explained. Each drill has a Success Goal for quantitative evaluation of daily performance.

With all basic skills, a list of technique objectives (the Keys to Success Checklist) is presented for qualitative evaluation. This format encourages the student athlete to evaluate both performance (Success Goals) and technique (Keys to Success Checklist) with the aid of an instructor or trained partner.

Instructor's Guides

The instructor's guide helps you implement the KS Model by offering seven procedural questions (representing Modules 1 through 7) for you to answer before following the step sequence (applying the KS Model). The introductory sections give guidelines for preparing your class for success, which includes tips on general class management, class organization techniques, class warm-up and cool-down, essential equipment, safety rules, creating an effective learning environment, and liability obligations.

Each step in the instructor's guide presents a strategy, concept, or skill; for each skill the guide provides a criterion checklist describing the typical characteristics of novice, intermediate, and advanced performers. The instructor's guide goes in-depth into skills analysis and correction (cognitive biomechanics) and identifies many learning activities and drills that are imaginative and have proven effective with groups of learners.

The instructor's guide also provides instructional aids for the teacher, including a knowledge structure overview for each activity; lists of equipment, audiovisual, and media aids; a scope and sequence chart; an individual program; a lesson plan; and a battery of test questions. All of these are designed to support the instructor in both teaching, coaching, and evaluation.

Application 9: The On-Campus Teaching Laboratory

In this final application, I describe an on-campus teaching laboratory in which you can implement the many components of the KS Model. The laboratory provides a realistic teaching environment that has been modified to facilitate your success. Now that you have been introduced to the different components of the KS Model and the Steps to Success Activity Series, it is your task to plan and deliver a complete unit of instruction, including evaluation.

The on-campus teaching laboratory places you in a small group (a group of three student teachers is ideal) where you assume total responsibility for teaching public school students who come to the university for instruction. The group's task is to design and teach a complete unit of instruction.

Team teaching is more difficult than teaching alone. The team must decide exactly what each person will teach and how, plus dozens of other issues as you go along. But this is the purpose of the exercise, to open up the teaching process to a dialogue that helps you understand yourself and others better, as both teachers and observers. As one student teacher delivers the lesson, the other two observe, using both subjective and objective methods. After each lesson, a feedback session is held to discuss observations and make suggestions for the next lesson.

By working together as a teaching group, peers help each other deal with the day-to-day realities of teaching. Many of the components of the KS Model are put into action, but in a non-threatening environment where there is time to discuss, analyze, assist one another, and talk issues through from week to week. This experience is also a rich one for public school students as a career experience and field trip, as most have never been in a university or a physical education department before.

Setting Up the Teaching Lab

An effective teaching laboratory can be created on-campus by bringing upper elementary, junior, or senior high students to the university for a one-hour class, once a week for 9 weeks. The optimum teaching arrangement is groups of three, with each student teacher delivering three lessons and observing six (one student teaches while two observe). An optimal class size is 10 to 16 students, except in high-risk situations such as climbing or kayaking, where the ratio should be no more than 6 to 1.

The on-campus teaching laboratory allows professors and supervisors the opportunity to see you teach before you go out to the schools. Let's look at a specific example. Two buses can bring approximately 110 students to your university or college each week. Ten 50-minute lessons can be scheduled, with 10 student teachers teaching and 20 observing each day. The public school teachers who come with the students can rove from class to class observing. However, the emphasis in the lab is on the student teachers assuming responsibility for the entire experience—planning, teaching, observation, discipline, evaluation, and liaison with public school teachers.

Student teachers should choose from a selection of appropriate activities. An appropriate activity is one for which there are adequate facilities and is also on the list of approved activities by the local school board or authorities. For example, a single gym can accommodate two to four activities at once (e.g., basketball, volleyball, wrestling, badminton); a utility room can accommodate dance and combative activities; pools can accommodate swimming, diving, kayaking, and snorkeling. A climbing wall is a big favorite (be sure the instructor is certified, work laterally, and keep the students below the 6-foot mark). Outdoor tennis courts, playing fields for orienteering and backpacking, squash and racquetball courts, and sport science labs for fitness and biomechanics units are additional possibilities.

Observation Methods

One of the keys to the success of the laboratory is the use of established observation techniques; you need to know both objective and subjective methods. Objective methods should be used first, because it is easier for peers to share and discuss this type of information with one another than subjective types. Subjective methods should be introduced after objective methods have been mastered, and then used in combination with objective methods. During the 2 weeks before the first laboratory class, you should become familiar with the categories on the observation form shown in Figure M8.18. Practice by observing a videotape of a class and then a live class.

Using the Observer Form

Figure M8.18 shows 12 basic observation categories.

Before beginning an observation session, fill out the top of the form. It is especially important to record the beginning and ending times of the lesson, because most calculations involve total class time. Your observation should begin when the teacher assumes control of the students within the instructional space. During the first two practice sessions, divide the categories with a partner. Over time, however, you should learn to observe in all categories at once.

1. Management Time. The management time category tells how much time is spent on events that are not directly related to presentation of the subject matter or content of the lesson (Siedentop, 1976). Typical management events in a lesson include starting class, taking roll, checking uniforms, making announcements, moving students from one formation or drill to another, fielding disruptions, disciplining, setting up and taking down equipment, and ending class.

To observe:

Record the number of seconds the student teacher spends on *each* management event.

TEACHING LABORATORY

OBSERVER FORM

Teacher's Name _____

Activity _____

Observer's Name _____

Date _____

Total Class Min _____ Beginning Time _____ Ending Time _____

Categories	Goal	Data Per Event	Total
1. Management Time	30 sec/episode, or 10% of total		
2. Managerial Prompts	1/1 ratio		
3. Instructional Time (Group)	15-30%		
4. Active Student Time (Group)	60-75%		
5. Teacher-Student Instructional Interactions	Jr. 2-3/min Sr. 1/mn		
6. Other Positive Interactions, Nonverbal & Verbal	Jr. 2-3/min Sr. 1/min		
7. All Negative Interactions Nonverbal & Verbal			

(Cont.)

Figure M8.18. The teaching laboratory observer form.

8. Placheks   95% Active

9. Voice   Projection
                                            Speed
                                            Detractors

10. Teaching Style   Command
                                            Practice
                                            Reciprocal

11. Other Suggestions

12. Constructive Advice for Next Session

1.

2.

TEACHER'S REPORT FROM PEER OBSERVER FEEDBACK SESSION

Notes:

Figure M8.18. Continued.

To determine lesson score:

1. Add up all times and divide by the number of events to get the average number of seconds used per managerial event.
2. Determine the percentage of management time by dividing the minutes of management time by total class minutes. For example, if class is 40 minutes and management time was 240 seconds (4 minutes), management time was 10% (4 ÷ 40).

Management time goal:

30 seconds per event, or 10% of total time in class

2. Managerial Prompts.   Managerial prompts are the number of times the teacher verbally prompts students in achieving a single goal, such as setting up equipment (Siedentop, 1976). A perfect ratio is 1:1 (one prompt:one event), the teacher gave only one verbal prompt for each management event.

To observe:

Note the number of verbal prompts the student teacher uses to accomplish *each* recorded management event.

To determine lesson score:

Divide the total number of verbal prompts (for all management events) by the number of events. For example, if in a complete lesson the teacher gave 30 directions for 6 events, the ratio is 5:1 (30 ÷ 6).

Management prompts goal:

1:1 is spectacular; 2:1 is very good

3. Instructional Time (Group).   Each occasion that instruction is given by a teacher to the group about the subject matter of the lesson is defined as an instructional event (Siedentop, 1976).

To observe:

Record by instructional event and in minutes and seconds the time the teacher spends teaching subject matter to the group as a whole.

To determine lesson score:

1. Divide the total time for group instruction by the number of instructional events to determine the number of seconds or minutes used per instructional event.
2. Determine the percentage of instructional time by dividing the minutes of instructional time by class minutes.

For example, if instructional time was 10 minutes and class is 40 minutes, instructional time is 25% (10 ÷ 40).

Instructional time (group) goal:

This will vary within a unit. Lessons at the beginning of a unit often have more group instruction time than those at the end, when students may be involved in individual practice and play. A range of 20% to 30% is normal.

4. Active Student Time (Group).   The time that students are physically active and working on the assigned tasks as a group (Siedentop, 1976) is classified as active student time (group).

To observe:

Record by event and in minutes and seconds the amount of time the class spends in physical activity as a group. All students must be moving or active for time to be recorded.

To determine lesson score:

1. Divide total activity time by the number of activity events.
2. Determine the percentage of active student (group) time by dividing the minutes of active time by the class minutes. For example, if active time was 20 minutes and class is 40 minutes, then the percentage is 50% (20 ÷ 40).

Active student (group) time goal:

Between 60% and 70%, except in activities such as wrestling and gymnastics, where it will be less.

The calculations for management time, instructional time, and activity time give the simplest overview of time utilization available for a physical education class. Their sum should total 100% of class time. Far more sophisticated observation systems are available, but this one is easy to use and gives students an immediate idea of their time utilization. Graph your times as a histogram (see Figure M8.19) after each lesson to see how your time utilization is changing. For example, Figure M8.19 shows that in Lesson 1, management events consumed more than 40% of class time and instruction an additional

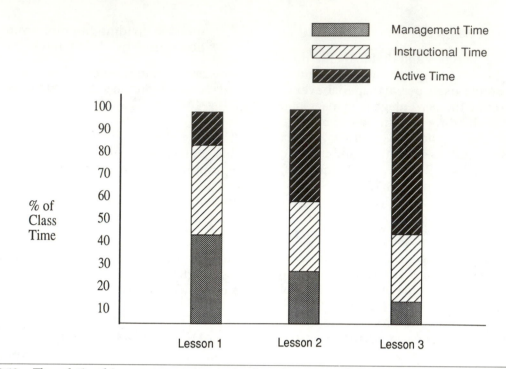

Figure M8.19. The relationships among management time, instructional time, and activity time for three lessons.

40%, leaving less than 20% of class time for physical activity. This type of balance often leads to problems with student discipline and motivation. But by Lesson 3, only 10% of time was spent on management and 30% on instruction, leaving 60% of class time for activity. The profile in Lesson 3 is the one you should try to achieve.

5. Teacher–Student Instructional Interactions. Teachers interact with students as individuals or in small groups about the subject matter of the class can involve skills analysis, correction, interpretation, reteaching, and review.

To observe:

Record the number of times the student teacher interacts with students individually or in a small group about the subject matter of the class.

To determine lesson score:

Determine the average number of interactions per minute by dividing the total number of interactions by the number of class minutes.

Teacher-student instructional goals:

2 to 3 interactions per minute for elementary and junior high students; 1 per minute for high school students

6. Other Positive Interactions. Any positive interactions that are not directly related to the subject matter being taught fall into this category.

To observe:

Record all positive interactions that are not instructional in nature.

To determine lesson score:

Determine the average number of other positive interactions per minute by dividing the total number of interactions by the number of class minutes.

Other positive interactions goals:

2 to 3 interactions per minute for elementary and junior high students; 1 per minute for high school students

7. Negative Interactions. A negative interaction, which can be verbal or nonverbal, is defined as one in which the objective of the class is lost, with a breakdown in communication and trust occurring between teacher and student. Negative interactions can be a challenge to define and manage. Observers should spend a considerable amount of time discussing this, and agree upon what is to be considered a negative interaction.

To observe:

Record each negative interaction, describing briefly what occurred.

To determine lesson score:

Determine the average number of negative interactions per minute by dividing the number of interactions by the number of class minutes.

8. Plachek. A plachek is defined (Siedentop, 1976) as a record of a teacher's ability to keep students on task throughout the class.

To observe:

1. Establish the frequency for conducting placheks (such as every 5 minutes); at each interval, scan the whole class from one side to the other for approximately 10 seconds.
2. Record the number of students off task and note their behavior.
3. Be sure to take measures only at predetermined times. Resist the temptation to take a plachek when you see students off task.

To determine lesson score:

Determine a percentage plachek score by totaling the number of students off task, obtain an average, and compare this to the number of studies in the class. For example, if a class has 20 students and 2 are off task on each plachek, then the overall plachek is 90%.

Plachek goal:

95% of the students on task throughout the whole class.

9. Voice. The following are important considerations:

- Projection (whether all students can hear)
- Speed (speaking too fast or too slow; giving students enough time to be attentive)
- Detractors (using repetitive expressions—ah, ok, now)

To observe:

Record observations about voice projection and speaking speed. Record types of detractors and the number of times they are used. Take note during the feedback session whether the student teacher also uses the detractor in a small-group discussion (if not, it may be a problem limited to large-group teaching).

10. Teaching Styles. Mosston's Spectrum of teaching styles helps teachers vary their teaching manner. The first three styles in the spectrum should be emphasized initially and are command, practice, and reciprocal. In command style, the teacher is in control of all events and instruction is to the group with everyone doing the same thing at the same time. In practice style, students are taught via a command style, but divide into smaller groups for practice and play. In the reciprocal style, students work in pairs; one performs what has been taught via the command and practice style while a peer observes and provides assistance. (See Mosston, [1972, 1986] for more information.)

To observe:

Record events that determine the style or styles being used. Be specific (for example, "When giving instruction on the set shot you used a direct, command style; you used a reciprocal style by dividing the students into threes for practice and feedback.").

Teaching styles goal:

To be aware of which style a teacher is using. To vary one's own style of teaching to better enable students to attain objectives.

11. Constructive Suggestions. Give no more than two constructive suggestions (ones that are realistic for the student teacher to accomplish in the next class).

Verbalizing the Lesson

The day before a lesson, the student teacher verbalizes it to the peer observers, to both prepare the observers and help the student teacher rehearse the phases of the lesson. Through this process corrections can be made and thought through. Observers should try to contribute reasonable suggestions for improving the lesson plan.

Class Day

The observers are not to become involved directly in the class except in an emergency. After the lesson is taught, the observers take 15 minutes to compile their results and then meet with the student teacher and go over each category. The course instructor should listen, directing any questions to the observers only. If asked a question, the instructor should respond to an observer, who then relays the information to the student teacher. (This is a reciprocal teaching strategy [Mosston, 1972] that keeps the observer's role at the forefront.)

The Written Report

You will end the laboratory experience by compiling a report on the classes that you taught, including the original lesson plans, the original observer reports, and the notes taken during each feedback session. These documents must be included because they form the basis for the report and are used in evaluating both student teachers and observers.

The report is done as a laboratory report. Graph the data for quantitative categories (management time, instructional time, activity time) and discuss each category and the time allocation changes (see Figure M8.19). For remaining subjective categories, discuss the observers' points. Conclude your report by discussing your perceived strengths and weaknesses.

Evaluation Criteria for the Teacher

The on-campus teaching laboratory should provide an atmosphere where you feel free to try out many of the components of the KS Model and to test your own goals and aspirations. You should expect to demonstrate the following as a student teacher:

- The ability to prepare a lesson plan following the guidelines in Module 8, and be thoroughly and professionally prepared for each lesson. (Teaching performance will improve given time and a secure environment in which to overcome nervousness.)
- The ability to explain your lesson plan to observers. (Students who find it difficult to describe their lessons often have not thought them through thoroughly. The preclass verbalization process helps more than any other factor to prevent problems during the class.)
- The ability to accept constructive advice from peers and adjust the lesson plan as warranted.
- Demonstrate proper conduct, including equipment and space management, appropriate dress, diplomacy, use of time, and interaction with the public school teachers.
- The ability to participate positively in the debriefing sessions, accepting advice and reflecting it in the next lesson plan as warranted.
- The ability to prepare a self-analysis for each lesson to answer three questions: (a) What did I do well? (b) How can I make these a permanent part of my teaching? and (c) What two things do I need to improve on, and how will I accomplish these in the next lesson?

Evaluation Criteria for the Observers

The observer's role is vital for two reasons: First, student teachers learn a lot about teaching by formally observing others in a realistic setting. Second, an observer must communicate, which is an important part of becoming a good teacher.

As an observer you should demonstrate the following:

- Mastery of the observation categories and the ability to record accurately, independently, and without disrupting the class.
- The ability to listen to a student teacher's lesson and to offer reasonable suggestions constructively.
- The ability to analyze results and draw up a composite report with a partner in 15 minutes.
- The ability to review each observation category with the student teacher in a constructive and supportive way.
- The ability to reflect on what has been observed and measured and to make realistic suggestions for improvement.

Conclusion

I have emphasized in this book the importance of being knowledgeable about what you teach. Teaching and coaching physical activity has an incredibly rich and challenging knowledge base, encompassing many disciplines and facets of human endeavor. Knowledge has been emphasized because it provides a never-ending world of stimulation and growth and allows the teacher to experiment, to challenge, and to welcome change. Perhaps as you exhibit these characteristics in your teaching, your student athletes will model through your example. I hope the KS Model helps you in this process and that you are able to chart new paths and meet new challenges every day.

Let knowledge grow from more to more
But more of reverence in us dwell;
That mind and soul, according well,
May make one music as before.
—Alfred Lord Tennyson

Knowledge Structure of Badminton

The following badminton structure was developed by a colleague, David Brecht, and me. Text analysis and stimulated recall were used in developing the structure, along with extensive co-teaching and observation of one another's teaching in a university course environment. The following structure has been used in beginning and advanced university badminton courses of 20 to 30 hours. The majority of enrolled students will one day be teaching in schools or coaching at interscholastic and club levels. The principles underlying the creation of this structure are elaborated in chapters 1 through 4 and in Module 1. The badminton structure is representative of structures designed for instructional settings. To be used in coaching, the physiological training and conditioning section would need to be more thoroughly developed, and advanced strategies would need to be added.

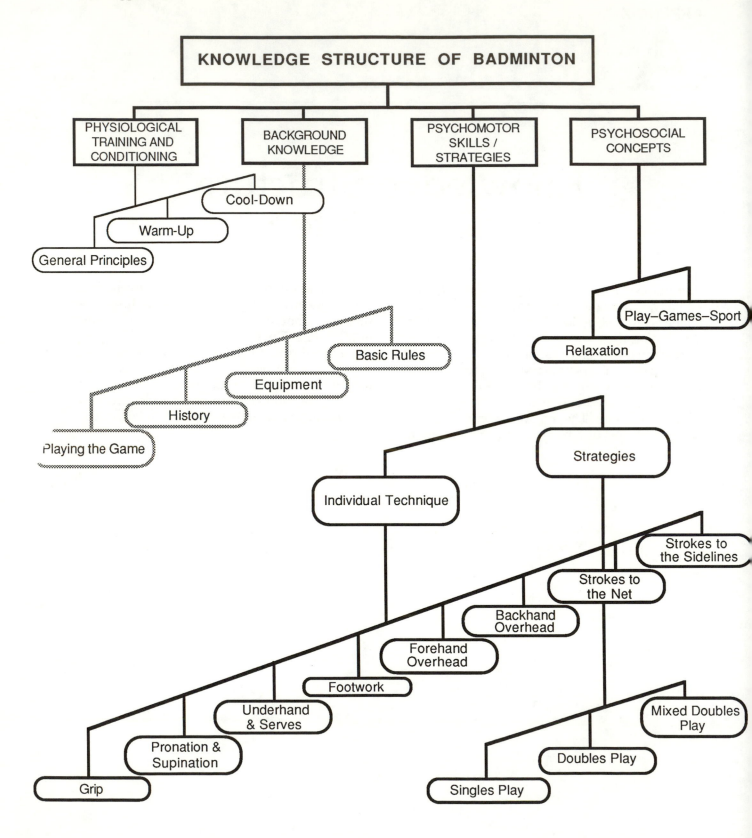

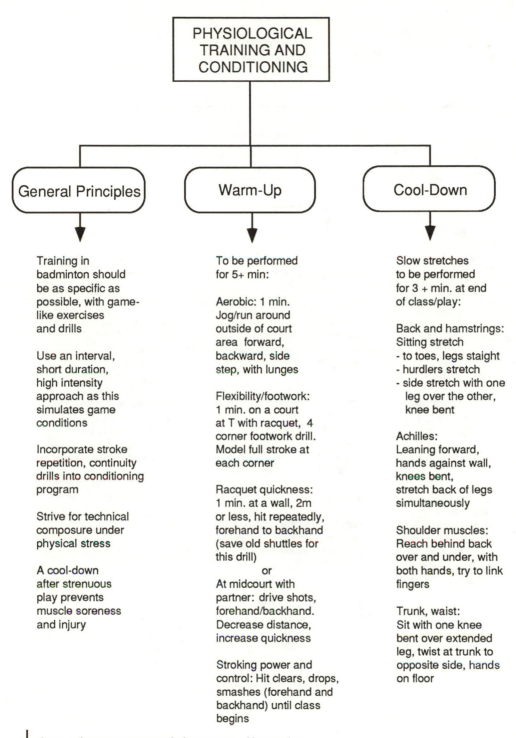

PHYSIOLOGICAL
TRAINING AND
CONDITIONING

General Principles

Warm-Up

Cool-Down

Training in
badminton should
be as specific as
possible, with game-
like exercises
and drills

Use an interval,
short duration,
high intensity
approach as this
simulates game
conditions

Incorporate stroke
repetition, continuity
drills into conditioning
program

Strive for technical
composure under
physical stress

A cool-down
after strenuous
play prevents
muscle soreness
and injury

To be performed
for 5+ min:

Aerobic: 1 min.
Jog/run around
outside of court
area forward,
backward, side
step, with lunges

Flexibility/footwork:
1 min. on a court
at T with racquet, 4
corner footwork drill.
Model full stroke at
each corner

Racquet quickness:
1 min. at a wall, 2m
or less, hit repeatedly,
forehand to backhand
(save old shuttles for
this drill)
or
At midcourt with
partner: drive shots,
forehand/backhand.
Decrease distance,
increase quickness

Stroking power and
control: Hit clears, drops,
smashes (forehand and
backhand) until class
begins

Slow stretches
to be performed
for 3 + min. at end
of class/play:

Back and hamstrings:
Sitting stretch
- to toes, legs staight
- hurdlers stretch
- side stretch with one
  leg over the other,
  knee bent

Achilles:
Leaning forward,
hands against wall,
knees bent,
stretch back of legs
simultaneously

Shoulder muscles:
Reach behind back
over and under, with
both hands, try to link
fingers

Trunk, waist:
Sit with one knee
bent over extended
leg, twist at trunk to
opposite side, hands
on floor

Arrows denote recommended sequence of instruction.
An ascending or descending order may be used. This is a personal choice.

References: Noble, 1986; Breen & Paup, 1983; Grice, 1981.

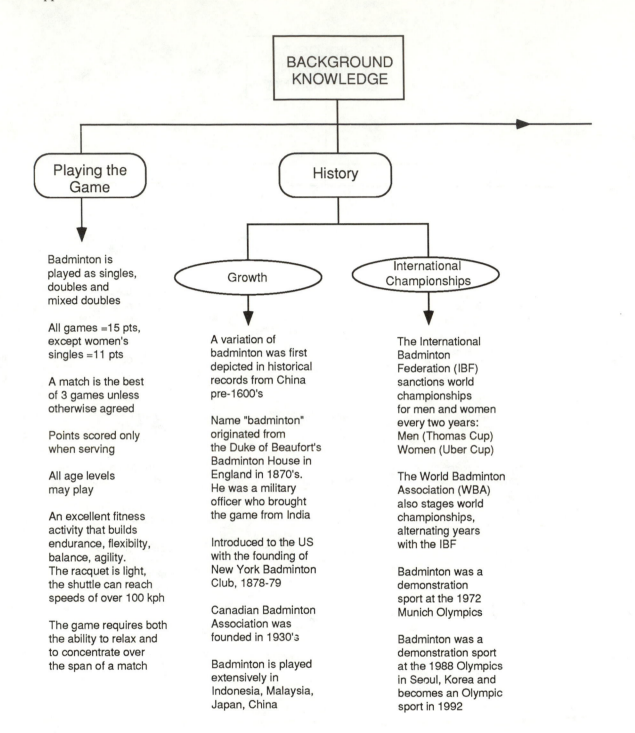

BACKGROUND KNOWLEDGE

Playing the Game

Badminton is played as singles, doubles and mixed doubles

All games =15 pts, except women's singles =11 pts

A match is the best of 3 games unless otherwise agreed

Points scored only when serving

All age levels may play

An excellent fitness activity that builds endurance, flexibilty, balance, agility. The racquet is light, the shuttle can reach speeds of over 100 kph

The game requires both the ability to relax and to concentrate over the span of a match

History

Growth

A variation of badminton was first depicted in historical records from China pre-1600's

Name "badminton" originated from the Duke of Beaufort's Badminton House in England in 1870's. He was a military officer who brought the game from India

Introduced to the US with the founding of New York Badminton Club, 1878-79

Canadian Badminton Association was founded in 1930's

Badminton is played extensively in Indonesia, Malaysia, Japan, China

International Championships

The International Badminton Federation (IBF) sanctions world championships for men and women every two years: Men (Thomas Cup) Women (Uber Cup)

The World Badminton Association (WBA) also stages world championships, alternating years with the IBF

Badminton was a demonstration sport at the 1972 Munich Olympics

Badminton was a demonstration sport at the 1988 Olympics in Seoul, Korea and becomes an Olympic sport in 1992

References: Breen & Paup, 1983; Grice, 1981.

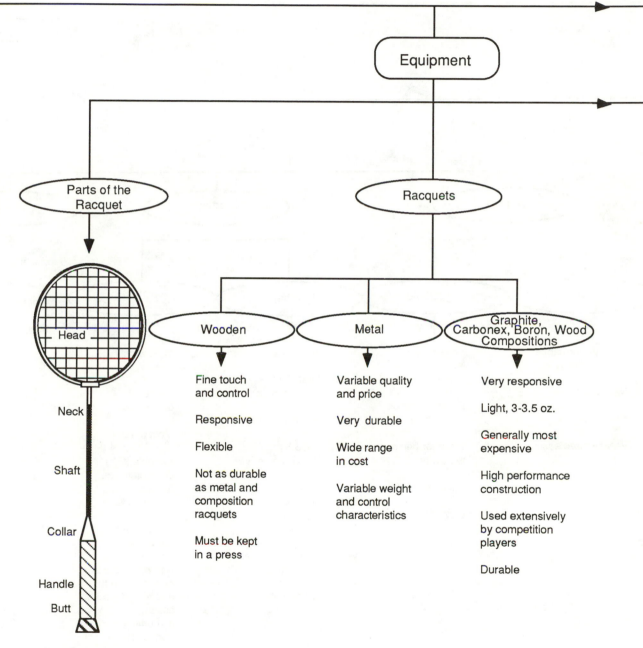

Equipment

Parts of the Racquet

Racquets

Head

Neck

Shaft

Collar

Handle

Butt

Overall length cannot exceed 680 mm (26.8") and width of head 230 mm (9.1")

Wooden

Fine touch and control

Responsive

Flexible

Not as durable as metal and composition racquets

Must be kept in a press

Metal

Variable quality and price

Very durable

Wide range in cost

Variable weight and control characteristics

Graphite, Carbonex, Boron, Wood Compositions

Very responsive

Light, 3-3.5 oz.

Generally most expensive

High performance construction

Used extensively by competition players

Durable

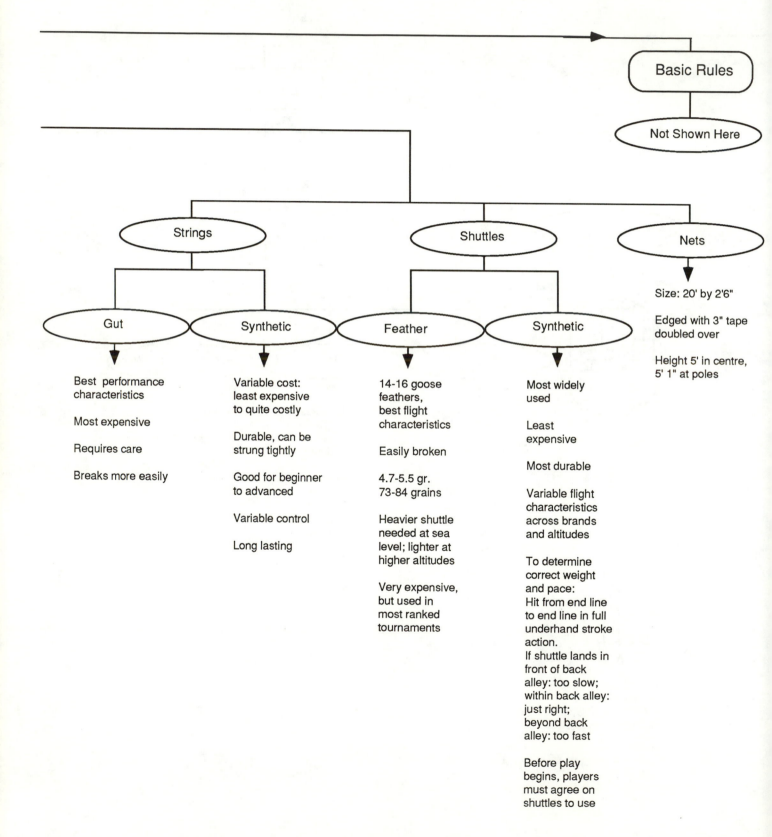

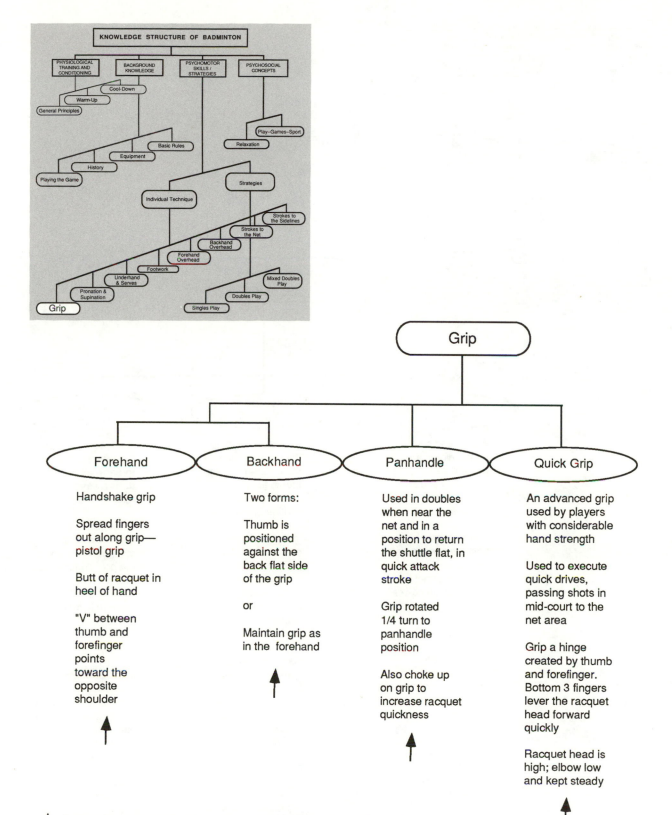

Grip

Forehand	Backhand	Panhandle	Quick Grip
Handshake grip	Two forms:	Used in doubles when near the net and in a position to return the shuttle flat, in quick attack stroke	An advanced grip used by players with considerable hand strength
Spread fingers out along grip—pistol grip	Thumb is positioned against the back flat side of the grip		Used to execute quick drives, passing shots in mid-court to the net area
Butt of racquet in heel of hand	or	Grip rotated 1/4 turn to panhandle position	
"V" between thumb and forefinger points toward the opposite shoulder	Maintain grip as in the forehand	Also choke up on grip to increase racquet quickness	Grip a hinge created by thumb and forefinger. Bottom 3 fingers lever the racquet head forward quickly
			Racquet head is high; elbow low and kept steady

Arrows denote recommended sequence of instruction, foot to head. An ascending or descending order may be used. This is a personal choice.

References: Badminton Canada, 1989; Bloss & Hales, 1987; Breen & Paup, 1983; Grice, 1981; Vickers & Brecht, 1987.

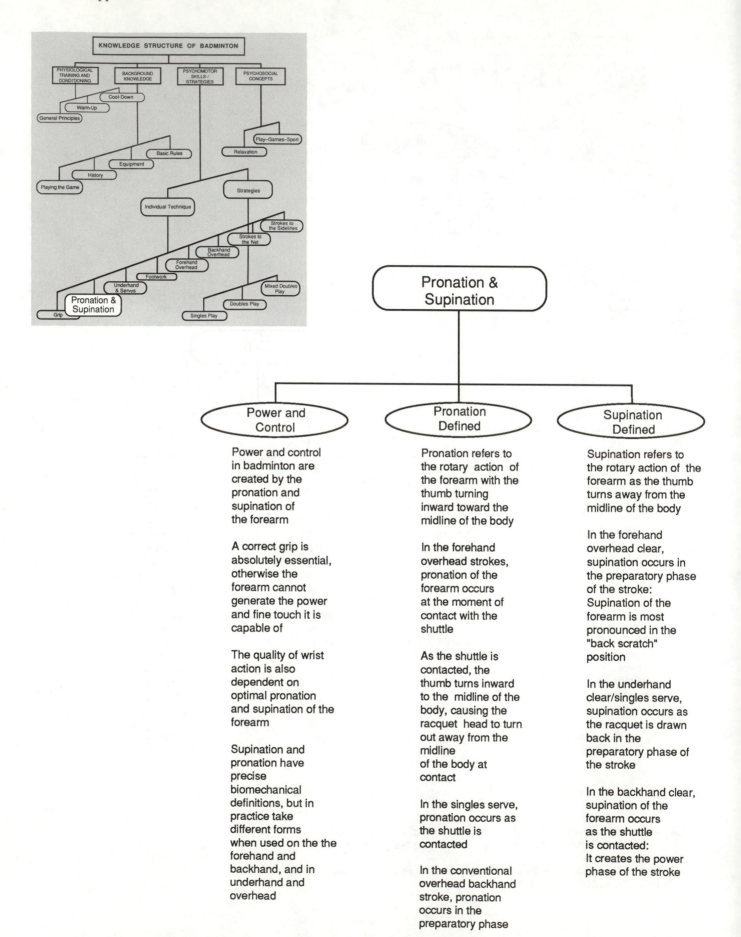

Pronation & Supination

Power and Control

Power and control in badminton are created by the pronation and supination of the forearm

A correct grip is absolutely essential, otherwise the forearm cannot generate the power and fine touch it is capable of

The quality of wrist action is also dependent on optimal pronation and supination of the forearm

Supination and pronation have precise biomechanical definitions, but in practice take different forms when used on the the forehand and backhand, and in underhand and overhead

Pronation Defined

Pronation refers to the rotary action of the forearm with the thumb turning inward toward the midline of the body

In the forehand overhead strokes, pronation of the forearm occurs at the moment of contact with the shuttle

As the shuttle is contacted, the thumb turns inward to the midline of the body, causing the racquet head to turn out away from the midline of the body at contact

In the singles serve, pronation occurs as the shuttle is contacted

In the conventional overhead backhand stroke, pronation occurs in the preparatory phase

Supination Defined

Supination refers to the rotary action of the forearm as the thumb turns away from the midline of the body

In the forehand overhead clear, supination occurs in the preparatory phase of the stroke: Supination of the forearm is most pronounced in the "back scratch" position

In the underhand clear/singles serve, supination occurs as the racquet is drawn back in the preparatory phase of the stroke

In the backhand clear, supination of the forearm occurs as the shuttle is contacted: It creates the power phase of the stroke

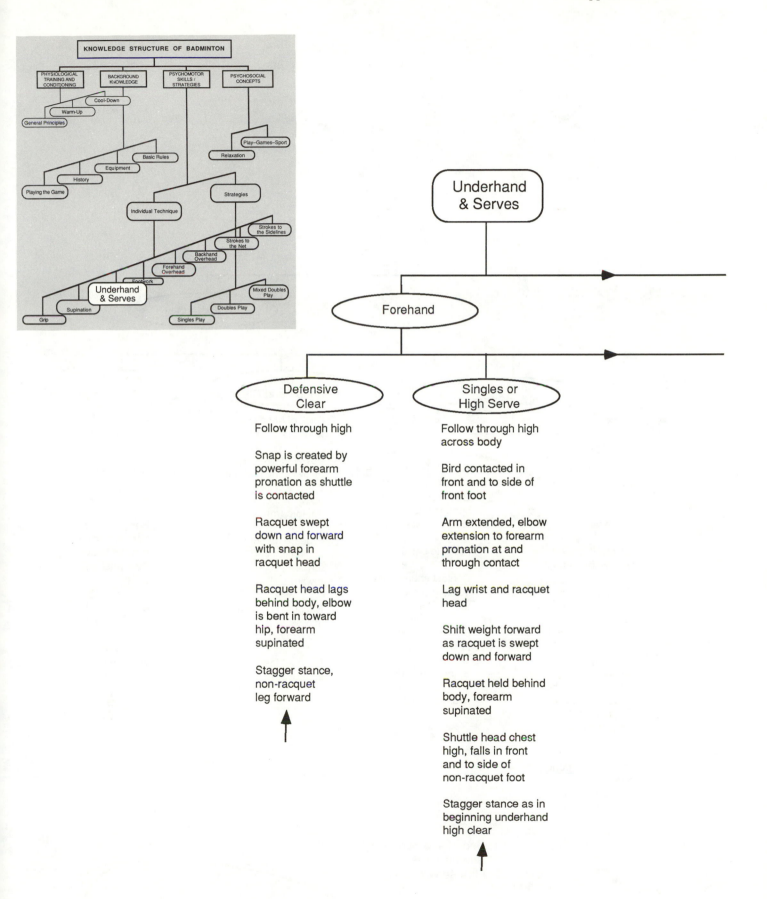

Underhand & Serves

Forehand

Defensive Clear

Follow through high

Snap is created by powerful forearm pronation as shuttle is contacted

Racquet swept down and forward with snap in racquet head

Racquet head lags behind body, elbow is bent in toward hip, forearm supinated

Stagger stance, non-racquet leg forward

Singles or High Serve

Follow through high across body

Bird contacted in front and to side of front foot

Arm extended, elbow extension to forearm pronation at and through contact

Lag wrist and racquet head

Shift weight forward as racquet is swept down and forward

Racquet held behind body, forearm supinated

Shuttle head chest high, falls in front and to side of non-racquet foot

Stagger stance as in beginning underhand high clear

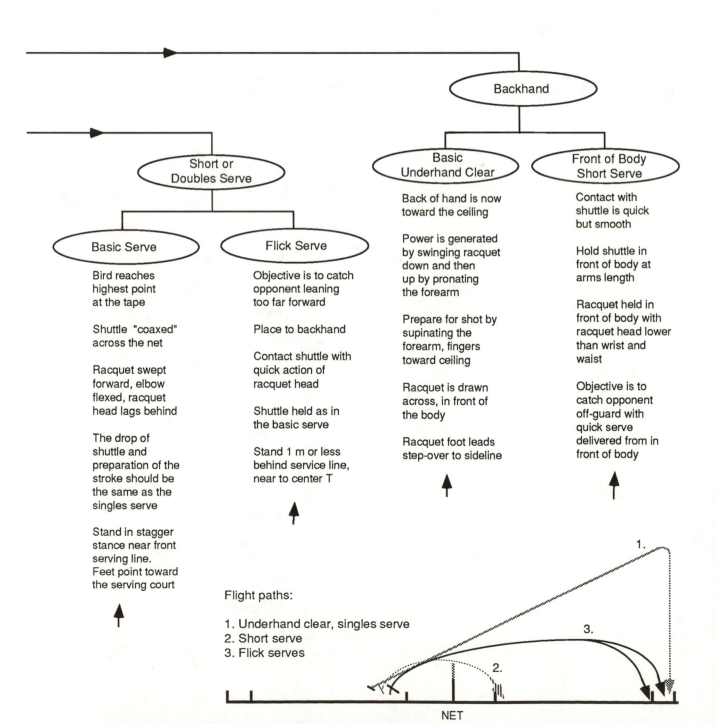

Backhand

Short or
Doubles Serve

Basic
Underhand Clear

Front of Body
Short Serve

Basic Serve

Flick Serve

Bird reaches
highest point
at the tape

Shuttle "coaxed"
across the net

Racquet swept
forward, elbow
flexed, racquet
head lags behind

The drop of
shuttle and
preparation of the
stroke should be
the same as the
singles serve

Stand in stagger
stance near front
serving line.
Feet point toward
the serving court

Objective is to catch
opponent leaning
too far forward

Place to backhand

Contact shuttle with
quick action of
racquet head

Shuttle held as in
the basic serve

Stand 1 m or less
behind service line,
near to center T

Back of hand is now
toward the ceiling

Power is generated
by swinging racquet
down and then
up by pronating
the forearm

Prepare for shot by
supinating the
forearm, fingers
toward ceiling

Racquet is drawn
across, in front of
the body

Racquet foot leads
step-over to sideline

Contact with
shuttle is quick
but smooth

Hold shuttle in
front of body at
arms length

Racquet held in
front of body with
racquet head lower
than wrist and
waist

Objective is to
catch opponent
off-guard with
quick serve
delivered from in
front of body

Flight paths:

1. Underhand clear, singles serve
2. Short serve
3. Flick serves

NET

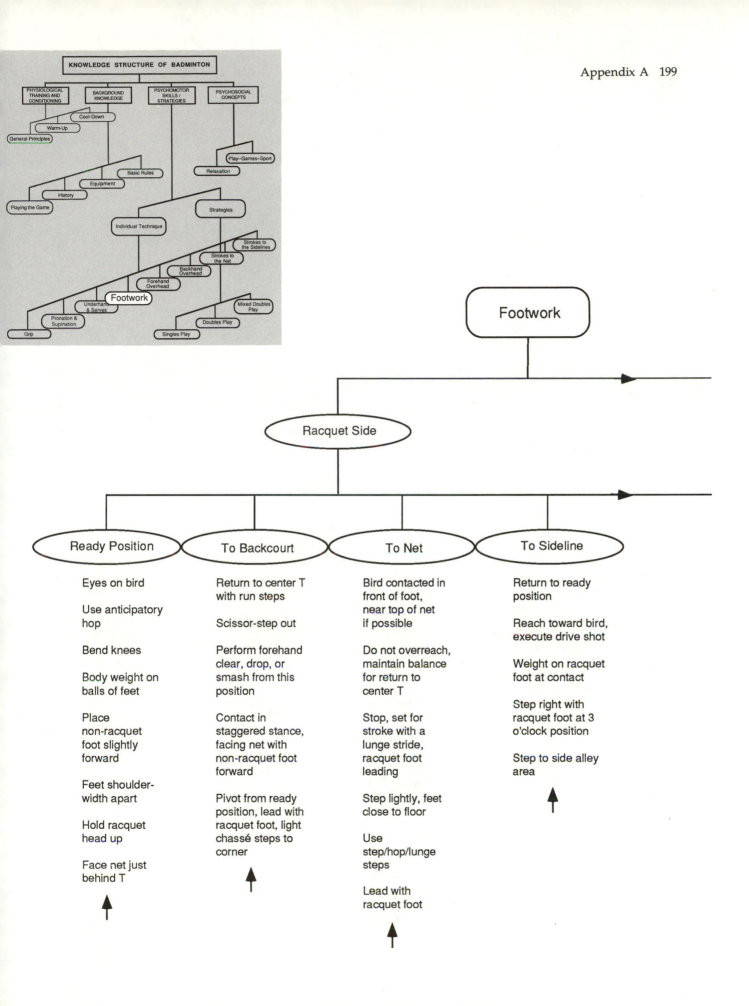

KNOWLEDGE STRUCTURE OF BADMINTON

Footwork

Racquet Side

Ready Position	To Backcourt	To Net	To Sideline
Eyes on bird	Return to center T with run steps	Bird contacted in front of foot, near top of net if possible	Return to ready position
Use anticipatory hop	Scissor-step out	Do not overreach, maintain balance for return to center T	Reach toward bird, execute drive shot
Bend knees	Perform forehand clear, drop, or smash from this position	Stop, set for stroke with a lunge stride, racquet foot leading	Weight on racquet foot at contact
Body weight on balls of feet	Contact in staggered stance, facing net with non-racquet foot forward	Step lightly, feet close to floor	Step right with racquet foot at 3 o'clock position
Place non-racquet foot slightly forward	Pivot from ready position, lead with racquet foot, light chassé steps to corner	Use step/hop/lunge steps	Step to side alley area
Feet shoulder-width apart		Lead with racquet foot	
Hold racquet head up			
Face net just behind T			

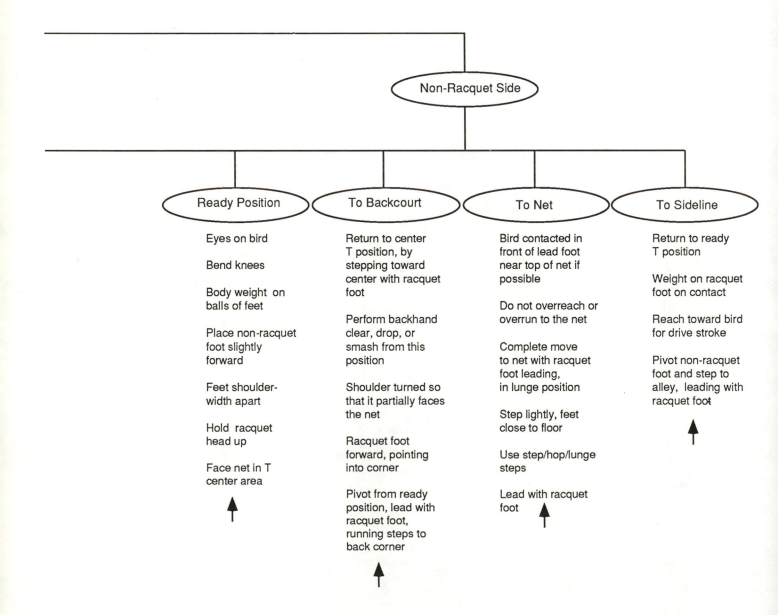

Non-Racquet Side

Ready Position

Eyes on bird

Bend knees

Body weight on balls of feet

Place non-racquet foot slightly forward

Feet shoulder-width apart

Hold racquet head up

Face net in T center area

To Backcourt

Return to center T position, by stepping toward center with racquet foot

Perform backhand clear, drop, or smash from this position

Shoulder turned so that it partially faces the net

Racquet foot forward, pointing into corner

Pivot from ready position, lead with racquet foot, running steps to back corner

To Net

Bird contacted in front of lead foot near top of net if possible

Do not overreach or overrun to the net

Complete move to net with racquet foot leading, in lunge position

Step lightly, feet close to floor

Use step/hop/lunge steps

Lead with racquet foot

To Sideline

Return to ready T position

Weight on racquet foot on contact

Reach toward bird for drive stroke

Pivot non-racquet foot and step to alley, leading with racquet foot

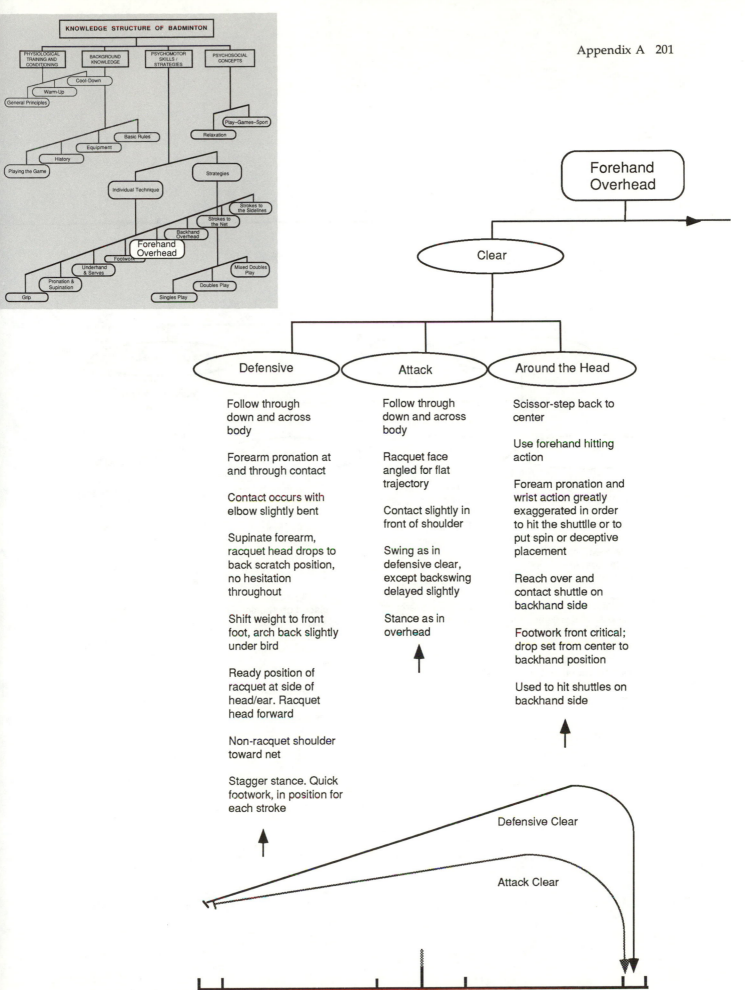

KNOWLEDGE STRUCTURE OF BADMINTON

PHYSIOLOGICAL TRAINING AND CONDITIONING

BACKGROUND KNOWLEDGE

PSYCHOMOTOR SKILLS / STRATEGIES

PSYCHOSOCIAL CONCEPTS

Cool-Down

Warm-Up

General Principles

Play–Games–Sport

Relaxation

Basic Rules

Equipment

History

Strategies

Playing the Game

Individual Technique

Strokes to the Sidelines

Strokes to the Net

Backhand Overhead

Forehand Overhead

Footwork

Mixed Doubles Play

Underhand & Serves

Pronation & Supination

Doubles Play

Grip

Singles Play

Forehand Overhead

Clear

Defensive

Follow through down and across body

Forearm pronation at and through contact

Contact occurs with elbow slightly bent

Supinate forearm, racquet head drops to back scratch position, no hesitation throughout

Shift weight to front foot, arch back slightly under bird

Ready position of racquet at side of head/ear. Racquet head forward

Non-racquet shoulder toward net

Stagger stance. Quick footwork, in position for each stroke

Attack

Follow through down and across body

Racquet face angled for flat trajectory

Contact slightly in front of shoulder

Swing as in defensive clear, except backswing delayed slightly

Stance as in overhead

Around the Head

Scissor-step back to center

Use forehand hitting action

Foream pronation and wrist action greatly exaggerated in order to hit the shuttlle or to put spin or deceptive placement

Reach over and contact shuttle on backhand side

Footwork front critical; drop set from center to backhand position

Used to hit shuttles on backhand side

Defensive Clear

Attack Clear

NET

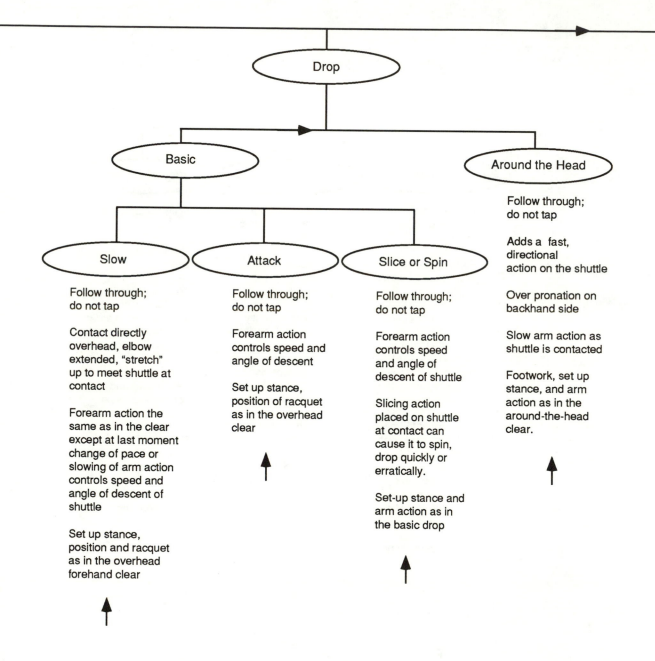

Drop

Basic

Around the Head

Follow through;
do not tap

Adds a fast,
directional
action on the shuttle

Over pronation on
backhand side

Slow arm action as
shuttle is contacted

Footwork, set up
stance, and arm
action as in the
around-the-head
clear.

Slow

Attack

Slice or Spin

Follow through;
do not tap

Contact directly
overhead, elbow
extended, "stretch"
up to meet shuttle at
contact

Forearm action the
same as in the clear
except at last moment
change of pace or
slowing of arm action
controls speed and
angle of descent of
shuttle

Set up stance,
position and racquet
as in the overhead
forehand clear

Follow through;
do not tap

Forearm action
controls speed and
angle of descent

Set up stance,
position of racquet
as in the overhead
clear

Follow through;
do not tap

Forearm action
controls speed
and angle of
descent of shuttle

Slicing action
placed on shuttle
at contact can
cause it to spin,
drop quickly or
erratically.

Set-up stance and
arm action as in
the basic drop

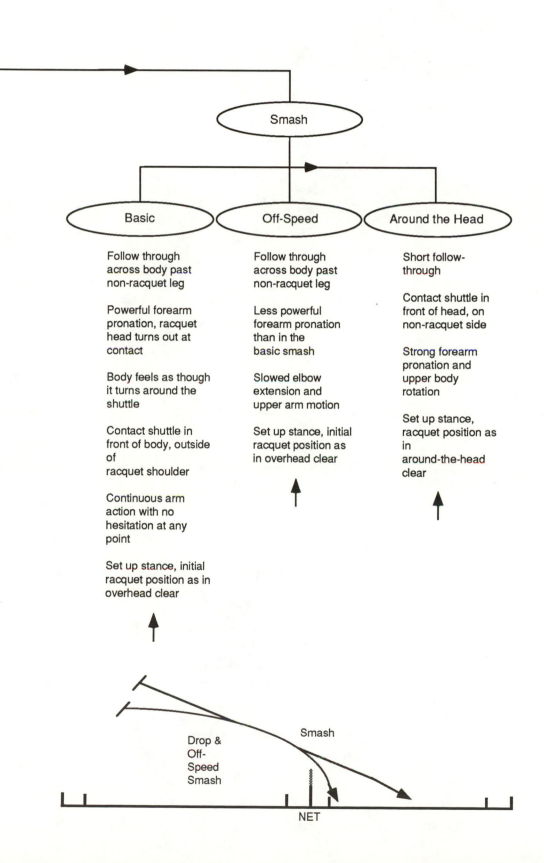

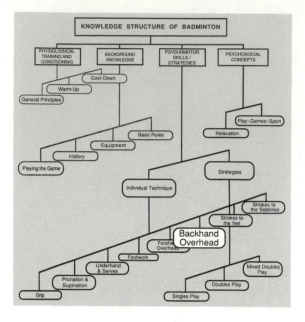

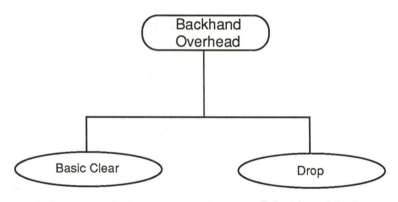

Backhand Overhead

Basic Clear

Follow-through is short

Contact high and even with shoulder, hit up towards ceiling

Power achieved through strong forearm supination at contact

Elbow leads stroke

Racquet drawn well back across body

Knees bent slightly, weight on racquet foot

Racquet foot leads pointing to backhand corner, back to net

Drop

Follow through is short

Contact in front of body and side of racquet shoulder

At contact, slow upper arm motion through supination

Arm action beginning phase as in overhead backhand clear

Set-up stance exactly as in overhead backhand clear

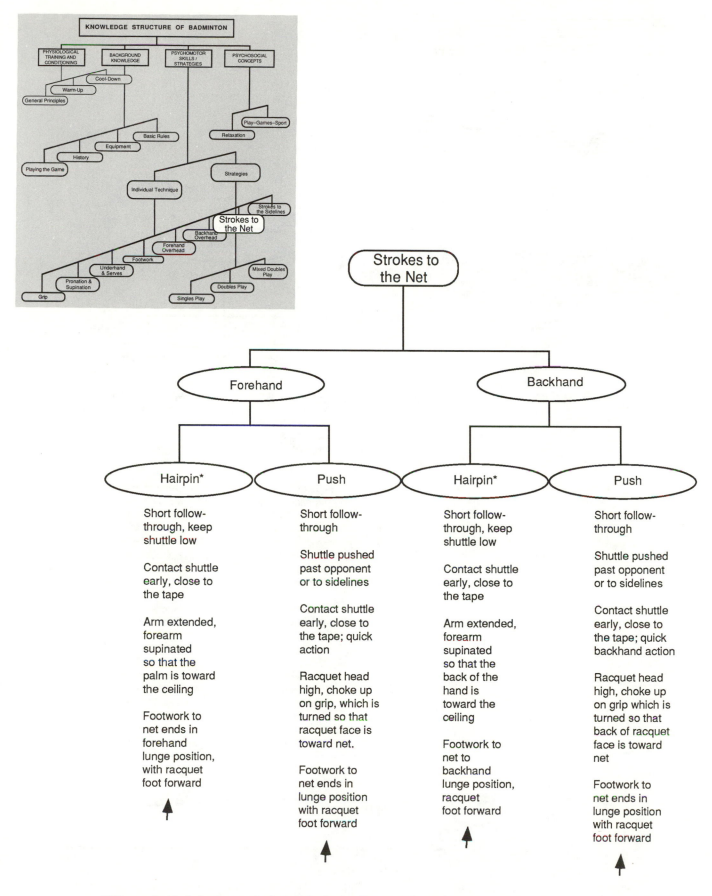

Strokes to the Net

Forehand

Hairpin*

Short follow-through, keep shuttle low

Contact shuttle early, close to the tape

Arm extended, forearm supinated so that the palm is toward the ceiling

Footwork to net ends in forehand lunge position, with racquet foot forward

Push

Short follow-through

Shuttle pushed past opponent or to sidelines

Contact shuttle early, close to the tape; quick action

Racquet head high, choke up on grip, which is turned so that racquet face is toward net.

Footwork to net ends in lunge position with racquet foot forward

Backhand

Hairpin*

Short follow-through, keep shuttle low

Contact shuttle early, close to the tape

Arm extended, forearm supinated so that the back of the hand is toward the ceiling

Footwork to net to backhand lunge position, racquet foot forward

Push

Short follow-through

Shuttle pushed past opponent or to sidelines

Contact shuttle early, close to the tape; quick backhand action

Racquet head high, choke up on grip which is turned so that back of racquet face is toward net

Footwork to net ends in lunge position with racquet foot forward

* "The perfect hairpin shot results in the shuttle crawling up and over the net and trickling down the other side" (Bloss & Hales, 1987, p. 34).

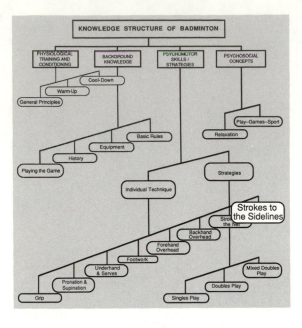

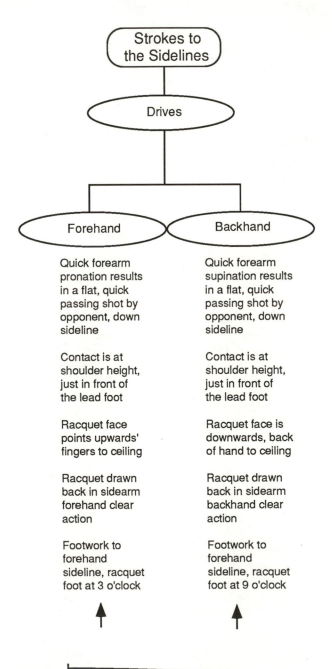

Strokes to the Sidelines

Drives

Forehand	Backhand
Quick forearm pronation results in a flat, quick passing shot by opponent, down sideline	Quick forearm supination results in a flat, quick passing shot by opponent, down sideline
Contact is at shoulder height, just in front of the lead foot	Contact is at shoulder height, just in front of the lead foot
Racquet face points upwards' fingers to ceiling	Racquet face is downwards, back of hand to ceiling
Racquet drawn back in sidearm forehand clear action	Racquet drawn back in sidearm backhand clear action
Footwork to forehand sideline, racquet foot at 3 o'clock	Footwork to forehand sideline, racquet foot at 9 o'clock

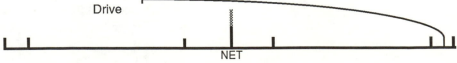

Drive

NET

Purpose : To keep flight of bird flat; to pass opponent

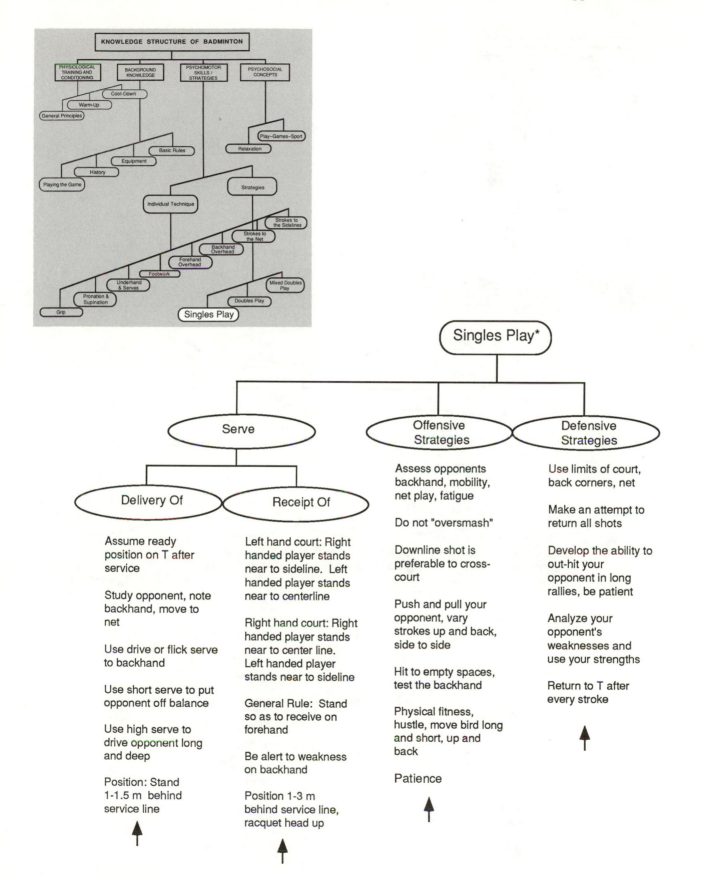

KNOWLEDGE STRUCTURE OF BADMINTON

PHYSIOLOGICAL TRAINING AND CONDITIONING — BACKGROUND KNOWLEDGE — PSYCHOMOTOR SKILLS / STRATEGIES — PSYCHOSOCIAL CONCEPTS

Cool-Down
Warm-Up
General Principles
Play–Games–Sport
Relaxation
Basic Rules
Equipment
History
Playing the Game
Strategies
Individual Technique
Strokes to the Sidelines
Strokes to the Net
Backhand Overhead
Forehand Overhead
Footwork
Underhand & Serves
Mixed Doubles Play
Pronation & Supination
Doubles Play
Grip
Singles Play

Singles Play*

Serve

Delivery Of

Assume ready position on T after service

Study opponent, note backhand, move to net

Use drive or flick serve to backhand

Use short serve to put opponent off balance

Use high serve to drive opponent long and deep

Position: Stand 1-1.5 m behind service line

Receipt Of

Left hand court: Right handed player stands near to sideline. Left handed player stands near to centerline

Right hand court: Right handed player stands near to center line. Left handed player stands near to sideline

General Rule: Stand so as to receive on forehand

Be alert to weakness on backhand

Position 1-3 m behind service line, racquet head up

Offensive Strategies

Assess opponents backhand, mobility, net play, fatigue

Do not "oversmash"

Downline shot is preferable to cross-court

Push and pull your opponent, vary strokes up and back, side to side

Hit to empty spaces, test the backhand

Physical fitness, hustle, move bird long and short, up and back

Patience

Defensive Strategies

Use limits of court, back corners, net

Make an attempt to return all shots

Develop the ability to out-hit your opponent in long rallies, be patient

Analyze your opponent's weaknesses and use your strengths

Return to T after every stroke

* Basic beginner strategy

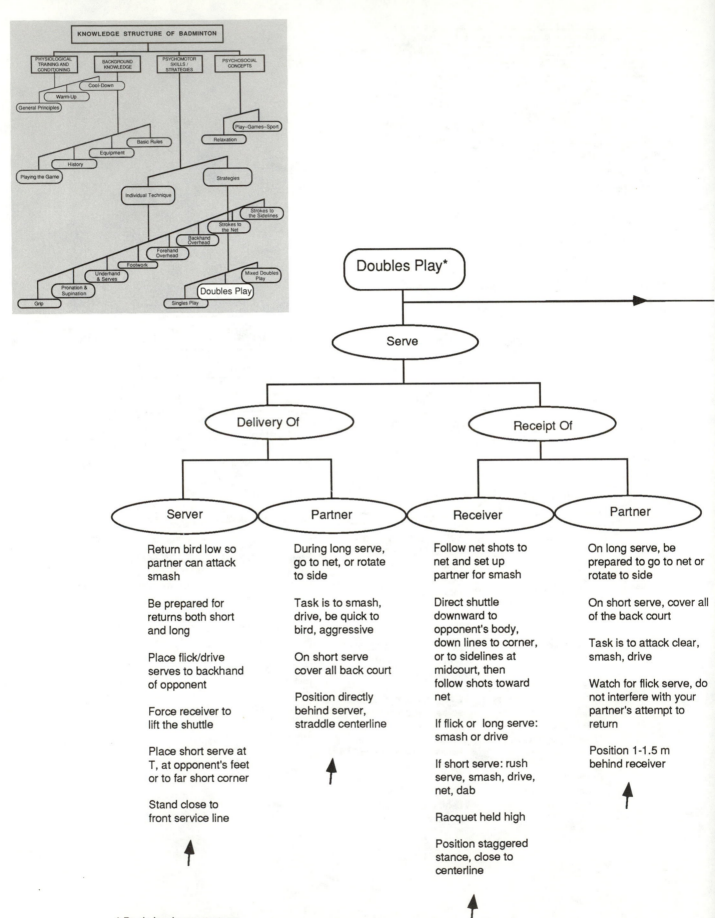

KNOWLEDGE STRUCTURE OF BADMINTON

Doubles Play*

Serve

Delivery Of

Receipt Of

Server

Return bird low so partner can attack smash

Be prepared for returns both short and long

Place flick/drive serves to backhand of opponent

Force receiver to lift the shuttle

Place short serve at T, at opponent's feet or to far short corner

Stand close to front service line

Partner

During long serve, go to net, or rotate to side

Task is to smash, drive, be quick to bird, aggressive

On short serve cover all back court

Position directly behind server, straddle centerline

Receiver

Follow net shots to net and set up partner for smash

Direct shuttle downward to opponent's body, down lines to corner, or to sidelines at midcourt, then follow shots toward net

If flick or long serve: smash or drive

If short serve: rush serve, smash, drive, net, dab

Racquet held high

Position staggered stance, close to centerline

Partner

On long serve, be prepared to go to net or rotate to side

On short serve, cover all of the back court

Task is to attack clear, smash, drive

Watch for flick serve, do not interfere with your partner's attempt to return

Position 1-1.5 m behind receiver

* Basic beginner strategy

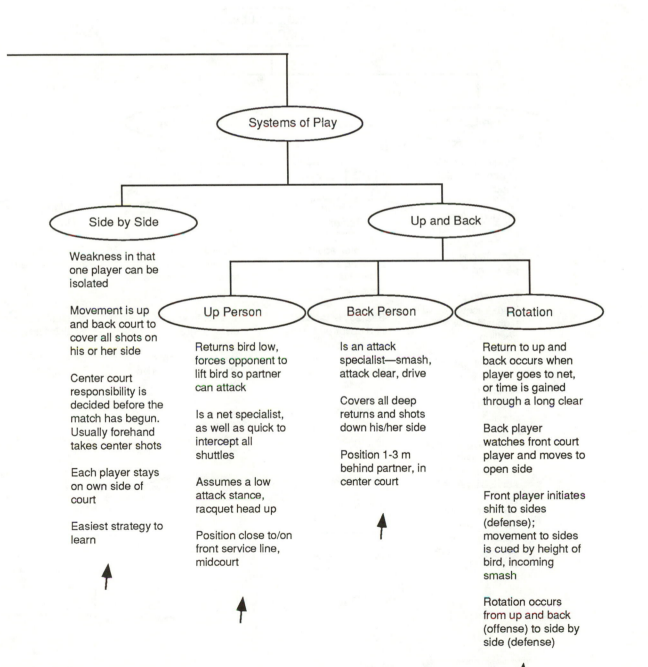

Systems of Play

Side by Side

Up and Back

Weakness in that one player can be isolated

Movement is up and back court to cover all shots on his or her side

Center court responsibility is decided before the match has begun. Usually forehand takes center shots

Each player stays on own side of court

Easiest strategy to learn

Up Person

Returns bird low, forces opponent to lift bird so partner can attack

Is a net specialist, as well as quick to intercept all shuttles

Assumes a low attack stance, racquet head up

Position close to/on front service line, midcourt

Back Person

Is an attack specialist—smash, attack clear, drive

Covers all deep returns and shots down his/her side

Position 1-3 m behind partner, in center court

Rotation

Return to up and back occurs when player goes to net, or time is gained through a long clear

Back player watches front court player and moves to open side

Front player initiates shift to sides (defense); movement to sides is cued by height of bird, incoming smash

Rotation occurs from up and back (offense) to side by side (defense)

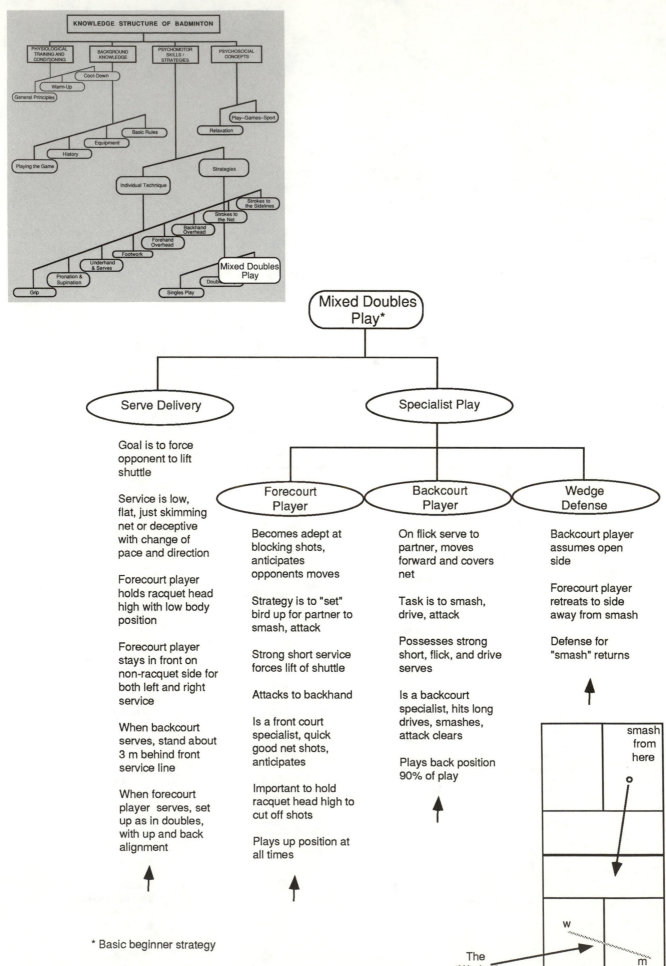

KNOWLEDGE STRUCTURE OF BADMINTON

Mixed Doubles Play*

Serve Delivery

Goal is to force opponent to lift shuttle

Service is low, flat, just skimming net or deceptive with change of pace and direction

Forecourt player holds racquet head high with low body position

Forecourt player stays in front on non-racquet side for both left and right service

When backcourt serves, stand about 3 m behind front service line

When forecourt player serves, set up as in doubles, with up and back alignment

Specialist Play

Forecourt Player

Becomes adept at blocking shots, anticipates opponents moves

Strategy is to "set" bird up for partner to smash, attack

Strong short service forces lift of shuttle

Attacks to backhand

Is a front court specialist, quick good net shots, anticipates

Important to hold racquet head high to cut off shots

Plays up position at all times

Backcourt Player

On flick serve to partner, moves forward and covers net

Task is to smash, drive, attack

Possesses strong short, flick, and drive serves

Is a backcourt specialist, hits long drives, smashes, attack clears

Plays back position 90% of play

Wedge Defense

Backcourt player assumes open side

Forecourt player retreats to side away from smash

Defense for "smash" returns

smash from here

The "Wedge"

* Basic beginner strategy

210

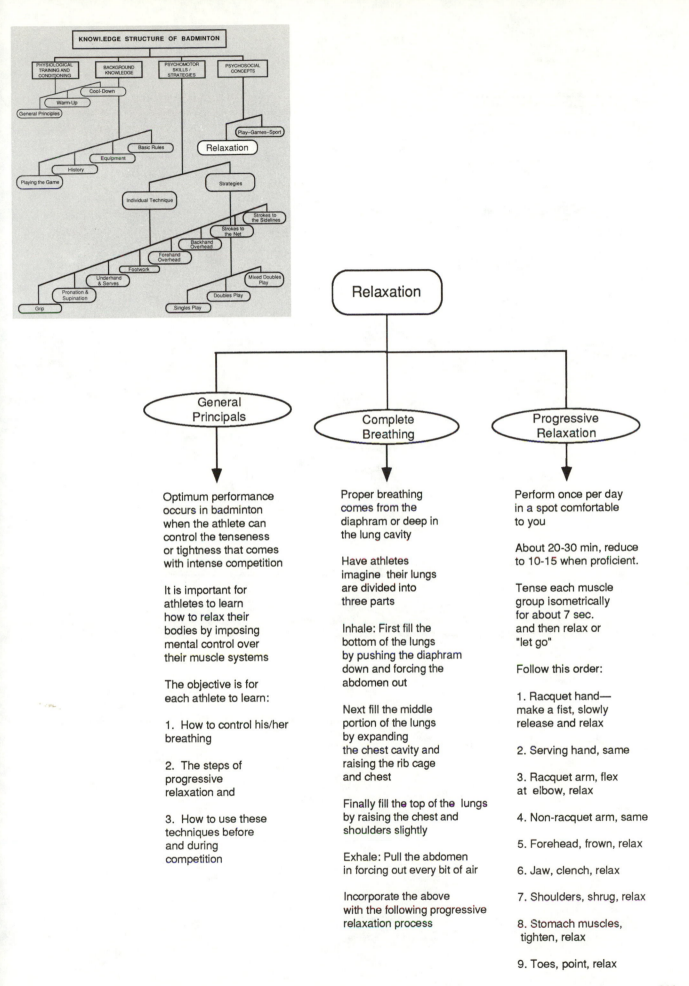

Relaxation

General Principals

Optimum performance occurs in badminton when the athlete can control the tenseness or tightness that comes with intense competition

It is important for athletes to learn how to relax their bodies by imposing mental control over their muscle systems

The objective is for each athlete to learn:

1. How to control his/her breathing

2. The steps of progressive relaxation and

3. How to use these techniques before and during competition

Complete Breathing

Proper breathing comes from the diaphram or deep in the lung cavity

Have athletes imagine their lungs are divided into three parts

Inhale: First fill the bottom of the lungs by pushing the diaphram down and forcing the abdomen out

Next fill the middle portion of the lungs by expanding the chest cavity and raising the rib cage and chest

Finally fill the top of the lungs by raising the chest and shoulders slightly

Exhale: Pull the abdomen in forcing out every bit of air

Incorporate the above with the following progressive relaxation process

Progressive Relaxation

Perform once per day in a spot comfortable to you

About 20-30 min, reduce to 10-15 when proficient.

Tense each muscle group isometrically for about 7 sec. and then relax or "let go"

Follow this order:

1. Racquet hand—make a fist, slowly release and relax

2. Serving hand, same

3. Racquet arm, flex at elbow, relax

4. Non-racquet arm, same

5. Forehead, frown, relax

6. Jaw, clench, relax

7. Shoulders, shrug, relax

8. Stomach muscles, tighten, relax

9. Toes, point, relax

211

References: Harris (1986); Suin (1986)

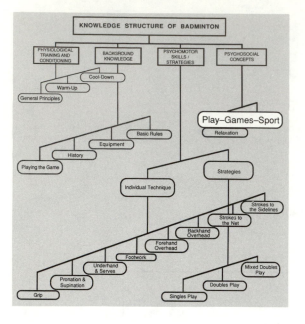

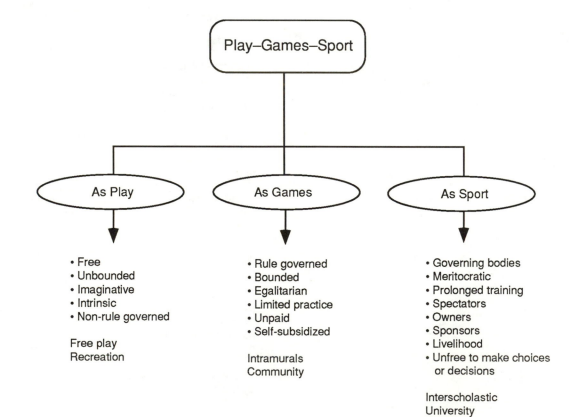

Reference: Lawson & Plachek (1981)

B

Knowledge Structure of Golf

The following golf structure was developed by Dede Owens and Linda Bunker, the authors of the golf Steps to Success Activity Series books, and me. A draft structure was first completed in a structured interview as described in Module 1. Final revisions were carried out using text analysis, with the Steps to Success golf books (Owens & Bunker, 1989a and 1989b. Adapted by permission). This structure has wide applicability and may be used in instructional settings ranging from public school to university credit teaching settings, as well as club and coaching settings.

Note: To conserve space, the Knowledge Structure of Golf does not detail the subcategories under ''Strategies'' nor the ''Psychological Concepts'' category.

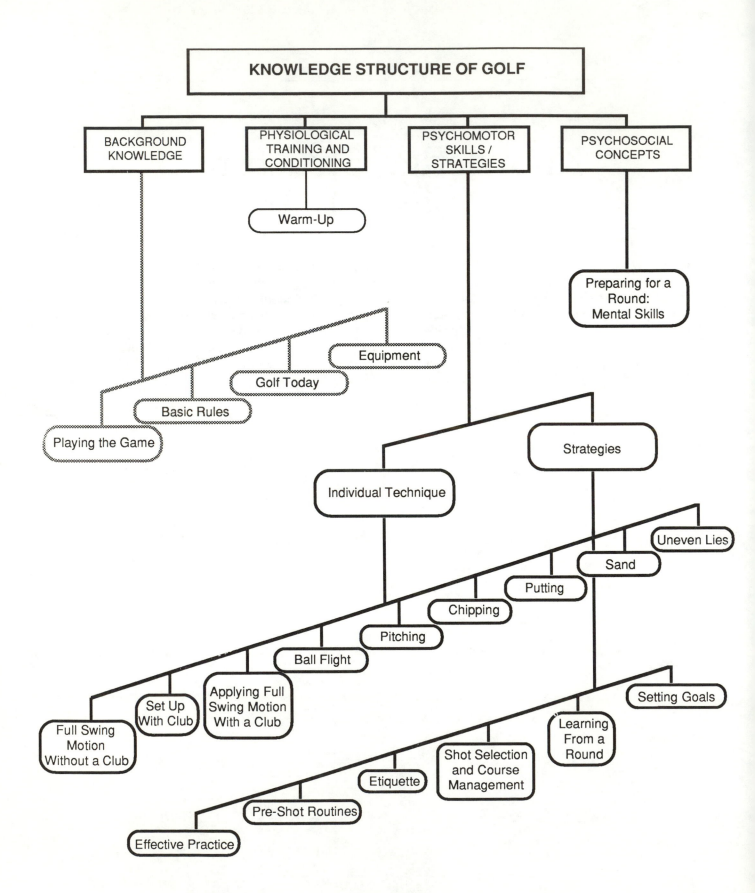

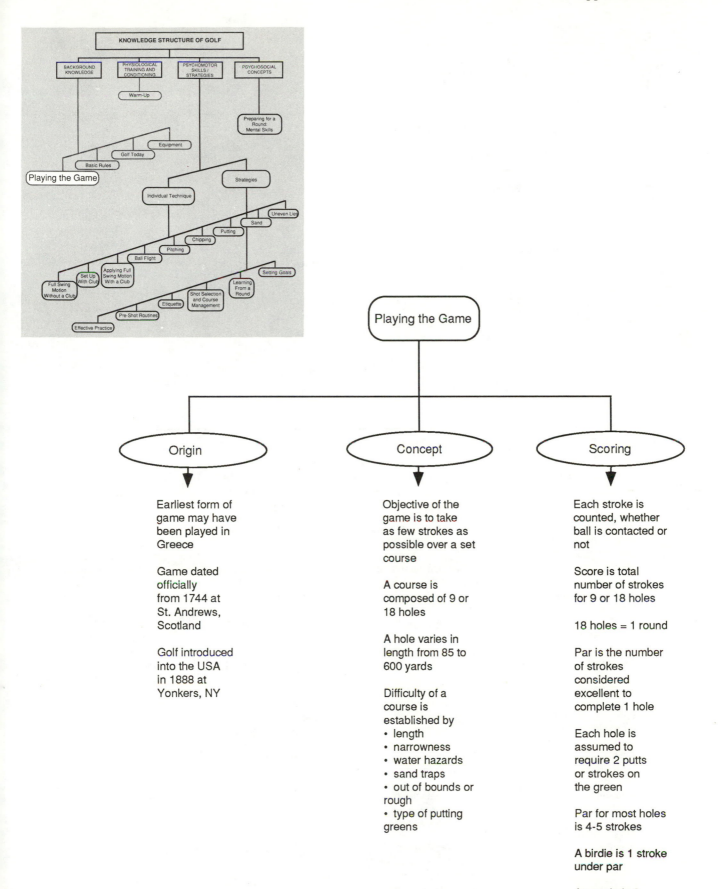

Playing the Game

Origin

Earliest form of
game may have
been played in
Greece

Game dated
officially
from 1744 at
St. Andrews,
Scotland

Golf introduced
into the USA
in 1888 at
Yonkers, NY

Concept

Objective of the
game is to take
as few strokes as
possible over a set
course

A course is
composed of 9 or
18 holes

A hole varies in
length from 85 to
600 yards

Difficulty of a
course is
established by
• length
• narrowness
• water hazards
• sand traps
• out of bounds or
rough
• type of putting
greens

Scoring

Each stroke is
counted, whether
ball is contacted or
not

Score is total
number of strokes
for 9 or 18 holes

18 holes = 1 round

Par is the number
of strokes
considered
excellent to
complete 1 hole

Each hole is
assumed to
require 2 putts
or strokes on
the green

Par for most holes
is 4-5 strokes

A birdie is 1 stroke
under par

An eagle is 2
strokes under par

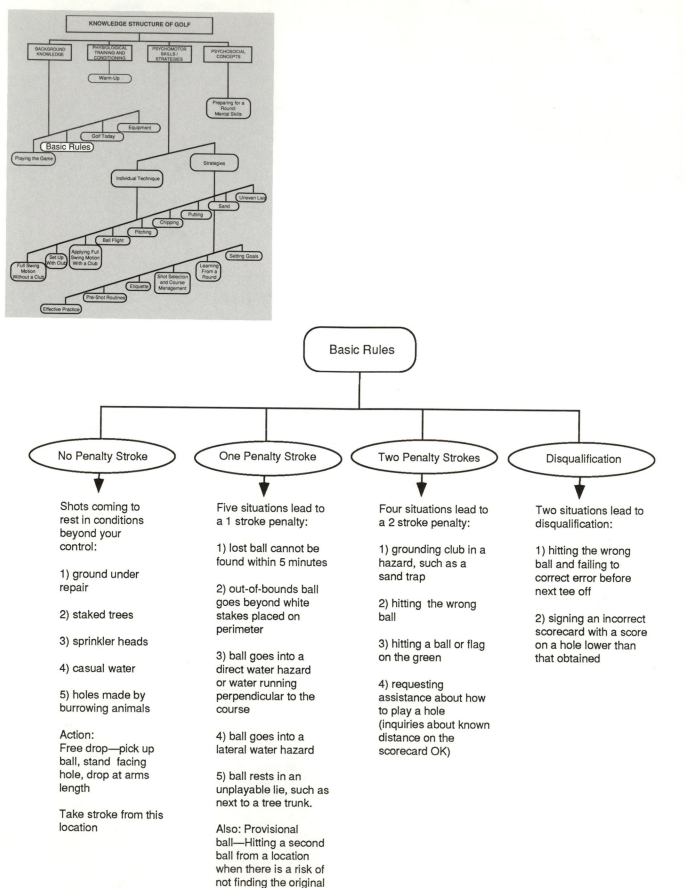

Basic Rules

No Penalty Stroke

Shots coming to rest in conditions beyond your control:

1) ground under repair

2) staked trees

3) sprinkler heads

4) casual water

5) holes made by burrowing animals

Action:
Free drop—pick up ball, stand facing hole, drop at arms length

Take stroke from this location

One Penalty Stroke

Five situations lead to a 1 stroke penalty:

1) lost ball cannot be found within 5 minutes

2) out-of-bounds ball goes beyond white stakes placed on perimeter

3) ball goes into a direct water hazard or water running perpendicular to the course

4) ball goes into a lateral water hazard

5) ball rests in an unplayable lie, such as next to a tree trunk.

Also: Provisional ball—Hitting a second ball from a location when there is a risk of not finding the original ball outside of a water hazard

Two Penalty Strokes

Four situations lead to a 2 stroke penalty:

1) grounding club in a hazard, such as a sand trap

2) hitting the wrong ball

3) hitting a ball or flag on the green

4) requesting assistance about how to play a hole (inquiries about known distance on the scorecard OK)

Disqualification

Two situations lead to disqualification:

1) hitting the wrong ball and failing to correct error before next tee off

2) signing an incorrect scorecard with a score on a hole lower than that obtained

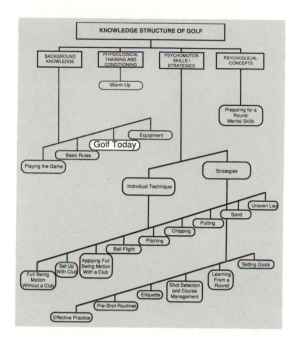

Golf Today

Etiquette

There are many unwritten rules in golf. You should be aware of the following:

1) only one golfer hits at a time

2) the person farthest from the hole hits first

3) the person with the longest putt hits first

4) play without delay

5) allow faster players to play through

6) hit safely; be sure no one is within range of swing or in path of ball

7) replace all divots

8) rake all sand bunkers

9) repair ball indents on green

10) be aware of and observe dress codes

The Handicap System

The handicap system allows players of differing abilities to play against one another

A handicap is an "equalizer" that is subtracted from your score at the end of a round

A low-handicap player scores close to par on every hole and has a handicap below 7

A high-handicap player rarely achieves par and has a handicap of 18 plus

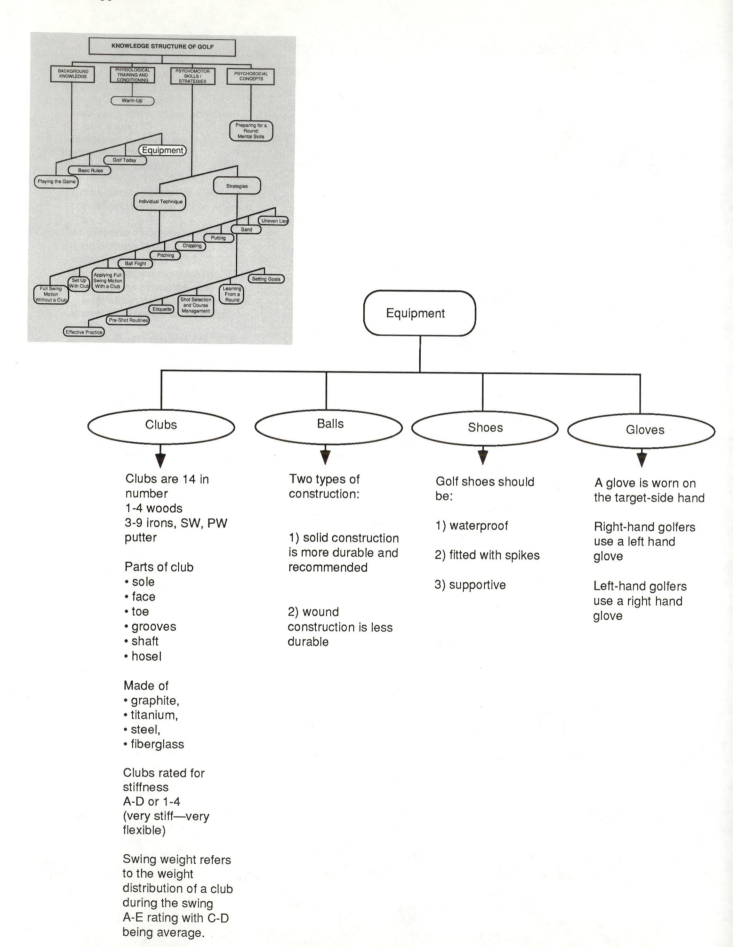

Equipment

Clubs

Clubs are 14 in
number
1-4 woods
3-9 irons, SW, PW
putter

Parts of club
• sole
• face
• toe
• grooves
• shaft
• hosel

Made of
• graphite,
• titanium,
• steel,
• fiberglass

Clubs rated for
stiffness
A-D or 1-4
(very stiff—very
flexible)

Swing weight refers
to the weight
distribution of a club
during the swing
A-E rating with C-D
being average.

Balls

Two types of
construction:

1) solid construction
is more durable and
recommended

2) wound
construction is less
durable

Shoes

Golf shoes should
be:

1) waterproof

2) fitted with spikes

3) supportive

Gloves

A glove is worn on
the target-side hand

Right-hand golfers
use a left hand
glove

Left-hand golfers
use a right hand
glove

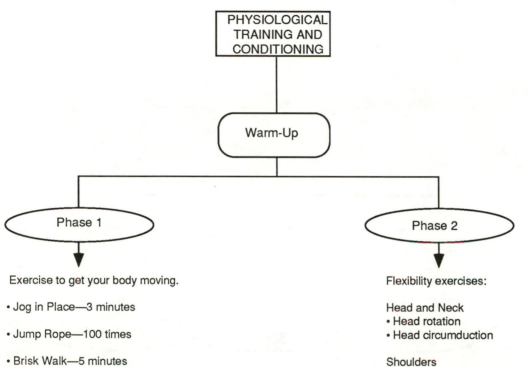

PHYSIOLOGICAL TRAINING AND CONDITIONING

Warm-Up

Phase 1

Exercise to get your body moving.

• Jog in Place—3 minutes

• Jump Rope—100 times

• Brisk Walk—5 minutes

Phase 2

Flexibility exercises:

Head and Neck
• Head rotation
• Head circumduction

Shoulders
• Arms across chest stretch
• Arm circumduction

Lower Back
• Trunk rotation
• Back stretch with legs crossed
• Trunk lateral flexion

Legs
• Trunk bend with crossed feet
• Sitting hamstring stretch

Arms and Hands
• Forearm rotation
• Radial-ulnar deviation

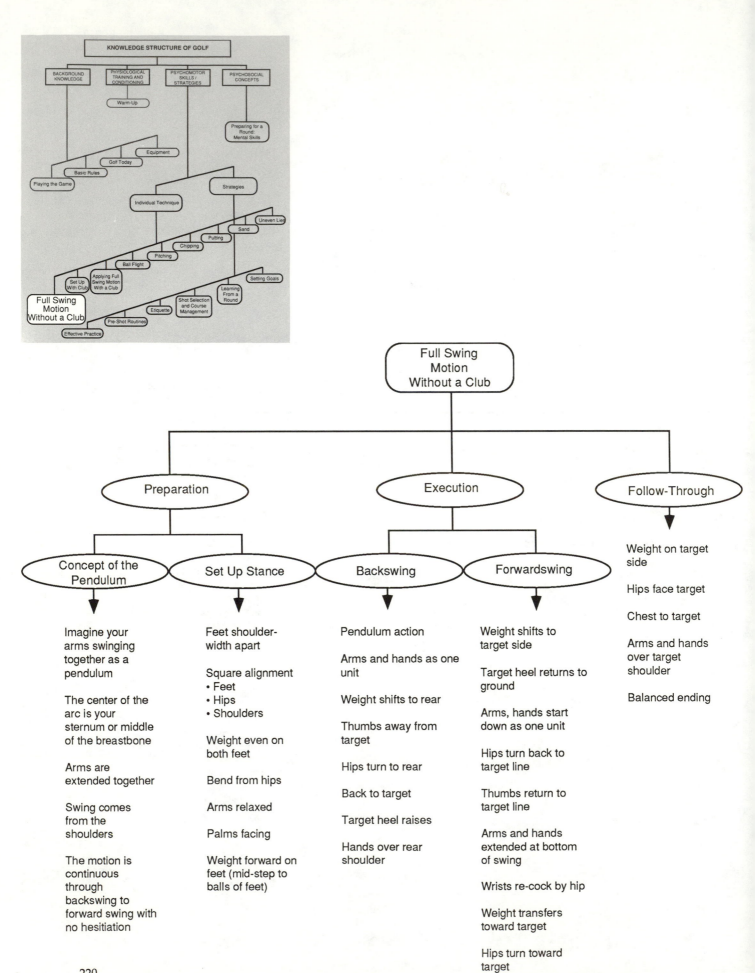

KNOWLEDGE STRUCTURE OF GOLF

BACKGROUND KNOWLEDGE · PHYSIOLOGICAL TRAINING AND CONDITIONING · PSYCHOMOTOR SKILLS / STRATEGIES · PSYCHOSOCIAL CONCEPTS

Warm-Up — Preparing for a Round: Mental Skills — Equipment — Golf Today — Basic Rules — Playing the Game — Individual Technique — Strategies — Uneven Lies — Sand — Putting — Chipping — Pitching — Ball Flight — Set Up With Club — Applying Full Swing Motion With a Club — **Full Swing Motion Without a Club** — Pre-Shot Routines — Etiquette — Shot Selection and Course Management — Learning From a Round — Setting Goals — Effective Practice

---

Full Swing Motion Without a Club

Preparation

Concept of the Pendulum

- Imagine your arms swinging together as a pendulum
- The center of the arc is your sternum or middle of the breastbone
- Arms are extended together
- Swing comes from the shoulders
- The motion is continuous through backswing to forward swing with no hesitiation

Set Up Stance

- Feet shoulder-width apart
- Square alignment
  • Feet
  • Hips
  • Shoulders
- Weight even on both feet
- Bend from hips
- Arms relaxed
- Palms facing
- Weight forward on feet (mid-step to balls of feet)

Execution

Backswing

- Pendulum action
- Arms and hands as one unit
- Weight shifts to rear
- Thumbs away from target
- Hips turn to rear
- Back to target
- Target heel raises
- Hands over rear shoulder

Forwardswing

- Weight shifts to target side
- Target heel returns to ground
- Arms, hands start down as one unit
- Hips turn back to target line
- Thumbs return to target line
- Arms and hands extended at bottom of swing
- Wrists re-cock by hip
- Weight transfers toward target
- Hips turn toward target

Follow-Through

- Weight on target side
- Hips face target
- Chest to target
- Arms and hands over target shoulder
- Balanced ending

220

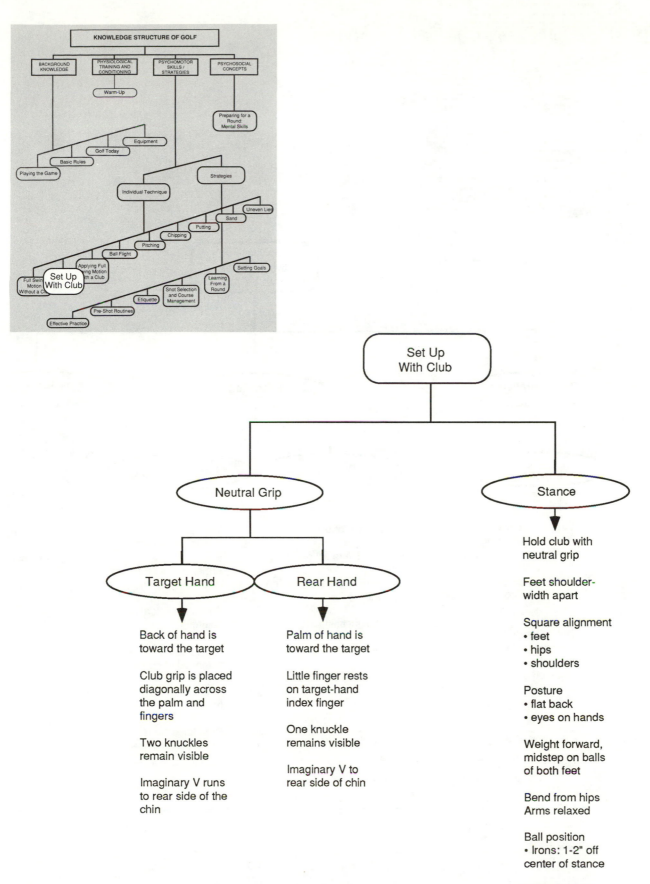

Set Up With Club

Neutral Grip

Target Hand

Back of hand is toward the target

Club grip is placed diagonally across the palm and fingers

Two knuckles remain visible

Imaginary V runs to rear side of the chin

Rear Hand

Palm of hand is toward the target

Little finger rests on target-hand index finger

One knuckle remains visible

Imaginary V to rear side of chin

Stance

Hold club with neutral grip

Feet shoulder-width apart

Square alignment
• feet
• hips
• shoulders

Posture
• flat back
• eyes on hands

Weight forward, midstep on balls of both feet

Bend from hips
Arms relaxed

Ball position
• Irons: 1-2" off center of stance

• Woods: 3-4" forward of center of stance

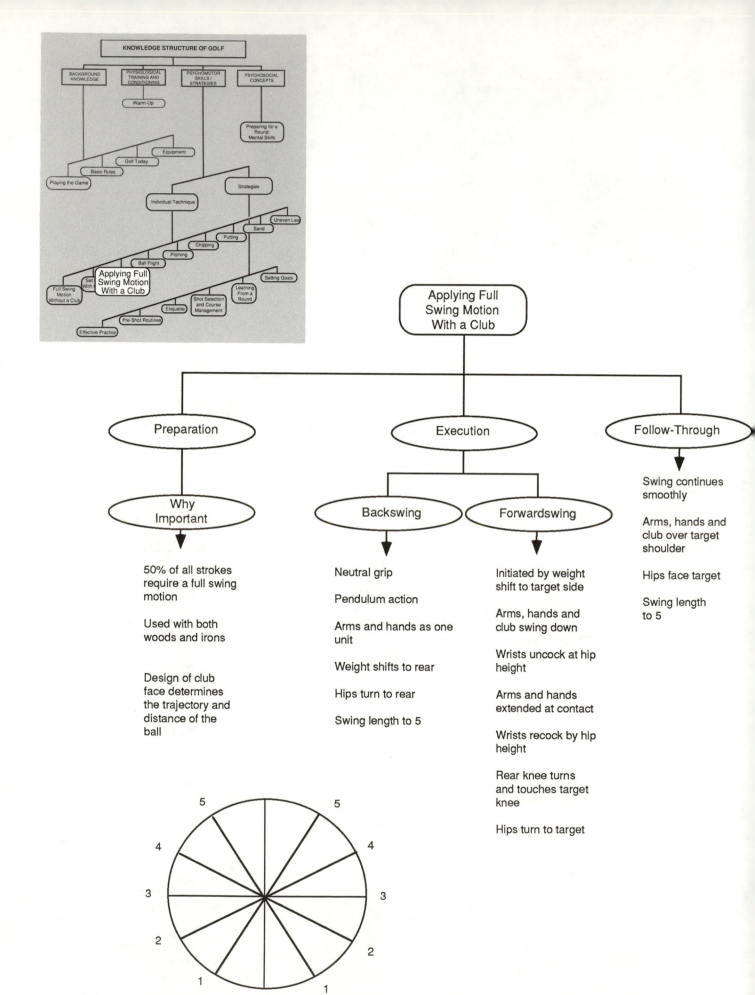

KNOWLEDGE STRUCTURE OF GOLF

BACKGROUND KNOWLEDGE · PHYSIOLOGICAL TRAINING AND CONDITIONING · PSYCHOMOTOR SKILLS / STRATEGIES · PSYCHOSOCIAL CONCEPTS

Warm-Up

Preparing for a Round: Mental Skills

Equipment

Golf Today

Basic Rules

Playing the Game

Individual Technique

Strategies

Uneven Lies

Sand

Putting

Chipping

Pitching

Ball Flight

Set Up With

Applying Full Swing Motion With a Club

Full Swing Motion Without a Club

Etiquette

Shot Selection and Course Management

Learning From a Round

Setting Goals

Pre-Shot Routines

Effective Practice

Applying Full Swing Motion With a Club

Preparation

Why Important

50% of all strokes require a full swing motion

Used with both woods and irons

Design of club face determines the trajectory and distance of the ball

Execution

Backswing

Neutral grip

Pendulum action

Arms and hands as one unit

Weight shifts to rear

Hips turn to rear

Swing length to 5

Forwardswing

Initiated by weight shift to target side

Arms, hands and club swing down

Wrists uncock at hip height

Arms and hands extended at contact

Wrists recock by hip height

Rear knee turns and touches target knee

Hips turn to target

Follow-Through

Swing continues smoothly

Arms, hands and club over target shoulder

Hips face target

Swing length to 5

222

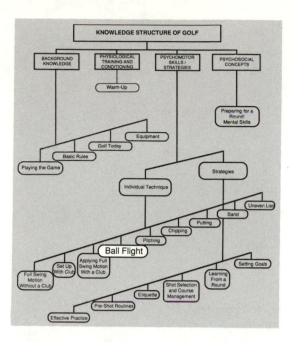

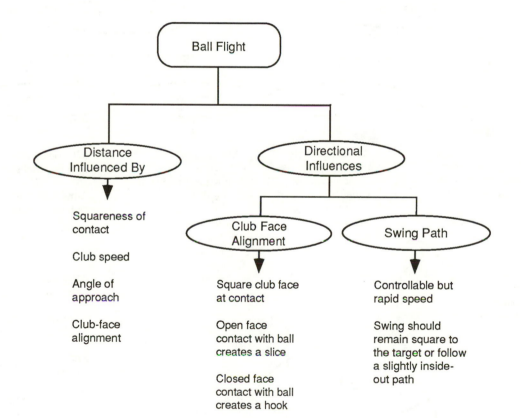

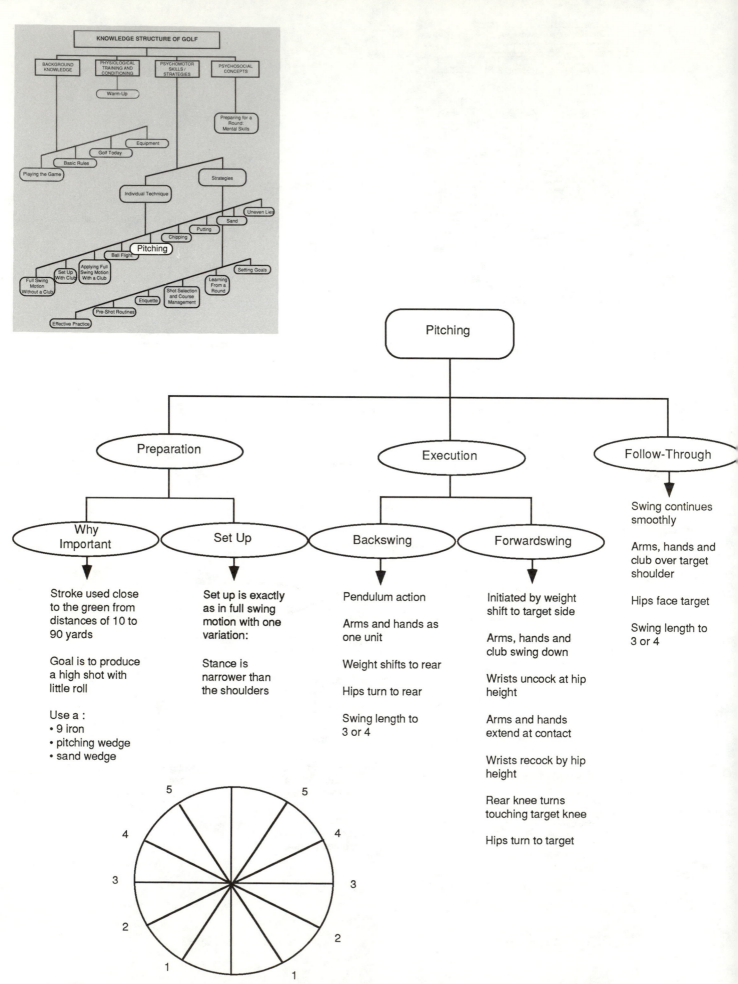

Pitching

Preparation

Why Important

Stroke used close to the green from distances of 10 to 90 yards

Goal is to produce a high shot with little roll

Use a :
• 9 iron
• pitching wedge
• sand wedge

Set Up

Set up is exactly as in full swing motion with one variation:

Stance is narrower than the shoulders

Execution

Backswing

Pendulum action

Arms and hands as one unit

Weight shifts to rear

Hips turn to rear

Swing length to 3 or 4

Forwardswing

Initiated by weight shift to target side

Arms, hands and club swing down

Wrists uncock at hip height

Arms and hands extend at contact

Wrists recock by hip height

Rear knee turns touching target knee

Hips turn to target

Follow-Through

Swing continues smoothly

Arms, hands and club over target shoulder

Hips face target

Swing length to 3 or 4

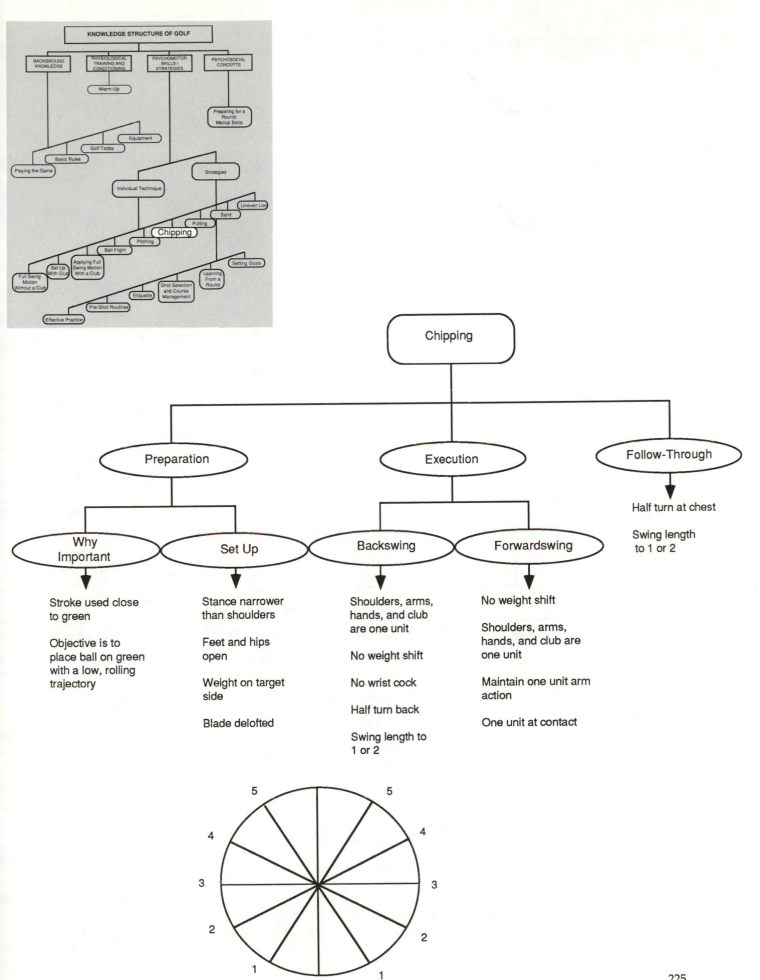

KNOWLEDGE STRUCTURE OF GOLF

BACKGROUND KNOWLEDGE | PHYSIOLOGICAL TRAINING AND CONDITIONING | PSYCHOMOTOR SKILLS / STRATEGIES | PSYCHOSOCIAL CONCEPTS

Warm-Up

Preparing for a Round: Mental Skills

Equipment

Golf Today

Basic Rules

Playing the Game

Strategies

Individual Technique

Uneven Lies

Sand

Putting

Chipping

Pitching

Ball Flight

Full Swing Motion Without a Club | Set Up With Club | Applying Full Swing Motion With a Club

Learning From a Round

Setting Goals

Shot Selection and Course Management

Etiquette

Pre-Shot Routines

Effective Practice

Chipping

Preparation

Why Important

Stroke used close to green

Objective is to place ball on green with a low, rolling trajectory

Set Up

Stance narrower than shoulders

Feet and hips open

Weight on target side

Blade delofted

Execution

Backswing

Shoulders, arms, hands, and club are one unit

No weight shift

No wrist cock

Half turn back

Swing length to 1 or 2

Forwardswing

No weight shift

Shoulders, arms, hands, and club are one unit

Maintain one unit arm action

One unit at contact

Follow-Through

Half turn at chest

Swing length to 1 or 2

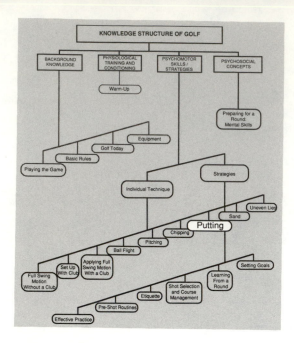

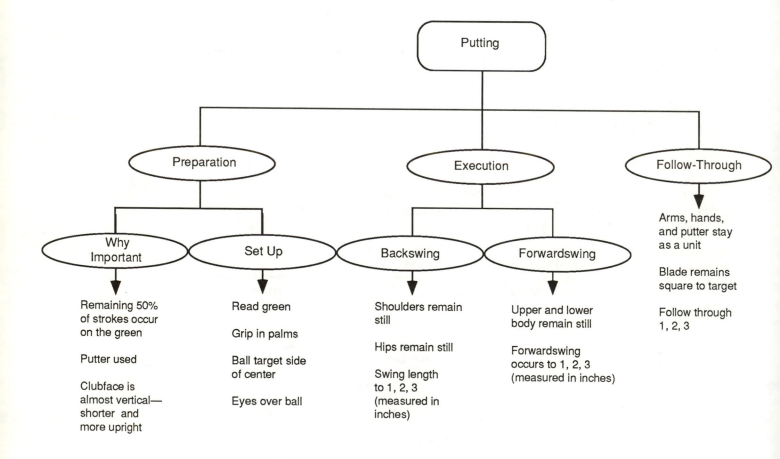

Putting

Preparation

Why Important

- Remaining 50% of strokes occur on the green
- Putter used
- Clubface is almost vertical— shorter and more upright

Set Up

- Read green
- Grip in palms
- Ball target side of center
- Eyes over ball

Execution

Backswing

- Shoulders remain still
- Hips remain still
- Swing length to 1, 2, 3 (measured in inches)

Forwardswing

- Upper and lower body remain still
- Forwardswing occurs to 1, 2, 3 (measured in inches)

Follow-Through

- Arms, hands, and putter stay as a unit
- Blade remains square to target
- Follow through 1, 2, 3

```
4 3 2 1 0 1 2 3 4
```

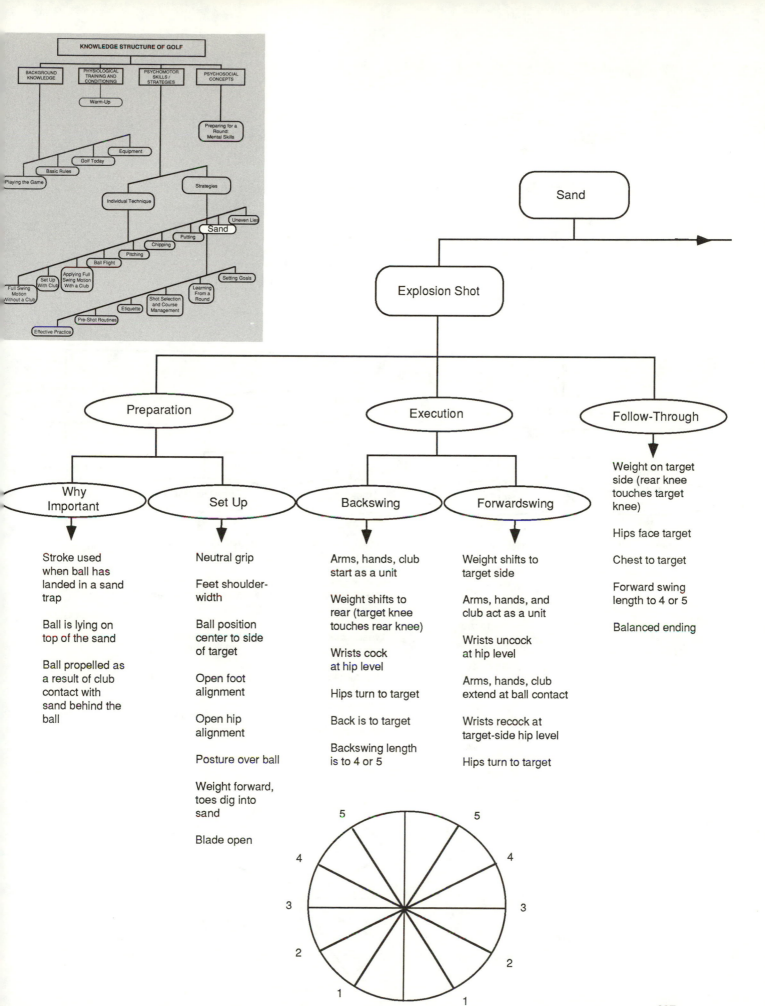

KNOWLEDGE STRUCTURE OF GOLF

Sand

Explosion Shot

Preparation

Why Important

Stroke used when ball has landed in a sand trap

Ball is lying on top of the sand

Ball propelled as a result of club contact with sand behind the ball

Set Up

Neutral grip

Feet shoulder-width

Ball position center to side of target

Open foot alignment

Open hip alignment

Posture over ball

Weight forward, toes dig into sand

Blade open

Execution

Backswing

Arms, hands, club start as a unit

Weight shifts to rear (target knee touches rear knee)

Wrists cock at hip level

Hips turn to target

Back is to target

Backswing length is to 4 or 5

Forwardswing

Weight shifts to target side

Arms, hands, and club act as a unit

Wrists uncock at hip level

Arms, hands, club extend at ball contact

Wrists recock at target-side hip level

Hips turn to target

Follow-Through

Weight on target side (rear knee touches target knee)

Hips face target

Chest to target

Forward swing length to 4 or 5

Balanced ending

227

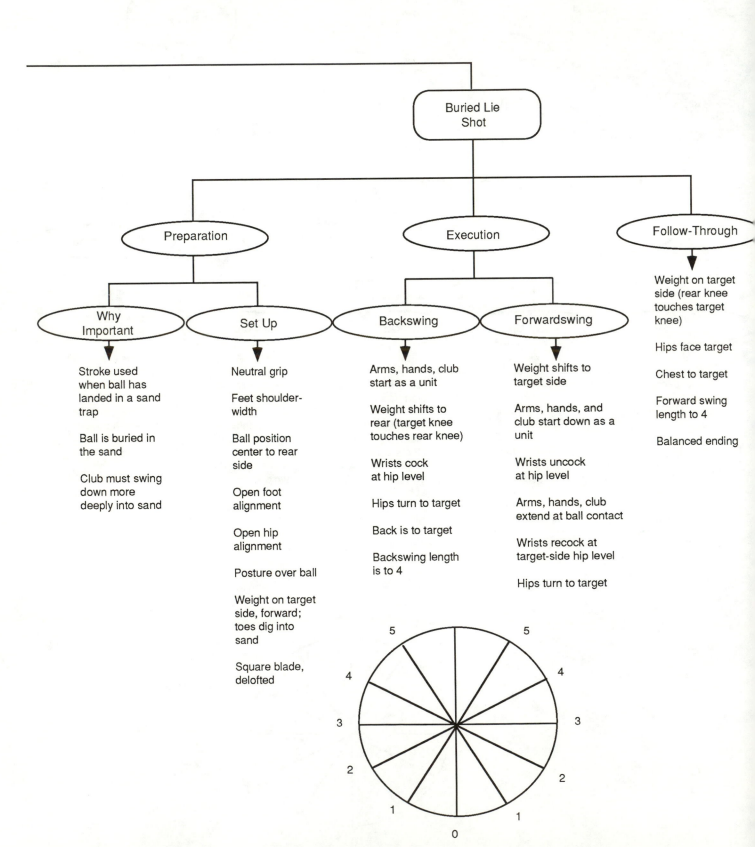

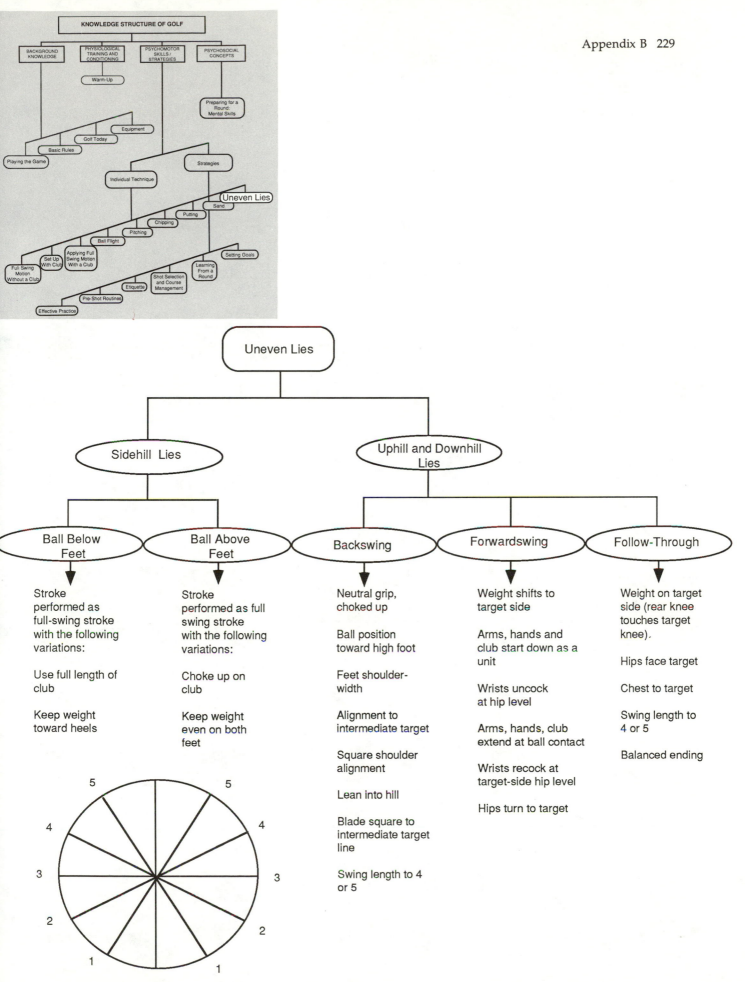

Uneven Lies

Sidehill Lies

Uphill and Downhill Lies

Ball Below Feet

Ball Above Feet

Backswing

Forwardswing

Follow-Through

Stroke performed as full-swing stroke with the following variations:

Use full length of club

Keep weight toward heels

Stroke performed as full swing stroke with the following variations:

Choke up on club

Keep weight even on both feet

Neutral grip, choked up

Ball position toward high foot

Feet shoulder-width

Alignment to intermediate target

Square shoulder alignment

Lean into hill

Blade square to intermediate target line

Swing length to 4 or 5

Weight shifts to target side

Arms, hands and club start down as a unit

Wrists uncock at hip level

Arms, hands, club extend at ball contact

Wrists recock at target-side hip level

Hips turn to target

Weight on target side (rear knee touches target knee).

Hips face target

Chest to target

Swing length to 4 or 5

Balanced ending

C

Knowledge Structure of Ice Hockey

The following ice hockey structure was created by a team of master coaches, sport scientists, elite athletes, and instructional design specialists. In a major research project funded by the Social Sciences and Humanities Research Council of Canada, ice hockey is being used as the prototype sport for developing a hypermedia system for sports teaching and coaching.

The first ice hockey structure was created by Don Kelm and me (Vickers & Kelm, 1984), using primarily text analysis techniques. This structure was extensively revised by Dr. George Kingston (head coach of the University of Calgary, assistant coach for Team Canada and the Minnesota North Stars, and currently head coach of the Norwegian National Team), and Robin Laycock, an ex-athlete of Dr. Kingston's and instructional design specialist. The physiological training and conditioning structure foundation materials were referenced from Physical Best, the new AAHPERD approach to physical fitness assessment and training (McSwegin et al., 1989), and by Dr. Howie Wenger (1986), an exercise physiologist from the University of Victoria and a specialist in ice hockey at both the community and elite levels (Team Canada).

The ice hockey structure was created for the elite coaching setting unrestricted by time, skill level, or other limitations. A wide variety of techniques has been used, including text analysis, analogical derivation, and structured interview techniques. There was also extensive use of stimulated recall: Many of the skills, strategies, and physiological testing and training materials in Appendix C have been filmed, edited, and placed on videotape/disc and software.

Note: To conserve space, the Knowledge Structure of Ice Hockey does not detail the categories "Background Knowledge," "Philosophy of the Game," and "Psychological Concepts," nor the subsections "Training Year" and "Nutrition."

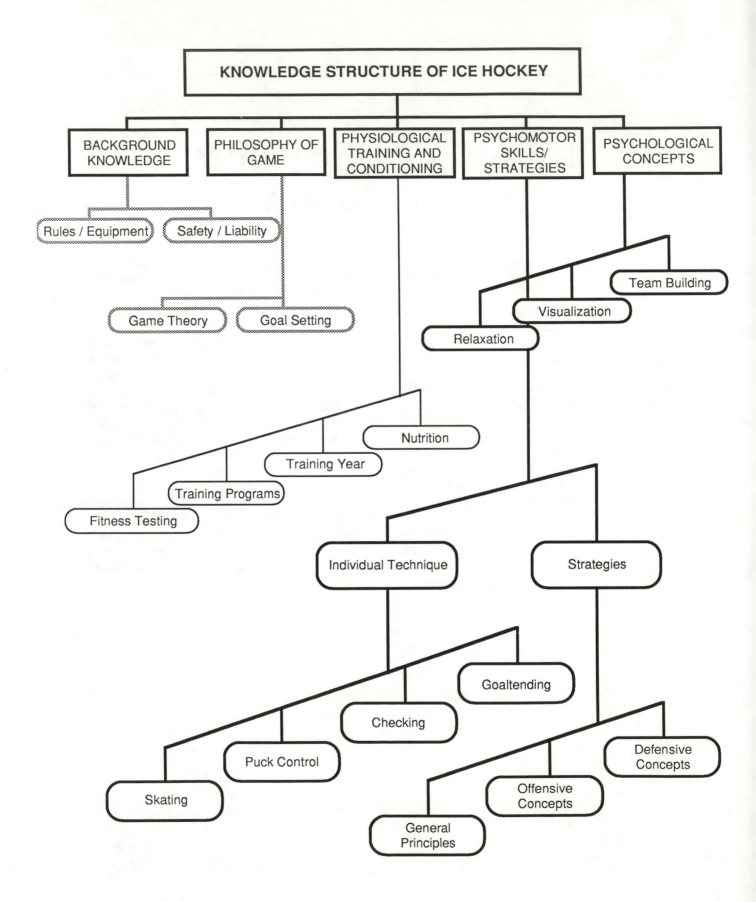

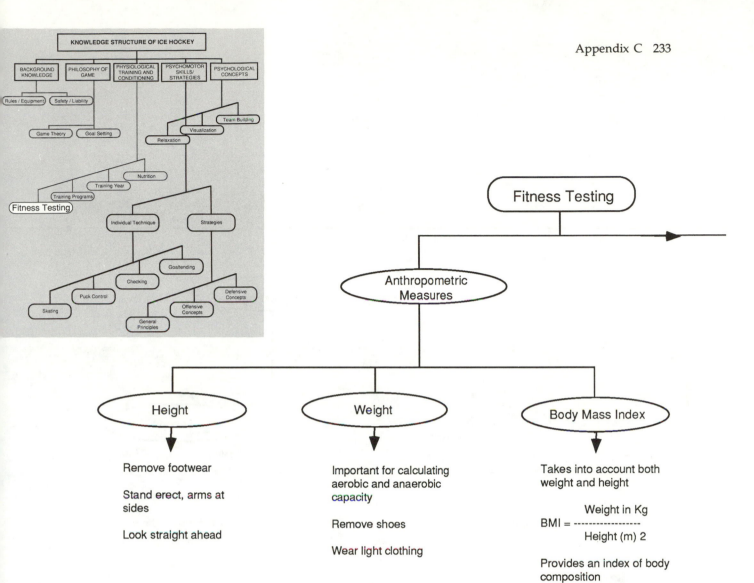

Fitness Testing

Anthropometric Measures

Height	Weight	Body Mass Index
Remove footwear	Important for calculating aerobic and anaerobic capacity	Takes into account both weight and height
Stand erect, arms at sides	Remove shoes	$BMI = \dfrac{Weight\ in\ Kg}{Height\ (m)\ 2}$
Look straight ahead	Wear light clothing	Provides an index of body composition

Recorded in cm.

Age	Boys		Girls	
Levels	1	2	1	2
6-7				
8-9				
10-11				
12-13				
14-15				
16-18				

Recorded in kg.

Age	Boys		Girls	
Levels	1	2	1	2
6-7				
8-9				
10-11				
12-13				
14-15				
16-18				

BMI Score

Age	Boys		Girls	
Levels	1	2	1	2
6-7				
8-9				
10-11				
12-13				
14-15				
16-18				

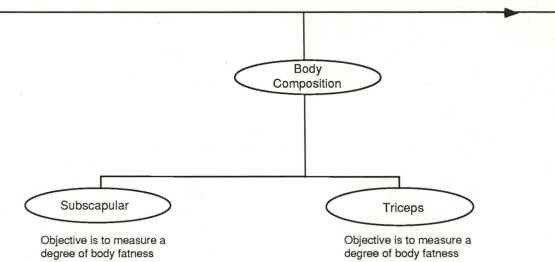

Body Composition

Subscapular

Objective is to measure a
degree of body fatness

Use skinfold calipers

Stand erect, relax

Take measure at the inferior
angle of the scapula

Recorded in mm.

Age	Boys		Girls	
Levels	1	2	1	2
6-7				
8-9				
10-11				
12-13				
14-15				
16-18				

Triceps

Objective is to measure a
degree of body fatness

Stand erect, arms at sides

Vertical fold at the midpoint
of back of the arm

Recorded in mm.

Age	Boys		Girls	
Levels	1	2	1	2
6-7				
8-9				
10-11				
12-13				
14-15				
16-18				

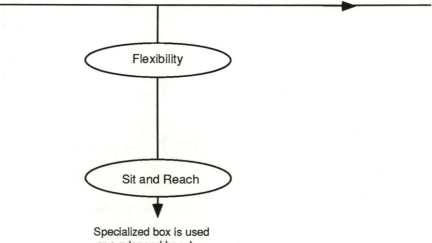

Flexibility

Sit and Reach

Specialized box is used
or a ruler and bench

Sit on floor, legs straight

Shoes off

Reach forward with both
hands as far as possible

One continuous motion

Recorded in mm.

Age	Boys		Girls	
Levels	1	2	1	2
6-7				
8-9				
10-11				
12-13				
14-15				
16-18				

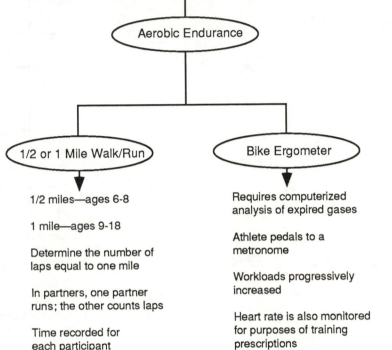

Aerobic Endurance

1/2 or 1 Mile Walk/Run

1/2 miles—ages 6-8

1 mile—ages 9-18

Determine the number of
laps equal to one mile

In partners, one partner
runs; the other counts laps

Time recorded for
each participant

Bike Ergometer

Requires computerized
analysis of expired gases

Athlete pedals to a
metronome

Workloads progressively
increased

Heart rate is also monitored
for purposes of training
prescriptions

Unit of measure is
ml/km/kpm

Age	Boys		Girls	
Levels	1	2	1	2
6-7				
8-9				
10-11				
12-13				
14-15				
16-18				

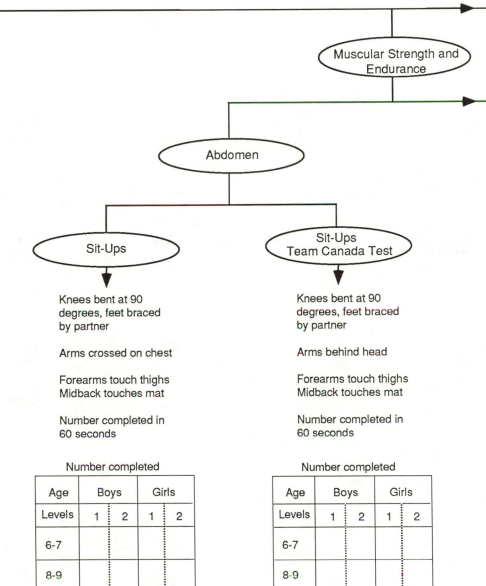

Muscular Strength and Endurance

Abdomen

Sit-Ups

Sit-Ups
Team Canada Test

Knees bent at 90
degrees, feet braced
by partner

Arms crossed on chest

Forearms touch thighs
Midback touches mat

Number completed in
60 seconds

Knees bent at 90
degrees, feet braced
by partner

Arms behind head

Forearms touch thighs
Midback touches mat

Number completed in
60 seconds

Number completed

Age	Boys		Girls	
Levels	1	2	1	2
6-7				
8-9				
10-11				
12-13				
14-15				
16-18				

Number completed

Age	Boys		Girls	
Levels	1	2	1	2
6-7				
8-9				
10-11				
12-13				
14-15				
16-18				

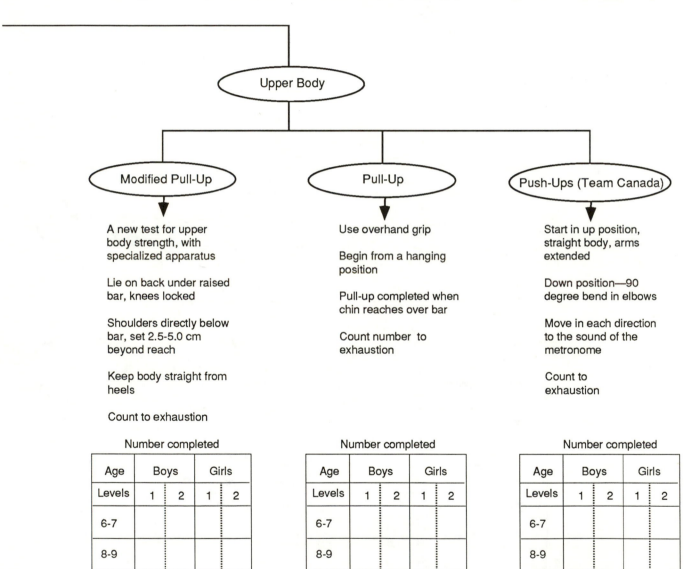

Upper Body

Modified Pull-Up

A new test for upper body strength, with specialized apparatus

Lie on back under raised bar, knees locked

Shoulders directly below bar, set 2.5-5.0 cm beyond reach

Keep body straight from heels

Count to exhaustion

Number completed

Age	Boys		Girls	
Levels	1	2	1	2
6-7				
8-9				
10-11				
12-13				
14-15				
16-18				

Pull-Up

Use overhand grip

Begin from a hanging position

Pull-up completed when chin reaches over bar

Count number to exhaustion

Number completed

Age	Boys		Girls	
Levels	1	2	1	2
6-7				
8-9				
10-11				
12-13				
14-15				
16-18				

Push-Ups (Team Canada)

Start in up position, straight body, arms extended

Down position—90 degree bend in elbows

Move in each direction to the sound of the metronome

Count to exhaustion

Number completed

Age	Boys		Girls	
Levels	1	2	1	2
6-7				
8-9				
10-11				
12-13				
14-15				
16-18				

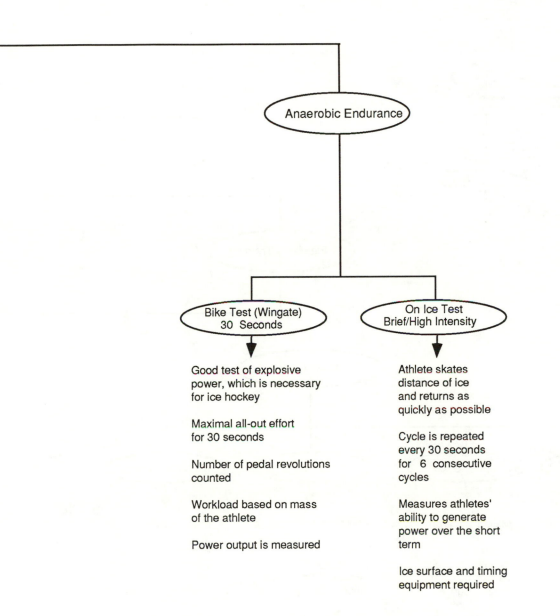

Anaerobic Endurance

Bike Test (Wingate) 30 Seconds

Good test of explosive power, which is necessary for ice hockey

Maximal all-out effort for 30 seconds

Number of pedal revolutions counted

Workload based on mass of the athlete

Power output is measured

On Ice Test Brief/High Intensity

Athlete skates distance of ice and returns as quickly as possible

Cycle is repeated every 30 seconds for 6 consecutive cycles

Measures athletes' ability to generate power over the short term

Ice surface and timing equipment required

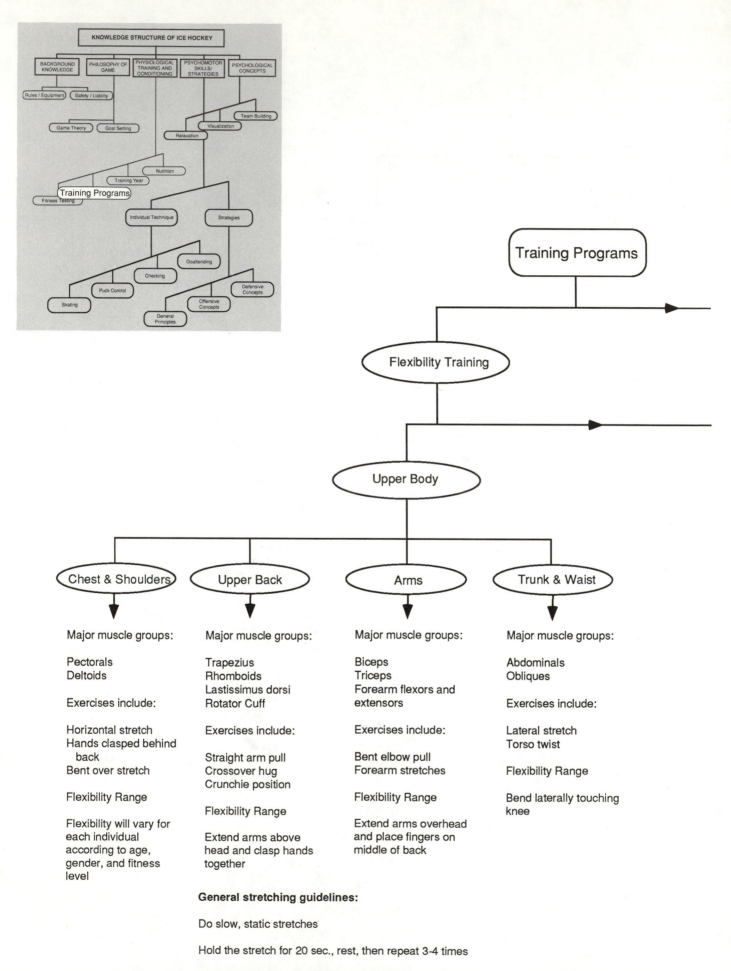

KNOWLEDGE STRUCTURE OF ICE HOCKEY

Training Programs

Flexibility Training

Upper Body

| Chest & Shoulders | Upper Back | Arms | Trunk & Waist |

Chest & Shoulders

Major muscle groups:

Pectorals
Deltoids

Exercises include:

Horizontal stretch
Hands clasped behind
  back
Bent over stretch

Flexibility Range

Flexibility will vary for
each individual
according to age,
gender, and fitness
level

Upper Back

Major muscle groups:

Trapezius
Rhomboids
Lastissimus dorsi
Rotator Cuff

Exercises include:

Straight arm pull
Crossover hug
Crunchie position

Flexibility Range

Extend arms above
head and clasp hands
together

Arms

Major muscle groups:

Biceps
Triceps
Forearm flexors and
extensors

Exercises include:

Bent elbow pull
Forearm stretches

Flexibility Range

Extend arms overhead
and place fingers on
middle of back

Trunk & Waist

Major muscle groups:

Abdominals
Obliques

Exercises include:

Lateral stretch
Torso twist

Flexibility Range

Bend laterally touching
knee

General stretching guidelines:

Do slow, static stretches

Hold the stretch for 20 sec., rest, then repeat 3-4 times

Do not force any stretch to the point of pain

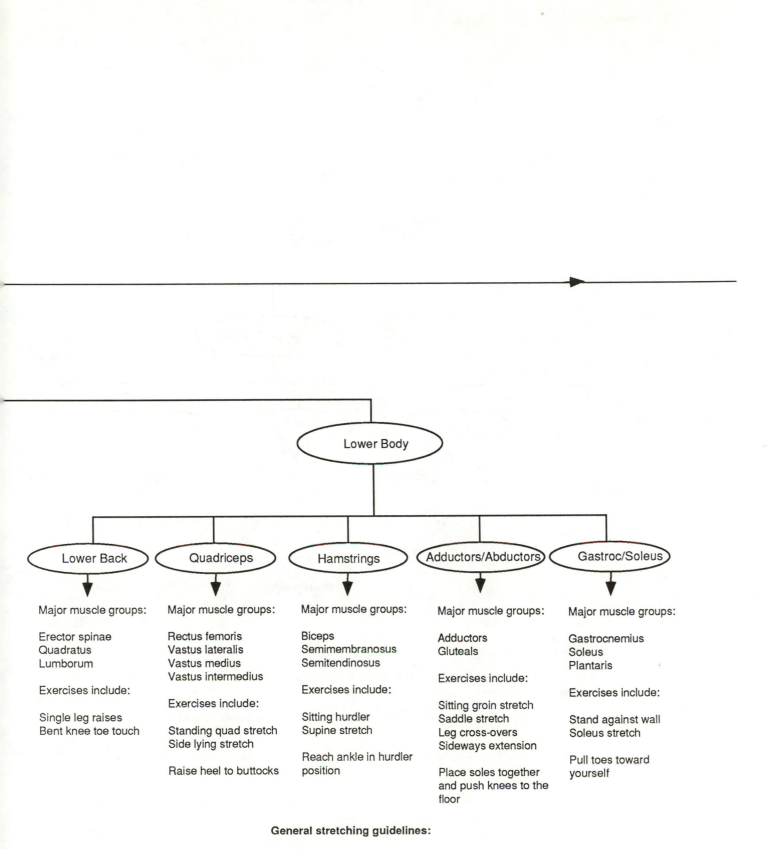

Lower Body

Lower Back

Major muscle groups:

Erector spinae
Quadratus
Lumborum

Exercises include:

Single leg raises
Bent knee toe touch

Quadriceps

Major muscle groups:

Rectus femoris
Vastus lateralis
Vastus medius
Vastus intermedius

Exercises include:

Standing quad stretch
Side lying stretch

Raise heel to buttocks

Hamstrings

Major muscle groups:

Biceps
Semimembranosus
Semitendinosus

Exercises include:

Sitting hurdler
Supine stretch

Reach ankle in hurdler position

Adductors/Abductors

Major muscle groups:

Adductors
Gluteals

Exercises include:

Sitting groin stretch
Saddle stretch
Leg cross-overs
Sideways extension

Place soles together and push knees to the floor

Gastroc/Soleus

Major muscle groups:

Gastrocnemius
Soleus
Plantaris

Exercises include:

Stand against wall
Soleus stretch

Pull toes toward yourself

General stretching guidelines:

Do slow, static stretches

Hold the stretch for 20 sec., rest, then repeat 3-4 times

Do not force any stretch to the point of pain

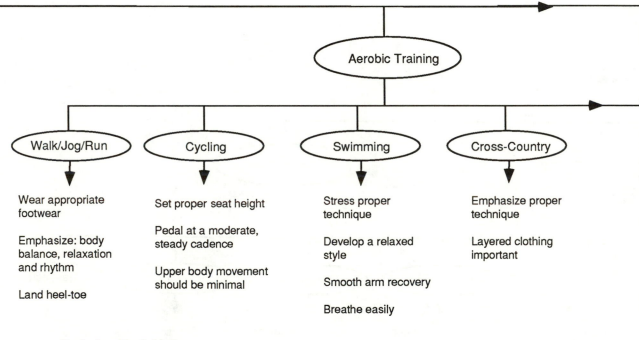

Basic Aerobic Guidelines:

Frequency: 3-4 times a week

Intensity: 60-80% of maximum heart rate (approximately 120-160 bpm)
Intensity will vary according to age and fitness level

Duration: minimum of 20 minutes long, slow work, gradually increase duration 20, 40, 50, 60 minutes of exercise

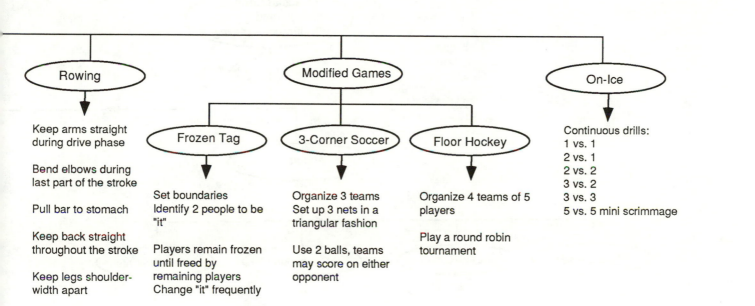

Rowing

Keep arms straight
during drive phase

Bend elbows during
last part of the stroke

Pull bar to stomach

Keep back straight
throughout the stroke

Keep legs shoulder-
width apart

Modified Games

Frozen Tag

Set boundaries
Identify 2 people to be
"it"

Players remain frozen
until freed by
remaining players
Change "it" frequently

3-Corner Soccer

Organize 3 teams
Set up 3 nets in a
triangular fashion

Use 2 balls, teams
may score on either
opponent

Floor Hockey

Organize 4 teams of 5
players

Play a round robin
tournament

On-Ice

Continuous drills:
1 vs. 1
2 vs. 1
2 vs. 2
3 vs. 2
3 vs. 3
5 vs. 5 mini scrimmage

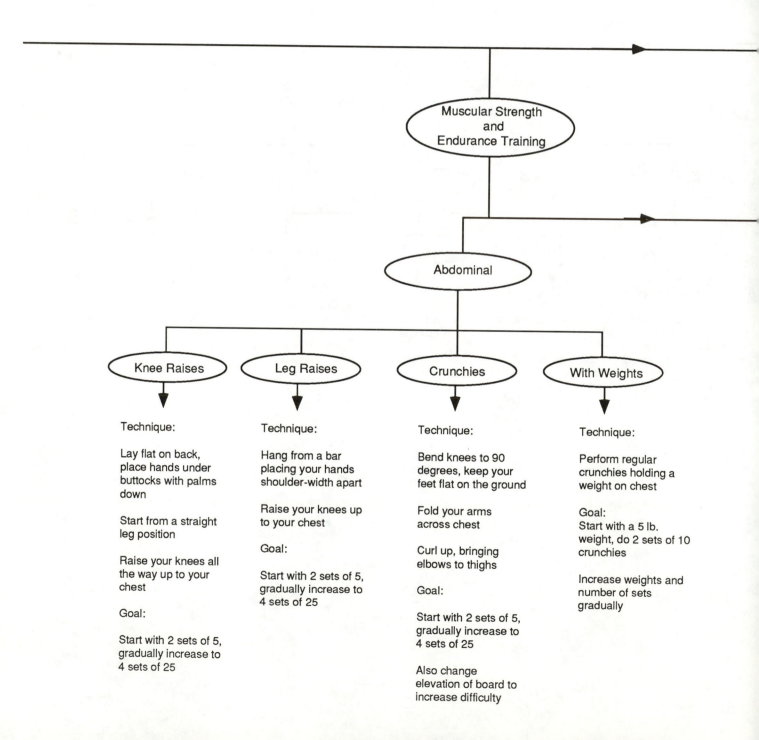

Muscular Strength and Endurance Training

Abdominal

Knee Raises

Technique:

Lay flat on back, place hands under buttocks with palms down

Start from a straight leg position

Raise your knees all the way up to your chest

Goal:

Start with 2 sets of 5, gradually increase to 4 sets of 25

Leg Raises

Technique:

Hang from a bar placing your hands shoulder-width apart

Raise your knees up to your chest

Goal:

Start with 2 sets of 5, gradually increase to 4 sets of 25

Crunchies

Technique:

Bend knees to 90 degrees, keep your feet flat on the ground

Fold your arms across chest

Curl up, bringing elbows to thighs

Goal:

Start with 2 sets of 5, gradually increase to 4 sets of 25

Also change elevation of board to increase difficulty

With Weights

Technique:

Perform regular crunchies holding a weight on chest

Goal:
Start with a 5 lb. weight, do 2 sets of 10 crunchies

Increase weights and number of sets gradually

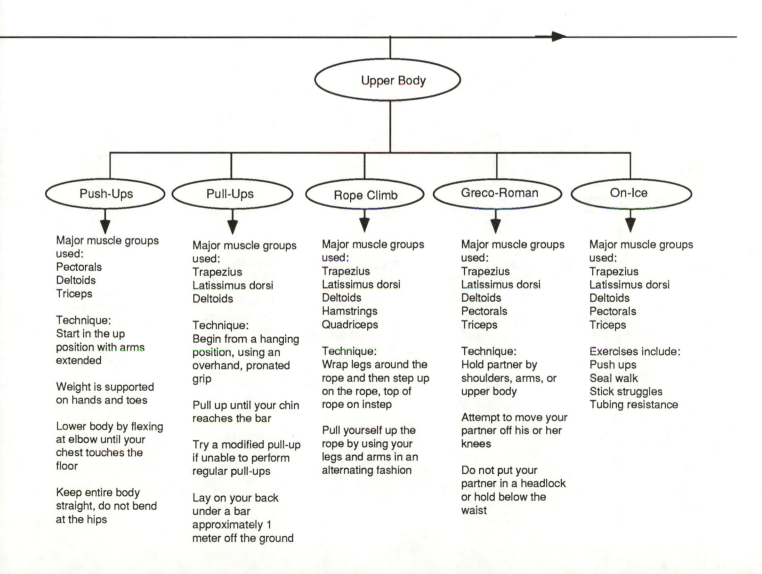

Upper Body

Push-Ups

Major muscle groups
used:
Pectorals
Deltoids
Triceps

Technique:
Start in the up
position with arms
extended

Weight is supported
on hands and toes

Lower body by flexing
at elbow until your
chest touches the
floor

Keep entire body
straight, do not bend
at the hips

Pull-Ups

Major muscle groups
used:
Trapezius
Latissimus dorsi
Deltoids

Technique:
Begin from a hanging
position, using an
overhand, pronated
grip

Pull up until your chin
reaches the bar

Try a modified pull-up
if unable to perform
regular pull-ups

Lay on your back
under a bar
approximately 1
meter off the ground

Rope Climb

Major muscle groups
used:
Trapezius
Latissimus dorsi
Deltoids
Hamstrings
Quadriceps

Technique:
Wrap legs around the
rope and then step up
on the rope, top of
rope on instep

Pull yourself up the
rope by using your
legs and arms in an
alternating fashion

Greco-Roman

Major muscle groups
used:
Trapezius
Latissimus dorsi
Deltoids
Pectorals
Triceps

Technique:
Hold partner by
shoulders, arms, or
upper body

Attempt to move your
partner off his or her
knees

Do not put your
partner in a headlock
or hold below the
waist

On-Ice

Major muscle groups
used:
Trapezius
Latissimus dorsi
Deltoids
Pectorals
Triceps

Exercises include:
Push ups
Seal walk
Stick struggles
Tubing resistance

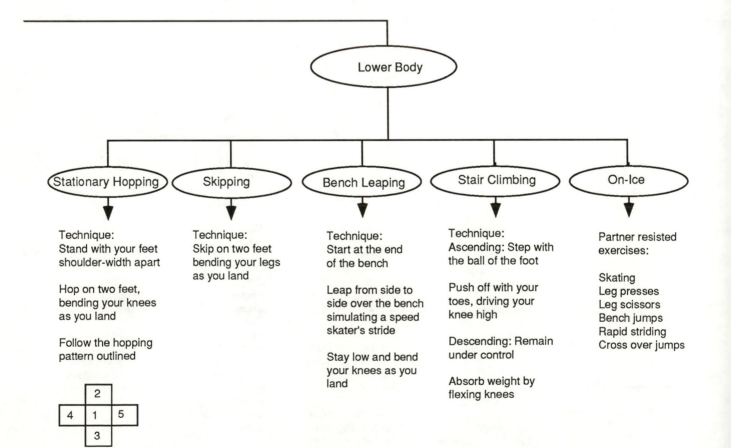

Lower Body

Stationary Hopping

Technique:
Stand with your feet
shoulder-width apart

Hop on two feet,
bending your knees
as you land

Follow the hopping
pattern outlined

	2	
4	1	5
	3	

Skipping

Technique:
Skip on two feet
bending your legs
as you land

Bench Leaping

Technique:
Start at the end
of the bench

Leap from side to
side over the bench
simulating a speed
skater's stride

Stay low and bend
your knees as you
land

Stair Climbing

Technique:
Ascending: Step with
the ball of the foot

Push off with your
toes, driving your
knee high

Descending: Remain
under control

Absorb weight by
flexing knees

On-Ice

Partner resisted
exercises:

Skating
Leg presses
Leg scissors
Bench jumps
Rapid striding
Cross over jumps

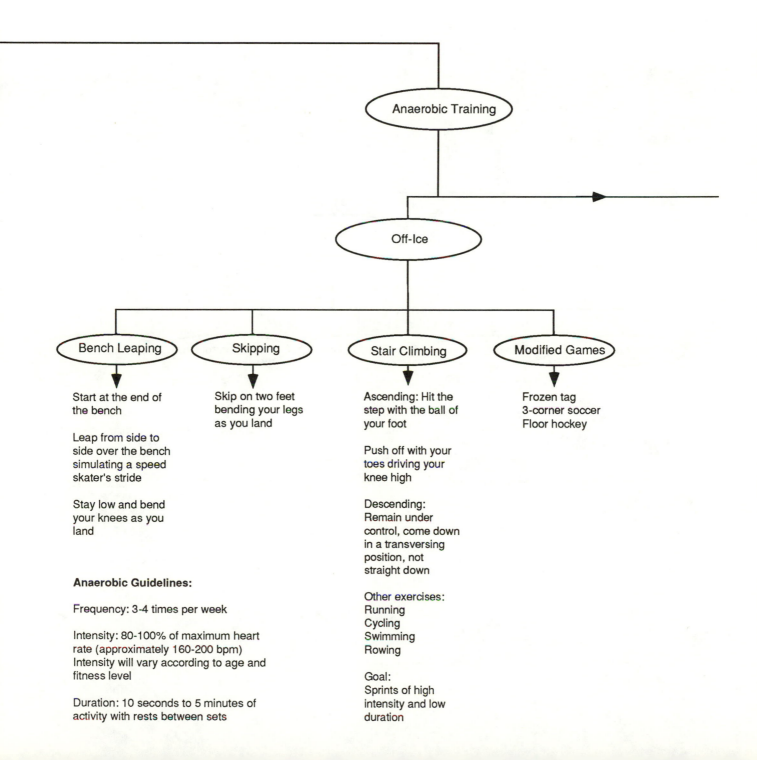

Anaerobic Training

Off-Ice

Bench Leaping

Skipping

Stair Climbing

Modified Games

Start at the end of
the bench

Leap from side to
side over the bench
simulating a speed
skater's stride

Stay low and bend
your knees as you
land

Anaerobic Guidelines:

Frequency: 3-4 times per week

Intensity: 80-100% of maximum heart
rate (approximately 160-200 bpm)
Intensity will vary according to age and
fitness level

Duration: 10 seconds to 5 minutes of
activity with rests between sets

Skip on two feet
bending your legs
as you land

Ascending: Hit the
step with the ball of
your foot

Push off with your
toes driving your
knee high

Descending:
Remain under
control, come down
in a transversing
position, not
straight down

Other exercises:
Running
Cycling
Swimming
Rowing

Goal:
Sprints of high
intensity and low
duration

Frozen tag
3-corner soccer
Floor hockey

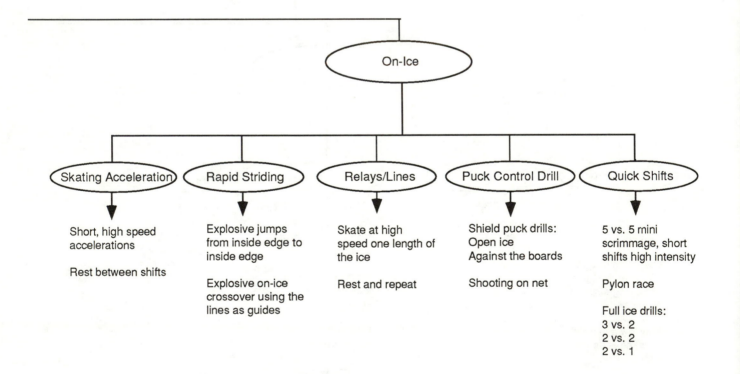

On-Ice

| Skating Acceleration | Rapid Striding | Relays/Lines | Puck Control Drill | Quick Shifts |

Short, high speed accelerations

Rest between shifts

Explosive jumps from inside edge to inside edge

Explosive on-ice crossover using the lines as guides

Skate at high speed one length of the ice

Rest and repeat

Shield puck drills:
Open ice
Against the boards

Shooting on net

5 vs. 5 mini scrimmage, short shifts high intensity

Pylon race

Full ice drills:
3 vs. 2
2 vs. 2
2 vs. 1

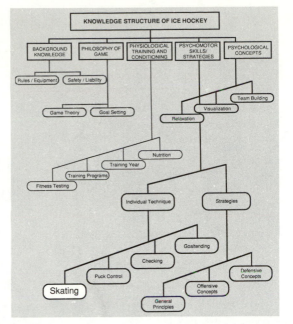

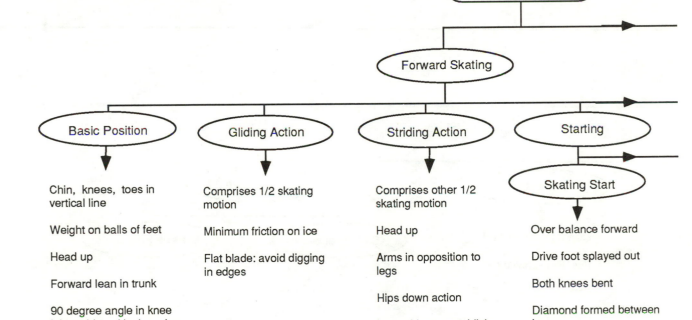

Skating

Forward Skating

Basic Position

Chin, knees, toes in vertical line

Weight on balls of feet

Head up

Forward lean in trunk

90 degree angle in knee joint achieved by lowering the hips

Ready (all sports) position

Gliding Action

Comprises 1/2 skating motion

Minimum friction on ice

Flat blade: avoid digging in edges

Striding Action

Comprises other 1/2 skating motion

Head up

Arms in opposition to legs

Hips down action

Lower hips to establish 90 degree knee joint angle

Vigorous full-blade push

Drive leg fully extended

Toe extended—splayed foot

Quick, low recovery of stride skate

Weight transfer for transition to ready glide leg for striding

Starting

Skating Start

Over balance forward

Drive foot splayed out

Both knees bent

Diamond formed between legs

Use inside edges

Vigorous push

Short, vigorous skating strides

Lengthen stride into regular skating motion

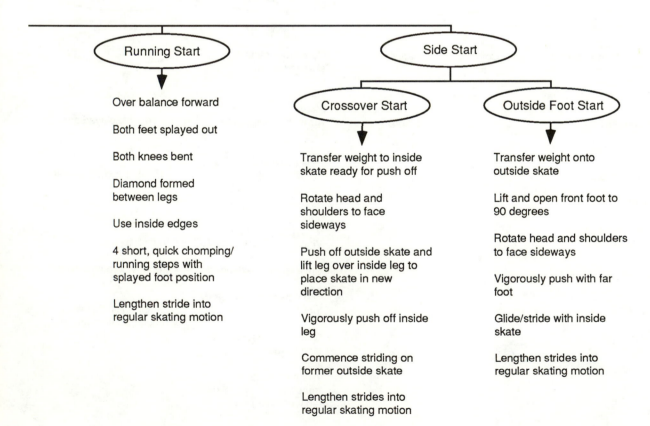

Running Start

Over balance forward

Both feet splayed out

Both knees bent

Diamond formed
between legs

Use inside edges

4 short, quick chomping/
running steps with
splayed foot position

Lengthen stride into
regular skating motion

Side Start

Crossover Start

Transfer weight to inside
skate ready for push off

Rotate head and
shoulders to face
sideways

Push off outside skate and
lift leg over inside leg to
place skate in new
direction

Vigorously push off inside
leg

Commence striding on
former outside skate

Lengthen strides into
regular skating motion

Outside Foot Start

Transfer weight onto
outside skate

Lift and open front foot to
90 degrees

Rotate head and shoulders
to face sideways

Vigorously push with far
foot

Glide/stride with inside
skate

Lengthen strides into
regular skating motion

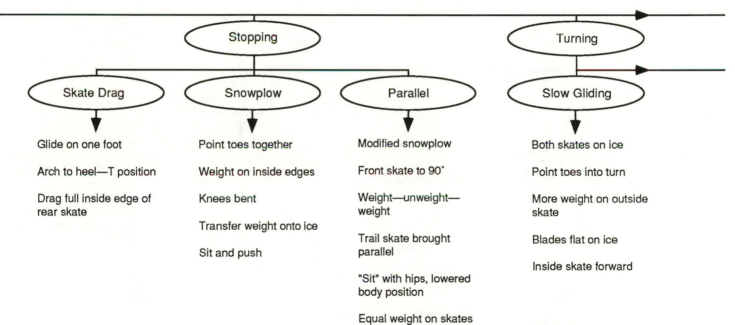

Stopping

Skate Drag

Glide on one foot

Arch to heel—T position

Drag full inside edge of
rear skate

Snowplow

Point toes together

Weight on inside edges

Knees bent

Transfer weight onto ice

Sit and push

Parallel

Modified snowplow

Front skate to 90˚

Weight—unweight—
weight

Trail skate brought
parallel

"Sit" with hips, lowered
body position

Equal weight on skates
on balls of feet

Push hard into ice

Turning

Slow Gliding

Both skates on ice

Point toes into turn

More weight on outside
skate

Blades flat on ice

Inside skate forward

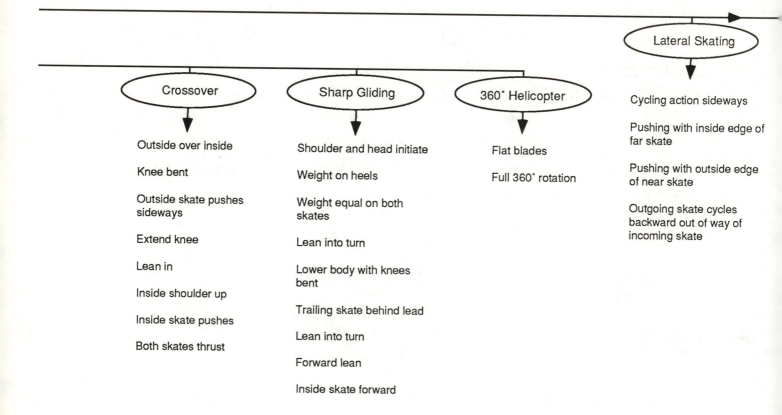

Lateral Skating

Cycling action sideways

Pushing with inside edge of far skate

Pushing with outside edge of near skate

Outgoing skate cycles backward out of way of incoming skate

Crossover

Outside over inside

Knee bent

Outside skate pushes sideways

Extend knee

Lean in

Inside shoulder up

Inside skate pushes

Both skates thrust

Sharp Gliding

Shoulder and head initiate

Weight on heels

Weight equal on both skates

Lean into turn

Lower body with knees bent

Trailing skate behind lead

Lean into turn

Forward lean

Inside skate forward

360° Helicopter

Flat blades

Full 360° rotation

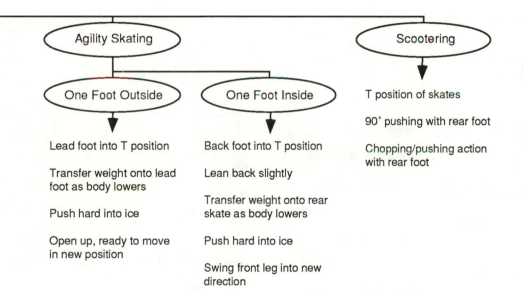

Agility Skating

One Foot Outside

Lead foot into T position

Transfer weight onto lead
foot as body lowers

Push hard into ice

Open up, ready to move
in new position

One Foot Inside

Back foot into T position

Lean back slightly

Transfer weight onto rear
skate as body lowers

Push hard into ice

Swing front leg into new
direction

Scootering

T position of skates

90° pushing with rear foot

Chopping/pushing action
with rear foot

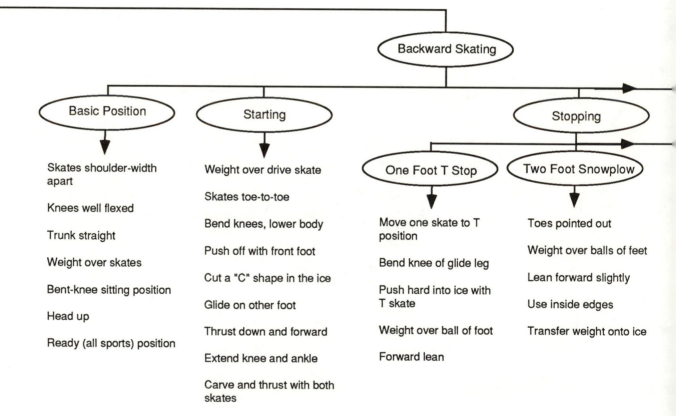

Backward Skating

Basic Position

Skates shoulder-width apart

Knees well flexed

Trunk straight

Weight over skates

Bent-knee sitting position

Head up

Ready (all sports) position

Starting

Weight over drive skate

Skates toe-to-toe

Bend knees, lower body

Push off with front foot

Cut a "C" shape in the ice

Glide on other foot

Thrust down and forward

Extend knee and ankle

Carve and thrust with both skates

Stopping

One Foot T Stop

Move one skate to T position

Bend knee of glide leg

Push hard into ice with T skate

Weight over ball of foot

Forward lean

Two Foot Snowplow

Toes pointed out

Weight over balls of feet

Lean forward slightly

Use inside edges

Transfer weight onto ice

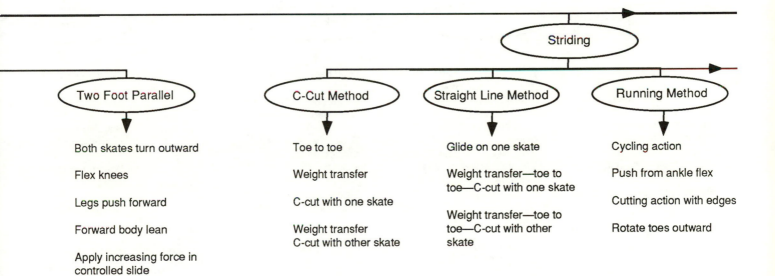

Striding

Two Foot Parallel	C-Cut Method	Straight Line Method	Running Method
Both skates turn outward	Toe to toe	Glide on one skate	Cycling action
Flex knees	Weight transfer	Weight transfer—toe to toe—C-cut with one skate	Push from ankle flex
Legs push forward	C-cut with one skate		Cutting action with edges
Forward body lean	Weight transfer C-cut with other skate	Weight transfer—toe to toe—C-cut with other skate	Rotate toes outward
Apply increasing force in controlled slide			

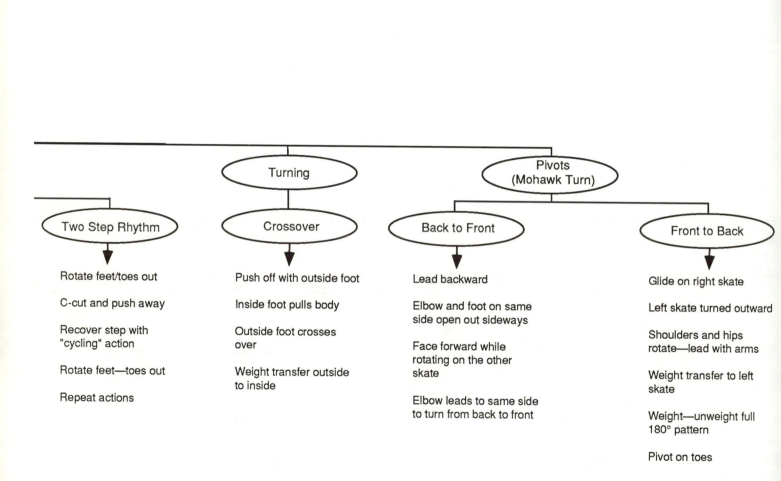

Turning

Two Step Rhythm

Rotate feet/toes out

C-cut and push away

Recover step with "cycling" action

Rotate feet—toes out

Repeat actions

Crossover

Push off with outside foot

Inside foot pulls body

Outside foot crosses over

Weight transfer outside to inside

Pivots (Mohawk Turn)

Back to Front

Lead backward

Elbow and foot on same side open out sideways

Face forward while rotating on the other skate

Elbow leads to same side to turn from back to front

Front to Back

Glide on right skate

Left skate turned outward

Shoulders and hips rotate—lead with arms

Weight transfer to left skate

Weight—unweight full 180° pattern

Pivot on toes

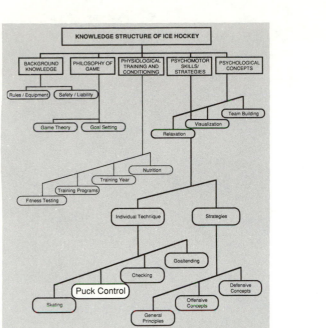

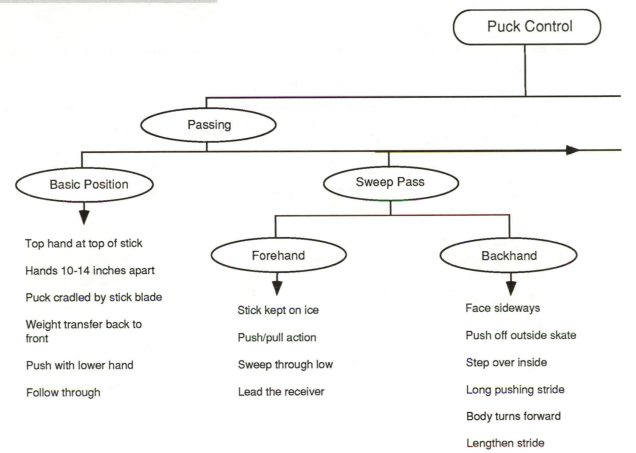

Puck Control

Passing

Basic Position

Top hand at top of stick

Hands 10-14 inches apart

Puck cradled by stick blade

Weight transfer back to front

Push with lower hand

Follow through

Sweep Pass

Forehand

Stick kept on ice

Push/pull action

Sweep through low

Lead the receiver

Backhand

Face sideways

Push off outside skate

Step over inside

Long pushing stride

Body turns forward

Lengthen stride

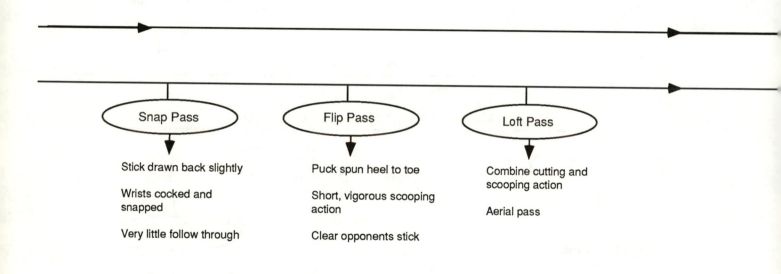

Snap Pass	Flip Pass	Loft Pass
Stick drawn back slightly	Puck spun heel to toe	Combine cutting and scooping action
Wrists cocked and snapped	Short, vigorous scooping action	Aerial pass
Very little follow through	Clear opponents stick	

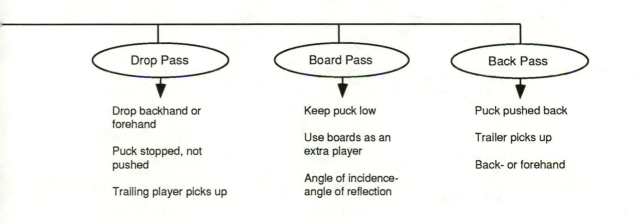

Drop Pass

Drop backhand or
forehand

Puck stopped, not
pushed

Trailing player picks up

Board Pass

Keep puck low

Use boards as an
extra player

Angle of incidence-
angle of reflection

Back Pass

Puck pushed back

Trailer picks up

Back- or forehand

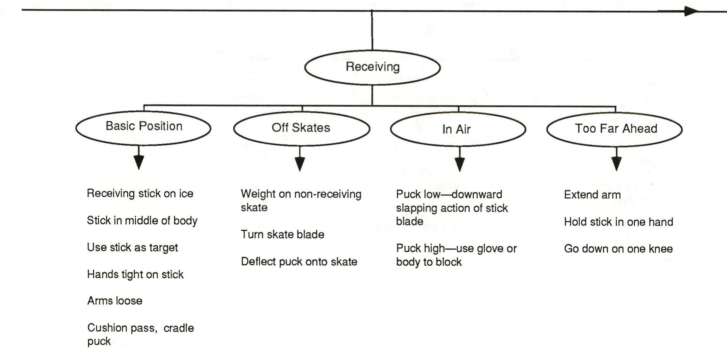

Receiving

Basic Position	Off Skates	In Air	Too Far Ahead

Receiving stick on ice

Stick in middle of body

Use stick as target

Hands tight on stick

Arms loose

Cushion pass, cradle puck

Blade at 90° angle to passed puck

Weight on non-receiving skate

Turn skate blade

Deflect puck onto skate

Puck low—downward slapping action of stick blade

Puck high—use glove or body to block

Extend arm

Hold stick in one hand

Go down on one knee

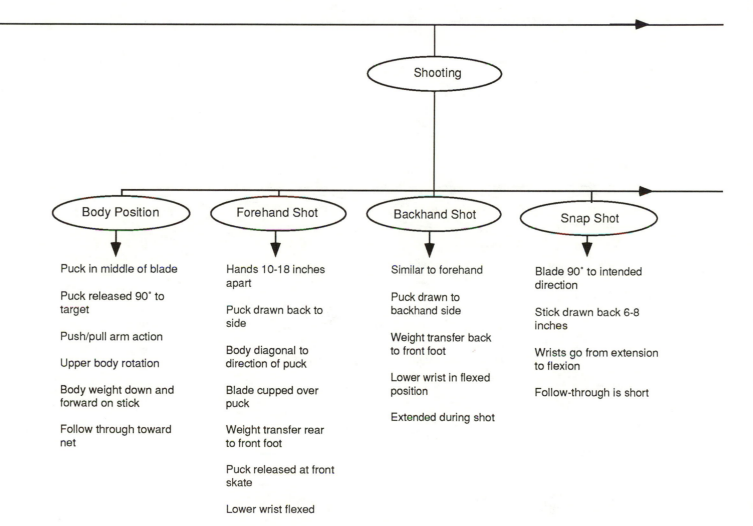

Shooting

Body Position

Puck in middle of blade

Puck released 90° to
target

Push/pull arm action

Upper body rotation

Body weight down and
forward on stick

Follow through toward
net

Forehand Shot

Hands 10-18 inches
apart

Puck drawn back to
side

Body diagonal to
direction of puck

Blade cupped over
puck

Weight transfer rear
to front foot

Puck released at front
skate

Lower wrist flexed

Weight transfer rear
to front foot

Backhand Shot

Similar to forehand

Puck drawn to
backhand side

Weight transfer back
to front foot

Lower wrist in flexed
position

Extended during shot

Snap Shot

Blade 90° to intended
direction

Stick drawn back 6-8
inches

Wrists go from extension
to flexion

Follow-through is short

```
────────────────────────────────────────────────────────────────────────▶
```

```
──────────┬──────────────┬──────────────┬──────────────┐
```

(**Slap Shot**)   (**Flip Shot**)   (**Rebounds**)   (**Tip Ins**)

▼   ▼   ▼   ▼

Puck in middle of blade

Body parallel to
direction of puck

Puck near the heel of
front skate

Lower hand slips down,
arm extended

Stick drawn back to
shoulder height

Lower arm rigid

Eyes on puck

Weight transfer back to
front foot

Pressure downward on
stick

Lower hand moved
down shaft

Open blade

Puck lifted

Follow through high

As a trailer, anticipate
rebound

Have stick ready for a
rebound

Once you shoot, turn
toward goal, not away

Shoot again or fake

Block goal tender's vision

Feet in open stance

Tight grip on stick

Angle the blade of stick

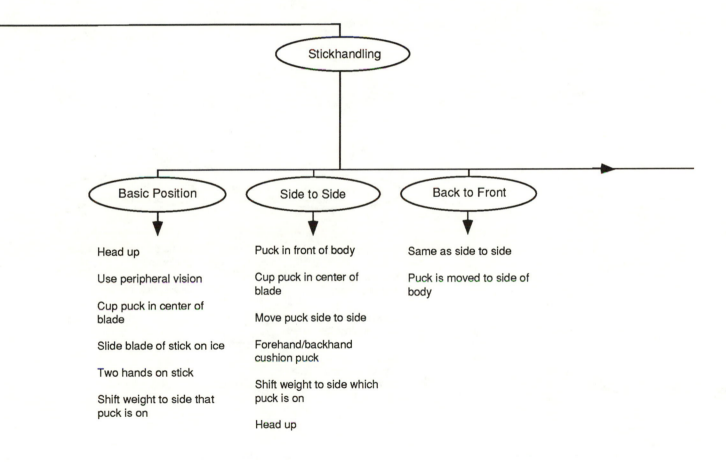

Stickhandling

Basic Position

Head up

Use peripheral vision

Cup puck in center of
blade

Slide blade of stick on ice

Two hands on stick

Shift weight to side that
puck is on

Side to Side

Puck in front of body

Cup puck in center of
blade

Move puck side to side

Forehand/backhand
cushion puck

Shift weight to side which
puck is on

Head up

Back to Front

Same as side to side

Puck is moved to side of
body

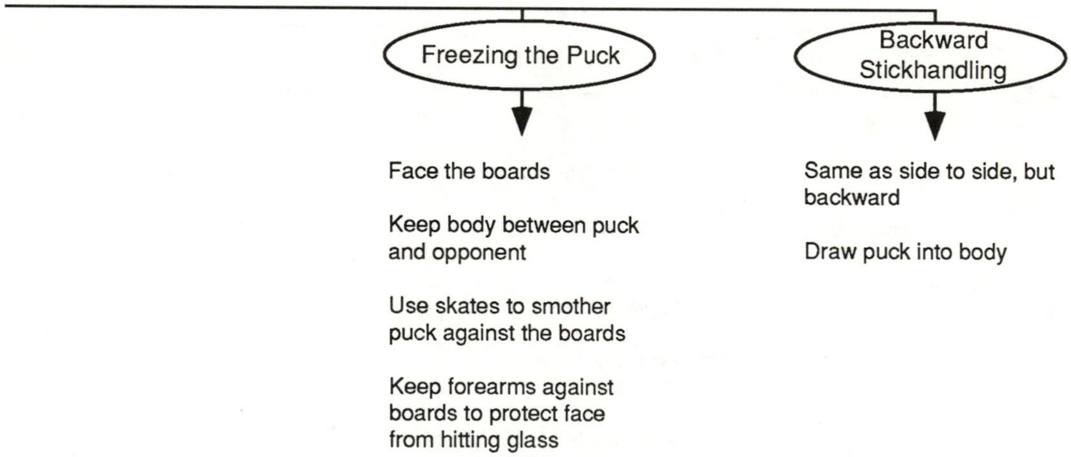

```
─────────────────────────────────────────────────────┐
```

(Freezing the Puck)   (Backward
                                           Stickhandling)

        ▼   ▼

Face the boards   Same as side to side, but
                                  backward
Keep body between puck
and opponent   Draw puck into body

Use skates to smother
puck against the boards

Keep forearms against
boards to protect face
from hitting glass

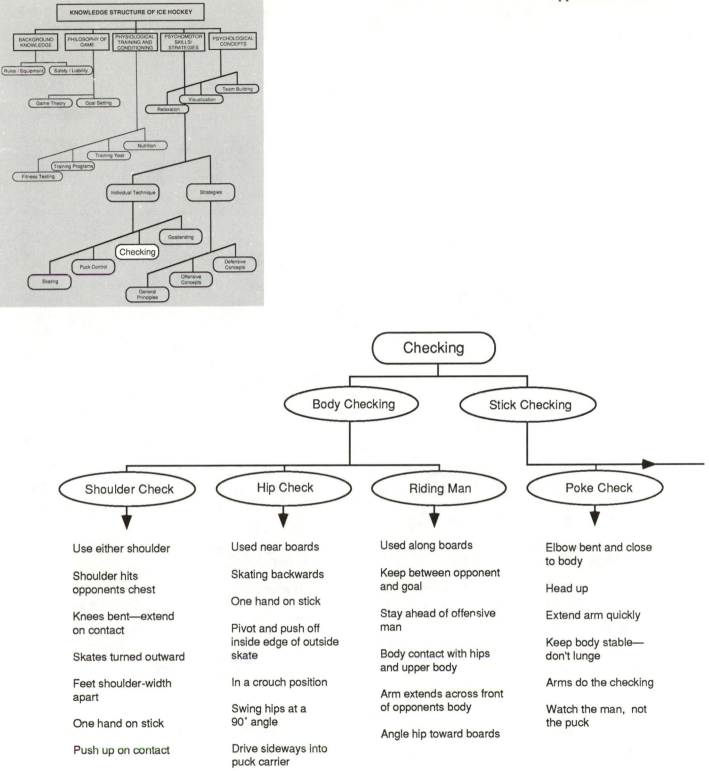

Checking

Body Checking — **Stick Checking**

Shoulder Check

Use either shoulder

Shoulder hits opponents chest

Knees bent—extend on contact

Skates turned outward

Feet shoulder-width apart

One hand on stick

Push up on contact

Hip Check

Used near boards

Skating backwards

One hand on stick

Pivot and push off inside edge of outside skate

In a crouch position

Swing hips at a 90° angle

Drive sideways into puck carrier

Riding Man

Used along boards

Keep between opponent and goal

Stay ahead of offensive man

Body contact with hips and upper body

Arm extends across front of opponents body

Angle hip toward boards

Poke Check

Elbow bent and close to body

Head up

Extend arm quickly

Keep body stable—don't lunge

Arms do the checking

Watch the man, not the puck

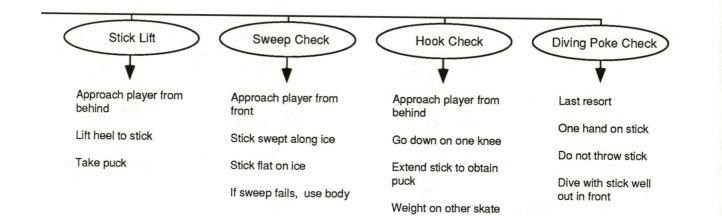

Stick Lift

Approach player from behind

Lift heel to stick

Take puck

Sweep Check

Approach player from front

Stick swept along ice

Stick flat on ice

If sweep fails, use body

Hook Check

Approach player from behind

Go down on one knee

Extend stick to obtain puck

Weight on other skate

Diving Poke Check

Last resort

One hand on stick

Do not throw stick

Dive with stick well out in front

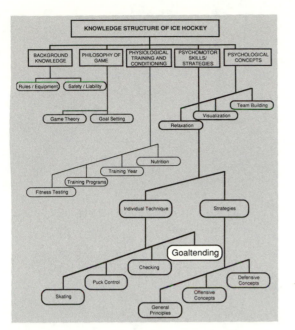

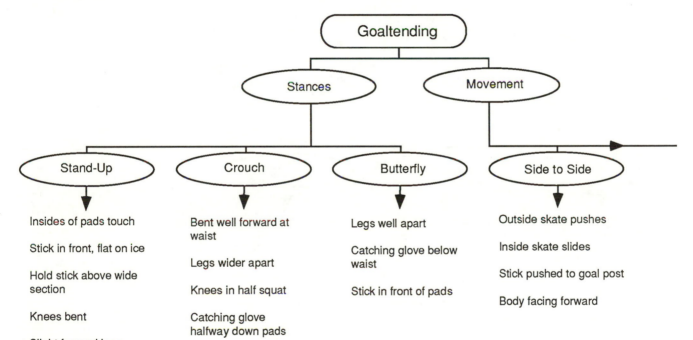

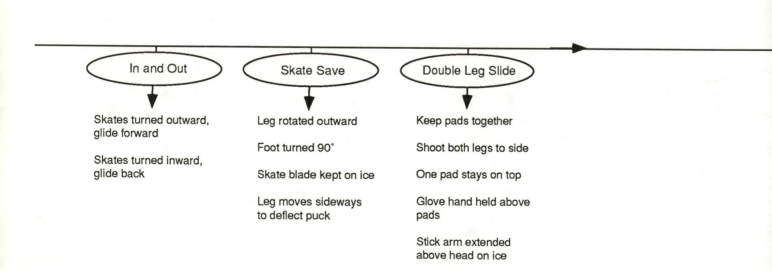

In and Out	Skate Save	Double Leg Slide
Skates turned outward, glide forward	Leg rotated outward	Keep pads together
Skates turned inward, glide back	Foot turned 90°	Shoot both legs to side
	Skate blade kept on ice	One pad stays on top
	Leg moves sideways to deflect puck	Glove hand held above pads
		Stick arm extended above head on ice

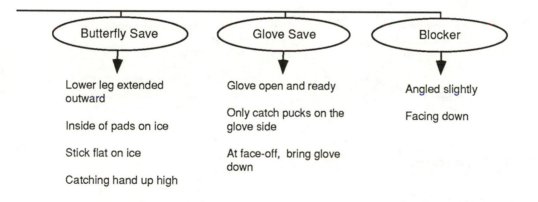

Butterfly Save

Lower leg extended outward

Inside of pads on ice

Stick flat on ice

Catching hand up high

Glove Save

Glove open and ready

Only catch pucks on the glove side

At face-off, bring glove down

Blocker

Angled slightly

Facing down

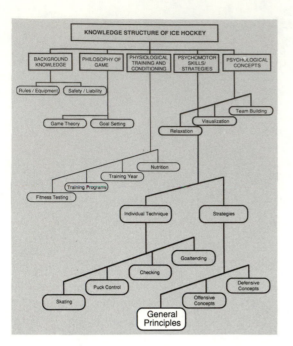

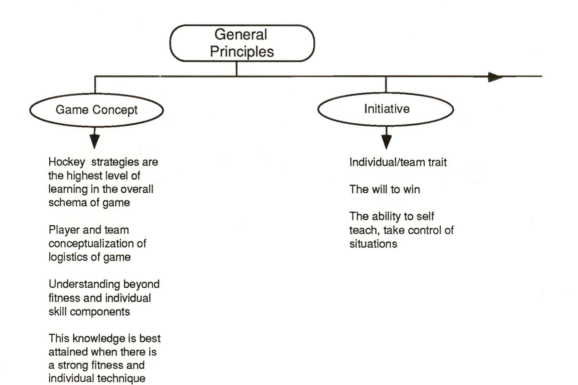

General Principles

Game Concept

Hockey strategies are the highest level of learning in the overall schema of game

Player and team conceptualization of logistics of game

Understanding beyond fitness and individual skill components

This knowledge is best attained when there is a strong fitness and individual technique base

Initiative

Individual/team trait

The will to win

The ability to self teach, take control of situations

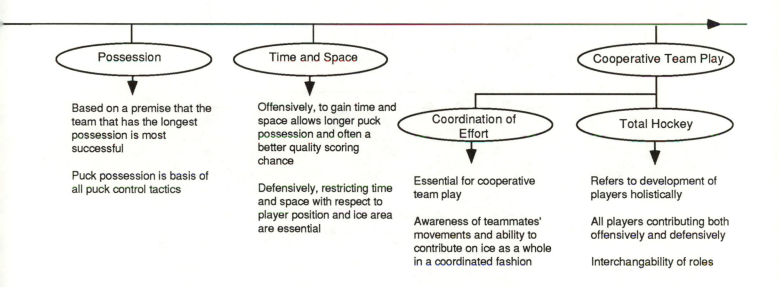

Possession

Based on a premise that the team that has the longest possession is most successful

Puck possession is basis of all puck control tactics

Time and Space

Offensively, to gain time and space allows longer puck possession and often a better quality scoring chance

Defensively, restricting time and space with respect to player position and ice area are essential

Cooperative Team Play

Coordination of Effort

Essential for cooperative team play

Awareness of teammates' movements and ability to contribute on ice as a whole in a coordinated fashion

Total Hockey

Refers to development of players holistically

All players contributing both offensively and defensively

Interchangability of roles

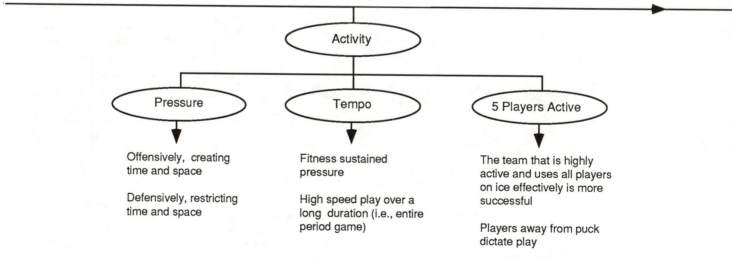

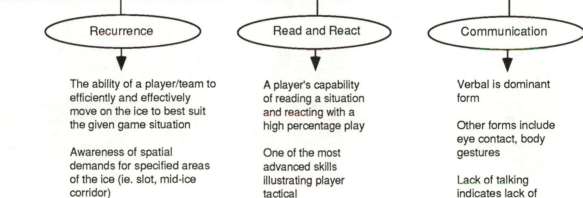

Recurrence

The ability of a player/team to efficiently and effectively move on the ice to best suit the given game situation

Awareness of spatial demands for specified areas of the ice (ie. slot, mid-ice corridor)

Read and React

A player's capability of reading a situation and reacting with a high percentage play

One of the most advanced skills illustrating player tactical conceptualization

Communication

Verbal is dominant form

Other forms include eye contact, body gestures

Lack of talking indicates lack of understanding of the game

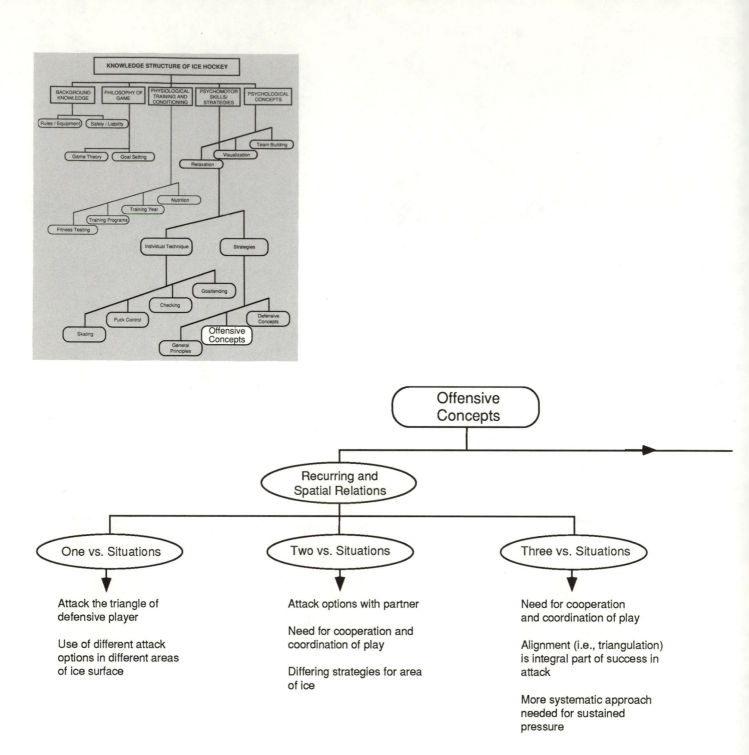

Offensive Concepts

Recurring and Spatial Relations

One vs. Situations	Two vs. Situations	Three vs. Situations
Attack the triangle of defensive player	Attack options with partner	Need for cooperation and coordination of play
Use of different attack options in different areas of ice surface	Need for cooperation and coordination of play	Alignment (i.e., triangulation) is integral part of success in attack
	Differing strategies for area of ice	More systematic approach needed for sustained pressure

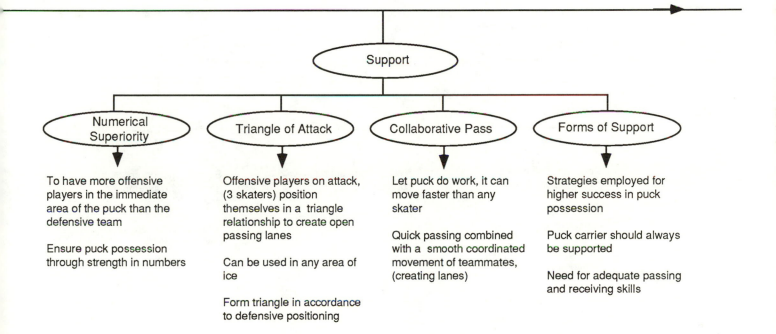

Support

Numerical Superiority

To have more offensive players in the immediate area of the puck than the defensive team

Ensure puck possession through strength in numbers

Triangle of Attack

Offensive players on attack, (3 skaters) position themselves in a triangle relationship to create open passing lanes

Can be used in any area of ice

Form triangle in accordance to defensive positioning

Collaborative Pass

Let puck do work, it can move faster than any skater

Quick passing combined with a smooth coordinated movement of teammates, (creating lanes)

Forms of Support

Strategies employed for higher success in puck possession

Puck carrier should always be supported

Need for adequate passing and receiving skills

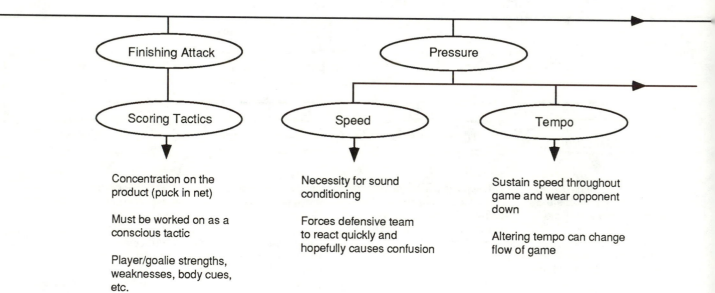

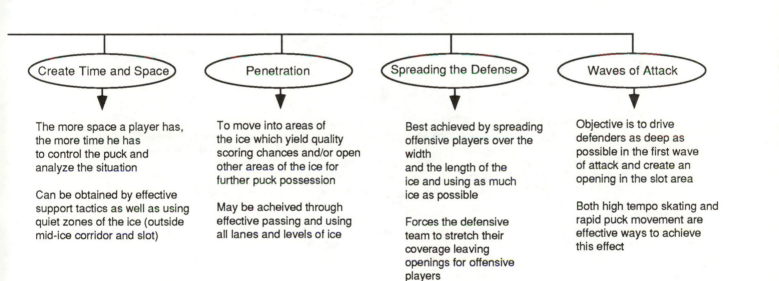

Create Time and Space

The more space a player has,
the more time he has
to control the puck and
analyze the situation

Can be obtained by effective
support tactics as well as using
quiet zones of the ice (outside
mid-ice corridor and slot)

Penetration

To move into areas of
the ice which yield quality
scoring chances and/or open
other areas of the ice for
further puck possession

May be acheived through
effective passing and using
all lanes and levels of ice

Spreading the Defense

Best achieved by spreading
offensive players over the
width
and the length of the
ice and using as much
ice as possible

Forces the defensive
team to stretch their
coverage leaving
openings for offensive
players

Waves of Attack

Objective is to drive
defenders as deep as
possible in the first wave
of attack and create an
opening in the slot area

Both high tempo skating and
rapid puck movement are
effective ways to achieve
this effect

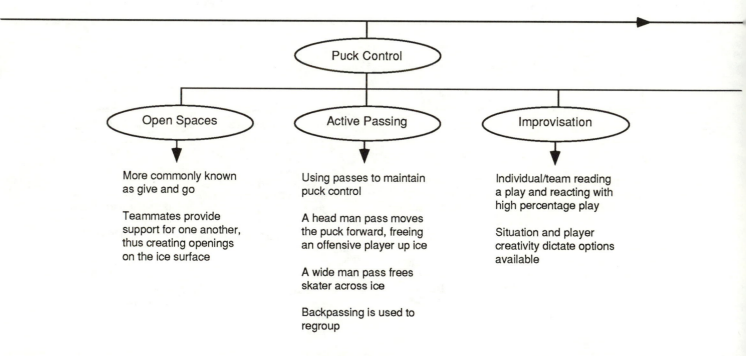

Puck Control

Open Spaces

More commonly known
as give and go

Teammates provide
support for one another,
thus creating openings
on the ice surface

Active Passing

Using passes to maintain
puck control

A head man pass moves
the puck forward, freeing
an offensive player up ice

A wide man pass frees
skater across ice

Backpassing is used to
regroup

Improvisation

Individual/team reading
a play and reacting with
high percentage play

Situation and player
creativity dictate options
available

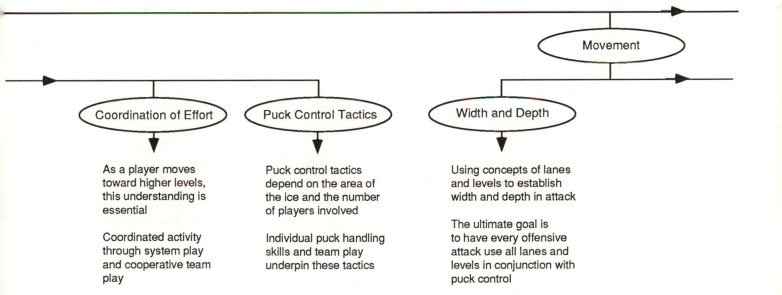

Coordination of Effort

As a player moves
toward higher levels,
this understanding is
essential

Coordinated activity
through system play
and cooperative team
play

Puck Control Tactics

Puck control tactics
depend on the area of
the ice and the number
of players involved

Individual puck handling
skills and team play
underpin these tactics

Movement

Width and Depth

Using concepts of lanes
and levels to establish
width and depth in attack

The ultimate goal is
to have every offensive
attack use all lanes and
levels in conjunction with
puck control

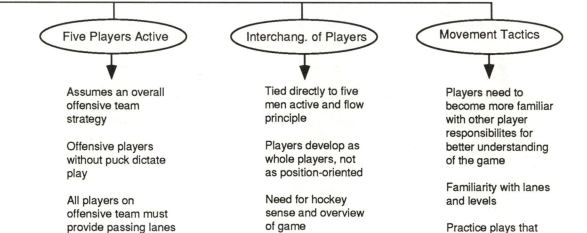

Five Players Active

Assumes an overall
offensive team
strategy

Offensive players
without puck dictate
play

All players on
offensive team must
provide passing lanes
and open ice for puck
carrier

Interchang. of Players

Tied directly to five
men active and flow
principle

Players develop as
whole players, not
as position-oriented

Need for hockey
sense and overview
of game

Movement Tactics

Players need to
become more familiar
with other player
responsibilites for
better understanding
of the game

Familiarity with lanes
and levels

Practice plays that
require position
changing

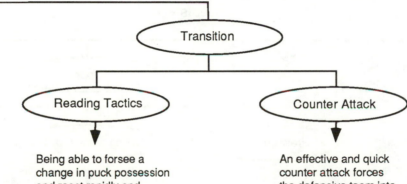

Transition

Reading Tactics

Being able to forsee a
change in puck possession
and react rapidly and
effectively to attack

Reacting from defense to
offense without losing puck
possession or position

Counter Attack

An effective and quick
counter attack forces
the defensive team into
a pressure situation

Effective reaction may
be lending support,
creating depth by drive
skating, and/or skating
at an opening

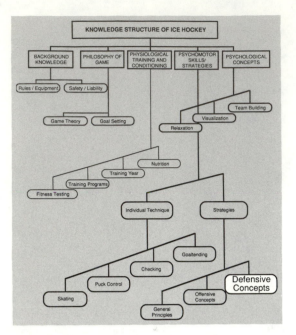

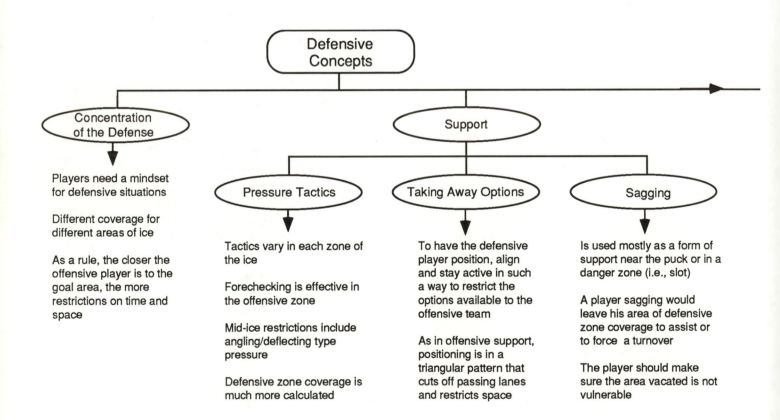

Defensive Concepts

Concentration of the Defense

Players need a mindset for defensive situations

Different coverage for different areas of ice

As a rule, the closer the offensive player is to the goal area, the more restrictions on time and space

Support

Pressure Tactics

Tactics vary in each zone of the ice

Forechecking is effective in the offensive zone

Mid-ice restrictions include angling/deflecting type pressure

Defensive zone coverage is much more calculated

Taking Away Options

To have the defensive player position, align and stay active in such a way to restrict the options available to the offensive team

As in offensive support, positioning is in a triangular pattern that cuts off passing lanes and restricts space

Sagging

Is used mostly as a form of support near the puck or in a danger zone (i.e., slot)

A player sagging would leave his area of defensive zone coverage to assist or to force a turnover

The player should make sure the area vacated is not vulnerable

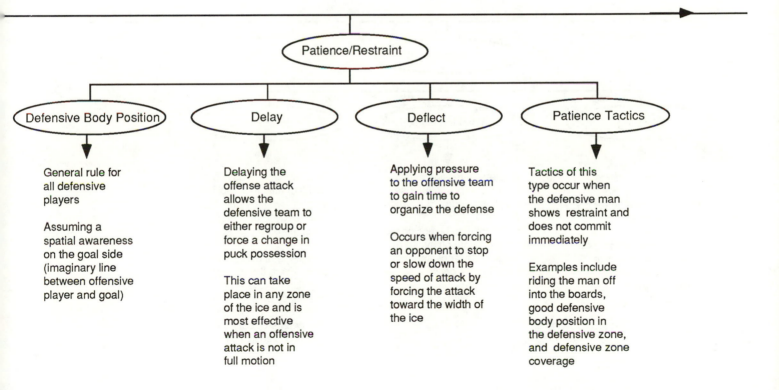

Patience/Restraint

Defensive Body Position

General rule for all defensive players

Assuming a spatial awareness on the goal side (imaginary line between offensive player and goal)

Delay

Delaying the offense attack allows the defensive team to either regroup or force a change in puck possession

This can take place in any zone of the ice and is most effective when an offensive attack is not in full motion

Deflect

Applying pressure to the offensive team to gain time to organize the defense

Occurs when forcing an opponent to stop or slow down the speed of attack by forcing the attack toward the width of the ice

Patience Tactics

Tactics of this type occur when the defensive man shows restraint and does not commit immediately

Examples include riding the man off into the boards, good defensive body position in the defensive zone, and defensive zone coverage

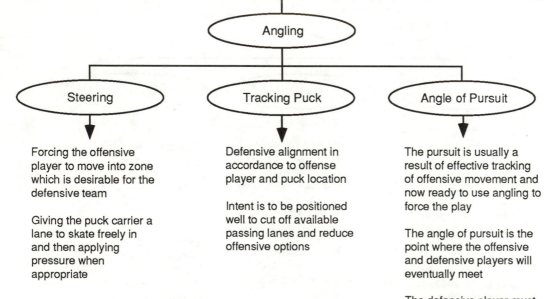

Angling

Steering

Forcing the offensive
player to move into zone
which is desirable for the
defensive team

Giving the puck carrier a
lane to skate freely in
and then applying
pressure when
appropriate

Tracking Puck

Defensive alignment in
accordance to offense
player and puck location

Intent is to be positioned
well to cut off available
passing lanes and reduce
offensive options

Angle of Pursuit

The pursuit is usually a
result of effective tracking
of offensive movement and
now ready to use angling to
force the play

The angle of pursuit is the
point where the offensive
and defensive players will
eventually meet

The defensive player must
stay on defensive side

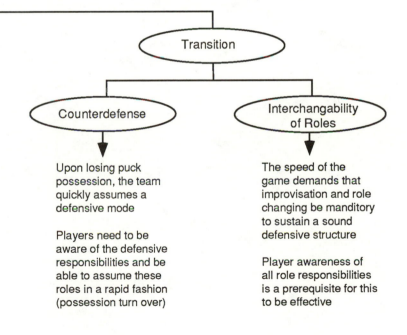

References

Abernethy, B., & Russell D. (1987). Expert-novice differences in an applied selective attention task. *Journal of Sports Psychology*, **9**, 326-345.

Allard, F. (1980). Perception in sport: Basketball. *Journal of Sport Psychology*, **2**, 14-21.

Allard, F., & Burnett, N. (1985). Skill in sport. *Canadian Journal of Psychology*, **39**(2), 294-312.

Allard, F., & Starkes, J.L. (1983). Perception in volleyball: The effects of competitive stress. *Journal of Sport Psychology*, **5**, 189-196.

Anderson, J.R. (1980). *Cognitive psychology and its implications*. San Francisco: W.H. Freeman.

Anderson, J.R. (1982). Acquisition of cognitive skill. *Psychological Review*, **89**(4), 369-406.

Anderson, J.R. (1983). *The architecture of cognition*. Cambridge, MA: Harvard University Press.

Ausubel, D.P. (1968). *Educational psychology: A cognitive view*. New York: Holt, Rinehart and Winston.

Badminton Canada. (1989). *Coaching badminton*. Ottawa: Author.

Bahill, A.T., & LaRitz, T. (1984). Why can't batters keep their eyes on the ball? *American Scientist*, **72**, 249-253.

Bard, C. (1980). Analysis of gymnastics judges' visual search. *Research Quarterly for Exercise and Sport*, **51**(2), 267-273.

Bard, C., & Fleury, M. (1976). Analysis of visual search activity during sport problem situations. *Journal of Human Movement Studies*, **3**, 214-222.

Bard, C., & Fleury, M. (1981). Considering eye movements as a predictor of attainment. In I.M. Cockerill & W.W. MacGillvary (Eds.), *Vision and sport* (pp. 28-41). Cheltenham, England: Stanley Thornes.

Bartlett, F.C. (1932). *Remembering*. Cambridge, England: Cambridge University Press.

Bergan, J.R. (1980). The structural analysis of behavior: An alternative to the learning-hierarchy model. *Review of Educational Research*, **50**(4), 625-646.

Bergan, J.R., & Stone, C.A. (1986). Psychometric and instructional validations of hierarchical domain structures. *Contemporary Educational Psychology*, **11**, 1-32.

Berliner, D.C. (1985). Laboratory settings and the study of teacher education. *Journal of Teacher Education*, **36**(6).

Block, J.H. (1971). *Mastery learning theory and practice*. New York: Holt, Rinehart and Winston.

Bloom, B.S. (1971). Mastery learning. In J.H. Block (Ed.), *Mastery learning theory and practice* (pp. 47-63). New York: Holt, Rinehart and Winston.

Bloss, M.V., & Hales, R.S. (1987). *Badminton*. Dubuque: William C. Brown

Boose, J., & Gaines, B. (1988). *Knowledge acquisition tools for expert systems* (Vol. 2). Toronto: Academic Press.

Bourne, L.E., Dominowski, R.L., & Loftus, E.F. (1979). *Cognitive processes*. Englewood Cliffs, NJ: Prentice-Hall.

Breen, J.L., & Paup, D.C. (1983). *Winning badminton*. N. Palm Beach, FL: The Athletic Institute.

Bressan, E., & Pieter, W. (1985). Philosophic processes and the study of human movement. *Quest*, **37**, 1-15.

Brookover, W.B., Beady, C., Flood, P., Schweitzer, J., & Wisenbaker, J. (1979). *School social systems and student achievement: Schools can make a difference*. New York: Praeger.

Brown, J. (1989a). *Teaching tennis: Steps to success*. Champaign, IL: Leisure Press.

Brown, J. (1989b). *Tennis: Steps to success*. Champaign, IL: Leisure Press.

Bruner, J.S. (1966). *Toward a theory of instruction*. New York: W.W. Norton.

Bruner, J.S. (1977). *The process of education*. Cambridge, MA: Harvard University Press.

Bruner, J.S. (1979). *On knowing: Essays for the left hand*. Cambridge, MA: Harvard University Press.

Bucher, C.A., & Koenig, C.R. (1978). *Methods and materials for secondary school physical education*. St. Louis: C.V. Mosby.

Carre, F.A., & Lashuk, M. (1986). Perceptions of grading procedures in physical education. *International Journal of Physical Education*, **23**(3), 9-14.

Carroll, J.B. (1963). A model of school learning. *Teachers College Record*, **64**, 723-733.

Carroll, W.R., & Bandura, A. (1982). The role of visual monitoring in observational learning of action patterns: Making the unobservable observable. *Journal of Motor Behavior*, **14**(2), 153-167.

Carroll, W.R., & Bandura, A. (1985). Role of timing of visual monitoring and motor rehearsal in observational learning of action patterns. *Journal of Motor Behavior*, **17**(3), 269-281.

Carroll, W.R., & Bandura, A. (1987). Translating cognition into action: The role of visual guidance in observational learning. *Journal of Learning Behavior*, **19**(3), 385-398.

Charniak, E., & McDermott, D. (1985). *Introduction to artificial intelligence*. Don Mills, ON: Addison-Wesley.

Chase, W.G., & Simon, H.A. (1973). Perception in chess. *Cognitive Psychology*, **4**, 55-81.

Chi, M.T.H. (1978). Knowledge structures and memory development. In R. Siegler (Ed.), *Children's thinking: What develops?* (pp. 73-96). Hillsdale, NJ: Lawrence Erlbaum Associates.

Chi, M.T.H., Feltovich, P.J., & Glaser, R. (1981). Categorization and representation of physics problems by experts and novices. *Cognitive Science*, **5**, 121-152.

Chi, M.T.H., & Glaser, R. (1980). The measurement of expertise: Analysis of the development of knowledge and skill as a basis for assessing achievement. In E.L. Baker & E.S. Quellmalz (Eds.), *Educational testing and evaluation* (pp. 37-47). Beverly Hills, CA: Sage.

Christina, R.W. (1987). Motor learning: Future lines of research. In M.J. Safrit & H.M. Eckert (Eds.), *The cutting edge in physical education exercise science research: American Academy of Physical Education Papers* (No. 20) (pp. 26-41). Champaign, IL: Human Kinetics.

Clancey, W.J. (1987). *Knowledge-based tutoring: The Guidon Program*. Cambridge, MA: MIT Press.

Clancey, W.J. (1988). The knowledge engineer as student: Metacognitive bases for asking good questions. In H. Mandel & A. Lesgold (Eds.), *Learning issues for intelligent tutoring systems* (pp. 81-113). New York: Springer-Verlag.

Clancey, W.J., & Hetsinger, R. (1984). NEO-MYCIN: Reconfiguring a rule-based expert system for application to teaching. In W.J. Clancey & E.H. Shortcliffe (Eds.), *Readings in medical artificial intelligence: The first decade* (pp. 361-381). Reading, PA: Addison-Wesley.

Clark, C.M. (1983). Research on teacher planning: An inventory of the knowledge base. In D.C. Smith (Ed.), *Essential knowledge for beginning educators* (pp. 5-15). Washington, DC: American Association of Colleges for Teacher Education.

Clark, C.M., & Elmore, J.L. (1981). *Transforming curriculum in mathematics, science, and writing: A case study of teacher yearly planning* (No. 99). East Lansing, MI: Michigan State University, Institute for Research on Teaching.

Clark, C.M., & Peterson, P.L. (1986). Teachers' thought processes. In M.C. Wittrock (Ed.), *Handbook of research on teaching* (3rd ed.). New York: Macmillan.

Clark, C.M., & Yinger, R.J. (1979). Teacher's thinking. In P.L. Peterson & H.J. Walberg (Eds.), *Research on thinking* (pp. 231-263). Berkley, CA: McCutchan.

Cockerill, I.M., & MacGillivary, W.W. (1981). *Vision and sport*. Cheltenham, England: Stanley Thornes.

Currie, J., & Dusterhoft, L. (1988). *Instructional design in jazz dance*. Unpublished manuscript.

Daughtery, H., & Lewis, C.G. (1979). *Effective teaching strategies in secondary physical education*. Philadelphia: W.B. Saunders.

Davies, I.K. (1976). *Objectives in curriculum design*. Toronto: McGraw-Hill.

Donald, J.G. (1980). Structures of knowledge and implications for teaching (Report No. 6). Vancouver: Centre for the Improvement of Teaching, University of British Columbia.

Donald, J.G. (1987). Learning schemata: methods of representing cognitive, content and curriculum structures in higher education. *Instructional Science*, **16**, 187-211.

Fitts, P.M., & Posner, M.I. (1967). *Human performance*. Belmont, CA: Brooks/Cole.

Funk & Wagnalls. (1978). *Standard college dictionary*. Toronto: Fitzhenry & Whiteside.

Gagné, R.M. (1974). Task analysis—Its relation to content analysis. *Educational Psychologist*, **11**(1), 11-18.

Gagné, R.M. (1977). *The conditions of learning* (3rd ed.). New York: Holt, Rinehart and Winston.

Gagné, R., & Briggs, L.J. (1979). *Principles of instructional design* (2nd ed.). New York: Holt, Rinehart and Winston.

Gagné, R.M., & Dick, W. (1983). Instructional psychology. *Annual Review of Psychology*, **34**, 261-295.

Gaines, B.R. (1987). Advanced expert system support environments. In B.R. Gaines & J. Boose (Eds.), *Proceedings of the 2nd Knowledge Acquisition for Knowledge-Based Systems Workshop* (pp. 8.0-8.14). Banff, AB: American Association of Artificial Intelligence.

Gaines, B.R. (1988). An overview of knowledge-acquisition and transfer. In B. Gaines & J. Boose (Eds.), *Knowledge acquisition for knowledge-based systems* (pp. 3-22). Toronto: Academic Press.

Gaines, B., & Boose, J. (Eds.) (1988). *Knowledge acquisition for knowledge-based systems* (Vol. 1). Toronto: Academic Press.

Gallistel, C.R. (1980). *The organization of action: A new synthesis*. Hillsdale, NJ: Lawrence Erlbaum Associates.

Gardner, H. (1985). *The mind's new science: A history of the cognitive revolution*. New York: Basic Books.

Gentile, A.M. (1972). A working model of skill acquisition with application to teaching. *Quest Monograph XVII*, 3-23.

Glaser, R. (1971). Instructional technology and the measurement of learning outcomes. Some question. In W.J. Popham (Ed.), *Criterion referenced measurement: An introduction* (pp. 5-16). Englewood Cliffs, NJ: Educational Technology Publications.

Glaser, R. (1976). Components of a psychology of instruction: Toward a science of design. *Review of Educational Research*, **46**(1), 1-24.

Glaser, R. (1984). Education and thinking: The role of knowledge. *American Psychologist*, **39**(2), 93-104.

Glencross, D.J. (1978). *Psychology and sport*. Toronto: McGraw-Hill.

Goc-Karp, G., & Zakrajsek, D.B. (1987). Planning for learning: Theory into practice. *Journal of Teaching in Physical Education*, **6**(4), 377-392.

Good, T.L., & Brophy, J.E. (1986). School effects. In M.C. Wittrock (Ed.), *Handbook of research on teaching* (3rd ed.). New York: Macmillan.

Gould, D.R., & Roberts, G.C. (1982). Modeling and motor skill acquisition. *Quest*, **33**(2), 214-230.

Greendorfer, S.L. (1987). Specialization, fragmentation, integration, discipline, profession: What is the real issue? *Quest*, **39**(1), 56-64.

Grice, W.A. (1981). *Badminton* (3rd ed.). Boston: American Press.

Harris, D.V. (1986). Relaxation and energyzing techniques for regulation of arousal. In J.M. Williams (Ed.), *Applied Sport Psychology*. Palo Alto, CA: Mayfield.

Harrison, J.W. (1987). A review of the research on teacher effectiveness and its implications for current practice. *Quest*, **39**(1), 36-55.

Hay, J.G. (1985). *The biomechanics of sports techniques* (3rd ed.). Englewood Cliffs, NJ: Prentice-Hall.

Haywood, K.M. (1986). *Life span: Motor development*. Champaign, IL: Human Kinetics.

Haywood, K.M., & Lewis, C.F. (1989a). *Archery: Steps to success*. Champaign, IL: Leisure Press.

Haywood, K.M., & Lewis, C.F. (1989b). *Teaching archery: Steps to success*. Champaign, IL: Leisure Press.

Hellison, D. (1978). *Beyond balls and bats: Alienated (and other) youths in the gym*. Washington, DC: American Alliance for Health, Physical Education, Recreation and Dance.

Hellison, D.R. (1985). *Goals and strategies for teaching physical education*. Champaign, IL: Human Kinetics.

Henry, F.M. (1964). Physical education—an academic discipline. *Proceedings of the 67th Annual Meeting of the National College Physical Education Association for Men* (pp. 6-9).

Hoffman, S.J. (1977). Competency-based training in skill analysis. In R.E. Stadilis (Ed.), *Research and practice in physical education*. Champaign, IL: Human Kinetics.

Hoffman, S.J. (1983). Clinical diagnosis as a pedagogical skill. In T. Templin & J.K. Olson (Eds.), *Teaching in physical education* (pp. 191-225). Champaign, IL: Human Kinetics.

Housner, L.D. (1981). *Skill in badminton*. Unpublished manuscript.

Housner, L.D., & Griffey, D.C. (1985). Teacher cognition: Differences in planning and decision making between experienced and inexperienced teachers. *Research Quarterly for Exercise and Sport*, **56**(1), 45-53.

Hubbard, A.W., & Seng, C.N. (1954). Visual movements of batters. *Research Quarterly*, **25**, 42-57.

Hunt, M. (1982). *The universe within. A new science explores the human mind*. Brighton, England: Harvester Press.

Hutchins, E. (1983). Understanding Micronesian navigation. In D. Gentner & A.L. Stevens (Eds.), *Mental models* (pp. 191-225). Hillsdale, NJ: Lawrence Erlbaum Associates.

Imwold, C.H., & Hoffman, S.J. (1983). Visual recognition of a gymnastics skill by experienced and inexperienced instructors. *Research Quarterly for Exercise and Sport*, **54**(2), 149-155.

Jewett, A.E. (1980). The status of physical education curriculum theory. *Quest*, **32**(2), 163-173.

Jewett, A.E., & Bain, L.L. (1985). *The curriculum process in physical education*. Dubuque, IA: William C. Brown.

Jewett, A.E., & Bain, L.L. (Eds.) (1987). The purpose process curriculum framework: A personal meaning model for physical education [Special Monograph]. *Journal of Teaching in Physical Education*, **6**(3), 1-366.

Johnson-Laird, P.N. (1982). Ninth Bartlett Memorial Lecture: Thinking as a skill. *Quarterly Journal of Experimental Psychology*, **34**(A), 1-29.

Johnson-Laird, P.N. (1988). *The computer and the mind: An introduction to cognitive science*. Cambridge, MA: Harvard University Press.

Joyce, B., & Weil, M. (1980). *Models of teaching* (2nd ed.). Englewood Cliffs, NJ: Prentice-Hall.

Kahneman, D. (1973). *Attention and effort*. Englewood Cliffs, NJ: Prentice-Hall.

Kemp, J.E. (1977). *Instructional design: A plan for unit and course development* (2nd ed.). Belmont, CA: Fearon-Pitman.

Kuhn, T.F. (1970). *The structure of scientific revolutions* (2nd ed.). Chicago: University of Chicago Press.

Lashuk, M. (March/April, 1984). A percentile method of grading physical education. *Canadian Association of Health, Physical Education, Recreation and Dance Journal*, 8-11.

Lawson, H.A. (1984). *Invitation to physical education*. Champaign, IL: Human Kinetics.

Lawson, H.A., & Morford, W.R. (1979). The cross-disciplinary nature of kinesiology and sport studies: Distinctions, complications, and advantages. *Quest*, **31**(2), 231-243.

Lawson, H.A., & Placek, J.H. (1981). *Physical education in the secondary schools: Curricular alternatives*. Boston, MA: Allyn and Bacon.

Leinhardt, G., & Smith, D. (1985). Expertise in mathematics instruction: Subject matter knowledge. *Journal of Educational Psychology*, **77**, 247-271.

Lenat, D.B. (1988). Computer software for intelligent systems [Special issue]. *Scientific American Trends in Computing*, **1**, 68-77.

Lindsay, P.H., & Norman, D.A. (1977). *An introduction to psychology* (2nd ed.). New York: Academic Press.

Logsdon, B., Barrett, K., Ammons, M., Broer, M., Halverson, L., McGee, R., & Roberton, M.A. (1977). *Physical education for children: A focus on the teaching process*. Philadelphia: Lea & Febiger.

Luxbacher, J. (in press-a). *Soccer: Steps to success*. Champaign, IL: Leisure Press.

Luxbacher, J. (in press-b). *Teaching soccer: Steps to success*. Champaign, IL: Leisure Press.

Mager, R.F. (1975). *Preparing instructional objectives* (2nd ed.). Belmont, CA: Fearon Publishers.

Magill, R.A. (1989). *Motor learning concepts and applications* (3rd ed.). Dubuque, IA: William C. Brown.

Marteniuk, R.G., & Romanows, S.K.E. (1983). Human movement organization and learning as revealed by variability of movement, use of kinetic information and Fourier analysis. In R.A. Magill (Ed.), *Memory and control of action* (pp. 167-197). Amsterdam: North Holland.

Martens, R., Burwitz, L., & Zuckerman, J. (1976). Modeling effects on motor performance. *Research Quarterly*, **47**(2), 277-291.

May, W. (1986). Teaching students how to plan: The dominant model and alternatives. *Journal of Teacher Education*, **37**(6), 6-12.

McClelland, J.L., Rumelhart, D.E., & PDP Research Group. (1986). *Parallel distributed processing: Explorations in the microstructures of cognition* (Vol. 2 [Psychological and biological models]). Cambridge, MA: MIT Press.

McSwegin, P., Pemberton, C., Petray, C., & Going, S. (1989). *Physical best: The American Alliance for Health, Physical Education, Recreation and Dance guide to physical fitness education and assessment*. Reston, VA: The American Alliance for Health, Physical Education, Recreation and Dance.

Merrill, D.M. (1983). Component display theory. In C.M. Reigeluth (Ed.), *Instructional design theories and models: An overview of their status* (pp. 279-334). Hillsdale, NJ: Lawrence Erlbaum Associates.

Miller, G.A. (1956). The magical number seven, plus or minus two: Some limits on our capacity for processing information. *Psychological Review*, **63**, 81-97.

Minsky, M. (1975). A framework for representing knowledge. In P.H. Winston (Ed.), *The psychology of computer vision*. Toronto: McGraw-Hill.

Morford, W.R., & Lawson, H.A. (1978). A liberal education through the study of human movement. In W. Considine (Ed.), *Alternative professional preparation in physical education*. Washington, DC: American Alliance for Health, Physical Education, Recreation and Dance.

Morford, W.R., Lawson, H.A., & Hutton, R.S. (1981). A cross disciplinary model for undergraduate education. In H.A. Lawson (Ed.), *Undergraduate education: Issues and approaches*. Washington, DC: American Alliance for Health, Physical Education, Recreation and Dance.

Morine-Dershimer, G. (1978-1979). Planning and classroom reality: An in-depth look. *Educational Research Quarterly*, **3**(4), 83-99.

Mosher, D., & Schutz, R. (1980). *Development of the UBC throwing test: Application of generalized theory*. Unpublished manuscript.

Mosston, M. (1972). *Teaching from command to discovery*. Belmont, CA: Wadsworth.

Mosston, M. (1981). *Teaching physical education*. Columbus, OH: C.E. Merrill.

Mosston, M., & Ashworth, S. (1986). *Teaching physical education* (3rd ed.). Columbus, OH: C.E. Merrill.

Newell, A., & Simon, H.A. (1972). *Human problem solving*. Englewood Cliffs, NJ: Prentice-Hall.

Noble, B.J. (1986). *Physiology of exercise and sport*. Toronto: Times Mirror/Mosby.

Norman, D.A. (1980). Twelve issues for cognitive science. *Cognitive Science*, **4**(1), 1-32.

Norman, D.A. (1980). What is cognitive science? In D.A. Norman (Ed.), *Perspectives on cognitive science* (pp. 1-11). Norwood, NJ: Ablex.

Norman, R.W. (1975). Biomechanics for the community coach. *Journal of Physical Education and Recreation*, **46**, 49-52.

Norman, R.W. (1976). How to use biomechanics knowledge in coaching. In J. Taylor (Ed.), *The fundamentals of coaching*. Ottawa, ON: The Coaching Association of Canada.

Owens, D., & Bunker, L.K. (1989a). *Golf: Steps to success*. Champaign, IL: Leisure Press.

Owens, D., & Bunker, L.K. (1989b). *Teaching golf: Steps to success*. Champaign, IL: Leisure Press.

Petrakis, E. (1986). Visual observation patterns of tennis teachers. *Research Quarterly for Exercise and Sport*, **57**(3), 254-259.

Pew, R.W. (1966). Acquisition of hierarchical control over the temporal organization of a skill. *Journal of Experimental Psychology*, **71**(5), 764-771.

Pew, R.W. (1974). Human perceptual-motor performance. In B.H. Kantowitz (Ed.), *Human information processing: Tutorials in performance and cognition* (pp. 1-39). Hillsdale, NJ: Lawrence Erlbaum Associates.

Polya, G. (1957). *How to solve it: A new aspect of mathematical method* (2nd ed.). Princeton, NJ: Princeton University Press.

Polya, G. (1981). *Mathematical discovery on understanding, learning, and teaching problem solving*. New York: John Wiley & Sons.

Potter, D.L., & Brockmeyer, G.A. (1989a). *Softball: Steps to success*. Champaign, IL: Leisure Press.

Potter, D.L., & Brockmeyer, G.A. (1989b). *Teaching softball: Steps to success*. Champaign, IL: Leisure Press.

Reber, A.S. (1985a). *Dictionary of psychology*. London: Hazell Watson & Viney.

Reber, A.S. (1985b). *The Penguin dictionary of psychology*. London: Penguin Books.

Reigeluth, C.M. (1983). *Instructional-design theories and models: An overview of their current status*. Hillsdale, NJ: Lawrence Erlbaum Associates.

Resnick, L.B. (1981). Instructional psychology. *Annual Review of Psychology*, **32**, 659-704.

Rink, J.E. (1985). *Teaching physical education for learning*. Toronto: Times Mirror/Mosby.

Ripoll, H., Papin, J.P., Guzennec, J.Y., Verdy, J.P., & Philip, M. (1985). Analysis of visual scanning patterns of pistol shooters. *Journal of Sport Sciences* **3**, 93-101.

Ripoll, H., Bard, C., & Paillard, J. (1986). Stabilization of head and eyes on target as a factor in successful basketball shooting. *Human Movement Science*, **5**, 47-58.

Rogers, C.R. (1980). *A way of being*. Boston, MA: Houghton Mifflin.

Rosch, E. (1975). Cognitive representation of semantic categories. *Journal of Experimental Psychology: General*, **104**, 192-233.

Rumelhart, D., Lindsay, P., & Norman, D. (1972). A process model for long term memory. In E. Tulving & W. Donaldson (Eds.), *Organization of memory* (pp. 127-135). New York: Academic Press.

Rumelhart, D.E., McClelland, J.L., & PDP Research Group. (1986). *Parallel distributed processing: Explorations in the microstructures of cognition* (Vol. 1 [Foundations]). Cambridge, MA: MIT Press.

Rumelhart, D.E., & Norman, D.A. (1976). Accretion, tuning and restructuring: Three modes of learning. In R.C. Anderson (Ed.), *Schooling and the acquisition of knowledge* (pp. 37-53). Hillsdale, NJ: Lawrence Erlbaum Associates.

Rumelhart, D.E., & Ortony, A. (1976). The representation of knowledge in memory. In R.C. Anderson (Ed.), *Schooling and the acquisition of knowledge* (pp. 99-135). Hillsdale, NJ: Lawrence Erlbaum Associates.

Ryle, G. (1949). *The concept of mind.* Middlesex, England: Penguin.

Schmidt, R.A., & White, J.L. (1972). Evidence for an error detection mechanism in motor skills: A test of Adams' closed loop theory. *Journal of Motor Behavior,* **4**, 143-153.

Schneider, W., & Shiffrin, R.M. (1977). Controlled and automatic human information processing: 1. Detection, search, and attention. *Psychological Review,* **84**, 1-66.

Schneider, W., & Shiffrin, R.M. (1984). Automatic and controlled processing revisited. *Psychological Review,* **91**(2), 269-276.

Shank, R.C., & Abelson, R. (1977). *Scripts, plans, goals, and understanding.* Hillsdale, NJ: Lawrence Erlbaum Associates.

Shaw, M.L.G., & Gaines, B.R. (1988). KITTEN: Knowledge Initiation and Transfer Tools for Experts and Novices. In B.R. Gaines & J. Boose (Eds.), *Knowledge acquisition tools for expert systems* (pp. 309-338). Toronto: Academic Press.

Shaw, M., & Woodward, B. (1988). Validation in a knowledge support system: Replication and consistency with multiple experts. *International Journal of Man-Machine Studies,* **29**, 329-350.

Shulman, L. (1986a). Paradigms and research in the study of teaching: A contemporary perspective. In M. Wittrock (Ed.), *Handbook of research in the study of teaching* (3rd ed.). New York: Macmillan.

Shulman, L.S. (1986b). Those who understand: Knowledge growth in teaching. *Educational Researcher,* **15**(2), 4-14.

Shulman, L.S. (September, 1987). Assessment for teaching: An initiative for the profession. *Phi Delta Kappan,* 38-44.

Siedentop, D. (1976). *Developing teaching skills in physical education.* Atlanta: Houghton Mifflin.

Siedentop, D., Herkowitz, J., & Rink, J. (1984). *Elementary physical education methods.* Englewood Cliffs, NJ: Prentice-Hall.

Siedentop, D., Mand, C., & Taggert, A. (1986). *Physical education: Teaching strategies for grades 5-12.* Palo Alto, CA: Mayfield.

Sinclair, G.D. (1979). The hierarchical development of skill in team games. *Pro Motion,* **23**(5), 5-9.

Sinclair, G.D. (1979). Practice organization. *Pro Motion,* **23**(6), 24-27.

Sinclair, G. (1983). Planning for improvement: A practice analysis profile. *Coaching Science,* 44-47.

Sinclair, G.D. (1985). Analyzing feedback style. *Coaching Review,* 60-65.

Sinclair, G.D. (1986). Designing the environment for the acquisition of team skills: The anatomy of practice organization. *Motor Skills Theory Into Practice,* **7/8**, 100-106.

Singer, R.N. (1980). *Motor learning and human performance: An application to motor skills and movement behaviors* (3rd ed.). New York: Macmillan.

Singer, R.N. (1982). *The learning of motor skills.* New York: Macmillan.

Singer, R.N., & Dick, W. (1980). *Teaching physical education: A systems approach* (2nd ed.). Boston: Houghton Mifflin.

Solso, R. (1979). *Cognitive psychology.* New York: Harcourt Brace Jovanovich.

Southard, D., & Higgins, T. (1987). Changing movement patterns: Effects of demonstration and practice. *Research Quarterly for Exercise and Sport,* **58**, 77-80.

Sparrow, W.A., & Irizarry-Lopez, V.M. (1987). Mechanical efficiency and metabolic cost as measures of learning a novel gross motor task. *Journal of Motor Behavior,* **19**, 240-264.

Stanely, S. (1977). *Physical education: A movement orientation* (2nd ed.). Toronto: McGraw-Hill Ryerson.

Strickland, R.H. (1989a). *Bowling: Steps to success.* Champaign, IL: Leisure Press.

Strickland, R.H. (1989b). *Teaching bowling: Steps to success.* Champaign, IL: Leisure Press.

Suin, R.M. (1986). *Seven steps to peak performance.* Toronto: Hans Huber.

Tharp, R.G., & Gallimore, R. (1976, January). What a coach can teach a teacher. *Psychology Today,* pp. 75-78.

Thomas, D.G. (1989a). *Swimming: Steps to success.* Champaign, IL: Leisure Press.

Thomas, D.G. (1989b). *Teaching swimming: Steps to success.* Champaign, IL: Leisure Press.

Tyler, R. (1949). *Basic principles of curriculum and instruction.* Chicago: University of Chicago Press.

Vickers, J.N. (1983). The role of expert knowledge structures in an instructional design model for physical education. *Journal of Teaching in Physical Education, 2*(3), 17-31.

Vickers, J.N. (1986). The resequencing task: Determining expert-novice differences in the organization of a movement sequence. *Research Quarterly, 57*(3), 260-264.

Vickers, J.N. (1987). The role of subject matter in the preparation of teachers in physical education. *Quest, 39*(2), 179-184.

Vickers, J.N. (1988). Knowledge structures of expert-novice gymnasts. *Human Movement Science, 7*(1), 47-72.

Vickers, J.N., & Brecht, D. (1987). *Badminton: A structures of knowledge approach*. Calgary: University of Calgary Printing Services.

Vickers, J.N., & Kelm, D. (1984). *Instructional design series: Introduction to ice hockey*. Unpublished manuscript.

Vickers, J.N., & Kingston, G.E. (1987). Modeling the master coach: Building an expert system for coaching. From D. Norrie (Ed.), *Learning in future education: Proceedings of the International Conference on Computer Assisted Learning in Secondary Education* (pp. 207-212). Calgary, AB: University of Calgary Printing Services.

Vickers, J.N., Rodney, D., & Rodney, W. (1984). *Instructional design series: Introduction to backpacking*. Unpublished manuscript.

Vickers, J.N., & Sinclair, G.D. (1982). The physical education teaching laboratory: Theory to practice on the campus. *Journal of Physical Education, Recreation and Dance, 72*, 16-18, 72.

Viera, B.L., & Ferguson, B.J. (1989a). *Teaching volleyball: Steps to success*. Champaign, IL: Leisure Press.

Viera, B.L., & Ferguson, B.J. (1989b). *Volleyball: Steps to success*. Champaign, IL: Leisure Press.

Wenger, H.A. (1986). *The key to hockey success*. Victoria, B.C.: British Columbia Amateur Hockey Association.

Wickelgren, W.A. (1973). The long and the short of memory. *Psychological Bulletin, 80*(6), 425-435.

Wickelgren, W.A. (1979). *Cognitive psychology*. Englewood Cliffs, NJ: Prentice-Hall.

Wickelgren, W. (1981). Human learning and memory. *Annual Review of Psychology, 52*, 21-52.

Winograd, T. (1975). Frame representation and the declarative/procedural controversy. In D.G. Bobrow & A. Collins (Eds.) *Representation and understanding: Studies in cognitive science*. New York: Academic Press.

Winter, D.A. (1979). *Biomechanics of human movement*. Toronto: John Wiley & Sons.

Index

DATE DUE

NOV 1 6 1991			
APR 2 6 1994			
FEB 1 3 2002			
NOV 0 3 2007			

DEMCO 38-297